TIME
HAS AN
END

5 And the angel which I saw stand upon the sea and upon the earth lifted up his hand to heaven,

6 And sware by him that liveth for ever and ever, who created heaven, and the things that therein are, and the earth, and the things that therein are, and the sea, and the things which are therein, that there should be time no longer:

7 But in the days of the voice of the seventh angel, when he shall begin to sound, the mystery of God should be finished, as he hath declared to his servants the prophets.

Revelation 10:5-7

HAROLD CAMPING

TIME HAS AN END

A BIBLICAL HISTORY OF THE WORLD
11,013 B.C. - 2011 A.D.

Vantage Press, New York

Table of Contents

Preface

This book is a study of the Bible that is concerned with the entire history of the world. We will learn from the Bible that God has pre-determined and pre-arranged and pre-planned in exquisite detail the entire program for this world including its salvation. We will understand that whenever anything happens, it has been precisely pre-planned by God. God is the Creator of time, and therefore, He is the Ruler of time (Colossians 1:16-17).

We will discover that the timeline of history is not governed by the rise and fall of civilizations or social structures, or anything else that mankind may consider of great value or importance. Rather, it is governed by the unfolding of God's pre-planned salvation program. It was planned and initiated in eternity past, unfolds in time, and will continue into eternity future (Romans 11:36; Ephesians 1:10). Between these two eternities are the approximately 13,000 years of the existence of this universe which, of course, includes our planet Earth.

Our purpose in this Bible study is to examine this timeline of God's pre-planned salvation program. This, of course, means that we will identify dates which may relate to the timing of the end of the world. Our conclusions, even those which relate to the future, will not be formed capriciously or for the purpose of gaining undue attention. As we discover important milestones along the timeline of history, we will see their strategic relationships to what the Bible discloses about future time events.

The Bible is a Book that is absolutely true and trustworthy. It is the centerpiece, the keystone of this study. There are many principles that should be kept in mind as we study the Bible, two of which are very important as we attempt to set forth the history of the world according to the true data set forth in the Bible.

Correction by the Bible

The first principle is that the Bible is the teacher and corrects the student of the Bible. The Bible declares in 2 Timothy 3:16:

All scripture is given by inspiration of God, and is profitable for doctrine, for reproof, for correction, for instruction in righteousness.

As we study the Bible, our conclusions are always subject to being corrected by the Bible. As a captain keeps a great ship on course by making very small adjustments in the ship's forward progress toward its destination, so the Bible keeps the student on course to truth by making correction in the student's thinking and doctrine whenever necessary. The Bible is the authority. It is the final word (Matthew 24:35; John 6:68). Without it, or if the student goes contrary to it, the student will most certainly stray off course (Psalm 119:105).

The necessity for these corrections is a result of the fact that however carefully we have studied a particular subject in the Bible, there is a second principle that also must be kept in mind. That is the principle which we can call "progressive revelation."

Progressive Revelation

What is progressive revelation? We should spend a moment examining this question. The Bible is the complete revelation of God's Word to the human race. We are not to add to it. We are not to take away from it (Deuteronomy 4:2; Revelation 22:18-19). It alone and in its entirety is the Word of God.

However, determining *when* any individual might receive truth from the Bible is another matter altogether. Before anything else, we must affirm that God alone gives understanding of His truth (Job 32:7-9; 38:36; Proverbs 16:1; Romans 8:28-29; Philippians 2:13). Then, in addition, we find demonstrated time and again in the Bible that God governs *when* that understanding will be given (Proverbs 21:1; Daniel 2:20-23; Luke 24:45; 2 Timothy 2:7; 1 John 5:20). There is a timetable known only to God as to when He plans to reveal, to whom He wishes, truth from the Bible. And that timetable reflects precisely each and every point in time when He knows the revealing of that truth is necessary in order to bring together all the intricacies of the unfolding of His salvation plan (Ephesians 1:9-12, 3:1-5).

God's schedule for revealing truth works perfectly in conjunction with His control of the affairs of men (Psalm 31:15). There are no conflicts; no emergency adjustments. Nothing happens incidentally or coincidentally. Nothing happens accidentally. God's timetable is always in play when anyone becomes aware of any of His truth. We will cite a few examples from the Bible. Jesus clearly told His disciples that the time would come when He would be killed and, after three days, He would rise again. Mark 8:31 declares:

And he began to teach them, that the Son of man must suffer many things, and be rejected of the elders, and of the chief priests, and scribes, and be killed, and after three days rise again.

Even though this is a plain, clear statement, it was not understood at all by the disciples (Mark 9:31-32). It was only after Christ's resurrection, as the disciples were reminded by the two men in shining garments, who stood outside the empty sepulcher, that they understood. Luke 24:6-8 informs us:

> **He is not here, but is risen: remember how he spake unto you when he was yet in Galilee, saying, the Son of man must be delivered into the hands of sinful men, and be crucified, and the third day rise again. And they remembered his words.**

This verse indicates that God had given them the revelation that Christ was to be killed and was to rise again, but it was not a revelation that became a part of their understanding until Christ had risen.

Likewise, we read in Ephesians 3:3-5:

> **How that by revelation he made known unto me the mystery; (as I wrote afore in few words, whereby, when ye read, ye may understand my knowledge in the mystery of Christ) which in other ages was not made known unto the sons of men, as it is now revealed unto his holy apostles and prophets by the Spirit.**

God is indicating that what had been a mystery was now made known to the Apostle Paul, **"that the Gentiles should be fellowheirs, and of the same body, and partakers of His promise in Christ by the gospel"** (Ephesians 3, verse 6). However, this truth had been written about repeatedly in the Bible. For example, Abram's name was changed to Abraham because he would be the father of many nations (Genesis 17:5-7). Another example is when Jesus told the disciples in Matthew 28:19:

> **Go ye therefore, and teach all nations, baptizing them in the name of the Father, and of the Son, and of the Holy Ghost:**

The truth that those whom God would save would include people from all nations of the world is taught in many places in the Bible. But while this truth was included in the Bible, which is God's revelation to mankind, only when Saul of Tarsus had become saved was this wonderful principle fully revealed.

Thus, we can know that, in the Bible, many truths are declared. But God may not reveal to students of the Bible an understanding of those truths until long after the student's first exposure to them. We can call this progressive revelation. That is, God has His own timetable for the giving of an understanding of those truths.

End Times

The principle of progressive revelation is especially emphasized in Daniel 12:8-9:

And I heard, but I understood not: then said I, O my Lord, what shall be the end of these things? And he said, Go thy way, Daniel: for the words are closed up and sealed till the time of the end.

In God's revelation, which is the Bible, God has a great many things to say about the end of the world and the details that lead up to the end of the world. But God has a timetable for the giving of understanding of these truths. We learn from this verse in Daniel 12 that this is definitely true of the details of God's plans for the end of the world. The true meaning of these end-time statements is not to be revealed until the time of the end. This is why many devout, God-fearing theologians of the past have endeavored to explain the meaning of Biblical end-time passages, but they have not even come close to the truth. This was not because of a lack of trust in the Bible. It simply was not the time that God had set up to reveal the meaning of these end-time passages.

Thus, we can expect that in our day, when the Biblical signs are showing that we must be close to the end of time (see, for example, Matthew 24; Romans 1; 2 Timothy 3), God is now revealing the meaning of a great many Biblical passages that deal with end-time truth to the minds of careful, diligent students of the Bible. The very fact that we can find great harmony in our understanding of Biblical passages that heretofore have been very obscure greatly encourages us that we have correctly understood this principle of progressive revelation. We can expect, therefore, that many passages of the Bible, which in earlier times have been somewhat mysterious, must now be re-examined. And we can expect that they can now be understood.

This also means that regardless of the time when we believe we have come to truth, we should still continue to study the question at issue because we may need further correction. If we have come to truth in regard to any teaching of the Bible, we will discover that continued study of the Bible will repeatedly affirm that truth. At the same time, as we continue to study the Bible and should find other teaching that contradicts or corrects what we had assumed to be true, we will know we earlier had not come to truth.

2 Timothy 3:16 Applied

About thirteen years ago, I wrote the book entitled *1994?* In it, I set forth a great amount of information derived solely from the Bible that suggested very strongly that there was a high likelihood that the world would come to an end sometime in the year A.D. 1994. Of course, the world did not end, and now, eleven years later, the world is still here.

However, during the past eleven years, God has been opening up to many who are studying the Bible considerable additional information which relates to the unfolding of God's salvation plan. When this additional information was integrated into the information which was set forth in the book *1994?*, we knew that indeed the year 1994 was an extremely important year. Moreover, we will discover that now, as we understand the Bible, it was the year 1994 in which Christ came a second time to begin the completion of the evangelization of His true people. We also have found considerable evidence that there is a high likelihood that the year 2011 will be the year in which the end will come. Nothing has changed in God's program. The Bible has simply made correction on our course toward truth!

We do know with absolute certainty that there will come a time when this world will come to its end (1 Corinthians 15:24). We also know that any reliable advance knowledge of such a dramatic event can only come from the Bible (Matthew 24:35; Mark 13:31; Luke 21:33).

We also know that about 7,000 years ago, in the year 4990 B.C., God destroyed the entire world by means of the Noachian Flood (Genesis 6:3, 7:4). It also appears that 120 years before the time of the Flood, God gave the inhabitants of that world the knowledge of the year when the Flood would occur (Genesis 6:3). Moreover, seven days before the Flood, God made clear the exact day when the Flood would begin (Genesis 7:4). We also know that God is the same yesterday, today, and forever (Hebrews 13:8). That is, the way God acted in the past tells us the way He will act in the present and in the future. Therefore, if He gave Noah such precise information concerning the timing of the Flood, we have every reason to believe that God has placed in the Bible similar information concerning the timing of the end of the world. Thus, we are greatly encouraged as we diligently search the Bible for anything and everything God might reveal to us.

It goes without saying that it is very hazardous to focus upon future dates about any matter, and certainly it would appear completely unwise in regard to the end of time. We immediately see the enormous risk of such an action. Throughout history, men have set dates and in every case, without exception, they were wrong in their prediction. Therefore it would appear that anyone who dares to set any kind of a date for the end of time is virtually guaranteed to be wrong.

Moreover, if the Bible teacher who dares to suggest a date is trusted by many, there may be confusion or hurt and disappointment in the lives of many of these trusting individuals. Having said this, let us look for a moment at the responsibility of a Bible teacher.

How Should One Teach the Bible?

If he is a true child of God, the Bible teacher will attempt to teach as accurately as possible. He will teach all that he, himself, has learned from the Bible. He will readily admit, of course, that he is not infallible in his teaching. As we have already pointed out, the purpose of the Bible is not only to bring an understanding of truth, but also to provide correction of that which has been wrongly understood. This does not mean, however, that the Bible teacher should be the least bit careless in his attempt to teach truth. He must be supremely careful and responsible as he teaches what he believes to be the truth of the Bible.

Ordinarily, if a very responsible teacher teaches a doctrine as Bible truth, but later he is corrected by further study of the Bible, it is not looked upon by others as a dreadfully serious matter. Fact is, there will be those who will sincerely appreciate the honesty of the teacher as he makes correction to his wrong doctrine.

However, when it comes to suggesting any kind of date for the end of time, many will vehemently oppose his efforts. These people might be included in one of three groups.

The first group could be those who are unalterably convinced that the Bible prohibits making any statements that suggest the timing of the end. Their objections will hopefully be answered in this study.

The second group would include those who believe fully that their Bible teacher does teach truth but who will selfishly use the end of time information for their own personal gain. For example, they may seek to purchase an automobile or some other object that they cannot possibly afford to buy. But if they can "buy now and pay later," they believe they can have the automobile now and never have to pay later because the end of the world will come first. But later on, if the teacher makes correction based on Biblical truth concerning future time, this group will find themselves trapped by their very wrongful ventures. (Those who engage in this kind of thinking and action deserve to be trapped because they have no idea of the nature and purpose of Bible truths.)

A third group will use the Bible teacher's error to discredit everything else he teaches. These people admit that the Bible teacher is ordinarily very accurate in his Bible teaching, but should his suggested end-time date prove to be wrong, they will seize upon the opportunity to call into question many other things he is teaching. Thus, these individuals will be given a convenient alibi to justify their unbelief of Biblical truth.

For these reasons, as well as possibly others, it certainly appears totally unwise for any credible Bible teacher to suggest any kind of end-time date.

But the Bible teacher must guard his relationship with God. He knows he must be obedient and speak the truth of God's Word. When he believes, after very careful study and prayer, that he understands any Biblical doctrine, he must teach that doctrine (Jeremiah 1:7-10,17, 20:9; Acts 20:26-27; Ephesians 4:14-15; 2 Timothy 2:2, 4:1-4). He must never be concerned about protecting himself from slander and reviling as he endeavors to be faithful to God's Word (1 Corinthians 4:1-4; 1 Peter 2:21-23). His first and only task is to please God, not to please men (2 Corinthians 5:9; Galatians 1:10).

Moreover, when the Bible teacher knows that we are living in a time when God is increasingly giving more enlightenment to serious Bible students (as we noted earlier, we can call this progressive revelation), the teacher knows also that trying to understand where our world is in God's timeline should be an even greater exercise than before — a matter to be taken more seriously today than at any other time in history (Revelation 22:6-7). God warns in Ezekiel 33 that when the watchman sees the enemy coming, but does not sound the alarm, the watchman will be under the wrath of God (Ezekiel 33: 6-8).

With regard to the idea that, in the past, no date setter has ever been correct, there is another side to this coin. We know that God's salvation program in time is real and ongoing (Acts 15:14-18). But also we know absolutely that there will be an end of time; the Bible says so (Revelation 10:5-6). And we know that there is a great deal of general evidence that the time of the end has drawn very close. Jesus tells us we must discern the times (Luke 12:35-57). And wonderfully, we affirm that a likely date for the end of time can be known – a date not set arbitrarily, but a date identified from and based upon all the information that the Bible gives us concerning the unfolding of God's grand salvation plan! (Matthew 24:39; 1 Thessalonians 5:4).

For several years now, we at Family Radio have been teaching that God has already come to bring judgment upon the local congregations, that is, He is already preparing them for the trial of Judgment Day. We therefore have been teaching that God has abandoned each and every local congregation so that the true believers in Christ, if they have not already been driven out, are commanded to come out. We, for several years, have been teaching that we are in the time of the latter rain during which God is bringing in the final harvest of those who are to be saved. This is the time when the Gospel is no longer under the care of the local congregations but is being sent into the world by individuals who are not under any church authority but who are definitely under the authority of the Bible.

For several years we at Family Radio have been teaching that we are already in this second part of the Great Tribulation (the latter rain) and, therefore, the end of the world can be only a relatively few years in the future (see *The End of the Church Age and After* and *Wheat and Tares* available free of charge from Family Radio). In this study of the history of the world, we are simply adding to all that we have already been teaching concerning the probable year for the end of the world.

But, someone can argue, "Is it not enough to repeatedly insist that Judgment Day is coming?" The answer is: If we are told when the enemy will be here, the warning will be far more insistent. It should be obvious that the cancer patient will react quite differently if his trusted, competent doctor tells him, "your cancer is terminal; you have six months to live," than if his doctor tells him, "you have cancer and some day you will die of that cancer." The giving of a timetable should clearly enhance the seriousness of the warning! In any case, we must remember that a faithful Bible teacher cannot pick and chose what he wishes to teach. He must teach everything he learns from the Bible (Acts 20:26-27). If he truly believes God has given a timeline to the end, then he must teach what he understands from the Bible concerning that timeline. True, he may delay teaching certain doctrines because he believes he is not properly prepared to teach them. It is always foolish for the teacher to teach something before he clearly understands it. But once that understanding is fully in his grasp, the Bible teacher must proclaim what the Bible has shown Him is God's message. The teacher is compelled to speak because he knows it is not his own word, but God's Word that He is declaring (Jeremiah 1:9; 20:9).

Why God Would Give Us End-Time Dates

But questions still linger in our minds. Why would God give us end-time dates? Why should we be concerned with knowing the possible year of the end of the world?

As we have already indicated, God's true people must publish to the world anything they can learn from the Bible about any subject. The true believer has no option. His role in the world is to teach all nations (Matthew 28:20) and what he teaches must be the whole counsel of God (Acts 20:26-27). Moreover, as we learned earlier, it is the duty of the true believer to warn the citizenry when danger is threatening (Ezekiel 33:1-10).

But consider the situation of those who are threatened by a very great hurricane or typhoon. People want to know, "Where will it make land fall?" That is, what is its path over the ocean, and where will it begin and continue its devastation on land?

Then people want to know "How strong is the hurricane?" How much damage will it do? And the people in the path of the hurricane desperately want to know, "When will it make landfall?" How fast is it moving down its destructive path?

Why are people in the potential path of this hurricane asking these questions? The answer is obvious. They want to know how severely this approaching hurricane will affect their life and property. Furthermore, they want to know how much time they have to prepare before its destruction begins. Likewise, people who are not ready for the return of Christ and the Judgment that will immediately follow must know the seriousness and the severity of the approaching end of time (Matthew 24:42-46).

Jonah Gives an Exact Time for Destruction to Happen

Significantly when Jonah was sent by God to Nineveh to warn of impending judgment on that great city, he not only published that the terrible judgment was coming, but he also gave a precise time when that judgment would fall.

We read in the Bible in Jonah 3:1-4:

And the word of the LORD came unto Jonah the second time, saying, Arise, go unto Nineveh, that great city, and preach unto it the preaching that I bid thee. So Jonah arose, and went unto Nineveh, according to the word of the LORD. Now Nineveh was an exceeding great city of three days' journey. And Jonah began to enter into the city a day's journey, and he cried, and said, Yet forty days, and Nineveh shall be overthrown.

In the experience of Jonah at Nineveh, we see the wonderful mercy of God in saving a great multitude of people. We can see the results of this salvation in how they responded to the warning in a God-pleasing way. Thus, the impending catastrophe was avoided.

We read in Jonah 3:5-10:

So the people of Nineveh believed God, and proclaimed a fast, and put on sackcloth, from the greatest of them even to the least of them. For word came unto the king of Nineveh, and he arose from his throne, and he laid his robe from him, and covered him with sackcloth, and sat in ashes. And he caused it to be proclaimed and published through Nineveh by the decree of the

king and his nobles, saying, Let neither man nor beast, herd nor flock, taste any thing: let them not feed, nor drink water: but let man and beast be covered with sackcloth, and cry mightily unto God: yea, let them turn every one from his evil way, and from the violence that is in their hands. Who can tell if God will turn and repent, and turn away from his fierce anger, that we perish not? And God saw their works, that they turned from their evil way; and God repented of the evil, that he had said that he would do unto them; and he did it not.

Time Has An End

In parallel fashion, God is warning the whole world that, in all likelihood, in the year 2011, the whole world will be destroyed. Sadly today, there is no evidence that the leaders and the people of our world are responding to this warning as the King of Nineveh did to Jonah's warning. However, there is surely the possibility for individuals all over the world to escape this awful destruction. All those who become saved will indeed be protected from this destruction. They are the individuals who are spoken of in Revelation 7:9-14 who are saved during this time of Great Tribulation during which God has already begun the judgment process (Jeremiah 25:26-29; 1 Peter 4:17). This explains why God has given so much calendar information in the Bible. As we carefully go down the timeline of history, we will see definite structure and harmony in the important historical events recorded in the Bible as they relate to each other. Thus, as we project them, based only on Biblical information, to the end of time, we will conceivably come to the year that possibly may very well be the last year of the history of the world.

We might recall that in Noah's day, the people of his world were given warning of the year of the Flood. But they remained in complete denial and perished in the flood. We have just noted that ancient Nineveh was given the precise day that total destruction would come upon them. They repented and pleaded for God's mercy. God did not bring destruction upon Nineveh, but He did bring horrific destruction upon the world of Noah's day.

Now, as we have already noted, the warning that the end of the world is almost here is making very, very little impact upon the peoples of the world. We would be very naive to believe that the whole world of today would react to the news that God is almost ready to bring the world to an end!

Would today's world cry to God for mercy? Well, the Bible informs us in Matthew 24:37-39:

But as the days of Noe were, so shall also the coming of the Son of man be. For as in the days that were before the flood they were eating and drinking, marrying and giving in marriage, until the day that Noe entered into the ark, and knew not until the flood came, and took them all away; so shall also the coming of the Son of man be.

On the other hand, God also tells us in Revelation 7:9-14 that there will be a great multitude that will become saved during these closing years before the end of time. Even as the Ninevites reacted to the preaching of Jonah, and cried to God for mercy, so there will be this remnant in our world today who in total are the great multitude who will react to the terrifying news that, in a few years, the end will come. May it be that a great many people will cry to God for His mercy as they become aware that the end of time has almost arrived!

It is our earnest, fervent prayer, as you become involved in the undertaking that is now before us, that you not become so bogged down or so engrossed in that which is seen that you miss the urgent, demanding message which constantly transcends the whole: YOU AND I MUST BE SAVED! We cannot escape the ultimate terror — the destruction and judgment that will fall when Christ returns at the end of time — unless God gives us His mercy and salvation. Oh, how wonderful is His mercy and salvation which He repeatedly reveals in the Bible! (Acts 4:10-12, 17:30-31) (see Chapter 13, "What Must I Do to Become Saved?"). God says in Acts 4:10-12:

Be it known unto you all, and to all the people of Israel, that by the name of Jesus Christ of Nazareth, whom ye crucified, whom God raised from the dead, even by him doth this man stand here before you whole. This is the stone which was set at nought of you builders, which is become the head of the corner. Neither is there salvation in any other: for there is none other name under heaven given among men, whereby we must be saved.

And God says in Acts 17:30-31:

. . . God . . . now commandeth all men everywhere to repent: because he hath appointed a day, in the which he will judge the world in righteousness by that man whom he hath ordained; whereof he hath given assurance unto all men, in that he hath raised him from the dead.

Having said all of the above, the end-time dates presented in this study are not being offered as absolute fact. They are being offered based upon our present knowledge of Biblical truth. Continued study of the Bible may result in correction being made at some future time if any errors have been made. We must never forget that the Bible is given not only to teach us doctrine but also to make correction in whatever doctrine we hold. Wherever we have correctly understood the Bible, however, the resulting date absolutely will be correct.

How then should we live in the face of a possible known date for the end? At Family Radio, on the one hand, we make decisions as if the end could be quite far away. For example, contracts are negotiated as if the future was altogether indefinite. We are the first ones to understand that we are not infallible in our conclusions, and that there may be correction at some time in the future. Yet, on the other hand, we fully realize the high likelihood that the dates set forth in this study are correct. Fact is, as we continue to study these matters, our conclusions are confirmed again and again. We find more and more evidence of the likelihood that 2011 could well be the end-time year. Thus, we are greatly stimulated to send forth the Gospel so that as many people as possible can hear the Gospel in the shortest possible time.

If this world is still in existence after the end of 2011, we will know that there is still much more we can learn from the Bible. Before that time, or at that time, we surely will receive correction from the Bible concerning any conclusions which prove to be in error.

TIME
HAS AN
END

*The reader is invited to send for any
of the following books which are available
from Family Radio free of charge.*

- **Adam When?**

- **The Prefect Harmony of the Numbers
  of the Hebrew Kings**

- **70 Weeks of Daniel 9**

- **The End of the Church Age**

- **Wheat & Tares**

- **When is the Rapture?**

Family Radio
P.O. Box 2140
Oakland, California 94621-9985
U.S.A.

1-800-543-1495

www.familyradio.com

Chapter 1
The Ultimate Terror — Judgment Day

We read in Isaiah 13:9:

Behold, the day of the LORD cometh, cruel both with wrath and fierce anger, to lay the land desolate: and he shall destroy the sinners thereof out of it.

This verse is summing up a very important, a supremely important, teaching of the Bible. It is describing the ultimate terror this world will soon face.

Significantly, as we come to that last day of ultimate terror, the world is being trained to think about and be frightened by terrorists. We are living in the day of terror. On September 11, 2001, two airplanes struck the World Trade Center in New York City, another airplane struck the Pentagon in Washington D.C., and one other airplane crashed in a field in Pennsylvania. About 3,000 people were killed within an hour, and suddenly, the whole world changed.

Prior to that terrible day, there were acts of terror here and there. A few were killed in one city or another city somewhere in the world. However, we in the United States, together with many peoples of the world, did not pay a whole lot of attention to these. These were news events that we read about in the newspaper or saw on TV, but they really did not register in our hearts with any seriousness. But come September 11, 2001, the temperature of the world changed dramatically. Suddenly, terror was on everybody's heart. Our government began to spend billions of dollars on security. Suddenly, everything changed.

Ever since September 11, 2001, any time there is a major event going on, security is of number one importance. This is not only true in our land, but in every land. For example, when I get on an airplane in Taiwan, it is clearly evident that security is of uppermost importance. Every bag put on the plane is carefully checked. Security officers look carefully to make sure there is nothing that could produce destruction. Terror is the name of the game. In September, 2004, when evil men seized more than 1,200 hostages at a school, and more than 330 people were killed, terror was in the hearts of those in Russia.

Terror is what is happening today all over the world. People in Israel live in constant terror because they never know when another bomb is going to explode. How many people have been beheaded in Iraq because of the brutal action of terrorists! And who knows what acts of terror may be occurring even as you are reading this book! Terror is a fact of this world, and all the people of the world must live with it. The big change or the focal point of all of this really began in 2001. We could say that the world has officially come into the age of terror. The world has been violently introduced into the age of terror.

The world has been violently introduced into the age of terror.

A Fictional Story of Terror

Now suppose there was someone in the world who was a very, very evil person, and yet, he also had a very brilliant mind. This is pure speculation. This is only imagination. This person does not exist, but I want you to suppose for a moment that this person does exist. This individual has somehow been able to assemble together enough components so that he was able to build a half dozen huge nuclear warheads. Not only has he been able to assemble these nuclear warheads, but also he has been able to put together several means of distribution.

This is an imaginary story, so we can make it as complex as we wish to make it. He is living in a hideout that is somewhere in the world, but nobody knows where it is, and it is impossible to find. This evil genius sends a message to all of the governments of the world. In this message, first of all, he gives enough information to show that he is completely able to do what he is threatening. The information he provides is so conclusive that there is no question at all about the fact that these governments will understand that he is able to perform what he plans to do. Not only that, but, in this message, he emphasizes that he has a very destructive mind. He is determined to destroy. We do not have to imagine that a man could have such a terrible desire in his mind. We see this kind of thinking all over the world today. We know that there are many who are ready to destroy.

The goal of this evil genius is to destroy as much of the world as possible. Therefore, in the message he sends to the governments of the world, he warns that soon, he is going to drop a nuclear bomb on one of the great cities of the world. It could be New York, it could be Tokyo, it could be London, it could be Beijing. He will not disclose which city. He also says that right after that, he is going to drop another nuclear bomb on another city. He warns that he plans to do this until his supply of a half dozen nuclear bombs has all been used up.

What do you suppose the governments of the world are going to do? They are going to start spending not billions of dollars but trillions of dollars trying to find this evil genius, trying to stop this from happening, if they possibly can. What do you suppose the people of the large cities are doing? They are frantic. They are paralyzed with fear. The whole world is paralyzed with fear, and they are all charging out of their cities and into the countryside. They do not want to be there when the bomb is dropped. When they carefully analyze the material that this evil genius has sent, it is very obvious that he is capable, totally capable, of performing what he plans to do. Thus, the world is totally paralyzed with fear. We have no trouble understanding that kind of scenario because we have seen examples of fright. Think of the example of when snipers can paralyze a whole state with fear so that the children are afraid to go to school and men are afraid to pump gas out in the open for fear that they might get a bullet in their heart.

A True Story of Terror

> *There is another scenario that is absolutely true*
> *that is infinitely more terrible than that described*
> *in that imaginary story.*

The above scenario is super awful. We are glad it is only a story. It is like a fairy tale that could never come true. However, there is another scenario that is absolutely true that is infinitely more terrible than that described in that imaginary story. It is going to happen even though the world pays no attention to it.

There is a God in heaven who wrote a book that was finished about 2,000 years ago. That book is called the Bible. There God has written what His plan is. He has written very, very plainly. He has written that there is going to come a day when God, in the Person of Jesus Christ, is going to return. He is going to come as the Judge of all the earth. At that time, every man, woman, and child who has not become saved is going to be subject to the eternal wrath of God (2 Thessalonians 1:7-10). Thus, the consequence for any unsaved person's life will be far worse than that of being killed by a nuclear weapon. It will mean that that person will be subject to the second death, eternal damnation.

God has warned the world. He has written about it again and again in the Bible, the Word of God, and He has indicated that this act of ultimate terror will happen. God has decreed that the time will come when He will end this world (2 Peter 3:10). It is the terror of God coming as the Judge of all the earth.

All of the evidence of the Bible shows that the time for Christ's return has drawn very, very close. It is very, very near, and He has indicated that He is going to come with great wrath and with fierce anger to destroy the sinners out of the land.

We read earlier that God warns in Isaiah 13:9:

Behold, the day of the LORD cometh, cruel both with wrath and

fierce anger, to lay the land desolate: and he shall destroy the sinners thereof out of it.

Christ is not an evil genius. He is holy righteous God. He is a God of great mercy and compassion. For over 13,000 years, He has been demonstrating His tremendous mercy in this sinful world. But in God's perfect righteousness, He must carry out God's Law (as set forth in the Bible) to bring to justice all of mankind who are guilty of sin.

We read in the Bible that Christ weeps in sorrow over the fact that He must do this (Luke 19:41). We read that He has no pleasure in the death of the wicked (Ezekiel 33:11). However, when this time of punishment comes, there will not, there cannot, be any pity or mercy. God must faithfully and righteously bring to trial and sentence to hell each and every one who is guilty.

Therefore, the Bible uses the language that Christ comes as a cruel God.

> *Repeatedly, God warns that the day will come when God will come to end the world.*

This kind of warning is sprinkled all through the pages of the Bible. Repeatedly, God warns that the day will come when God will come to end the world. Everyone who is not a genuinely-saved child of God is going to be caught in the net of the wrath of God. They will receive a blow that is far more terrible than being destroyed by a nuclear weapon. Each and every unsaved person will be caught and will stand for judgment. It will be too late for salvation. Those who stand for judgment will end up eternally under the wrath of God, under eternal damnation (Revelation 20:12-15). Nothing could be worse than that. It is a terror that is indescribable in its horror. Our present age of terror becomes completely insignificant in comparison to this gigantic terror that is fast approaching.

God Can and Will Do What He Has Planned

Immediately, this question must be raised. In our imaginary story, the evil genius was able to prove to the world governments that he had the ability to carry out his threat of terror. Is God able to carry out His threat of the ultimate terror of Judgment Day?

We need to go to 2 Peter Chapter 3. God has given us this letter in the Bible. He has given the document to us, and He is showing us that He is perfectly capable of doing what He has planned. Nothing can be done to prevent what God has planned. We read in 2 Peter 3, verses 3 and 4:

> **Knowing this first, that there shall come in the last days scoffers, walking after their own lusts, and saying, Where is the promise of his coming? . . .**

In other words, many people are saying, "We have this letter from this person who says He will destroy the world in the very near future, but we don't believe it. We just do not think it could happen."

In answer to this, God effectively says, "Now wait a minute, wait a minute, look who is speaking." In 2 Peter 3, verses 5 and 6, we read:

> **For this they willingly are ignorant of, that by the <u>word of God</u> the heavens were of old, and the earth standing out of the water and in the water: whereby the world that then was, being overflowed with water, perished.**

Oh, when did that happen? When did such a flood happen? To find out, we must go back to Genesis Chapter 6. There, within the account of the Universal Flood, we read in verse 3:

> **And the LORD said, My spirit shall not always strive with man, for that he also is flesh: yet his days shall be an hundred and twenty years.**

God Gave a Timetable

God had given a timetable for something to happen. At the end of 120 years, something awful was going to happen. The world had become very wicked at that time. Oh, yes, it was about 7,000 years ago, and the world was not nearly as populated as it is today. However, the Bible tells us what God did to the world at the end of that 120 years. It is a true and trustworthy declaration. God can set a timetable, and He can make it happen. We read in Genesis 6, verses 5-7:

> **And GOD saw that the wickedness of man was great in the earth, and that every imagination of the thoughts of his heart was only evil continually. And it repented the LORD that he had made man on the earth, and it grieved him at his heart. And the LORD said, <u>I will destroy man whom I have created from the face of the earth; both man, and beast, and the creeping thing, and the fowls of the air; for it repenteth me that I have made them</u>** [emphasis added].

In this statement, God is effectively saying, "I am going to destroy this world." You mean God was going to destroy the whole earth? Come on, that is an impossibility. How could He do that? Let us learn how He did it.

God commands Noah to build an ark. It is a huge boat. It is an impossible idea. This man and his family are to build this huge craft that is 450 feet long and 75 feet wide and 45 feet high with three floors in it so that it has a ceiling height of every floor that is about 14 or 15 feet. It is a craft that is to be built on dry land. Noah has 120 years to complete the task (Genesis 6:3, 14-16).

Certainly, by the end of 120 years, everyone on the earth of that day knew about this idiot Noah. Look what he is doing. He is spending all of his efforts building this ridiculous boat on dry land. Why, there never could be enough water to float that craft, much less do what Noah is preaching about — destroy the whole earth! Noah was a preacher of righteousness (2 Peter 2:5). Therefore, he would have been preaching, "God is going to destroy this earth. You have to repent. You must turn away from your sins." Nobody listened. Nobody listened except his own family: his wife, his three sons and their respective wives. They were the only ones who listened (Genesis 6:18).

Then came the day, and all the animals began to congregate in order to be put into this huge boat. Two of each kind of dinosaur (they could have been baby dinosaurs), two of every animal that had the breath of life, two of every bird that had the breath of life, they all had to be brought into that ark. Noah had to bring seven pairs of all the clean animals (Genesis 7:2-3, 7-9). There were only a few of this kind of animal, like sheep and oxen and turtle doves (see Leviticus Chapter 11). In our mind's eye, we can see a huge crowd all around the ark, watching. People are watching, watching, but no one is repenting. How could anybody destroy this earth? Look what that crazy man Noah is up to. Look at the effort he is putting forth. Certainly, this is a ridiculous thing that we are looking at. After a while they are going to come out of that ark, and we are really going to laugh at them.

Then God shut the door, and the waters began to pour down (Genesis 7:10-16). In all likelihood, God put the earth on a path so that it would pass through a great rain cloud in deep space because for 40 days and 40 nights, it rained and rained and rained (see *Adam When?*, pg. 182, available free of charge from Family Radio). The waters rose above the highest mountains of those days. Since water seeks its own level, when the highest mountain was covered, it meant that the whole face of the planet was covered with water. So, we read in Genesis Chapter 7, verse 10:

And it came to pass after seven days, that the waters of the flood were upon the earth.

Verses 18 and 19 tell us:

And the waters prevailed, and were increased greatly upon the earth; and the ark went upon the face of the waters. And the waters prevailed exceedingly upon the earth; and all the high hills, that were under the whole heaven, were covered.

Verses 20 through 23 go on:

Fifteen cubits upward [*that is, the waters covered the highest mountains by at least 22.5 feet*] **did the waters prevail; and the mountains were covered. And all flesh died that moved upon the earth, both of fowl, and of cattle, and of beast, and of every creeping thing that creepeth upon the earth, and every man: all in whose nostrils was the breath of life, of all that was in the dry land, died. And every living substance was destroyed which was upon the face of the ground, both man, and cattle, and the creeping things, and the fowl of the heaven; and they were destroyed from the earth: and Noah only remained alive, and they that were with him in the ark.**

Proof that the Deluge Did Happen

Now, it is significant that we have very clear evidence of this great Flood as we look at the fossil records. The unbelieving scientists and theologians and archeologists say something happened a million or more years ago that caused the fossils in the rocks. They speak of dinosaurs that lived 20 million or 50 million or 80 million years ago, but they will not at all consider the fact of the flood of Noah's day. They do not at all realize that the fossils in the rocks are clear evidence that such a flood did occur.

Ordinarily, bones do not fossilize. They slowly return to dust. Thus, a very special and unique situation was required to produce the immense quantities of fossils presently found in sedimentary rock. The only reason the fossils are there is because of the cataclysmic nature of the Flood. The animals were caught in huge mud slides. Under the pressure and heat that generated from the mud floes, the mud floes turned to sedimentary rock, that is, rock that is laid down by water, and the bones that were in it fossilized. Thus, we have striking evidence that this Flood did occur.

So, what does God say in 2 Peter? He says in 2 Peter 3:5-6:

For this they [*these scoffers*] **willingly are ignorant of, that by the word of God the heavens were of old, and the earth standing out of the water and in the water: whereby the world that then was, being overflowed with water, perished.**

By the Flood of Noah's day, God has clearly demonstrated that God will not only carry to full fruition any threats that He makes, but He is absolutely able to carry out His threats. Therefore, it is absolutely necessary to listen carefully when God gives us a warning.

God once again sounds the warning of the ultimate act of terror — Judgment Day! God has repeatedly sounded this warning in the Bible. We saw the warning in Isaiah 13:9. But also God declares in 2 Peter 3, verse 7:

But the heavens and the earth, which are now, by the same word are kept in store, reserved unto fire against the day of judgment and perdition of ungodly men.

We read in 2 Peter 3, verse 10:

But the day of the Lord will come as a thief in the night; in the which the heavens shall pass away with a great noise, and the elements shall melt with fervent heat, the earth also and the works that are therein shall be burned up.

Later on, as another example, we see that the four cities of Sodom and Gomorrah and Admah and Zeboim had become very wicked. It became God's purpose to destroy them. He told Abraham that He was going to destroy these cities. He even came into the city of Sodom and told Lot, his wife, his daughters and sons-in-law, that the time had come. He was going to destroy this city. You have to get out! Lot and his two daughters reluctantly obeyed, but Mrs. Lot's heart was still in Sodom. The next thing, fire and brimstone came down, and the whole city and all the individuals — men, women, children, babies, everybody — was incinerated because God brought this enormous holocaust on Sodom, Gomorrah, Admah, and Zeboim (Genesis 19:1-29; Deuteronomy 29:23).

> *God is illustrating His absolute ability*
> *to carry out His warnings.*

By means of these events, God is illustrating His absolute ability to carry out His warnings. He is effectively indicating, "Look, when I tell you there is going to come a time when I will return and bring this world into judgment, you better listen to me. You better listen to me because I have clearly demonstrated in history my complete ability to carry out my threats."

For a Long Time, God Has Been Warning

The Bible was completed about A.D. 95, and for the last 1,900 years, the world has had the Bible. Theologians and Bible scholars and curious people have read the Bible, and they have seen that, at some time in the future, there is a Judgment Day coming. Someday, that dreadful event is to occur. But they say it is in the future, in the wild blue yonder, so to speak. Because it is in the far future, it is nothing that we really have to be concerned about.

Nevertheless, it is something that is gnawing at the heart of man. Even secular men talk about doomsday. They talk about a final end of some kind, but they do not speak about it with great fear or trembling. It is more of a curiosity. It is something that they can think about a little tiny bit, but basically, it is not of great concern. Are we not making this world better and better for mankind? Are we not solving our problems left and right? Are we not making more and more medical discoveries so that we are able to prolong life? Are we not finding ways in which to begin to abolish war? Are we not becoming one world so that we are able to adjudicate grievances in various countries? Surely, we are somehow going to make this world a better place.

Yet the Bible keeps persisting there is going to be a Judgment Day.

Now let us return for a moment to our imaginary story. We imagined an evil genius, and in this world, only a very evil person would be a terrorist today. Remember in our fictitious story, this evil genius was able to convince the governments of the world that he would drop a nuclear weapon on a large city. He indicated that he has the capability to do it, and so the whole world is in stark terror. Everyone is absolutely paralyzed with terror. They are paralyzed with fear as they wonder, "What is going to happen?" We know this would be the reaction of the world to such a threat because we see the terror that is already in the hearts of people as a result of the things that are happening today. We are in an era of terror today. It is the present legacy of the world.

Let us compare the threat of this evil genius with the declaration from Almighty God Himself. As we have noted, God repeatedly insists that there will come a time when He will destroy this whole world and every human being on it who has the breath of life and who has not become a genuinely-saved child of God. It will not be a physical death. It will be something infinitely more terrible.

Unsaved man will be destroyed by being cast into hell forevermore, and this world will be consumed by a holocaust. It is going to be burned by fire, and it will come to an end.

As we have noted, secular man, who couldn't care less about what the Bible warns, is hardly affected by this warning. But what about the theologians and Bible students who earnestly study the Bible?

At any time in history, those who were warned by the Bible could agree, "Yes, someday there will be a Judgment Day. That is going to happen, but praise the Lord, not in our generation. We do not have to worry about it, even though all around us people die, and we think how unfortunate that may be. We know the Biblical truth that, on the last day, they will be resurrected to face the Judgment Throne (John 5:28-29; 12:48); but Judgment Day is far in the future. They died; we buried them; the world keeps going. We are busy trying to build our business. We are still trying to make this world a better place to live. We are still trying to solve our health problems. We are still trying to get a cure for cancer and a cure for heart disease or whatever. We are still working hard at this, and we are making a lot of progress, are we not? Are not people beginning to live a little bit longer, and do we not have a little bit better quality of life in some ways? Do we not have nicer things and a whole lot more toys that we can play with and new electronic gadgets of one kind or another? We are happier! Is not this what happiness is? Are we not obtaining what we are looking for? Even though we have some doubts about how well we will be doing, nonetheless, we are getting along very well. And so, our friend died. Too bad; too bad he cannot enjoy this world anymore."

Fact is, God is a holy God. He is an absolutely perfect God who has demonstrated beyond any question at all that, someday, He is going to come and destroy this world (Psalms 98:9; 99:1-5). At that dreadful time, all of the unsaved are going to be sent to hell to experience eternal damnation. Read again the Scripture passages we have already cited. And there are plenty more, many of which will be included in this book. God uses the most lurid language possible as He warns of this dreadful event. Repeatedly, He speaks of the terrible nature of this event. Repeatedly, He emphasizes that it will impact every human being on the face of the earth. God has written profusely about this awful event and has demonstrated that He can do it and that He will do it.

It Is About To Occur

...probably the vast majority of the people who are living today will still be living when Christ comes again.

Now we have come to a time when we sense more and more that this terrible event is about to envelop the whole earth. We are near that moment. In fact, there is enough evidence to believe that probably the vast majority of the people who are living today will still be living when Christ comes again. All of the evidence is pointing to the fact that we are near the end. The Bible teaches that, just before the end of the world, there will be a period of Great Tribulation. We read in Matthew 24:21:

For then shall be great tribulation, such as was not since the beginning of the world to this time, no, nor ever shall be.

This Great Tribulation will be immediately followed by the return of Christ. In Matthew 24:29-30, God declares:

Immediately after the tribulation of those days shall the sun be darkened, and the moon shall not give her light, and the stars shall fall from heaven, and the powers of the heavens shall be shaken: and then shall appear the sign of the Son of man in heaven: and then shall all the tribes of the earth mourn, and they shall see the Son of man coming in the clouds of heaven with power and great glory.

The return of Christ is at the end of the world.

A great amount of evidence shows that we are now in that period of Great Tribulation. Since the Bible teaches that the Great Tribulation is the last great event before the return of Christ, we know that Judgment Day is almost here. Immediately after the tribulation of those days, Christ will return. Therefore, we know that we are very close to the end. It is not in the wild blue yonder any longer. It is not "someday, someday this will happen." We have to say it is ALMOST READY TO HAPPEN!

When we examine the Bible carefully, we can know that there is a very high probability that most of us who are alive today will still be alive when Christ comes again. (The Bible indicates this in passages like Matthew 24:40-41 and 1 Thessalonians 4:17.) I believe we are very close. We are moving rapidly to the end of the world and Judgment Day. In Family Radio, we have been teaching for months and even years that we are already in the time of the Great Tribulation (see *The End of the Church Age and After* and other studies from Family Radio). We know we are very near the end.

When we see what is happening in the world, whether it is the World Trade Center tragedy, the terrible terror events that are happening in Israel, Iraq, or anywhere else in the world, we know we have entered into an age of terror. Acts of terror are occurring everywhere, and, in one sense, we can say these are warnings pointing to the ultimate act of terror, Judgment Day.

The likelihood is, however, that we also have to look at these tragic events a little differently. What is happening in the world today is actually a distraction. It is a distraction and a diversion from where men's minds ought to be. We can look at the physical characteristics of present acts of terror and realize that we must do something about it. We all agree that not only must we do something, but we can do something about it. We can marshal our money and our efforts, and we can stamp out this kind of terror.

If the world could only realize the awful predicament it is really in!

But simultaneously, almost entirely unknown to the world, there is this infinitely greater terror that is stalking the world. It is the return of Jesus Christ to judge the world, and almost nobody is paying attention to it. Virtually nobody is in fear or trembling. If the world could only realize the awful predicament it is really in! Every human being on the face of the earth who does not know the salvation that is in Jesus Christ should be trembling in fear. They should hardly be able to sleep at night!

Just think, in the next few years, some time shortly, Christ is coming, and He is coming to end this world. It is going to be total destruction. It means that if I am unsaved, I am going to be brought to trial. It means that I have to answer for my life, for my sins (Ecclesiastes 12:14; 2 Corinthians 5:10). It means that I am going to be found guilty and be cast into hell forevermore. How terrible! How terrible! How can I sleep at night when I think about these things?

These warnings of the Bible are absolutely true and trustworthy. As we study the Bible carefully, surely, we have to admit, yes, it is indeed very, very true. That means that this terrible event, this terrible holocaust, this terrible thing, that is infinitely more terrible than what is going on today as we are being terrified by terrorists, will happen. It is infinitely more awful than what an evil genius could pull off, if such a thing could ever exist. The ultimate terror is not fanciful; it is not "may be."

The ultimate terror is the fact that God has declared that He is going to come and destroy this world. He has written about it all through the pages of the Bible. He has clearly indicated He has full capability to do it. He has demonstrated His total capability to do it. No matter what security system all of the governments of the world can put together, this awful event cannot be stopped. They can provide every nickel of their government budgets to attack this problem, but there is no way that they can stop it from happening. There is no way that they can stop God from doing it. There is no place where they can find security. Even if they could dig a cave into the bowels of the earth, 10 miles down, and somehow get all of the people down there, they would not be safe because God will find everybody wherever they might be (1 Thessalonians 5:3; Hebrews 12:25-26). There is no protection. None whatsoever.

This scenario that God paints on the pages of the Bible, in which He warns that He is coming to destroy the wicked in His great wrath, is absolutely true. Since it is absolutely true, one would wonder why every unsaved person in the world is not paralyzed with fear? How can it be that every person is not stricken with fright?

One of the reasons, of course, is that, if they hear about it, they will scoff. Remember, God said in 2 Peter 3, verse 3, that scoffers will come. They effectively say, "Ah, come on, do we have to believe that? That is just a scare tactic. Come on, a good God would not do that, He loves the earth. He would never do that." Oh? Won't He? Won't He? Read Genesis Chapters 6 and 7 again, and read about Sodom and Gomorrah (Genesis Chapter 19). Read about what He did to Judah in 587 B.C., when He threatened to bring Babylon against Jerusalem. He did bring Babylon against Jerusalem and totally destroyed it (2 Kings Chapter 25). Look up all of the places where God says, "I will do it," and He did it.

Anyone can deceive himself, and stick his head in the sand like the proverbial ostrich, and say, "It will not happen," but that will not change the fact that it will happen. IT IS GOING TO HAPPEN! What a terrible thing! What an enormous predicament the world is in!

Who Should Be Warning the World?

> *To whom has God assigned the responsibility to sound the warning?*

Is it the task of our government to warn the world of the reality of this ultimate terror? To whom has God assigned the responsibility to sound the warning? Certainly, it is not the government. Fact is, warning the world is precisely the task that God has given to each and every true believer in Christ (Matthew 28:19-20; Romans 10:14; 2 Corinthians 5:20; 2 Timothy 4:1-5). That is exactly why God assigns the task of preaching the Gospel to you, if you have become a true believer, and to me and to all who become true believers.

Incidentally, to "preach" means to "publish" or "proclaim" the Gospel, and when God uses the word "preach," He is not necessarily talking about a man who is an elder in his church and who has been ordained in some way to be the preacher. Every true believer is a preacher. They are to proclaim the Gospel. THIS IS WHY TRUE CHRISTIANS EXIST TODAY. They have one task and that is to proclaim the Gospel. Given the awfulness of and the certainty of this ultimate terror, it is of the utmost seriousness that each and every true believer realize how utterly important it is to faithfully sound the warning.

We know that no matter how carefully the true Christian warns the world (that this terrible judgment is coming, and that it is so bad that everyone ought to be paralyzed with fear so much so that they cannot sleep tonight because they are climbing the walls worrying about it), most people will not listen to the warning. The heart of man is so dead, it is so much in rebellion (Jeremiah 5:23; 17:9), that most people of the world will pay no attention. They will say, "Well, I know you are saying all of those things, but first of all, you must prove to me that the Bible is true. You must prove that the Bible is the Word of God. You claim that it is, but I do not buy it. I just don't buy it. Now, this is the end of the matter, don't disturb me. I have to keep building my business, and I have to keep trying to find some happiness in this life." That is what is on the minds of men.

But you see, it is God's business to decide whose minds He wants to open up (Psalm 65:4; Acts 16:14; 1 Corinthians 2:14). If we go to Romans Chapter 10, we can read the instructions God gives to the true believers who have been mandated to sound the warning.

Remember, in connection with the terrorists of today, the government can spend billions of dollars on security trying to protect the citizenry. However, the government cannot spend five cents nor five trillion dollars to try to protect the people from this super-duper terror that is going to strike this world in a very few years. They are powerless to do anything to protect anybody. In this matter, the governments are completely helpless.

...there is protection, and that protection is in Christ.

Wonderfully, however, there is protection, and that protection is in Christ. If anyone does become a true believer, and only God can make someone a true believer, it means that he is safe and secure (Psalm 46:1-3). This is so because when that awful day comes, he, together with all the true believers, will be caught up to be with Christ in the air (1 Thessalonians 4:17). They are not going to experience one figment of trouble because, during that last day's terror, when

Christ comes on the clouds of glory as the Judge of all the earth, and all of these prophecies and all of these declarations of judgment and the wrath of God are taking place, the true children of God will be absent. They will be with Christ in the air. They will not be here. They are safe and secure. It is the maximum security. It is total security. It is a security that is as real and wonderful as it is real and terrible that God is going to come to terrorize the world as He brings the unsaved into eternal damnation.

How Can I Escape?

At this point, many of our readers could rightfully exclaim, "Now that I have been frightened beyond measure, what can I do? Is there any hope for me? You describe those who are true believers in Christ and who, therefore, will not come under this awful judgment. They are to publish the news about this impending disaster to the world. But what good is that? Is there any hope for me? I am just hearing about this ultimate act of terror."

There is great hope for you! We must look at the Bible for the evidence that this great hope exists.

The Bible's Book of Jonah

In the Old Testament of the Bible, there is a small book with the title "Jonah." In it, God gives a vivid illustration that sets forth the wonderful mercy of God.

The historical setting of the book of Jonah is the great city of Nineveh, a capital city of the nation of Assyria circa 750 B.C. Nineveh was a very secular wicked city that knew little or nothing about the God we know of in the Bible. Fact is, it was the enemy of Israel. To this city, at the command of God, came the Israelite prophet Jonah. Jonah very reluctantly came to Nineveh with a mandate from God to declare terrible news. Jonah was to warn the city that, because of the wickedness of Nineveh, in forty days, God planned to destroy the city (Jonah 1:1-3; 3:1-4).

The reluctant prophet Jonah brought no supernatural activity to demonstrate he was a prophet sent by God. He came to this great city with only a message from God. It was an awful, reprehensible message. That message did not infatuate the Ninevites with, "God loves you and has a wonderful plan for you." Instead, this message of doom and gloom declared, "**Yet forty days, and Nineveh shall be overthrown**" (Jonah 3:4). Nineveh was to be destroyed by God.

The reaction to this startling terrible message should have been one of anger and complete distrust. The Ninevites logically should have killed this prophet for daring to suggest that the great city of Nineveh was about to be destroyed. How could it be that this lone prophet would dare to intimidate a great world-class city with such a message of catastrophic oblivion? Anyone who would take this prophet seriously would have to be out of his mind!

But something happened that does not make any kind of logical, reasonable, sense. God tells us in Jonah 3:5-8:

> **So the people of Nineveh believed God, and proclaimed a fast, and put on sackcloth, from the greatest of them even to the least of them. For word came unto the king of Nineveh, and he arose from his throne, and he laid his robe from him, and covered him with sackcloth, and sat in ashes. And he caused it to be proclaimed and published through Nineveh by the decree of the king and his nobles, saying, Let neither man nor beast, herd nor flock, taste any thing: let them not feed, nor drink water: but let man and beast be covered with sackcloth, and cry mightily unto God: yea, let them turn every one from his evil way, and from the violence that is in their hands.**

How could it be that these words of God spoken by this reluctant prophet caused such an unexpected and dramatic reaction? The individual citizens of Nineveh would have learned very little from a lone prophet moving through the city preaching over a period of forty days. The amount of Biblical information reaching the ears of every citizen of this city of more than 120,000 (Jonah 4:11) would have been minuscule! Most of them, at best, would have heard only the indictment: "You are sinners. This city is under the wrath of God. On such a day of the month of this year, God is going to destroy this city."

What caused them to cry mightily to God at the same time they were turning from their evil ways? Did they have absolute assurance that God would see and hear them and thus withdraw His anger and judgment from this city? The next verse tells us they had no such assurance. We read in Jonah 3:9:

> **Who can tell if God will turn and repent, and turn away from his fierce anger, that we perish not?**

> *...they were a people that had come to believe the reality of God's warning.*

This verse shows us that they were a people that had come to believe the reality of God's warning. They understood that only God Himself could intercede for them to set aside the punishment. They also had come to fully recognize that it was their sins that had brought them to this terrible predicament. And they realized that maybe -- maybe -- God would have mercy on them.

Now, dear reader, what about you? We cannot leave our cities, and we cannot leave the world to escape the approaching holocaust. Holocaust is the right word because the Bible calls hell a lake of fire (Revelation 21:8), and God speaks of Himself as a consuming fire (Hebrews 12:29). We need — yes, it is imperative that we have — God's mercy! God's mercy is our only hope for deliverance from the awful, terrible Judgment Day which is almost upon us! (Hebrews 2:1-3a; 1 Peter 2:9-10).

God's Solution

Wonderfully, God has a divine plan by which people can escape the horrible consequences of the ultimate terror that is coming. We read in Romans 10:14:

> **How then shall they call on him in whom they have not believed? and how shall they believe in him of whom they have not heard? and how shall they hear without a preacher?**

In other words, God here has set up His divine plan. It begins with hearing the Word of God. We read in Romans 10, verse 17:

> **So then faith cometh by hearing, and hearing by the word of God.**

Now, what is the Word of God? It is the Bible. It is the key; it is the key to the needs of the world. It is the key to the whole terrible situation of ultimate terror that is going to come. We do not know the exact month or day or hour, but judgment is going to come, and it is very, very close at hand. And just as God saved the Ninevites, so today, God is saving many through the proclamation of His Word (Revelation 7:9-14). The Bible is the key. It is the solution to the security problem.. But how then are the peoples of the world, more than six billion of them, going to hear the Word of God?

Preaching, Proclaiming, Prophesying, Warning

God declares that His Word is to be preached. Let us ask again, "who are the preachers?" Normally, we think of a preacher as someone who stands in the pulpit because he has been specially ordained to preach the Gospel. During the church age, the Bible called for qualified men to be elders and deacons. They were the ones who were particularly called upon to minister the Word of God in the congregation (1 Timothy 3:1-7). But, in Acts Chapter 2, God indicated that beginning with Pentecost in A.D. 33, every genuine believer was called upon to be a prophet, that is, like Jonah the prophet, he or she was to do the work of a prophet which is to prophesy. To prophesy simply means to declare the Word of God. God declares in Acts 2, verse 17:

> **And it shall come to pass in the last days, saith God, I will pour out of my Spirit upon all flesh: and your sons and your daughters shall prophesy . . .**

From that time in A.D. 33 till the end of the world, every genuine believer -- man, woman, and child -- has become a prophet. When God makes spiritually-dead sinners spiritually alive, they are commissioned, qualified and mandated to bring the Gospel. During the church age, bringing the Gospel was under the oversight and guidance of the local congregation. Now that the church age has come to an end, it is the responsibility of each individual believer to declare this precious Word of God to the world (see *The End of the Church Age and After* and *Wheat and Tares*, available from Family Radio).

In Luke 8:38, we read about a man who was filled with evil spirits, and God healed him. He was an ordinary man. He was just someone like you or me who had become saved. When the evil spirits were cast out of him, he became a dramatic picture of someone who was taken out of the kingdom of Satan and was translated into the kingdom of the Lord Jesus Christ. That is, he had become saved. He was no longer subject to Judgment Day. He was told by the Lord Jesus in Luke 8, verse 39:

> **Return to thine own house, and shew how great things God hath done unto thee. And he went his way, and published throughout the whole city how great things Jesus had done unto him.**

The word "published" is the identical Greek word that elsewhere in the Bible is translated "preached." He could not keep still. "Look what happened to me, look how good the Lord Jesus is, look how he healed me from my terrible suffering! Look how He healed me!" So, he became a preacher. It was not that he now headed up a church and a congregation. He himself is the preacher.

Furthermore, we read in Luke Chapter 12 that God tells the true believers where they are to preach. Look at verse 3:

Therefore whatsoever ye have spoken in darkness shall be heard in the light; and that which ye have spoken in the ear in closets shall be proclaimed [*same word*, "preached"] **upon the housetops.**

In Mark 13:15, God is describing the Great Tribulation. In this context, God commands:

And let him that is on the housetop not go down into the house, . . .

What are they doing on the housetop? Luke Chapter 12, verse 3, tells us that they are proclaiming the Gospel. They are proclaiming the Gospel to the world. God commands the true believers in Luke 12:3:

Therefore whatsoever ye have spoken in darkness shall be heard in the light; and that which ye have spoken in the ear in closets shall be proclaimed upon the housetops.

> *The key is the Word of God. It must be proclaimed!*

In other words, God is commanding true believers in this time of Great Tribulation to get busy proclaiming the Word of God. Why? Why? We can know why when we think about the enormous danger the world is in. This super-duper terrorist act of all time, Christ returning and destroying the whole world, is about to happen, and the true believers have the key. Only true believers have the key. The key is the Word of God. It must be proclaimed! It must be gotten out there to the world, and the true children of God are not to come off the housetops. "Do not go back into the house or your church to try and get more information or whatever. You stay on the housetop. You stay out in the world and keep sounding the alarm. It is my program," God is saying. "As individuals, each one of you has a task to proclaim the Gospel, to preach the Gospel."

Therefore, we read in Romans Chapter 10, verse 14:

How then shall they call on him in whom they have not believed? and how shall they believe in him of whom they have not heard? and how shall they hear without a preacher?

That is the way God gets the Gospel out. Throughout the church age, God assigned the local churches the task of preaching. Now, in this day, He has assigned that task to individuals.

Again let me underscore how important that is. This world is on the edge of the greatest tragedy it has ever, ever known. It is a tragedy that makes every other tragedy like a kindergarten class or like a child's play thing. In this age of terror, no terrorist, not even the potential terror that would come if our fictitious evil genius were real, can remotely terrorize the world as God is doing. This is the ultimate terror as Christ warns that He is coming with His righteous wrath. He is coming with His furious anger to destroy the wicked by sending them to hell. He tells us about the role of the true believer in Romans 10:14, where we read:

> **How then shall they call on him in whom they have not believed? and how shall they believe in him of whom they have not heard? and how shall they hear without a preacher?**

And Romans 10:15 tells us:

> **And how shall they preach, except they be sent? as it is written, How beautiful are the feet of them that preach the gospel of peace, and bring glad tidings of good things!**

Does it take a church or a congregation to send a preacher? The answer is: No. No. True believers are sent out by God Himself. God says in 2 Corinthians 5:20:

> **. . . we are ambassadors for Christ . . . .**

And He says in Acts 1:8:

> **. . .ye shall be witnesses . . . unto the uttermost part of the earth.**

God says in Mark 16:15:

> **. . . Go ye into all the world, and preach the gospel . . . .**

He is telling each one of us who is a true believer, "You are to do the proclaiming. You are to publish the Gospel." The need to warn the world is not tomorrow, it is not next week or next year, it is now! Never in the history of the world has the need to warn the world been as urgent or serious as it is today. God warns in Ezekiel 33:2-9:

Son of man, speak to the children of thy people, and say unto them, When I bring the sword upon a land, if the people of the land take a man of their coasts, and set him for their watchman: if when he seeth the sword come upon the land, he blow the trumpet, and warn the people; then whosoever heareth the sound of the trumpet, and taketh not warning; if the sword come, and take him away, his blood shall be upon his own head. He heard the sound of the trumpet, and took not warning; his blood shall be upon him. But he that taketh warning shall deliver his soul. But if the watchman see the sword come, and blow not the trumpet, and the people be not warned; if the sword come, and take any person from among them, he is taken away in his iniquity; but his blood will I require at the watchman's hand. So thou, O son of man, I have set thee a watchman unto the house of Israel; therefore thou shalt hear the word at my mouth, and warn them from me. When I say unto the wicked, O wicked man, thou shalt surely die; if thou dost not speak to warn the wicked from his way, that wicked man shall die in his iniquity; but his blood will I require at thine hand. Nevertheless, if thou warn the wicked of his way to turn from it; if he do not turn from his way, he shall die in his iniquity; but thou hast delivered thy soul.

The watchman can only be those who have been designated by God to give warning. They are the true believers who have been given the task to send the Gospel into all the world.

The enemy that is coming is Christ as the Judge. The unsaved of the world are the enemies of Christ (Colossians 1:21). Thus, Christ is the enemy of the unsaved world.

Thus, this passage is warning the true believers that they have no option. They know that Judgment Day is coming as the ultimate act of terror that will strike this earth. If they do not sound the warning, they themselves will come under the judgment of God (Ezekiel 33:6, 8). The language of this Biblical passage is so emphatic that it permits no argument. We who are true believers must sound the warning to the whole world that Judgment Day is almost here.

In Isaiah 34:1-4, God declares:

Come near, ye nations, to hear; and hearken, ye people: let the earth hear, and all that is therein; the world, and all things that come forth of it. For the indignation of the LORD is upon all nations, and his fury upon all their armies: he hath utterly de-

stroyed them, he hath delivered them to the slaughter. Their slain also shall be cast out, and their stink shall come up out of their carcases, and the mountains shall be melted with their blood. And all the host of heaven shall be dissolved, and the heavens shall be rolled together as a scroll: and all their host shall fall down, as the leaf falleth off from the vine, and as a falling fig from the fig tree.

The nations, the earth, must hear. The language of verse 2, **"... He hath utterly destroyed them, He hath delivered them to the slaughter,"** is in the past tense. This emphasizes the absolute certainty that this slaughter (Judgment Day) will happen. Already in God's mind it has happened, because God is the great "I am," the ever-present One (Exodus 3:14; John 8:58).

This world is on the edge of oblivion. It is right on the edge. It is like the world is living on a volcano, a huge volcano. This volcano has not erupted for a thousand years, so fields have been planted, and cities have been built on that volcano. However, a group of scientists has been studying that volcano, and they suddenly realize that this volcano is ready to erupt. And when it does erupt, it is such a major eruption that it will utterly destroy all the cities that have been built on this volcano. And so, they run through the streets of the city, screaming to anyone who will listen, "We have got to get out! We have got to get off this volcano! There is going to be an explosion that will destroy all of us if we do not immediately get away from this volcano!" This is the kind of thing the world is facing today as the righteous God is soon to come with the ultimate terror.

> *The terrible fact is that there is a comet coming.*

Sometimes we read about people who warn that there are comets or asteroids out there. If a large comet or a large asteroid would strike this earth, it could bring this world to its end. But then they add, "Wonderfully, we don't see anything out there that will threaten us for maybe the next million and a half years, as near as we can tell." The terrible fact is that there is a comet coming. There is an asteroid coming. It is already on the way and it is coming from heaven. It is God and His wrath and His fury! It is going to strike, and God has given us enough information so that we can be absolutely sure it will strike. Moreover, we know it is going to strike very, very soon. It is not in the wild blue yonder. It is not someday. It is going to strike very, very soon.

People, can you understand what the position of the true believer is? God has saved a significant number of people who, before God saved them, were facing this terrible judgment just like everyone else was (Ephesians 2:1-3). But because God has saved these sinners, He has given them the task to warn. The Gospel of Salvation, which true Christians preach, is the only security system that exists in the world. Only the true believers put their confidence in the Bible and understand that this will happen (1 Thessalonians 2:13).

God's True People Must Sound the Warning

Only the true believers in Christ are in a position where they can send out the Gospel. They are the only people who absolutely trust the Bible. They are the only people who have been commissioned, and qualified, and commanded to sound the warning. We read in Romans 10:17:

So then faith cometh by hearing, and hearing by the word of God.

The Word of God must be sent out into the world. Without the true children of God intensely wanting to be obedient to Him, proclaiming or publishing His Word to the world, there will be no warning to the world of this impending holocaust. This is God's plan. Those whom God has saved are to publish the Word. The Bible declares that true believers cannot preach or publish or proclaim except they be sent (Romans 10:14-15). The moment a person becomes a true believer, he is automatically sent out. This is God's plan. This is the role that God has assigned to His true people: sent into the world to publish, to proclaim, the Gospel.

How important is this Gospel? Can you now begin to see some things tying together? How important is the Gospel to the world? This world is on that volcano that is ready to erupt. This world is at that moment when God is about to terrorize the world like it has never been terrorized before, as He comes in judgment to destroy. Who is there in this world who can provide any answer for security? We cannot marshal all of the political money or the political entities to provide security. We cannot marshal all of the scientists and try to figure out a way to provide security. There is no security that the world governments or scientists can provide.

However, there is a way of escaping that holocaust, and the people God has saved are holding the solution right in their hands! The answer is the Word of God. In the Word of God, God tells us all about this ultimate act of terror. He commands His true people to send out that Word, publish it on the housetops and proclaim that Word to the world. This is imperative because the world is ready to blow. The world is ready to receive the maximum destruction, the maximum holocaust, it will ever, ever face; and God has commissioned you, if you are a true believer, and me, as custodians of that Word: sent by God to proclaim that Word to the world.

Can you see what life is all about? Hey, look, you have a business to take care of; you have an office job; you have to make a living. We are all busy with life. We all have plenty to do in this life, and we find that most of our attention is focused on taking care of our family. We are planning to buy a new house; we are planning to take a vacation next year. We are doing all of the normal things that the world is doing. Everything is under control. It is just so nice when we are thinking about buying some new clothes, and these are all the things we care about. Oh, yes, on Sunday, many of us fellowship together, and we sing some songs, and we have some nice Christian conversation with each other. We feel spiritually refreshed, and now we go back to work on Monday morning, and we go back to school, and everything appears to be fine.

> *There is only one possibility of security and*
> *that security is in the Lord Jesus.*

Another week goes by and it is another week closer to d-day. It is another week closer to the holocaust, closer to the act of terror that is going to happen, which those who trust the Bible know about. They know it is going to happen because they trust the Bible. They have learned that the Bible is the Word of God, and God does not play games. God is not fooling around. God is not just giving idle warnings (Ezekiel 8:17-18; 21:8-10). God has given a message. He has told us that this holocaust is going to happen, and it is going to happen very soon. It is going to impact the whole world. There is only one possibility of security and that security is in the Lord Jesus.

True Christians have trusted the Bible, and yet, do they just kind of fold their hands and live out their lives, effectively declaring, "Who cares about the world? Who cares? What difference does that make? Let them go to hell if they want to go to hell." This is very crude language but is this not the way it seems to be, to such a high degree? Unfortunately, many who say they are Christians are not true Christians at all. Is this the way we live our lives? "Just let people go, we are not going to worry about them." The fact is, this is not the way God designed a true believer.

God has made <u>saved</u> people, <u>new</u> people. He has made them changed people. He has commanded them to "Occupy till I come" (Luke 19:13). He has commanded them to be His ambassadors. God is evangelizing the world through the true believers. To them has been given the responsibility to evangelize the world. Because this is God's divine plan, those of us who call ourselves true believers ought to be extremely agitated about this. Our whole lifestyle ought to change radically. We ought to have an entirely different focus for our life. We should recognize that this terrible act of terror is almost ready to happen. We should clearly recognize it is no longer business as usual. We cannot go on with our normal life the way we have in the past. There is a world out there, six billion people and more, who are going to be incinerated. Not just suddenly annihilated, but they are going to be eternally, continually incinerated in hell. They are going to be in the lake of fire forevermore. They are going to be under the wrath of God forevermore. And the only solution is Christ.

What About Election?

Now we know that Christ has elected those who are to become saved (2 Thessalonians 2:13; 1 Peter 1:2). Therefore, since God does all the work required to save the elect, why does anyone have to be concerned?

We must remember God's election program is not our business. That is God's business. Why do you think God has commanded His true people to go into all the world with the Gospel? Why do you think He tells them to stay on the housetops and not go down into the house? Do you recall that God declares in Luke 12:3:

Therefore whatsoever ye have spoken in darkness shall be heard in the light; and that which ye have spoken in the ear in closets shall be proclaimed upon the housetops.

To be on the housetop is a figure of speech that the true believers are ceaselessly to send out the Gospel. Is this just conversation? Is God just kind of making some small talk with us? No way. These are expressed commands of God. This is what God desires. This is what He wants. This is what He commands. This is His plan. It is through the true believers that God sends the Gospel so that His lost sheep will become saved (Isaiah 55:11; Matthew 28:19-20; Luke 19:10; John 10:11,16; 20:21; Acts 1:8; Romans 10:14-17). These are the ones He still has to bring in before that final day when Christ comes. It is altogether God's business. It is not up to man to make that decision. We know the ones God still must bring in are a great multitude because Revelation 7, verse 9, says:

After this I beheld, and, lo, a great multitude, which no man could number, of all nations, and kindreds, and people, and

tongues, stood before the throne, and before the Lamb, clothed with white robes, and palms in their hands.

This great multitude consists of all those who become saved. And where did they come from? They came out of Great Tribulation.

Life Is No Longer the Same

What I am trying to get across to you and to me is that life is no longer business as usual. Today is the day when God's true people have an absolutely important task. It is an insistent task, and we who are true believers in Christ as our Savior are the only ones with the message that the whole world must hear. That message is that Judgment Day is almost here.
And Judgment Day is super awful. It is no wonder that, in Revelation Chapter 6, verses 15-17, God warns that when Christ comes:

. . . the kings of the earth, and the great men, and the rich men, and the chief captains, and the mighty men, and every bondman, and every free man, hid themselves in the dens and in the rocks of the mountains; and said to the mountains and rocks, Fall on us, and hide us from the face of him that sitteth on the throne, and from the wrath of the Lamb: for the great day of his wrath is come; and who shall be able to stand?

These are the very words that God is saying to us. These words are similar to the message God brings all through the Bible. In 2 Peter Chapter 3, for example, God reminds us of what He did in the Flood of Noah's day. He says in 2 Peter 3, verses 3 and 4:

Knowing this first, that there shall come in the last days scoffers, walking after their own lusts, and saying, Where is the promise of his coming? for since the fathers fell asleep, all things continue as they were from the beginning of the creation.

You and I know that many who call themselves Christians are very nonchalant about this whole business, but they are not actually saying out loud, "Where is the promise?" Many say they do believe Christ is coming. But many of us are demonstrating that it is not really important at all that He is coming. What is so big about this? Effectively, we are saying, "I have to get on with my life. I want my children to go to college. I want to build this new house, and I want to have this other thing and that other thing. I and my family are getting along very well, thank you. Don't bother me."

If we really knew in our hearts and accepted the fact that the end of the world is near, we could not be nonchalant. We would have to be trembling with fear for our loved ones. We would have to be trembling with fear for the world. We would be exercising every muscle of our existence and of our strength in order somehow to tell more people about this. We would have an enormous compulsion to tell anyone and everyone that this holocaust is coming (2 Corinthians 5:11). It is coming. In His Word, God tells us in 2 Peter 3, verses 5 and 6:

> **For this they willingly are ignorant of, that by the word of God the heavens were of old, and the earth standing out of the water and in the water: whereby the world that then was, being over-flowed with water, perished.**

These are facts that God is declaring. God is saying, "Remember, remember, go back to the Flood of Noah's day. Did I not say I was going to destroy the whole world? I did destroy it! So what are you doing about this warning that I intend to destroy the whole world by fire?" Remember, God says in 2 Peter 3:7:

> **But the heavens and the earth, which are now, by the same word are kept in store, reserved unto fire against the day of judgment and perdition of ungodly men.**

He goes on to say in 2 Peter 3:10:

> **But the day of the Lord will come as a thief in the night; in the which the heavens shall pass away with a great noise, and the elements shall melt with fervent heat, the earth also and the works that are therein shall be burned up.**

Is this just poetic language? Is this just small talk? Is this exaggeration? No way. These are warnings from Almighty God. It is Almighty God who is speaking. Is this something that will happen hundreds of years down the corridors of time? No way. It is coming very close.

I am trying to get a very serious message across to each one of us. Life is not the same. We have to get this serious message into our thick skulls, into our hardened hearts. We have to begin to understand that we are living in a most serious time. Throughout history, God has warned that Judgment Day is coming.

When Christ comes to judge the unsaved, it will be the end of time. There will be no more grace, no more mercy. Please read again the Scriptures we have included here! Understand that at the end of time, there will be no more salvation. It will mean that it is settled once and for all that anyone who is unsaved at that point is going to stand before the Judgment Throne of God and end up in hell forevermore.

For the genuine believers, the real crisis is not that we are at the end of the church age (see *The End of the Church Age and After*, available free of charge from Family Radio). That is not the issue.

As God completes the evangelization of the world, He has assigned the task to individual true believers to publish, to preach, to proclaim the Word of God. This is the assignment that He has given us if we are true believers, and that is why we understand that we are to be on the housetops. This is the task that we have to do. The real crisis for the true believer is that the completion of God's salvation program for this world is so near. Time is so very short.

Please let me repeat, This is not "business as usual." Each one of us who claims to be a genuine believer has to ask, "Oh, Lord, what can I do?" I can witness to my loved ones. I can stand on a street corner and pass out tracts that proclaim the Gospel. I can encourage people to read the Bible.

Incidentally, I am in awe at what God is doing presently through Family Radio as we are able to reach whole continents with the Gospel. It is the very same Gospel that can be heard in so many cities in the United States. It is the whole counsel of God that Family Radio tries to bring. We are trying to be as faithful as possible to the Word of God.

They dare not say, "That's not for me. . . ."

God has placed an enormous responsibility in the lives of each and every true believer. They dare not say, "That's not for me. There are plenty of others who are available to carry out the task of warning the world. They will provide the funds. They will see to it that the work is done." If that is our thinking, then we better ask the question, "Am I really a true child of God?" (2 Corinthians 13:5). I am very, very candid about this because God commands the true people of God to remain on the housetops, and it is from the housetops that the Gospel is to be proclaimed. If we do not obey this command, it is because we are not truly saved (Matthew 24:42-51).

If we have been healed of our spiritual illness, we, like the demoniac who was healed of his demons (Luke 8:26-39), should be proclaiming to anyone who will listen what God has done in our life.

In Romans 10:17, we read:

So then faith cometh by hearing, and hearing by the word of God.

True believers know that the only faith which will secure the souls of people in this world is the faith of Jesus Christ. Only when God gives this faith to the sinner, and God accepts this faithfulness of Christ which justifies the sinner, will that sinner be in safety (Galatians 2:16, 20; Ephesians 3:14-19; Revelation 19:7-9, 11-14). Only then will that sinner be secure. Only then will that sinner not be incinerated in hell forevermore. Only then is there any kind of safety.

So what is the remedy for the world? They must hear the Word of God. That is why in our task today, as individual true believers, there is only one purpose, and that purpose is to get the Word of God out into the world.

> *The crisis is the authority of the Word of God.*

Earlier, I indicated that the crisis today is not the end of the church age. The crisis is the authority of the Word of God. That is the real crisis: The authority of the Bible. All kinds of people will hear this kind of message, and they will say, "Is he trying to scare people? Is he trying to get people to send money to Family Radio?" They can scorn and they can scoff all they want but the fact is that if people are not going to listen seriously to this kind of message, the question must be asked: "What do they think about the Word of God?" It is the Bible that is at issue. It is the Bible that is at issue (Amos 8:11).

The Final Minutes

The time is desperate; it is critical. It is super, super critical. It has never been more desperate. We have never been closer to the end than we are today. Never, never. It has never been so close. The trumpet is about to sound! We can almost hear the sound of the trumpet as we will hear it when Christ does come (1 Corinthians 15:52; Revelation 1:7). Yet God gives opportunity to warn the world. If we are truly saved, this concern should be burning in our souls all the time. How can we reach more people? What else can we do? We have got to reach the peoples of the world. The true believers, proclaimers of the Gospel, are the only early-warning security system for this granddaddy of all terrorists' activities that is going to come. And it is coming.

It is going to come. And yet, is it not true that we continue to live out our lives very complacently? Be honest about it. We are very complacent. Every day, if, really, God is working in our lives as true children of God, we ought to be thinking, it will not be long now, and that great terror is going to strike. Who can I warn? How can I help to tell somebody that it is time. And I know, as I warn, there will be scoffers. I know that my friends will think I am crazy. I know they will think I have lost my mind. I know all of that will happen. But that is beside the issue. I will not worry about how or what they think of me. I have got to warn. I have got to warn. There have been no individuals in the entire history of the world who, as true believers, have had a more insistent task than I have today.

We are in the final inning of the game.

Friends, we are in the wrap-up. We are in the final inning of the game. We are in the final minutes of the ball game. It is almost time for Christ to come. Beloved ones, do you get the picture? Do you get the picture? On the one hand, we are living in the most exciting time of history. But on the other hand, we are living in the most terrible time of the history of the world.

The Bible has threatened throughout its pages that the time will come when Christ will return to judge all the unsaved of the earth. Let us read again from Isaiah Chapter 13, verse 9:

Behold, the day of the LORD cometh, cruel both with wrath and fierce anger, to lay the land desolate: and he shall destroy the sinners thereof out of it.

Isaiah, under the inspiration of the Holy Spirit, wrote these words 2,800 years ago. Thus, it was 2,800 years ago that God was already warning mankind, and that warning has been sounded again and again throughout the Bible. However, today, it is not 2,800 years ago. In all likelihood, it is in your lifetime, and it may even be in my lifetime, that the day of the Lord will come, **"cruel both with wrath and fierce anger."**

Cruel! How can that be? God is a merciful God, a compassionate God. But now God says the day cometh with cruelty. Why? You see, there is no longer any mercy when Christ comes.

Oh, today there is mercy! Today there is mercy! Today there is still a great multitude that no man can number who are being saved! But when Christ appears on the clouds of glory on the last day, Judgment Day, there will be no mercy! There will be countless people at the Judgment Throne arguing in some way with God, saying, "But, oh, God, look how I have lived for you. Look at all of the good things I have done, and look at this and look at that. Oh, God, are you not a merciful God?" And God is effectively saying, "You never did become saved, and now it is too late. I must send you into eternal damnation because I never knew you! It is too late! The time is gone." That, my dear ones, is what God teaches in the Bible (Matthew 7:21-23).

I wish that I could be accused of, "Wow, are you exaggerating! Are you getting carried away!" I wish that could be an honest accusation, but it is not. I am not getting carried away. I wish I could be ten times more excited about this! I wish I could tremble 50 times more than I am trembling as I think about where the world is! And please remember, when you read about the various acts of terror that are going on, and they are going on, that is a diversion. That is a diversion to get our minds off the real problem. The real problem is that the greatest terror of all is almost here. It is almost here.

God is teaching that He has become cruel with wrath and fierce anger to lay the land desolate, and He shall destroy the sinners out of it. Isaiah 13:10a says:

For the stars of heaven and the constellations thereof shall not give their light.

There are times in the Bible, when God talks about stars, that He is referring to His eternal people (Genesis 15:5; Galatians 3:29; Hebrews 11:12). When Christ comes, the true believers no longer can bring the light of the Gospel to the world because God is finished with this world. Isaiah 13:10b says:

. . . the sun shall be darkened . . . .

Ordinarily, Christ is looked upon as the sun that rises with healing in His wings (Malachi 4:2). He, as the very essence of the Gospel light (John 8:12; Ephesians 5:13-14), is no longer saving. The sun is darkened. Isaiah 13:10c says:

. . . and the moon shall not cause her light to shine.

The moon, at times, is a picture of the Law of God (Psalm 72:1-2, 5-7; Jeremiah 31:35-36; Romans 6:14; Revelation 12:1). The whole Bible is the Law of God (Matthew 5:17-18; 24:35). And while God sometimes uses the word "moon" in the sense of bringing judgment (Isaiah 24:16-23; Joel 2:31; Acts 2:20; Revelation 6:12), in this setting, as in several others (Ezekiel 32:7-8; Joel 2:10; 3:15; Matthew 24:29; Mark 13:24), it does not give light, that is, God is speaking of the fact that there will be no more light of the Gospel. It is too late. It is too late! You can beg and cry and weep for mercy, and you can hope that there is still some possibility, but it is all gone. No wonder God says in Hebrews 2:3a:

How shall we escape, if we neglect so great salvation . . .

Of course, we know we cannot get anybody saved, God has to save them (Matthew 19:25-26). But we read in Romans 10:17:

So then faith cometh by hearing, and hearing by the word of God.

Read the Bible! Read the Bible!

So, again, if we are truly a person saved by God, truly a child of God, and thus an ambassador for Christ, what is our task? It is to get the Word of God out to the multitudes of the world. On the Family Radio program "The Open Forum," people call with their problems. They are being told that whatever their problems are, no man can truly help. God is the only solution. God speaks to us from the pages of the Bible (John 6:63). Therefore, read the Bible. Read the Bible! Read the Bible! Read it prayerfully, asking God to give you some understanding. Read it praying that you might be obedient to what you are commanded in the Bible. The task of the true believer is to encourage people to read the Bible (John 5:39; Romans 10:14-17; 2 Timothy 2:24-25).

If you are one of Christ's ambassadors and you are sharing the Gospel with someone, and he is arguing about a theological point, say, "Look, I don't know. I am not an expert in that; but let me tell you, you must read the Bible. Keep reading the Bible. Keep reading the Bible. I, as a Christian, find reading the Bible extremely valuable. In fact, God has given Sunday as a marvelous opportunity to read the Bible, study it, meditate upon it, and pray for obedience to it (Isaiah 58:13-14). In the Bible, I find the Gospel (Psalm 19:7-11). God's Gospel of Salvation is the only security system that can give any protection from this gigantic, super terrible terror that is about to happen."

God has given the responsibility to true believers to function as an early-warning security system. As true believers proclaim God's Word, they sound the alarm: "This day of terror is about to happen!" It will happen. Without any question whatsoever, it <u>will</u> happen. And it will happen very soon!

Chapter 2
Does God Exist?

The foregoing chapter describing the ultimate terror "Judgment Day" presupposes that there is a God. If we could know that God did not exist, then obviously, there would be no Judgment Day. If there were no Judgment Day, the ultimate act of terror described in this study could not happen. Thus, the worst terror this world would then face is further terrorist activity by evil men.

> *If we could know that God did not exist, then obviously, there would be no Judgment Day.*

Indeed, there are those who desperately try to prove that there is no God. Consequently they dream up such fantasies as evolution. In spite of the utterly impossible nature of evolution, there are those with brilliant minds who tenaciously cling to this preposterous idea. They must do this because if they admit there is a being that created this universe then they logically would know that they must someday answer to this Creator Being.

They know this intuitively because God has created mankind in the image of God (Genesis 1:27). The Bible tells us about the way mankind was created. In Romans 1:18-20, God informs us:

> **For the wrath of God is revealed from heaven against all ungodliness and unrighteousness of men, who hold the truth in unrighteousness; because that which may be known of God is manifest in them; for God hath shewed it unto them. For the invisible things of him from the creation of the world are clearly seen, being understood by the things that are made, even His eternal power and Godhead; so that they are without excuse . . .**
> .

Furthermore, in Romans 2:14-16, God declares:

> **For when the Gentiles , which have not the law, do by nature the things contained in the law, these, having not the law, are a law unto themselves: which shew the work of the law written in their hearts, their conscience also bearing witness, and their thoughts the mean while accusing or else excusing one another; in the day**

when God shall judge the secrets of men by Jesus Christ according to my gospel.

> *...while people would wish there were no higher being called God, deep in their hearts they know there is a God with whom they somehow must relate.*

Thus, while people would wish there were no higher being called God, deep in their hearts they know there is a God with whom they somehow must relate. Genesis 1:27 informs us that man was created in the image or likeness of God. Even though that image was severely marred by man's sin, mankind cannot claim that he has no knowledge whatsoever of God.

Man's problem with God becomes very serious because mankind was created in the image of God. Therefore, all mankind knows consciously or subconsciously that he has sin in his life. In his heart, he knows there is something terribly wrong when acts of murder, or stealing, or other vicious acts against his fellow man are committed. He also knows fundamentally that somehow the scales of justice must be balanced. The only Judge who is qualified to perfectly accomplish this is that Infinite Being who created this universe.

Thus, to many, the idea of the existence of a Creator Being, who is called God, is a completely unacceptable idea. Therefore, to avoid this altogether unacceptable conclusion, they have concocted such crazy ideas as evolution.

Evolution's Absurdities

The notion called evolution can easily be shown to be utterly impossible. Consider a simple object like a table. How did that table come into existence? No one can deny that a human being designed it and then carefully constructed it. Under no circumstance can anyone conclude that over a long period of time that table somehow evolved. Every person with even the slightest intelligence knows that.

Jump now to a human being with his more than three billion pairs of DNA in his genome. Obviously, the design of the human genome is a million times more complex than the design of the table. Thus, if a simple object like a table requires a designer, certainly a being as complex as a human being also requires a designer. Furthermore, if this table had to be manufactured by someone after it was designed, it should be immediately obvious that a human being also has to be made by someone. For that matter, everywhere we look in this universe we find millions of objects far more complex than a simple table. If a simple table could not be a product of evolution, then neither can any of these other millions of objects in the universe be a product of evolution.

The very fact that intelligent men and women slavishly maintain the idea of evolution is a fact in itself that proves there is a God who created the universe. The conduct of these individuals in believing in the supposed reality of such a preposterous idea as that of evolution in itself indicates that deep in their being, perhaps in their subconscious mind, they know that there must be a divine creator. What other reason could there be that would cause intelligent men and women to try to believe in such an impossible concept as evolution?

We might take note once more of the truths we are given in the Bible that show why some humans insist on believing in evolution. In Genesis 1:27, we read:

So God created man in his own image, in the image of God created He him; male and female created He them.

God further teaches in Romans 1:18-20, which we quoted and want to quote again because of the importance of this statement:

For the wrath of God is revealed from heaven against all ungodliness and unrighteousness of men, who hold the truth in unrighteousness; because that which may be known of God is manifest in them; for God hath shewed it unto them. For the invisible things of him from the creation of the world are clearly seen, being understood by the things that are made, even His eternal power and Godhead; so that they are without excuse . . . .

Remember, again, we read from Romans 2:14-16, where God instructs us:

For when the Gentiles , which have not the law, do by nature the things contained in the law, these, having not the law, are a law unto themselves: which shew the work of the law written in their hearts, their conscience also bearing witness, and their thoughts the mean while accusing or else excusing one another; in the day when God shall judge the secrets of men by Jesus Christ according to my gospel.

Significantly, God takes note of the foolishness of those who try to deny the existence of God by indicating so in both Psalm 14:1 and in Psalm 53:1 where we read:

The fool hath said in his heart, there is no God.

Frankly, they are in complete denial.

Given all of the foregoing information, one should not be surprised that it is especially the individuals with great human intelligence who would be most desirous to somehow prove the truthfulness of evolution. With superior human intelligence that God Himself gave them, they know there must be a Creator Being, and that Creator Being is someone to whom the human race must answer. But in their panic to silence this totally unacceptable conclusion, they have developed and tenaciously cling to this impossible idea of evolution. Frankly, they are in complete denial.

We have learned from Romans 2:14-16 that God's law is written on the hearts of man. We can see this principle in action in a number of ways. One way we see this is when we note that primitive peoples offered sacrifices to appease the angry gods. Not infrequently these sacrifices often included human sacrifices. Intuitively they concluded a life must be sacrificed as some kind of an ultimate payment for their wrongdoing.

As we have already learned from Romans 2, God's law to some degree is an integral part of man's personality. Therefore, naturally he knows there is some kind of a higher being that governs his life. Apart from the Bible, he knows very little about this higher being. He does know, however, that he must somehow find that intelligence -- he must find this higher being -- so that he can pay suitable homage to this being. He may decide therefore that it is the sun, the moon, or the constellations of the stars that is the supreme intelligence. He therefore will worship the sun, or he may follow the ideas of astrology. Or, it is possible that some animal is that supreme intelligence that he must recognize and worship. Thus, like the ancient Egyptians, an image of a calf is worshiped. Or it may be that this supreme intelligence called God can be designed by the worshiper himself. So he carves a tree or a rock until it resembled some kind of living person. In this way the Buddhist pays homage and worships a Buddha carved from a tree and gilded with scarlet, silver, and gold paint.

In our modern sophisticated society, we have been influenced to some degree by the Bible. So we believe there is a higher being whom we cannot see who has ultimate control over our life. Or, if we want to demonstrate our own superior intelligence, we can follow the lead of the atheists and evolutionists and attempt to insist that there is no God. As we witness their rejection of the existence of God, we can know how greatly mankind can be in denial of the fact that there is a Supreme Intelligence who rules the world.

> *The big problem is: where do we have*
> *information about this Supreme Being?*

The big problem is: where do we have information about this Supreme Being? Countless books have been written to explain this Supreme Intelligence whoever or whatever it may be. Worldwide religions like Buddhism or Islam have been developed in an effort to describe this higher being and how man is to relate to him. Unfortunately, all of these attempts to find this higher being and properly worship him are developed by the minds of men. Therefore, whatever wisdom that is offered can be no greater than that which is in man's mind alone.

As we saw earlier in this study, the world all around us with its billions of complex structures cries out for an acknowledgment that there must be an infinite mind that has designed and created this vast universe. Where can we go to find out about this great intelligence? Since man is simply one of the creatures who inhabits this universe, he is not qualified to find this supreme God. This is so even though he strives mightily to come to a solution as to who is this God.

The Bible Reveals the Complete Truth

Wonderfully, this Supreme Being Himself has revealed who this Supreme Intelligence is. Amazingly, He has written a book (2 Peter 1:20-21), which we call the Bible, in which He describes very much about Himself as well as how He brought this universe into existence. The Bible therefore is the most amazing and important book in the entire world. No other book can stand in its shadow. No other book is so absolutely true and trustworthy as the Bible (John 17:17) (see Preface).

Because the Bible is so impeccably true and trustworthy, it immediately becomes unacceptable to mankind. This is so because it describes in detail who mankind is and how humans fit into God's long-range plans. The Bible reveals that mankind was created in the image of God and therefore is accountable to God (Romans 1:18-23; 2:14-16). It reveals that God created mankind to serve God perfectly (Genesis Chapters 1-3; Revelation 22:3). And the Bible sets forth all the rules and principles mankind is to obey for the service of God (Matthew 4:4).

Among these laws is the law concerning the perfect justice of God (Romans Chapters 1-6). This law stipulates that if an individual disobeys any of the Biblical laws, he must someday stand before God as the Righteous Judge to answer for his breaking of God's law. The Bible calls this act of disobeying any of God's law sin. And because sin is rebellion against God, the Creator and Judge of the world, the penalty for sin described by God's law is an enormous penalty. That penalty is to be damned forever in a place the Bible calls **"the lake of fire"** (Revelation 20:15). It is a place where **"the smoke of their torment ascendeth up for ever and ever"** (Revelation 14:11).

Because mankind knows he has sinned, he therefore finds the Bible to be a totally unacceptable book.

Because mankind knows he has sinned, he therefore finds the Bible to be a totally unacceptable book. He absolutely does not want to think about a penalty for sin as great as that of eternal damnation. Consequently, as we have learned earlier, he blindly tries to become an atheist or an evolutionist. Or, he tries to design or become part of a religion with which he can be comfortable. In any event he tries very hard to believe the Bible is not God's book and that it has no authority over his life.

Unfortunately, this kind of thinking cannot and will not change the fact that the laws of the Bible will be carried out. Whether this individual likes it or not, in time he will be standing before the judgment throne of God to answer for his sins. God has a complete knowledge of each and every sin that each and every individual has committed (Hebrews 4:13). These sins may be sins of the mind, or of action, or of words, but each sin will be found out. Any one of the sins is sufficient to cause the sentence of eternal damnation to be decreed (James 2:10-13).

The fact is, if we want to be completely honest and realistic about our life, we must learn everything we possibly can about ourselves. And there is no other book that can begin to tell us about ourselves as the Bible is able to do (Psalm 119). Wonderfully, the Bible not only discloses to us the awful consequence of sin, but it also has much to say about the magnificent plan God has provided whereby a great multitude which no man can number will be rescued by God (Hebrews 7:25; 9:26b-28). This is God's salvation plan whereby many individuals will come to know that Jesus Christ is their Savior.

Mankind wants a salvation over which he can have some control.

However, even God's plan of salvation is altogether unacceptable to mankind. The Bible indicates this plan depends entirely on God's mercy and God's sovereign decision as to whom God has named to become saved (Romans

9:14-24). Because of man's sinful condition, he will never come to Christ on Christ's terms (John 5:38, 40). Those terms emphasize that an individual can make no contribution whatsoever to his salvation (Ephesians 2:8-9). He must wait entirely upon God's mercy as to whether or not he will become saved (Lamentations 3:26). This also is unacceptable to mankind. Mankind wants a salvation over which he can have some control. This he believes will more certainly make it possible for him to become saved, if and when he wishes to do so. At the same time, it is subconsciously satisfying to his ego that he is able to make some contribution to the grand work of his salvation (Romans Chapter 3 and Chapter 11:5-6).

The consequence of all this is that most individuals will find fault with the Bible (Psalm 50:16-17; Romans 9:20). They will argue that it is no more authoritative than any other religious book. For example, they believe that the Islamic Qoran or some book of that nature has equal authority. Or, they will readily believe those who claim the Bible has errors and contradictions within it. Or possibly they will simply ignore the Bible because they are too busy with their life.

Additionally, there will be those who might acknowledge the Bible as God's holy book, but they will pick and choose among the wealth of Biblical statements to extract those statements that appear to support what they wish to believe God's salvation plan should be (Matthew 23:23). In other words, the problem mankind faces is not that of the integrity or the truth or the authority of the Bible. The problem is that people ordinarily will not humbly submit to the Bible as the Word of God which is of supreme importance to each and every human being (Luke 12:57; John 7:24).

Only God Can Convince You

Arguments are frequently set forth as to why we are to believe that the Bible is the trustworthy Word of God. But no matter how convincing these arguments may be, these arguments will not cause anyone to begin to trust the Bible as the authoritative Word of God. This is so because it absolutely requires an action by God Himself working in the life of an individual to cause that individual to humble himself in the presence of the Bible, trusting that indeed the Bible is the Holy Word of God and is to be obeyed (John 3:21; Philippians 2:13). Therefore, the most meaningful way to address the question of the authority of the Bible is by means of the Bible itself. The words that we will quote are God's words. They are the voice of Almighty God Himself. In other words, we don't have to defend the authority and the trustworthiness of the Bible. The Bible is always constant and consistent. It is the sinful nature and lack of understanding of man that casts doubt on or brings disagreement about the teachings of Scripture. We know that only God Himself can give an individual spiritual understanding so that he will trust implicitly in God's Word the Bible.

With these principles in mind let us listen to God's own words concerning the nature and truth of the Bible.

Psalm 2:1-4:

> **Why do the heathen rage, and the people imagine a vain thing? The kings of the earth set themselves, and the rulers take counsel together, against the LORD, and against his anointed, saying, let us break their bands asunder, and cast away their cords from us. He that sitteth in the heavens shall laugh: the Lord shall have them in derision.**

Psalm 2:8-11:

> **Ask of me, and I shall give thee the heathen for thine inheritance, and the uttermost parts of the earth for thy possession. Thou shalt break them with a rod of iron; thou shalt dash them in pieces like a potter's vessel. Be wise now therefore, O ye kings: be instructed, ye judges of the earth. Serve the LORD with fear, and rejoice with trembling.**

Psalm 108:4:

> **For thy mercy is great above the heavens: and thy truth reacheth unto the clouds.**

Psalm 117:2:

> **For his merciful kindness is great toward us: and the truth of the LORD endureth for ever. Praise ye the LORD.**

Isaiah 40:13-15:

> **Who hath directed the Spirit of the LORD, or being his counsellor hath taught him? With whom took he counsel, and who instructed him, and taught him in the path of judgment, and taught him knowledge, and shewed to him the way of understanding? Behold, the nations are as a drop of a bucket, and are counted as**

the small dust of the balance: behold, he taketh up the isles as a very little thing.

Isaiah 40:17:

All nations before him are as nothing; and they are counted to him less than nothing, and vanity.

Isaiah 40:28:

Hast thou not known? hast thou not heard, that the everlasting God, the LORD, the Creator of the ends of the earth, fainteth not, neither is weary? there is no searching of his understanding.

Isaiah 41:4:

Who hath wrought and done it, calling the generations from the beginning? I the LORD, the first, and with the last; I am he.

Isaiah 46:9-10:

Remember the former things of old: for I am God, and there is none else; I am God, and there is none like me, declaring the end from the beginning, and from ancient times the things that are not yet done, saying, My counsel shall stand, and I will do all my pleasure:

Isaiah 48:3:

I have declared the former things from the beginning; and they went forth out of my mouth, and I shewed them; I did them suddenly, and they came to pass.

Matthew 24:35:

Heaven and earth shall pass away, but my words shall not pass away.

John 17:17:

Sanctify them through thy truth: thy word is truth.

In the first chapter of Romans, God makes this series of statements in which he assures us that every unsaved individual knows deep in his heart there is a God who is the Creator. He is God to whom they must answer. We have quoted these verses before, but they are so important, we are going to quote them again. We read in Romans 1:19-21:

Because that which may be known of God is manifest in them; for God hath shewed it unto them. For the invisible things of him from the creation of the world are clearly seen, being understood by the things that are made, even his eternal power and Godhead; so that they are without excuse: because that, when they knew God, they glorified him not as God, neither were thankful; but became vain in their imaginations, and their foolish heart was darkened.

And then God goes on to say in Romans 1:28-32:

And even as they did not like to retain God in their knowledge, God gave them over to a reprobate mind, to do those things which are not convenient . . . God, that they which commit such things are worthy of death, not only do the same, but have pleasure in them that do them.

God knows the hearts and minds of all mankind (Jeremiah 17:10). In these verses, God is speaking to us and assuring us that, without question, each and every human being is quite aware that there is a God to whom he must answer.

Since God has put a knowledge of God in the heart of each and every human being, it is God's purpose that they should also be told that the Bible is the Word of God (Jeremiah 22:29; 36:1-3; John 20:30-31). To assist them in this knowledge, God makes many statements whereby they can know the Bible is God's Word. Some of these are as follows:

2 Peter 1:21:

For the prophecy came not in old time by the will of man: but holy men of God spake as they were moved by the Holy Ghost.

2 Timothy 3:16:

All scripture is given by inspiration of God, and is profitable for

doctrine, for reproof, for correction, for instruction in righteousness.

Isaiah 42:9:

Behold, the former things are come to pass, and new things do I declare: before they spring forth I tell you of them.

Prophecies Given and Fulfilled

As we read these verses, we learn that God is emphasizing that one important way we can know that the Bible is true is, whenever God prophesied concerning a future event, that future event always came to pass. For example, there are numerous prophetic statements sprinkled throughout the Old Testament that give details concerning the coming of the Lord Jesus as Messiah. Such details as the city in which He was to be born (Micah 5:2), the tribe of Israel from which He was to come (Genesis 49:10), and the ugly reception He would receive from the Jewish people (see Psalm 22, Isaiah 53, and many other references) were all prophesied hundreds of years before they were literally fulfilled.

An excellent illustration of this characteristic of the Bible can be seen in a noteworthy fulfillment of events that were prophesied concerning the nation of Israel. The Bible predicted that, with the exception of a small percentage of the people of this nation, as a nation they would never accept Jesus as the Messiah. The Bible indicates this rejection would continue all the way to the end of the world (Isaiah 6:9-12; Amos 8:14; Mark 11:13-14; Romans 11:5-10, 25).

This prophecy is remarkable for two reasons. The first is that, in A.D. 70, Jerusalem was completely destroyed by the Romans, and for almost 1,900 years after this, the nation of Israel had no homeland. Effectively, they had disappeared from the world scene as a viable nation among the nations of the world. Therefore, how could they continue to reject Christ all the way to the end of the world, if they no longer existed as a nation that could reject Him?

The second reason this prophecy is remarkable is the importance of the name Jesus Christ on the world scene. Every nation has its favorite sons that they are proud to own and acknowledge because of the contributions that they have made to the world. Jesus Christ is a true Israelite from the tribe of Judah and the family of David. One would think that by now Israel would be only too ready to acknowledge Him as one of their favorite sons even though they may not agree altogether with His theological teachings. However the Bible already prophesied almost 2,000 years earlier that Israel would continue to reject Him all the way to the end of the world.

To make this prophecy become true they would have to again become a nation. Indeed, they would have to become a nation existing close to the end of the world. Only in this way would there be credible evidence that they would still be rejecting Christ all the way to the end of the world. This prophecy is given in the words of Romans 11:25:

> **For I would not, brethren, that ye should be ignorant of this mystery, lest ye should be wise in your own conceits; that blindness in part is happened to Israel, until the fulness of the Gentiles be come in.**

The whole chapter of Romans 11 is speaking of the sad fact that, except for a remnant chosen by grace, the nation of Israel would remain in blindness. Verses 5 through 8 declare this fact:

> **Even so then at this present time also there is a remnant according to the election of grace. And if by grace, then is it no more of works: otherwise grace is no more grace. But if it be of works, then is it no more grace: otherwise work is no more work. What then? Israel hath not obtained that which he seeketh for; but the election hath obtained it, and the rest were blinded (according as it is written, God hath given them the spirit of slumber, eyes that they should not see, and ears that they should not hear;) unto this day.**

Verse 25 prophesies that this blindness would continue until the fulness of the Gentiles would come in (that is, the Gentiles' coming to a saved relationship with Christ). In other words, as long as one non-Jew remained anywhere in the world that was to become saved and still remained unsaved, this blindness would still be on national Israel. Thus, this prophecy virtually demands that Israel would have to exist as a nation very near the end of the world. Only in this way could there be a clear indication that this prophecy had been fulfilled.

Fact is, the Bible prophesies in another place that before the end of the world Israel would be a nation once again. This fact is found when we understand the language of Mark 13:28-29 where we read:

> **Now learn a parable of the fig tree; When her branch is yet tender, and putteth forth leaves, ye know that summer is near: so ye in like manner, when ye shall see these things come to pass, know that it is nigh, even at the doors.**

This whole chapter of Mark is speaking of the time of the great tribulation, which comes just before the end of the world.

Frequently, God uses the figure of the fig tree to represent the nation of Israel. For example, in Mark 11, Jesus cursed a fig tree indicating it would never again bear fruit. This incident recorded in Mark Chapter 11, verses 12-14, and verses 20-21, is pointing to the fact that Israel, represented by the fig tree, would never again as a nation bear spiritual fruit (that is, trust in Jesus as their Savior). But the Mark 13:28-29 reference also discloses that as a harbinger of the nearness of the end of the world, it would again be a nation. It would be a fig tree with leaves. That is, it is a fig tree that represents Israel as a viable nation. But this fig tree would produce no spiritual fruit precisely as God prophesied concerning it in Romans 11:25. That is, as a nation they would reject Christ as their Messiah.*

Therefore, these two prophesies of Mark 13 and Romans 11, while sounding quite different from each other, in actuality are teaching the same truth, namely, that, very close to the end of the world, Israel would again be a nation. But they would be a nation that would still be rejecting Christ.

To our amazement and astonishment, these prophecies literally came true. In 1948, after almost 1,900 years of non-existence as a nation, Israel again became a nation with their own homeland. Moreover, after having continued more than 50 years since then as a viable nation among the nations of the world, Israel still rejects Christ as their Messiah even as Romans 11:25 had prophesied.

This prophecy is only one among a great many that the Bible has predicted would eventually come true and did come true. God repeatedly has demonstrated that He has the power, ability and authority to make each and every one of His prophesies come to pass.

One of the greatest prophesies of the Bible is yet to be fulfilled: the return of Jesus Christ and the end of the world. We dare to look into these prophesies because we know we can trust the Bible. As we see how God has worked out His salvation plan down through the ages, we will see how He will bring history to a grand and awesome conclusion for which we all must be ready!

> *We should be impressed with the fact that only God could have written the Bible.*

All of the information in this study is based upon prophecies from the Bible. As you read this study, I trust you will begin to understand that this writing is a result of the meticulous accuracy of the Bible, not the surmisings of man. And this study serves to put on display God's faithfulness in bringing these prophecies to fulfillment. We should be impressed with the fact that only God could have written the Bible.

Scholars can rave about other books that they have written, but they are nothing compared to the exquisite accuracy and integrity of the Bible. Need we say more to defend the Bible as God's Word? Indeed, all we must do is begin to carefully read it. But there is more that should be propounded before we begin to examine the Bible's teachings concerning the unfolding of God's plan for the history of the world. We should realize that the Bible is a divine instruction book for the human race.

THE BIBLE: An Instruction Book

When any of us purchase a computer or any complicated piece of equipment, the device normally comes with instructions concerning its use. In very similar fashion, God has given the earth to mankind. But He, too, has provided an instruction book to assist us in realizing the greatest blessings as we live on this earth. In His divine mercy and wisdom, He gave this book to mankind. This book is the Bible.

The instructions given with the purchase of a sophisticated instrument, or even a simple piece of furniture that must be assembled before it can be used, usually do not describe the object's density or chemical composition or any other intricate details concerning the materials used in the manufacture of the purchased object. Hopefully, however, there is enough information given so that maximum usage and enjoyment of the equipment can be obtained.

> *...the Bible is an exceptionally extraordinary instruction book that the Creator of all things has given to us!*

Similarly, God, in His instruction book the Bible, does not give us details of the chemical composition of any of the billions of objects He has created. He, in His instruction book, does not give details concerning electrons and radio-magnetic waves. But He does tell us how and when this universe came into being (Genesis 1:1; John 1:1-3). He does tell us how to best relate to everything God has created so that we can have the most blessed life (Deuteronomy 30:19-20;

Matthew 11:28-30). Indeed, the Bible is an exceptionally extraordinary instruction book that the Creator of all things has given to us!

Not only has the God of the universe given these instructions in the Bible, He has also created mankind with an ability to read and have some understanding of these instructions. Thus, we should begin to see that the Bible is supremely important.

If a complex instrument like a computer is given to an individual who has received no instruction whatsoever in the science of computer technology, and no instructions come with the computer, what is the likelihood that he will ever benefit from the use of that computer? It is more likely that, in a short time, he will have destroyed that computer because he made all the wrong attempts to make it work.

Likewise, mankind, without the instruction book the Bible, cannot achieve the security and happiness he desires. Fact is, the Bible shows that if anyone follows the rules of the Bible, there is a possibility he can have the absolute highest blessing and happiness. That blessing is to become eternally a child of God, serving Him and reigning with Him for evermore (Romans Chapter 8). Truly we must realize that the Bible is a super-supremely valuable book of instructions that God has given to mankind. What a pity that people do not want to carefully read this instruction book.

We might take note that sometimes instruction manuals that come with complex objects are difficult to understand. The more complex the instrument is, the more likely it will be that the instructions may be difficult to follow. Thus we should not be surprised when we discover that the Bible is difficult to understand. The Bible gives us information about an infinite God who has no beginning and who spoke and brought this world into existence (Psalm 147:4-5; Isaiah 48:12-13; Colossians 1:16-17; 1 Timothy 1:17). The Bible speaks about God's perfect justice that demands eternal damnation for those who violate even the smallest of God's rules (James 2:10-12). It also describes a love in which God Himself, in the person of the Lord Jesus Christ, made payment for sin on behalf of the rebellious humans He came to save (John 3:14-16, 10:11-15). You will recall that God created mankind to serve God perfectly (Matthew 5:48; 1 Peter 1:15-16). Yet, without the impartation of salvation by God to man, mankind is doomed to fall short of the perfection God demands (Romans 3:23). Thus, instead of having the highest blessing and maximum happiness, man ends up under the wrath of God, under eternal damnation (John 3:36). The Bible tells us that when God saves a man, He removes rebellion from the heart of man (Ephesians 2:12-17), so that once again, he can serve God acceptably (Hebrews 12:28).

As sinful humans, we cannot understand these awesome actions of God. We only argue and exclaim that we cannot trust the Bible. For example, we may contend that the Bible cannot be any more trustworthy than any other book that calls itself the Word of God.

However, God comes to the rescue! God can cause people to approach the Bible very humbly, recognizing that it is God Himself who is speaking (Psalm 65:4; Jeremiah 30:2; Romans 2:4). God Himself can work in the minds and hearts of men to make them begin to understand more clearly the instructions given in the Bible (Psalm 119).

This does not mean that those to whom God begins to give understanding of the Bible will become experts in Bible truth, increasingly being able to clearly understand each and every verse of the Bible (2 Peter 3:16-18). Rather it means that those who are assisted by God, in the person of the Holy Spirit (1 Corinthians 2:9-10), to understand the Bible will primarily and most importantly begin to understand that they are sinners who unquestionably deserve the eternal wrath of God as payment for their sins (Ezra 9:6, 13; Psalm 119:9; 1 Timothy 1:15). And they will increasingly understand that only God Himself, in the person of the Lord Jesus Christ, can make payment for sins (1 John 1:8 - 2:2). Of all of the truths set forth in this instruction book, these may be considered to be foundational if other truths of the Bible are to be understood (Hebrews 5:13-6:2).

How wonderful that God has given us such a magnificent instruction book! What a pity that most people do not want to carefully read it!

But much more must be said about the Bible .We shall see next that it is the supreme law book of the universe.

The Bible is the Supreme Law Book of God

The peoples of the world have little or no awareness of the fact that the Bible is a law book. Even among serious Bible students, the same ignorance of the Bible exists. However, in this study, we will see that the Bible reveals its major character as a law book. For example, in it God sets forth the laws, decrees, ordinances, statutes, and commandments by which God governs. The Bible sets forth all the rules and principles mankind is to obey for the service of God (Deuteronomy 10:12-13, 31:24-26; Micah 6:8).

> *Surprisingly, God Himself has made Himself subject to the same laws to which mankind is subject.*

Surprisingly, God Himself has made Himself subject to the same laws to which mankind is subject. In Psalm 138:2 we read:

I will worship toward thy holy temple, and praise thy name for thy lovingkindness and for thy truth: for thou hast magnified thy word above all thy name.

This remarkable and surprising citation spoken by God Himself and given as a tenant of God's holy Law informs us that God Himself is subject to the Word of God. The Word of God is the Bible, which is the Law of God. The words "laws," "statutes," "decrees," "ordinances," and "commands," etc., are synonyms found many hundreds of times in the Bible. For example, in the longest Psalm of the Bible (Psalm 119), which has more than 170 verses, we see that virtually each and every verse makes reference to the Law of God. The Bible (the Law book) stipulates how each human being is to conduct himself. The King, who rules over mankind and who has established the laws by which he is to live, is God Himself. He created this world together with mankind to bring praise and glory to Himself as the matchless Creator (Deuteronomy 4:32-40; Romans 11:36; Revelation 4:11). He created mankind in His own image and likeness and placed him in a beautiful perfect universe (Genesis 1:27-2:9; Isaiah 45:18).

However, because mankind was created in the image of God, God immediately established laws by which mankind was to live as they serve God as their King (Psalm 97:7-10a). If humans were to continue in the perfection in which they were created, they would have to continue to be as righteous as God Himself is righteous (Matthew 5:45-48). They, therefore, would have to perfectly obey all of the commands set forth in God's Law book (Galatians 3:10).

Therefore, to test man's fidelity to God, God immediately set up the testing arena by which our first parents -- Adam and Eve -- could be tested. God had already begun to lay down laws by which they were to live as God's servants. They were placed in a beautiful garden and commanded to dress (till) it and keep it (Genesis 2:15).

But, also in that beautiful garden, God placed a tree, giving it a very intriguing name: **"the tree of the knowledge of good and evil"** (Genesis 2:9b). God then gave Adam and Eve the command that they could eat of every tree in the garden, but in the day that they would eat of the tree of the knowledge of good and evil, they would surely die. Genesis 2:16-17 says:

And the LORD God commanded the man, saying, Of every tree of the garden thou mayest freely eat: but of the tree of the knowledge of good and evil, thou shalt not eat of it: for in the day that thou eatest thereof thou shalt surely die.

Already therefore, in the second chapter of Genesis, we can understand that God is a God of law. He sets forth the laws by which mankind is to live, and also indicates that penalty which will be placed on the law breaker. To these first laws given to mankind in Genesis Chapter 2, God eventually added many hundreds of additional laws. All of these laws are recorded in the Bible, the Law book of God.

> *The law given to Adam called for death as the penalty*
> *for breaking the law.*

The establishment of law also requires the prescribing of penalties for breaking that law. The law given to Adam called for death as the penalty for breaking the law (Genesis 2:17). As God continued to write His Law book the Bible, God became more and more specific as to what that death was. It was not physical death. It was a death far more terrible. When God created man in His own image, He created mankind to live forever even as God continues to live forever (Genesis 3:22). However, God's Law book, the Bible, also sets forth the principle that when man sins (breaks the Law of God, 1 John 3:4), the penalty is eternal damnation. Mankind will still exist forever in the future, but instead of living in the highest good and happiness, they are to be punished for their sins by being cast into Hell for all eternity as payment for their sins (Jeremiah 17:4; Matthew 25:46; Luke 12:5; Romans 2:7-8; 6:22-23; Revelation 14:11).

God has established the law and has decreed the punishment He requires as a consequence of breaking that law. But also required is a judge to adjudicate the matter. The Law book (the Bible) therefore tells us who the judge is.

The Judge is God Himself, who created man and who established the law. In Psalm 7:8, God declares:

The LORD shall judge the people . . . .

In Psalm 9:8, the citation is given:

And he shall judge the world in righteousness, he shall minister judgment to the people in uprightness.

However, if there is a judge who must judge the world, there must be a trial at which judgment will be made. God describes that trial in 2 Corinthians 5:10:

For we must all appear before the judgment seat of Christ; that every one may receive the things done in his body, according to that he hath done, whether it be good or bad.

This trial will take place at the end of the world. We read in John 12:48:

He that rejecteth me, and receiveth not my words, hath one that judgeth him: the word that I have spoken, the same shall judge him in the last day.

We see therefore that the trial will occur on the last day of this world's existence.

To know more about this trial we can turn to Revelation 20:11-12, where we read:

And I saw a great white throne, and him that sat on it, from whose face the earth and the heaven fled away; and there was found no place for them. And I saw the dead, small and great, stand before God; and the books were opened: and another book was opened, which is the book of life: and the dead were judged out of those things which were written in the books, according to their works.

How to Escape the Wrath of God

Thus far, then, we have before us some basic truths that show that the Bible is a law book. Since all mankind have sinned against God, all mankind stand guilty and can expect to receive punishment for that sin (Romans 2:3, 3:19). However, the Bible also discloses to us that there is a way of escape from the wrath of God. That way of escape is a result of the amazing mercy of God (Psalm 103:10-11). That way of escape is also an integral part of the law of God.

Remember earlier we learned that God Himself is subject to this same law book. He is the way of escape that has been set forth in the law book. The Bible decrees that since Christ is God, He has to carefully and meticulously carry out all that the Bible says about how this way of escape would occur. This is very important because Christ Himself as very God is the One who is to be the Savior (Isaiah 43:11; Luke 2:11; John 17:1-4; Hebrews 1:1-3, 8). He is the One who must bear the enormous wrath of God in order to provide the means by which this way of escape will operate (Isaiah 53:6; Romans 3:24-25; 2 Corinthians 5:21; 1 Peter 3:18). We are also delighted to know that this is all spelled out and set forth in the law book (the Bible) and that God Himself must perfectly carry this out because He has placed Himself under that law.

That way of escape is the gospel of God's grace (Ephesians 2:8). It is the good news of salvation (Hebrews 2:3a). It is a plan by which God's perfect justice is perfectly satisfied (Romans 3:23-26). It is a plan by which there will be many who escape the consequences of their sins (Isaiah 53:11). Instead of being cast into hell on the last day, they will end up in the highest bliss forevermore as sons of God reigning with Christ in the new heaven and new earth (Romans 8:16-18; 1 John 3:2; Revelation Chapter 21).

As we have learned from Psalm 138:2, the Word (the Law) of God is above His name. Therefore, when God in His great wisdom designed His plan of salvation, the Law of God could not be set aside or violated in anyway. Sin was sin. The wages of sin was death (Romans 6:23a). The death God had in mind consisted of those who were guilty of sin being eternally damned to Hell. The way of escape rigorously had to meet all of the requirements demanded by the Law of God.

When we carefully analyze what was required by God's Law as satisfaction or payment for the sins of those God would save, the solution is beyond our wildest imagination. It is an incredible act of God's love, mercy, and grace. Only an all-wise and perfectly loving God could conceive of such a plan and carry it out to fulfillment. In so doing, He must keep the Law of God perfectly.

The plan called for finding a substitute or stand-in for guilty man. That substitute would have to meet the following very rigorous qualifications.

1. He must be a human being because it was humans who rebelled against God by transgressing His perfect laws (1 Corinthians 15:21).

2. He must be a perfect human being without any sins of his own (2 Corinthians 5:21; 1 Peter 2:21-22).

3. He must be able to bear an enormous load of sin because every sin of every individual for whom he would become a substitute would have to be laid on him. He must bear the guilt for each and every one God intended to save from the wrath of God (Isaiah Chapter 53; Romans 5:11-19; 1 Peter 2:24).

4. He would have to be an individual who was able to endure a super enormous punishment for the sins that were to be laid on him and not be utterly and forevermore consumed in his attempt to pay for those sins (Romans 4:25; 1 Corinthians 15:20-22).

5. He had to be entirely willing to experience this horrible wrath of God that He Himself, being a perfect person, did not deserve at all (Matthew 16:21-23; Luke 22:41-42; 1 Peter 3:18).

Could such a person be found? God's perfect righteousness demanded that the rescue plan for sinful man could not violate in the slightest degree any part of the Law of God. The Bible reports that God looked for such an individual but none could be found. In Isaiah 63:5 we read:

> And I looked, and there was none to help; and I wondered that there was none to uphold: therefore mine own arm brought salvation unto me; and my fury, it upheld me.

Of course, such a qualified person did not exist anywhere. Remember we read in Romans 3:10-12:

> As it is written, There is none righteous, no, not one: there is none that understandeth, there is none that seeketh after God. They are all gone out of the way, they are together become unprofitable; there is none that doeth good, no, not one.

Given this sad fact, that there could not be a human anywhere that could begin to provide the way of escape, God Himself had to do the impossible. God Himself, in the person of the Lord Jesus Christ, took on a human nature (Philippians 2:5-8). Christ, who, by God, is called the Son of God, also became the Son of man. By being born of Mary (Matthew 1:18-25; Galatians 4:4-5), He took on a human nature. He thus met the qualification of being part of the human race.

He Himself, however, had no sin. We read in 2 Corinthians 5:21:

> For he hath made him to be sin for us, who knew no sin; that we might be made the righteousness of God in him.

God then gave to Christ all those whom God had chosen to save (to experience this way of escape from hell). We read in John 6:37:

> All that the Father giveth me shall come to me; and him that cometh to me I will in no wise cast out.

In John 17:2, we read that, as Jesus is praying, He declares:

> As thou hast given him power over all flesh, that he should give eternal life to as many as thou hast given him.

However, in order for Christ to have these who were given to Him eternally, He had to provide payment for their sins. Otherwise, they would have to first spend eternity in Hell to pay for their sins. Since eternity is forever, Christ would never be able to take them into heaven as His own. Therefore, the sins of these individuals, every dirty, rotten, awful one of them, were laid on Jesus Christ who had been named by God to be their Substitute or stand-in. Again note 2 Corinthians 5:21:

For he hath made him to be sin for us, who knew no sin; that we might be made the righteousness of God in him.

We read in Isaiah 53:5-6:

But he was wounded for our transgressions, he was bruised for our iniquities: the chastisement of our peace was upon him; and with his stripes we are healed. All we like sheep have gone astray; we have turned every one to his own way; and the LORD hath laid on him the iniquity of us all.

The "us all" in these verses are all those whom God had elected to be His people and who had been given to Christ by the Father (John 17:2, 9, 11-12, 24). The Law book (the Bible) further declares in Ephesians 1:3-7:

Blessed be the God and Father of our Lord Jesus Christ, who hath blessed us with all spiritual blessings in heavenly places in Christ: according as he hath chosen us in him before the foundation of the world, that we should be holy and without blame before him in love: having predestinated us unto the adoption of children by Jesus Christ to himself, according to the good pleasure of his will, to the praise of the glory of his grace, wherein he hath made us accepted in the beloved. In whom we have redemption through his blood, the forgiveness of sins, according to the riches of his grace.

Since Christ was the Substitute provided by God to satisfy the demands of God's Law book on behalf of those whom God planned to save, Christ had to be and was altogether willing to endure a punishment that would be equal to that which should have been endured by each and every one whom God had elected to become saved (Hebrews 9:26b-28). Only because Jesus never ceased to be God was it possible for Him to carry out this enormous requirement (Isaiah 63:5; Luke 22:41-42; John 10:28-30).

Only God can see all the sins of which Jesus has become guilty.

The trial of Jesus was about to begin. The Judge was God Himself. But in God's perfect justice, the Judge must also be represented by a human judge. God selected Pontius Pilate who represented Caesar, the highest ruler of the world in that day, to be that judge (Matthew 27:2). Jesus is to be brought to trial to discover His guilt or innocence. Only God knows that Jesus is terribly guilty. Only God can see all the sins of which Jesus has become guilty because each and every sin of each and every person whom God had given to Christ had been laid upon Him (Isaiah 53:6). Fact is, Jesus could have never returned to heaven unless full payment had been made for every one of those sins (John 17:1-5; Hebrews 1:1-3).

What a terrible situation! Jesus realizes the enormous punishment He must bear to satisfy the perfect justice of God. There could be no lessening of the punishment demanded by God's Law. There could be no pity or mercy shown Christ. He was guilty before God's perfect Law. God was under the Law of God (the Bible) so that He had to perfectly exact a punishment that would be completely equal to that which should have been endured by each and every one of those whom God had elected to salvation. That punishment was the fact that each of them should spend an eternity in hell.

No wonder, as Jesus is preparing to go before Pilate, the sweat is pouring off His body like great drops of blood to the ground (Luke 22:44). No wonder He prays in astonishment, **"Father, if it be possible, let this cup pass from me"** (Matthew 26:39). The cup is the cup of God's wrath that He must endure until the payment for each and every sin that had been laid on Him had been made (Mark 14:23-24; John 18:11).

No one will ever know the awful suffering Jesus was beginning to suffer. We do not know how God was punishing Him (Isaiah 53:10). We obtain a little insight as we see Him hanging on the cross. The cry is wrenched from His lips, **"My God, My God, why hast thou forsaken me?"** (Matthew 27:46). We will never understand the supreme horror of God forsaking God. For as Christ suffered, He never ceased to be God (Matthew 27:54; Philippians 2:8-11).

He was nailed to a cross to show the world that He had become cursed by God. We read in Galatians 3:13:

Christ hath redeemed us from the curse of the law, being made a curse for us: for it is written, Cursed is every one that hangeth on a tree.

As we see Him in the Garden of Gethsemane, piteously praying that the cup of God's wrath might pass from Him, we also see His perfect obedience, His perfect willingness to be the Substitute as He declares, **"not my will but thine be done"** (Luke 22:42b). Christ was the perfectly willing Substitute.

He was also the perfectly capable Substitute. Before the daylight hours ended that Friday afternoon, we hear the wonderful words from the lips of Jesus from the cross, **"It is finished"** (John 19:30). He, for sin, had fully paid the penalty demanded by the Law of God. The Law of God had been fully satisfied. God could now legally forgive the sins of those whom God had elected to become saved (Isaiah Chapter 53; Romans 5:11-19).

We thus see that as God provided a way of escape for the elect of God so that they would never have to stand for judgment, the perfectly righteous justice and integrity of God was perfectly maintained (Romans 3:26). In 2 Corinthians 5:10 we read that every human being has to stand before the judgment seat (Greek: bema) of Christ. When Jesus stood before Pilate to receive the condemnation of God for the sins that had been laid on Him, the same Greek word (bema) is used by God in describing Pilate's judgment seat (Matthew 27:19; John 19:13).

Thus, by Jesus having been found guilty for sin and making payment for sin as God brought His wrath on Him, the requirements of 2 Corinthians 5:10 (that each and every person must be tried before the judgment seat of Christ) was completely satisfied for His elect. That is why God can declare in Romans 8:1:

There is therefore now no condemnation to them which are in Christ Jesus . . .

That is why the Law also declares in Revelation 3:10:

Because thou hast kept the word of my patience, I also will keep thee from the hour of temptation, which shall come upon all the world, to try them that dwell upon the earth.

The word "temptation" in this verse should be translated "trial." This verse is assuring true believers in Christ that they will never be brought to trial. This is so because Christ as their Substitute has already stood for trial on their behalf.

We thus should see that the whole context and message of the Bible is very legal. It is no wonder the Bible repeatedly speaks of itself as the law.

However, one of the major messages of the Bible -- that it is the law book -- is frequently obscured because of the complex language God uses. It is also obscured by the numerous historical events that are recorded throughout the Bible. But when we begin to understand that the Bible is a law book, we can be greatly helped in our understanding of phrases that are otherwise very difficult and complex. We also are helped in our understanding of those historical events that are recorded all through the Bible. Invariably we find that sin brings judgment. This is true whether it is a sin of a wicked nation like Babylon (Jeremiah Chapters

50 and 51), or sin taking place in a holy place like the temple in Jerusalem (John 2:13-17), or in the local congregations at the end of the church age (Jeremiah 6:10-19; Matthew 24:15). The more clearly we understand the Bible to be a book of law, the more clearly we will understand the otherwise more difficult parts of the Bible. Of course, we must never forget that it is only God who can lead us into any truth (John 14:6, 16:13, 17:17).

This brings us to the present situation that exists in the world. More than six billion people are living today. Unless they have become saved, each and every one is destined to stand before the judgment seat of Christ to answer for their sins. And as this study will show, we are only a short time from that awful event. Already we have learned that the final judgment has already begun. This is so because God's judgment is presently upon all of the local congregations throughout the world (1 Peter 4:17) (see *The End of the Church Age and After* and *Wheat and Tares*, available from Family Radio).

But now we should begin our study of the timeline of the unfolding of God's magnificent salvation plan. In the process, we will learn much about God's timetable for the end of the world.

Writers of history are interested in a variety of events they feel are especially to be considered as significant markers of the passage of time. The rise and fall of civilizations, the development of scientific knowledge, the occurrence of significant wars of the past, or the appearance of certain notable or notorious rulers are some of the markers that emphasize the movement of time throughout the history of the world.

However, the Bible, which is the only true and trustworthy document that embraces, with perfect accuracy, the history of the world, utilizes an entirely different kind of time marker. It shows us that the timeline of history is governed by the unfolding of God's salvation plan which He has provided for the world.

Because the Bible is extremely accurate and true in all that it declares, we can know that, from the Bible, we have a perfect record of the history of the world.

The Creation of Time

> *In between these two "everlastings" is the time of the existence of the planet Earth.*

The Bible is the supreme law book that proclaims the message of salvation by our Lord Jesus Christ. We have already examined to a tiny degree this amazingly perfect legal solution to the problem of sinners and their transgression of God's law. Now the Bible speaks of Jesus being from everlasting to everlasting (Psalm 41:13). In between these two "everlastings" is the time of the existence of the planet Earth. When God created this universe, He also created time. Fact is, on the fourth day of creation, He created the magnificent celestial clock which is our solar system. The sun, the planets, the earth and the moon are all integral parts of this huge celestial clock that ticks off the days, the months, the seasons and the years. We read in Genesis 1:14-18:

> **And God said, Let there be lights in the firmament of the heaven to divide the day from the night; and let them be for signs, and for seasons, and for days, and years: and let them be for lights in the firmament of the heaven to give light upon the earth: and it was so. And God made two great lights; the greater light to rule the day, and the lesser light to rule the night: he made the stars also. And God set them in the firmament of the heaven to give light upon the earth, and to rule over the day and over the night, and to divide the light from the darkness: and God saw that it was good.**

We do not readily recognize that when God planned the salvation program for the planet Earth, He established a very precise time frame for the unfolding of this marvelous salvation program. We do know that before God created this universe and before He had created time, He had already designed His entire salvation program. He had already named each and every person that He planned to save. God's method of saving was already worked out. The Bible reports that Christ as the sacrificial lamb was **"slain from the foundation of the world"** (Revelation 13:8b). However, along with these super important details of God's salvation plan, God also developed a very detailed time program that pre-scheduled each event in this salvation plan. God summarizes this principle by the language of Ecclesiastes 3:1, where we read:

> **To every thing there is a season, and a time to every purpose under the heaven.**

This verse emphasizes that there is a time to every purpose under the heaven. That is, time is of essence wherever God's will is to be done. This principle is further detailed in the next seven verses of Ecclesiastes Chapter 3 as God declares that there is:

> **A time to be born, and a time to die; a time to plant, and a time to**

pluck up that which is planted; a time to kill, and a time to heal; a time to break down, and a time to build up; a time to weep, and a time to laugh; a time to mourn, and a time to dance; a time to cast away stones, and a time to gather stones together; a time to embrace, and a time to refrain from embracing; a time to get, and a time to lose; a time to keep, and a time to cast away; a time to rend, and a time to sew; a time to keep silence, and a time to speak; a time to love, and a time to hate; a time of war, and a time of peace.

Each of the statements in these seven verses relates to aspects of the unfolding of God's salvation plan. God illustrates this as He, at various junctures in His salvation plan, speaks of the particular event being addressed as occurring in accordance with a previously-planned time program.

For example, in Acts 7:17, God speaks of Israel in Egypt. This verse states:

But when the time of the promise drew nigh, which God had sworn to Abraham, the people grew and multiplied in Egypt.

Or again, in Mark 1:15, where God says:

... The time is fulfilled, and the kingdom of God is at hand: repent ye, and believe the gospel.

The phrase "the time is fulfilled" indicates that this moment when Jesus began to preach in Galilee was in accord with a previously-planned timetable.

The same principle is stated in connection with the first coming of Christ. Galatians 4:4 declares:

But when the fulness of the time was come, God sent forth his Son, made of a woman, made under the law.

The same kind of language is found in Ephesians 1:10, where we read:

That in the dispensation of the fulness of times he might gather together in one all things in Christ, both which are in heaven, and which are on earth; even in him.

Similar language is used in Luke 9:51 where we read:

And it came to pass, when the time was come that he should be received up, he steadfastly set his face to go to Jerusalem.

When God speaks about the time plan for the end of the world, He declares in Daniel 8:19:

. . . Behold, I will make thee know what shall be in the last end of the indignation: for at the time appointed the end shall be.

Similarly, in Habakkuk 2:3, God says:

For the vision is yet for an appointed time, but at the end it shall speak, and not lie: though it tarry, wait for it; because it will surely come, it will not tarry.

From the above Biblical references, we should understand that God's whole salvation plan for this earth was carefully pre-programmed to follow a very precise time schedule.

> *God's whole salvation plan for this earth was carefully pre-programmed to follow a very precise time schedule.*

Now we should realize why God has put so much time information in the Bible. Earlier, we briefly looked at Acts 7:17 in which the time for Israel to go out of Egypt is spoken of as having almost come. Then, within the next few verses, God makes four distinct time references. In Acts 7:20, we read:

In which time Moses was born, and was exceeding fair, and nourished up in his father's house three months.

In Acts 7:23, we read:

And when he was full forty years old, it came into his heart to visit his brethren the children of Israel.

Also, in Acts 7:30, God says:

And when forty years were expired, there appeared to him in the

wilderness of mount Sina an angel of the Lord in a flame of fire in a bush.

And in Acts 7:36, we read:

He brought them out, after that he had shewed wonders and signs in the land of Egypt, and in the Red sea, and in the wilderness forty years.

Obviously, the amount of time required for each event to occur is a very important part of the Gospel message.

> *...the whole Bible is a calendar that details the various important milestones in the unfolding of God's Gospel plan.*

Thus, we should not be surprised when we learn that the whole Bible is a calendar that details the various important milestones in the unfolding of God's Gospel plan. To understand this calendar will be one important goal of this study. We will discover that these important milestones did not occur in any random or haphazard form. Instead, we will discover that each event is time-related to other important events in a very distinct pattern that must have been previously carefully designed.

One curious fact is that there was also a time for God to enlighten the minds of His people, so that they might know this Biblical calendar of history. Amazingly, it is only in our generation that this calendar has been found in the Bible. Why God waited until this time when we have come almost to the very end of time before He made the calendar known is a puzzle in itself.

We can speculate that because the Bible does not reveal a probable date for the end of the world, people have not taken seriously the idea of a judgment day. A day of reckoning has been largely dismissed because it always has been projected so far into the distant future. But the teaching of the Bible is that at any time that awful day is close at hand. This is so because when a person dies, the next moment he will experience will be the moment he has been resurrected to stand before Christ as the Judge.

Perhaps God did not want to encourage premature discussion of this subject which, to some, is very interesting and enticing but which might intrude upon the most important focus of the Bible – salvation. Perhaps this is one of the reasons for Jesus' words in Acts 1:7 after the disciples asked Him if this were the time that He would **"restore again the kingdom to Israel"** (Acts 1:6b). Jesus replied to them:

> **. . . It is not for you to know the times or the seasons, which the Father hath put in his own power.**

However, as we have come very close to the very end of history, a discussion of the possible timing of the end of time itself, enhances the warning that Christ is coming as the Judge of all the earth. Thus the need for salvation is greatly magnified. It should cause mankind to search the Bible more carefully than ever in an effort to find truth.

This surely gives major insight into what God teaches in Daniel 12, that is, the principle of progressive revelation. Daniel 12 teaches that there are many things in the Bible that are sealed up until the time of the end. That is, as we come to the end of the world, there are many teachings of the Bible that God did not allow earlier searchers of Bible truth to understand but which are now becoming increasingly understood.

Certainly it is the duty of a faithful Bible teacher to share those doctrines which he has come to understand as God has opened his understanding to Bible truth.

True Believers Are Watchmen

Moreover, the Bible teaches that the true believers are watchmen. We read in Ezekiel 33:2-6:

> **Son of man, speak to the children of thy people, and say unto them, When I bring the sword upon a land, if the people of the land take a man of their coasts, and set him for their watchman: if when he seeth the sword come upon the land, he blow the trumpet, and warn the people; then whosoever heareth the sound of the trumpet, and taketh not warning; if the sword come, and take him away, his blood shall be upon his own head. He heard the sound of the trumpet, and took not warning; his blood shall be upon him but he that taketh warning shall deliver his soul. But if the watchman see the sword come, and blow not the trumpet, and the people be not warned; if the sword come, and take any person from among them, he is taken away in his iniquity; but his blood will I require at the watchman's hand.**

Remember we read, for example, in Luke 12:37-38:

Blessed are those servants, whom the lord when he cometh shall find watching: verily I say unto you, that he shall gird himself, and make them to sit down to meat, and will come forth and serve them. And if he shall come in the second watch, or come in the third watch, and find them so, blessed are those servants.

The watchmen, the true believers, are faithfully to sound the warning concerning what they can know from the Bible concerning the closeness of Judgment Day.

In any case, at this time in history, when we have approached very close to the time when the world will come to an end, God has revealed the fact that the Bible gives us a detailed calendar of the history of this earth. As God opens our understanding of this very interesting and important subject, we learn afresh how difficult it is to understand the Bible. Fact is, God has hidden the necessary Biblical information concerning the Calendar of the Bible to such a degree that no Bible students or theologians have come to an understanding of it until our day.

Incidentally, we must understand that an enlarged understanding of this important subject did not come because someone is smarter or more worthy or more holy than those who in the past have searched the Bible for truth. It is only because we are now living at a time when God is revealing many truths of the Bible to His true believers who are earnestly searching the Word. God has prophesied concerning this matter. Daniel 12:9 declares:

. . . Go thy way, Daniel: for the words are closed up and sealed till the time of the end.

Eternity Past

We will learn in this study that time began in the year 11,013 B.C. However, God's law book, the Bible, reaches into eternity past. We, of course, do not understand eternity. Our minds were designed to identify with time. Time is regulated by the great celestial clock that God spoke into existence on the fourth day of creation. But prior to the first day of creation, time did not exist. There did exist eternity however, which our human knowledge cannot measure. The best we can say is that what existed before time was "eternity past."

We will also learn that there is an "eternity future." We will see that this concept identifies with the end of time which will come on the day that Christ, the Judge of all the earth, comes to end this earth's existence. At this point, however, let's read several passages that give a little insight into eternity past.

In speaking about eternity past God uses the phrase "from everlasting." We read, for example, in Psalm 41:13:

Blessed be the LORD God of Israel from everlasting, and to everlasting. Amen, and Amen.

Again, in Psalm 90:2, we read:

Before the mountains were brought forth, or ever thou hadst formed the earth and the world, even from everlasting to everlasting, thou art God.

God also uses language such as "before the foundation of the world." Now in this present universe, planet earth is the most important planet because it serves as the locale for God's salvation program. Therefore God uses the words "before the foundation of the world" to refer to eternity past. We read in John 17:24:

Father, I will that they also, whom thou hast given me, be with me where I am; that they may behold my glory, which thou hast given me: for thou lovedst me before the foundation of the world.

Again, we read in Ephesians 1:4 as God speaks of His grand plan of salvation:

According as he hath chosen us in him before the foundation of the world, that we should be holy and without blame before him in love:

Or, in yet another example, 1 Peter 1:18-20, speaks about Christ as the Savior:

Forasmuch as ye know that ye were not redeemed with corruptible things, as silver and gold, from your vain conversation received by tradition from your fathers; but with the precious blood of Christ, as of a lamb without blemish and without spot: who verily was foreordained before the foundation of the world, but was manifest in these last times for you,

By these Biblical citations we learn that not only did there exist an eternity before the creation of time but that also God's plan of salvation was worked out in meticulous detail before the first day of creation.

Because God is infinite in every aspect of His being,
He knew every individual who would be born...

Because God is infinite in every aspect of His being, He knew every individual who would be born at any time during the duration of the history of the world, even before He created time. God also knew that our first parents, Adam and Eve, whom He would create, would rebel against His law and plunge the whole human race into rebellion against God (Romans 5:12). As a consequence, that rebellion could only bring the righteous justice and wrath of God against mankind. But because God is a God of salvation, the Bible tells us that He would choose to withhold His wrath from many who are just as deserving of eternal punishment as all the others. Therefore, in eternity past, before time began, God had already chosen those whom He would save. He already had prepared for their salvation by choosing to become their substitute in Christ, **"in him dwelleth all the fulness of the Godhead bodily"** (Colossians 2:9). The Lord Jesus Christ was to be their Savior so that in principle, He, as the great I AM, the ever-present One (John 8:58; John 17:5), was **"the Lamb slain from the foundation of the world"** (Revelation 13:8b).

Earlier, we learned that the death of Christ was payment for each and every sin of those whom He came to save. Since Christ, in principle, was slain from the foundation of the world, we may conclude that He knew about each and every sin that would ever be committed by those He came to save.

In addition to the verses quoted above, we read in Matthew 25:34, where God says:

Then shall the King say unto them on his right hand, Come, ye blessed of my Father, inherit the kingdom prepared for you from the foundation of the world:

We also read in Hebrews 4:3 where God says:

For we which have believed do enter into rest, as he said, As I have sworn in my wrath, if they shall enter into my rest: although the works were finished from the foundation of the world.

> *God's great and wonderful salvation plan was the motivating*
> *cause for His creation of this amazing planet Earth.*

Thus, we learn that God's great and wonderful salvation plan was the motivating cause for His creation of this amazing planet Earth. We, therefore, should not at all be surprised to learn that what governs the timeline of earth's history is the unfolding of God's marvelous work of salvation. Everything connected with God's salvation program works to unfold the greatest event in all of history. No earthly story, no human saga, no sprawling epic can come within an eternity of matching what God is declaring in His Word the Bible. Fact is, God's magnificent salvation plan is the very substance and essence of history. How then, and when, and where did it all begin?

Before the start of any great trip, whether it be a journey to the South Pole or the ascent to the top of the earth's highest mountain or a trip to the moon, enormous and detailed preparations must be made. So, too, before the beginning of the unfolding of God's salvation program, enormous preparations were made. In no particular chronological order, those preparations included but were not limited to the following.

- Creation of the universe to demonstrate the glory of God as Creator.
- Creation of time.
- Creation of the planet earth, the locale where God's salvation program would be developed and which eternally would identify with mankind.
- Creation of mankind in the image and likeness of God.
- Naming of Christ to be the Savior.
- God's choosing of all those who were to become saved.
- Creation of angels to be servants of God. Some would be used of God as His servants in His salvation program. Some would rebel and become instrumental in the rebellion of mankind.
- Creation of the great celestial time clock (our solar system) to mark the passage of time and also to provide types and figures of various aspects of God's salvation program.
- Establishment of the law of God which began rather simply and finally was expanded to become the entire Bible.
- Christ, in principle, dying for the sins of those who were chosen

to salvation so that, from the moment mankind sinned, salvation was an existent reality.

- Establishing a testing arena where our first parents could be tested concerning their obedience to God. This testing arena was the beautiful Garden of Eden, which was located in the perfect world that God had created. This garden was to typify how the perfect kingdom of God (consisting of those who would become saved), would exist in a world which would become altogether sinful. (See also *The Glorious Garden of Eden*, by Harold Camping, available from Family Radio free of charge.)
- Establishment of the seventh-day Sabbath as a day of rest. God Himself rested on the seventh day of creation. This was a tremendous sign pointing to the fact that we must never try to achieve salvation by our own efforts. (See also *Sunday: The Sabbath*, by Harold Camping, available from Family Radio.)
- The institution of marriage which would point to the beautiful fact that man would become married to Christ. (See also *What God Hath Joined Together,* by Harold Camping, available from Family Radio, free of charge.)

Within a very short time, the whole salvation plan was set into motion.

- Desiring to be a king like God, the angel Lucifer rebelled against God.
- Taking on the form of a serpent, Lucifer tempted Eve so that she disobeyed God by eating the forbidden fruit.
- Eve gave the forbidden fruit to Adam. He, too, in disobedience, ate of it.
- Mankind became spiritually dead. They no longer were energized by God, and God no longer dwelt within them.
- Also known as Satan or the devil, the serpent was cursed but was given the right to rule over mankind.
- Mankind was cursed and became completely infected by sin because God no longer energized them. The whole human race became subject to eternal damnation both in body and soul.
- Adam and Eve were driven out of the Garden of Eden wherein was the tree of life. The cherubim with a flaming sword were placed at the entrance of the garden. The cherubim with the flaming sword represented God as the Judge. God was portraying that the only

way for anyone to get into the kingdom of God (the Garden of Eden) wherein Christ (the tree of life) is, is for that person first to be judged for his sins. This meant that no one could ever come into heaven where Christ is unless he first spent an eternity in hell paying for his sins. Because eternity is forever, this excluded all mankind from heaven, unless a capable and willing substitute could be found to pay for their sins.

- The earth itself was cursed so that it became, in many ways, an enemy of man. Thorns, thistles, poisonous animals, poisonous bacteria, carnivorous animals, etc. resulted from this curse. Immediately man's life span began to become shorter and shorter.
- Adam and Eve discovered their physical nakedness which was a picture of their spiritual nakedness; that is, God could readily see their sin-infected personality.
- God killed animals and provided animal skins to cover the nakedness of Adam and Eve. This action was pointing to the essence of God's salvation plan that must unfold. The killed animals represented Christ as the Savior who must die, that is, He must suffer eternal damnation, for the sins of God's chosen people.

All of the above is from the most reliable history book of all ages. It is completely without error and will stand any test it may be given. The Bible is God's supernal revelation of truth to each and every one of us.

Now that we have briefly outlined the fundamental elements of God's marvelous salvation plan, we should go through the Bible to discover from its pages God's calendar that is set forth which is, indeed, the oldest and best calendar, yes, the perfect calendar of the history of the world. Once we have accomplished this, we can again begin at the beginning and from there proceed down the timeline of history, giving some details that relate to all-important milestones in the unfolding of God's salvation plan.

Chapter 3
Calendar Patriarchs

Discovering the calendar of history is no easy matter. God has intentionally buried all the necessary information concerning this important subject deep in the language of the Bible. Only in God's own timetable will He open our understanding concerning this.

To begin our search, we have to remember several very significant truths. The first is that the Bible is the Word of God. Therefore, regardless of how difficult or complicated the language of the Bible may appear to be, it is absolutely true and trustworthy.   .

Secondly, we must keep in mind that any understanding we may receive must come from the Bible.

Thirdly, God wrote the Bible in such a way that each conclusion we come to must stand the scrutiny of any and every verse of the Bible that relates to the same subject. This verification of the Bible by the Bible is the only way we can be assured that our conclusions are correct.

Fourthly, we must understand that each word in the original languages of the Bible is completely accurate, exactly how God intended every word to be. Those words came from the mouth of God (Jeremiah 1:9, 36:2; Ezekiel 33:7; 2 Timothy 3:16; 2 Peter 1:21). Even though we may have great difficulty understanding a particular word or phrase, the truth conveyed by that very word or phrase is altogether trustworthy because it is given to us by God Himself.

The fifth truth that encourages us is the fact that at this present time in history the evidence is mounting that we are very close to the end of the world. By means of the Bible, God is revealing much additional information concerning this momentous truth -- truth that had been denied earlier Bible students.

Verbal Clues to Lineage Patterns of Biblical Speech

We shall now attempt to develop a chronology of history from the Biblical statements, approaching the Bible in the manner we have discussed. We must begin this search with the study of the genealogical record of Genesis Chapters 5 and 11. If further light could be given to arrive at a proper understanding of these important chapters, a great stride forward would be taken toward the development of a consistent statement regarding the exact date of Adam, the Flood, and other phenomena of history. Such new information and interpretation would point up anew the true believer's trust in the total accuracy and authority of the Bible, especially with regard to the early chapters of Genesis which long have been open to dispute.

> *The Bible must be accepted as God's inerrant word to man*
> *and is, therefore, entirely trustworthy.*

Again, I must emphasize that as a fundamental starting point, one basic fact must be acknowledged as a presupposition upon which this study rests. It is that we will receive enlightenment from God's Word only when we recognize it as His infallible revelation. **"For the prophecy came not at any time by the will of man: but holy men of God spoke as they were moved by the Holy Ghost"** (2 Peter 1:21; 2 Timothy 3:16). The Bible must be accepted as God's inerrant word to man and is, therefore, entirely trustworthy.

Inspired Verbs

As we examine the genealogical record of Genesis 5 and 11, is there anything distinctive in the language pattern used that might give us a clue to the understanding of these chapters? The verses do seem very similar to each other. Although there are two that are definitely different from the others, and we will consider those in a moment, all the other genealogical notices in this chapter follow the same pattern: namely, when 'A' had lived 'x' years, he begot 'B.' For example, Genesis 5:12 says, **"And Cainan lived seventy years, and begat Mahalaleel."** There is no indication that Cainan gave his son the name of Mahalaleel. The passage simply says he begat Mahalalel.

Now let us look more intently at these two passages that stand apart from the usual pattern. The first is Genesis 5:3 which records the genealogical descent of Seth from Adam. Genesis 5:3:

> **And Adam lived an hundred and thirty years, and begat a son in his own likeness, after his image; and called his name Seth.**

Adam begat a son and called his name Seth. The second passage is verses 28 and 29, which tell us about the relationship of Lamech to Noah. Genesis 5:28-29 records:

> **And Lamech lived an hundred eighty and two years, and begat a son: And he called his name Noah, saying, This same shall comfort us concerning our work and toil of our hands, because of the ground which the LORD hath cursed.**

Lamech begat a son and called his name Noah.

The phrase **"called his name,"** which is the Hebrew **"qara shem,"** gives us help with at least a few of the names in these chapters. A search of the Bible reveals no instance where such a phrase is used in connection with the naming of a person, where the person named was not an immediate child or was not immediately related to the person doing the naming. Many examples might be given to show this. Genesis 21:3, **"And Abraham called the name of his son that was born unto him, whom Sarah bare to him, Isaac."** Genesis 25:25, **"And the first came out red, all over like an hairy garment; and they called his name Esau."** This phrase is used in describing the births of all the sons of Jacob; for example, we read in Genesis 29:32:

> **And Leah conceived, and bare a son, and she called his name Reuben: for she said, Surely the LORD hath looked upon my affliction; now therefore my husband will love me.**

The phrase is also used in Genesis 38 where the five sons of Judah are noted in verses 3, 4, 5, 29, and 30. This particular indisputable father-son relationship is underscored in 1 Chronicles 2:4 by the statement, **"All the sons of Judah were five."** Interestingly, the same phrase, *qara shem*, is used in Isaiah 7:14, where God prophesied that a virgin would bear a son and call his name Immanuel. It is used also in Genesis 5:2 where God called the man **"Adam."** We know, of course, from the other Biblical data that there were no humans before Adam. From all of this evidence, we can be quite sure that wherever the clue phrase, *qara shem* occurs, we can be certain that an immediate son is being described and not a grandson or some more remote descendant.

...wherever the clue phrase, qara shem occurs, we can be certain that an immediate son is being described...

Returning to the Genesis account with this knowledge concerning the Bible's use of the clue phrase **"called his name,"** we discover in Genesis 4:25 and in Genesis 5:3 that Seth was undoubtedly an immediate son of Adam, for in both of these verses *qara shem* is used. We find, too, in Genesis 4:26:

> **And to Seth, to him also there was born a son; and he called his name Enos:**

Thus, we can know that Enosh was an immediate son of Seth. Likewise, on the same grounds we can know that Noah was the immediate son of Lamech (Genesis 5:28-29).

Thus, we may conclude on the basis of the information found in the verses cited above that when Adam was 130 years old, Seth was born to him. When Adam was 235 years old and Seth was 105, Enosh, the grandson of Adam was born. Similarly, when Lamech was 182 years of age, Noah was born.

Noah's and Terah's Sons

Two other generations are named in the genealogical accounts of Genesis 5 and 11 which can be shown to be of an immediate father-son relationship. In neither of these is the clue phrase **"called his name"** used, but sufficient information is given in other Biblical references so that we can know this. The first of these is in relationship to Noah's son, Shem. In Genesis 5:32 we read:

And Noah was five hundred years old: and Noah begat Shem, Ham, and Japheth.

We can know that these must be immediate sons by the testimony of Genesis 9:18 which reads:

And the sons of Noah, that went forth of the ark, were Shem, and Ham, and Japheth: and Ham is the father of Canaan.

And Genesis 7:13 states that Noah, Shem, Ham, and Japheth, together with their wives, entered the ark. We read in I Peter 3:20 that there were eight souls in the ark. These verses lead us to the inescapable conclusion that Shem was an immediate son of Noah, and not a grandson or later descendant.

The other generation that can be known to represent an immediate father-son relationship is that of Terah and Abram. Genesis 11:26 declares:

And Terah lived seventy years, and begat Abram, Nahor, and Haran.

The verses which follow give additional information which points conclusively to the relationship that existed. Genesis 11:27-28 declares:

Now these are the generations of Terah: Terah begat Abram, Nahor, and Haran; and Haran begat Lot. And Haran died before his father Terah in the land of his nativity, in Ur of the Chaldees.

Verse 31 continues:

And Terah took Abram his son, and Lot the son of Haran his son's son, and Sarai his daughter in law, his son Abram's wife; and they went forth with them from Ur of the Chaldees, to go into the land of Canaan; and they came unto Haran, and dwelt there.

This language surely has reference to an immediate family relationship. Thus, Abram could only have been the son of Terah, and not his grandson or some later descendant.

Some further clarification might be helpful at this point. Although Genesis 11:26 would seem to indicate that all three of Terah's sons, Abram, Nahor, and Haran, were born when he was 70 years old, this cannot have been the case unless they were triplets. Verse 32 clearly states that Terah died in Haran at the age of 205 years. Upon his father's death, Abram left Haran at the age of 75 (Acts 7:4; Genesis 12:4). We must, therefore conclude that Terah was actually 130 years of age at the time of Abram's birth, and that either Nahor or Haran was the oldest of the three brothers, one having been born when their father was 70. In the genealogies, Abram is probably mentioned first because he was the important figure in God's redemptive plan for man.

Thus far, we have established that Seth, Enosh, Noah, Shem, and Abram were all immediate sons of their fathers, named in the record of Genesis 5 and 11. We are left with the remaining names in these two chapters. Are they immediate sons or are they later descendants? The phrase "*qara shem*" is not used anywhere in the Bible in connection with these names to indicate an immediate father-son relationship. Neither is there other evidence in Scripture which conclusively suggests this kind of relationship. Is there Scriptural evidence to indicate that these verses are speaking of other than a father-son relationship? There is indeed as we shall now see.

Patriarchal Periods

An analysis of the language used in Chapters 5 and 11 reveals a pattern that is unique only to these chapters. A typical passage is that of Genesis 5:15-17:

And Mahalaleel lived sixty and five years, and begat Jared: And Mahalaleel lived after he begat Jared eight hundred and thirty years, and begat sons and daughters: And all the days of Mahalaleel were eight hundred ninety and five years: and he died.

These verses set forth truth that might be written as the following equation:

When "**A**" was "**x**" years old, he begat a son, "**B.**"
"**A**" then lived "**y**" years after he begat "**B**"
and begat other sons and daughters.

This language pattern is used to describe men from Adam all the way to Terah, the father of Abraham. The account of Genesis 5 adds that, thus, all the days of "**A**" were (x + y) years and he died. This was added probably because of the extreme longevity of these ancients. By this added phrase there could be no misunderstanding regarding these long life-spans.

How are we to understand these verses? Is "**B**" the son of "**A**" or is he a later descendant of "**A**"? The word "**begat**" does not help us. In some cases in the Bible it is used where unquestionably an immediate father-son relationship is in view. For example, in 1 Chronicles 1:34, where we read that Abraham begat Isaac. On the other hand, begat is sometimes used where a descendant later than an immediate son is in view. In Matthew 1:8, for example, we read that Joram begat Uzziah. But Ahaziah, Joash, and Amaziah should come between Joram and Uzziah (2 Chronicles Chapters 21-26). Thus, in this case "**begat**" could have reference only to a descendant later than a son.

A casual comparison of Genesis 11:16-17 with Genesis 10:25 would seem to offer a solution. The typical language pattern of Genesis 5 and 11 is followed in Genesis 11:16-17, where we read:

> **And Eber lived four and thirty years, and begat Peleg: And Eber lived after he begat Peleg four hundred and thirty years, and begat sons and daughters.**

And in Genesis 10:25 we find recorded:

> **And unto Eber were born two sons: the name of one was Peleg; for in his days was the earth divided; and his brother's name was Joktan.**

Do these verses appear to say that Peleg was an immediate son of Eber? If this is so, in Genesis 11:16-17 the word "**begat**" must necessarily be understood as a reference to an immediate father-son relationship. Since at first this appears to be true for Genesis 11:16-17, we would suspect that this would be true of all of the other verses of Genesis 5 and 11 which follow the same language pattern.

Yet the problem with this reasoning is that other language found in Genesis 10 indicates that the reference to "sons," as it is used in Genesis 10:25, does not at all ensure that an immediate father-son relationship is in view, i.e., that Peleg was the immediate son of Eber. In the same chapter, for example, we read in verse 31, **"These are the sons of Shem, after their families, after their tongues, in their lands, after their nations."** But in this verse, **"sons"** has reference to all of the descendants of Shem. Thus, the word **"sons"** does not prove that a reference is made to the immediate son of the father. It might be noted that Matthew 1:1 also illustrates this truth, for there we read, **"The book of the generation of Jesus Christ, the son of David, the son of Abraham."**

Moreover, when we look at Eber and Peleg more carefully, we will discover evidence that suggests very strongly that Peleg could not have been the immediate son of Eber. In Genesis 10:25 we read:

> **And unto Eber were born two sons: the name of one was Peleg; for in his days was the earth divided; and his brother's name was Joktan**.

This statement is repeated in 1 Chronicles 1:19, which suggests that God appears to be calling attention to these facts as though they are of great importance. From Genesis 11:16-19 we discover that Eber begat Peleg, and Peleg begat Reu.

Genesis 11:16-19:

> **And Eber lived four and thirty years, and begat Peleg: And Eber lived after he begat Peleg four hundred and thirty years, and begat sons and daughters. And Peleg lived thirty years, and begat Reu: And Peleg lived after he begat Reu two hundred and nine years, and begat sons and daughters.**

Let us now assume for the moment that Peleg was an immediate son of Eber and that Reu was an immediate son of Peleg. Since according to Genesis 11:16-18, Eber was 34 years old when Peleg was born and presumably 30 years later bore Reu, the result would look like this:

Eber born	34 years	Peleg born	Eber lived 464 years		Peleg died	Reu died	Eber died
			Peleg lived 239 years				
			30 years				
				Reu lived 239 years			

We can see from the diagram that these three men must have been contemporaries, with Eber the oldest. But if Eber had actually been born earlier than Peleg and Reu, and if he had outlived both Peleg and Reu (as the diagram shows), so that he was the patriarch, so to speak, of the clan, one would surely think it would have been a matter of divine record that he, instead of Peleg, lived when the earth was divided. Thus, we are led again to the conclusion that the term **"begat"** as used in Genesis 5 and 11, must have, at least in some instances, reference to some relationship other than that of an immediate father-son.

As we reflect further on the question at hand, two passages must be examined. These passages suggest an answer to our problem that can be shown to make abundant sense. The first is that of Genesis 7 and 8 where the dates of the flood events are referenced to the age of Noah. Genesis 8:13 records:

> **And it came to pass in the six hundredth and first year, in the first month, the first day of the month, the waters were dried up from off the earth: and Noah removed the covering of the ark, and looked, and, behold, the face of the ground was dry.**

Genesis 7:6 indicates that the six hundred years was the age of Noah when the flood came. This leads us to an important question: Could the calendars of ancient peoples have been tied to the life spans of certain individuals?

The second passage is in the New Testament where Christ declare in Matthew 24:34:

> **Verily I say unto you, This generation shall not pass, till all these things be fulfilled.**

In this reference, Christ is speaking of events that will take place just before His return. He, therefore, insists that "this generation" will continue for at least two thousand years, for this much time has elapsed and all of the events of which he was prophesying in Matthew 24 have not yet happened. As a matter of fact, this present generation is the generation of Jesus Christ.[1] We speak of years today as **"A.D."** which means the Year of Our Lord. The events of today are dated exactly as they were in Noah's day: by reference to the birth date of a person.

Footnote

[1] The Greek work translated in this verse is *genea*. It is translated **"generation,"** **"age,"** and **"nation"** in the King James Bible. It could have reference in this verse to the nation of the Jews who would endure until Christ's return. More likely, it refers to the generation of evil that has existed all through history and will exist until the end of time.

> *The events of today are dated exactly as they were in Noah's day:*
> *by reference to the birth date of a person.*

Since this method of dating events, which was practiced in Noah's day, was suggested by Jesus Himself, and is actually the practice used today, could not this have been the method described in Genesis 5 and 11? If so, then Eber, Peleg, and Reu were patriarchs who followed each other in history. Each in turn was the reference point for his period or generation in history. This makes abundant sense and would provide for continuity and clarity in historical reckoning.

Thus, we see that when the Bible records that Eber was 34 year old when Peleg was born and lived 430 years after the birth of Peleg, fathering other sons and daughters (Genesis 11:16), it means literally that when Eber was 34 years of age, a son was born to him. This might have been his first (immediate) son or it might have been a second, third, or even a fourth removed in his line of direct descendants. Significantly, the Bible does not record that Eber **"called his name Peleg"** because as a point of fact Peleg was not born until about the time Eber died. The son born to Eber at age 34 was an ancestor of Peleg, but his name is nonessential insofar as God's record is concerned. The important fact to remember is that the patriarchal successor to Eber was Peleg. Peleg was a direct descendant, and Eber at 34 was the progenitor of the Peleg line. The result should look like this:

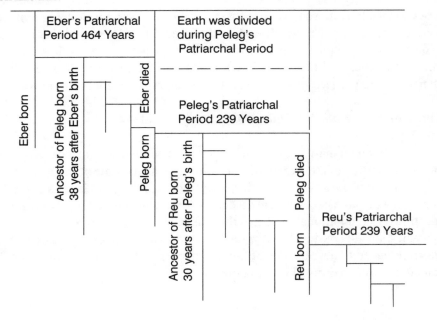

We are suggesting at this point in our study that the language of Genesis 5 and 11 which follows the equation, **"A"** lived **"x"** years and begat **"B"** and **"A"** lived after he begat **"B"** for **"y"** years, is actually a calendar. Exceptions to the patriarchal calendar are introduced, namely, Adam begetting Seth, Seth begetting Enosh, and Lamech begetting Noah. Yet these exceptions are distinguished by the phrase **"called his name,"** thus showing Seth, Enosh, and Noah to be immediate sons. Of course some of our conclusions are still tentative; but as we consider more and more data, we will discover how close to the truth we are.

Patriarchal Periods on the Family Tree

In our study thus far we have seen that when the phrase **"called his name,"** the Hebrew *qara shem,* is used in the Bible, it has reference to an immediate son. Thus, we know that Seth was the immediate son of Adam, Enosh was the immediate son of Seth, and Noah was the immediate son of Lamech. We have also determined that in two cases where this key phrase is not used in connection with close relatives, there is sufficient evidence in other parts of the Bible to assure us that they are related to each other on an immediate father-son basis. Thus, we know with certainty that Shem was an immediate son of Noah and that Abraham was an immediate son of Terah.

Finally, we discovered that the other individuals named in the genealogical records of Genesis 5 and 11 are probably not related as immediate descendants. In fact, we have seen that the Bible offers some evidence that they were not closely related at all. Rather, we offered the suggestion that the year of birth of one individual coincided with the death year of the person named before him in the ancestral table. Thus, we proposed that each of these remaining characters are patriarchal leaders, each heading his own ancestral division.

The Key that Unlocks Genesis Chapters 5 and 11

Though it may seem a bit removed from our discussion, it develops that an understanding of the Israelite's genealogy during the time of their sojourn in Egypt provides the key that confirms our understanding of Genesis 5 and 11. When we study the genealogical descent of Levi, who entered Egypt as a son of Jacob, we find additional evidence that substantiates our patriarchal calendar. We will show that during the Egyptian sojourn a kind of calendar existed which was referenced to descendants of Levi, with each of his descendants being the calendar patriarch during his entire lifetime.

To develop this point, let us now examine the various Biblical references which relate to the descendants of Levi, who entered Egypt with his brothers and his father Jacob, when Joseph had become prime minister. These references are as follows (<u>emphasis</u> added).

Genesis 46:11: **And the sons of Levi; Gershon, Kohath, and Merari.**

Exodus 2:1-10: **And there went a <u>man of the house of Levi, and took to wife a daughter of Levi. And the woman conceived, and bare a son:</u> and when she saw him that he was a goodly child, she hid him three months. And when she could not longer hide him, she took for him an ark of bulrushes, and daubed it with slime and with pitch, and put the child therein; and she laid it in the flags by the river's brink. And his sister stood afar off, to wit what would be done to him. And the daughter of Pharaoh came down to wash herself at the river; and her maidens walked along by the river's side; and when she saw the ark among the flags, she sent her maid to fetch it. And when she had opened it, she saw the child: and, behold, the babe wept. And she had compassion on him, and said, This is one of the Hebrews' children. Then said his sister to Pharaoh's daughter, Shall I go and call to thee a nurse of the Hebrew women, that she may nurse the child for thee? And Pharaoh's daughter said to her, Go. And the maid went and called the child's mother. And Pharaoh's daughter said unto her, Take this child away, and nurse it for me, and I will give thee thy wages. And the woman took the child, and nursed it. And the child grew, and she brought him unto Pharaoh's daughter, and he became her son. And <u>she called his name Moses:</u> and she said, Because I drew him out of the water.**

Exodus 6:16-20: **And these are the names of the sons of Levi according to their generations; Gershon, and Kohath, and Merari: <u>and the years of the life of Levi were an hundred thirty and seven years.</u> The sons of Gershon; Libni, and Shimi, according to their families. And the sons of Kohath; Amram, and Izhar, and Hebron, and Uzziel: <u>and the years of the life of Kohath were an hundred thirty and three years</u>. And the sons of Merari; Mahali and Mushi: these are the families of Levi according to their generations. <u>And Amram took him Jochebed his father's</u>**

---

sister to wife; and she bare him Aaron and Moses: and the years of the life of Amram were an hundred and thirty and seven years.

Exodus 7:7: **And Moses was fourscore years old, and <u>Aaron fourscore and three years old, when they spake unto Pharaoh.</u>**

Numbers 26:58-60: **. . . And Kohath begat Amram. And the name of Amram's wife was Jochebed, the daughter of Levi, whom her mother bare to Levi in Egypt: and she bare unto Amram Aaron and Moses, and Miriam. The sons also of Aaron; Nadab, and Abihu, Eleazar, and Ithamar.**

1 Chronicles 6:1-3: **The sons of Levi; Gershon, Kohath, and Merari. And the sons of Kohath; Amram, Izhar, and Hebron, and Uzziel. And the children of Amram; Aaron, and Moses, and Miriam. The sons also of Aaron; Nadab, and Abihu, Eleazar, and Ithamar.** [emphasis added]

The Time Bridge

Some interesting observations which impinge on our study can be noted about these references to the descendants of Levi.

1. The phrase **"called his name"** (*qara shem*) is nowhere used in these references except in Exodus 2:10 where the child of this passage is named Moses by the Egyptian princess.
2. It is very clear from the detail given in Exodus 2:1-10 as well as the use of the phrase *qara shem* that Moses was the son of the unnamed man and woman of Exodus 2:1.
3. With all of the other detail given in Exodus 2:1-10, it is significant that Amram and Jochebed are not named as the father and mother of Moses as Exodus 6:20 would appear to indicate. Why are the names Amram and Jochebed omitted from the detailed account of Exodus 2:1-10 if they were Moses' father and mother?
4. There is no evidence of an immediate father-son relationship in any of these accounts except in the Exodus 2:1-10 account which relates Moses to an unnamed father and mother.
, 5. The life spans of Levi and only two of his descendants are noted as are the ages of Moses and Aaron at the time of the Exodus (Exodus 6:16-20;

Exodus 7:7). Doesn't this appear rather strange? What purpose could God have in mind in giving us the ages of just these men? Is there a possibility that in these verses a time bridge was built across the period from Jacob's descent into Egypt to the Exodus?

Parents and Patriarchs

We shall begin to answer these difficult questions by attempting to arrive at the age of Levi when he entered Egypt. This information is essential if we are to correlate the various time notices given in the Bible that refer to the Israelites' sojourn in Egypt. In particular, if we can relate Levi's age to the age of his father Jacob who was 130 years old when he entered Egypt (Genesis 47:9), we will have the correlation we are seeking.

We do know that Levi's younger brother Joseph was 39 years of age when Jacob was 130 because Joseph was 30 when he was made ruler over Egypt (Genesis 41:46); and it was during the second year of the famine, or nine years later, that he revealed himself to his brothers (Genesis 45:6). Thus, we know that Jacob was 91 years of age when Joseph was born (130 - 39 = 91).

Can we now discover how much younger Joseph was than Levi? The solution to this question depends upon whether Jacob spent 20 years or 40 years in Haran with his Uncle Laban. If he spent 20 years, the time sequence would work out something like this: Jacob worked seven years for Rachel (Genesis 29:20). Deceived into marriage with Laban's older daughter, Leah, Jacob was forced to serve another seven years for Rachel, whom he apparently married at the beginning of this second seven years (Genesis 29:30). Since Jacob worked six years for the flocks he received from Laban (Genesis 31:41), and these six years followed the birth of Joseph (Genesis 30:24), all of Jacob's children, with the exception of Benjamin, must have been born during the period that he worked the second seven years which was for Rachel. With Levi being the third son and Joseph the last born during this period, Levi must have been at least four years older than Joseph.

To conclude that so many children were born to Jacob during the second seven-year period while he was working to pay for Rachel is difficult. Presumably during this period Leah bore four children, none of whom were twins (Genesis 29:31-35); she then ceased bearing (Genesis 29:35), and because she ceased bearing she gave Zilpah, her maid, to Jacob to father two sons (Genesis 30:9-13) and finally she bore two more sons and a daughter (Genesis 30:16-21). To conclude that all of these events occurred during a seven year period seems quite impossible.

Jacob: Forty Years in Haran

What alternative to a 20-year sojourn in Haran does the Bible offer? Genesis 29:18-30, clearly indicates that Jacob worked the first fourteen years as payment for Rachel and Leah. Genesis 30:25-32 indicates that following Joseph's birth, Jacob made a contract with Laban to work in return for keeping as his own spotted and speckled sheep. Genesis 31:41 summarizes his work for Rachel and Leah and indicates that he worked for a period of six years for his flocks. Genesis 31:41:

> **Thus have I been twenty years in thy house; I served thee fourteen years for thy two daughters, and six years for thy cattle: and thou hast changed my wages ten times.**

This is the key verse that we should examine very carefully. God wrote this verse in such a way that superficially it appears to teach that Jacob was in Haran for a total of twenty years. Fact is, this is the understanding most Bible scholars derive from this verse. Because this conclusion is altogether incorrect they are deprived of very essential information required to understand the biblical calendar.

This verse indicates there were three major divisions of time during which Jacob lived in Haran. They are:

1. 14 years to obtain Leah and Rachel as wives.

2. 20 years enjoying the hospitality of living in his Uncle Laban's house.

3. 6 years of working for his oddly marked cattle during which time he was not in Laban's house.

We know that Jacob was not in Laban's house during this final six year period because of what we read in Genesis 30:35-36. There we read that Laban moved three day's journey from Jacob.

> **And he removed that day the he goats that were ringstraked and spotted, and all the she goats that were speckled and spotted, and every one that had some white in it, and all the brown among the sheep, and gave them into the hand of his sons. <u>And he set three days' journey betwixt himself and Jacob</u>: and Jacob fed the rest of Laban's flocks.**

This information that Jacob was no longer in the house of Laban during this six year period is further attested to by the citation of Genesis 31:22:

And it was told Laban on the third day that Jacob was fled.

With this information in mind we can now understand Genesis 31:41. The first 14 years Jacob worked to obtain Leah and Rachel. During the next 20 years he lived with his family in Laban's house. Therefore, from the time he married Leah and Rachel until he was no longer living in the house of Laban was a period of 7 plus 20 years or 27 years. During these 27 years Jacob became the father of eleven sons and one daughter. The last son born to him was Joseph. We read that it was shortly after Joseph was born that Jacob worked the final six years to obtain the cattle which he owned at the time he left Haran (Genesis 30:25-33).

Joseph was born to Rachel shortly before the final six years (Genesis 30:25). Remember during this final six years, Jacob was not in the house of Laban. The timing would have been as follows.

Jacob arrives in Haran at the age of	60
He works seven years for Rachel and is then married to Rachel and Leah. He is then	67
For the next 20 years, he with his growing family live in the house of Laban	
Reuben is born to Leah the following year when Jacob is	68
Simeon is born next to Leah when Jacob is	69
Levi is born next to Leah when Jacob is	70 or 71
Jacob finishes his second seven year contract for Rachel when he is	74
With his growing family he lives 20 years in the house of Laban. In the 18th or 19th year of this period Joseph is born. Jacob is	91
At the end of this 20 year period wishes to leave Haran. He is	92 or 93

> He works six years longer for his flocks but
> during this six years he is not in the house of
> Laban   100

Thus, Levi was about 22 years older than Joseph. Since Joseph was 39 years of age when Jacob came to Egypt, Levi at that time would have been 39 + 22 = 61 years of age. Since Levi was the third son born to Leah (Genesis 29:31-34), and since Jacob became married to Leah after being in Haran seven years, Levi would have been born about the 11th or 12th year after Jacob went to Haran.

The Perfect Tally

One other piece of evidence points precisely to the 21-year age differential and also shows how time was reckoned during the Egyptian sojourn. In fact, it also gives us the Biblical evidence for understanding the language of Genesis Chapters 5 and 11.

We previously saw that Joseph was 39 when Jacob and his family entered Egypt. Since Levi, as we have seen, must have been about 22 years older than Joseph, he would have been 61 when Jacob's family entered Egypt. Since Levi died at the age of 137 (Exodus 6:16), 76 years (137 - 61) of his life would have been spent in Egypt.

Let us recall the premise which we established. In the absence of evidence that the Genesis genealogies specifically indicate an immediate father-son relationship, we may assume the relationship to be one which interrelates individual patriarchs living their entire lifetime as the family head. Let us apply this principle to the family of Levi. In Exodus 6:16-20, we saw the genealogical sequence of Levi. His 137 years were followed by Kohath's 133 years which in turn were followed by Amram's 137 years; Amram was followed by Aaron. Since we know that Levi lived 76 years in Egypt (if our 22 year assumption is correct), and since the Bible indicates that Aaron was 84 years old at the time of the Exodus, all of the ingredients are available to establish the chronological sequence during the Egyptian sojourn. Remember that the death year of one patriarch coincides with the birth year of the next, thus, the result must look like this:

Levi's time in Egypt (137 - 61)	76 years
Kohath's period of patriarchal leadership	133 years
Amram's period of patriarchal leadership	137 years

Aaron's age at the time of the Exodus (Exodus 7,: 7 Numbers 33:8-9)	84 years
	————
Total	430 years

This sum tallies exactly with Israel's sojourn in the land of Egypt, which we read was 430 years in Exodus 12:40-41:

Now the sojourning of the children of Israel, who dwelt in Egypt, was four hundred and thirty years. And it came to pass at the end of the four hundred and thirty years, even the selfsame day it came to pass, that all the hosts of the LORD went out from the land of Egypt.

Thus, we see that our assumption is correct that in certain situations there existed a patriarchal calendar with one patriarch living his entire lifetime as the family head. God indicates to us that the generation or patriarchal period of Kohath followed the period of Levi and commenced in the year that ended Levi's period. Similarly, Amram's generation followed Kohath's. Aaron's generation began at the death of Amram. In this way the Bible gives us a time bridge covering the Israelites sojourn in Egypt that is identical with the 430 years of Exodus 12:40.

There is one other fact we must determine if we are to accurately understand the Biblical method of Calendar keeping during the 430 year period of Israel's Egyptian experience. That fact is concerned with the age of Aaron at the time Israel went out of Egypt.

In Exodus 7:7 we read:

And Moses was fourscore years old, and Aaron fourscore and three years old, when they spake unto Pharaoh.

Additionally in Numbers 33:38-39:

And Aaron the priest went up into mount Hor at the commandment of the LORD, and died there, in the fortieth year after the children of Israel were come out of the land of Egypt, in the first day of the fifth month. And Aaron was an hundred and twenty and three years old when he died in mount Hor.

Later we will learn that Israel left Egypt on the fourteenth day of the first month of the Biblical Calendar which was March 22, 1447 B.C. of our modern calendar.

Forty years and three days later they crossed the Jordan River into the land of Canaan on the tenth day of the first month. This corresponds to March 25, in the year 1407 B.C. of our calendar.

Returning now to the death of Aaron it is reported in Numbers 33:38-39 we learn he died at the age of 123 in the first day of the fifth month which was about seven months before Israel crossed the Jordan River. That is, Aaron would have been in the wilderness about 39½ years. Remember Aaron stood before Pharaoh when he was 83 (Exodus 7:7). Therefore, by the time Israel left Egypt he would have become 84 years of age in order to have been 123 years of age when he died (84 + 39 = 123 years).

While Exodus 6:16-19 refers to the generations of Levi by name, significantly Kohath and Amram are the only two patriarchs of all of those named whose ages have been written into the genealogical record. Obviously, the family of Levi, from Kohath to Amram and finally to Aaron, was the patriarchal family selected during the 430-year bondage in Egypt to establish the calendar during this period. The method of doing this would have been similar to that done by their forefathers before Abraham.

This, I believe, is the reason why the ages of Levi, Kohath, and Amram have been recorded, and one of the reasons why we are given so many details that relate to the ages of Joseph and Moses. It is why the parents of Moses are not named Amram and Jochebed in Exodus 2:1, when so many other details concerning the birth of Moses are given. Amram and Jochebed were not the immediate parents of Moses. Moses was of the patriarchal family of Amram. Amram must have died the year of Aaron's birth.

It also throws a spotlight of revelation upon God's prophecy to Abram in Genesis 15:13-16, where he tells Abram that his descendants would be oppressed 400 years in a land that was not theirs, and that they would return to their own land in the fourth generation. Levi was the first, Kohath the second, Amram the third, and Aaron the fourth in the prophetic sequence.

Thus, God in His wonderful wisdom has placed in our hands a key that unlocks the hitherto perplexing genealogies of Genesis 5 and 11. The key is the chronological record of the Israelite's sojourn in Egypt. By properly understanding the timetable of the Egyptian sojourn, we establish the evidence for understanding Genesis 5 and 11. God gave considerable information about the Egyptian sojourn so that this key could be found.

Genesis Chapters 5 and 11 Are A Calendar

To return to the genealogies of Genesis 5 and 11, we have already pointed out that in the cases of Adam and Seth, Enosh and Lamech, Noah and Shem, and finally Terah and Abraham, the Bible indicates conclusively the existence of immediate father-son relationships. But all of the other names recorded, we must assume, were the patriarchal heads of families and followed each other chronologically even as they did in the case of Levi, Kohath, Amram, and Aaron.

Genesis 5 and 11 are actually a calendar.

When we reflect a bit further on the conclusions of our foregoing study, we discover that Genesis 5 and 11 are actually a calendar. Think for a moment of our present calendar. We speak of an event that happened in the year 1950, for instance. What we mean is that this event occurred in the year of our Lord 1950 or that 1950 is the 1950th year after the birth of Christ. This is the generation or patriarchal period, if you will, of Jesus Christ. Jesus, the Lord of all history, in Matthew 24:34 used the language of man's earliest history when he described the certainty of God's plan until the end of the age. We read in Matthew 24:34:

Verily I say unto you, This generation shall not pass, till all these things be fulfilled.

This was the same situation that existed in man's early history. The time was divided into patriarchal periods or generations even as the New Testament period is the generation of Jesus Christ and as the Egyptian sojourn was so divided. Thus, for example, when Methuselah died, bringing to an end his generation, a man who was born in the year of Methuselah's death was selected to be the next reigning patriarch or at least the next man for calendar reference. After Methuselah, this was Lamech. None of the conditions of his selection are given except that he had to be a descendant of Methuselah. Therefore, the Bible indicates that Methuselah was 187 years old when he begat Lamech; that is, when he was 187, the forefather of Lamech was born to Methuselah (Genesis 5:25). This notice establishes the certainty of Lamech's blood descent from Methuselah by showing where his forefather tied into the life of Methuselah.

The selection of the next patriarch had to include a birth date coinciding with Methuselah's death date to ensure a rational history. Had he been born one or more years earlier an overlap would have occurred which would have blurred history. If Lamech had been born one or more years later than Methuselah's death, a gap would have occurred which would have confused history. Therefore, when a citizen of the world of that day spoke of an event occurring in the year Methuselah 950, only one year in history answered to this date. Again, if he spoke of the year Lamech 2, only one year answered to this date, and he knew precisely how many years transpired from Methuselah 950 to Lamech 2.

Time Begins

We will now develop the Biblical Calendar as we carefully analyze the Biblical citations beginning with the time of Creation as the year zero. Later we will tie our findings into our modern calendar, and then we will find that the creation date is the year 11,013 B.C.

We read in Genesis 1:26-27:

And God said, Let us make man in our image, after our likeness: and let them have dominion over the fish of the sea, and over the fowl of the air, and over the cattle, and over all the earth, and over every creeping thing that creepeth upon the earth. So God created man in his own image, in the image of God created he him; male and female created he them.

God then adds in Genesis 1:31 and Genesis 2:1-3:

And God saw every thing that he had made, and, behold, it was very good. And the evening and the morning were the sixth day. Thus the heavens and the earth were finished, and all the host of them. And on the seventh day God ended his work which he had made; and he rested on the seventh day from all his work which he had made. And God blessed the seventh day, and sanctified it: because that in it he had rested from all his work which God created and made.

These verses clearly teach that the universe together with mankind was created during a period of six 24-hour days at the very beginning of time. We know that they were 24-hour days because the Bible also tells us in Genesis 1:14 and 19:

And God said, Let there be lights in the firmament of the heaven to divide the day from the night; and let them be for signs, and for seasons, and for days, and years:

And the evening and the morning were the fourth day.

In these verses God takes us to the very threshold of time, to the very beginning moment of the creation of this world. We therefore can assign the year "zero" to this beginning of the timeline of God's Calendar.

The next important calendar reference is found in Genesis 5:3-5 where we read:

> **And Adam lived an hundred and thirty years, and begat a son in his own likeness, after his image; and called his name Seth: and the days of Adam after he had begotten Seth were eight hundred years: and he begat sons and daughters: and all the days that Adam lived were nine hundred and thirty years: and he died.**

One hundred thirty years after Adam was created, he bore a son whose name was called Seth.

This is now the year 130 in our developing calendar.

We then read in Genesis 5:6-8:

> **And Seth lived an hundred and five years, and begat Enos: and Seth lived after he begat Enos eight hundred and seven years, and begat sons and daughters: and all the days of Seth were nine hundred and twelve years: and he died.**

Is Enos an immediate son of Seth or is he a descendant (grandson, great grandson, etc.)? As we have noted, the word "begat" does not necessarily indicate an immediate father-son relationship. So, we can begin to discover the answer to this question regarding Enos, in Genesis 4:26. There we read:

> **And to Seth, to him also there was born a son; and he called his name Enos: then began men to call upon the name of the LORD.**

The phrase "called his name" assures us that Enos was an immediate son of Seth. Thus the calendar develops showing that Seth was born in the year 130, and Enos was born 105 years later in the year 235. The Bible then declares in Genesis 5:9-11:

> **And Enos lived ninety years, and begat Cainan: And Enos lived after he begat Cainan eight hundred and fifteen years, and begat sons and daughters: and all the days of Enos were nine hundred and five years: and he died.**

To understand these verses, we must search the Bible to discover if there exists any other information that shows whether Enos was the immediate father of Cainan. Not only do we not find any other indication that Cainan was an immediate son of Enos, but we also find that the phrase "called his name" is not used. Therefore we can be certain that Cainan was not an immediate son. We can also be certain that during the life time of Enos, the Calendar was referenced to Enos. And we can be certain that when the Bible uses the word "begat" in a genealogy, it does not necessarily indicate an immediate father-son relationship.

But if this is so, why then does Genesis 5:9 record that **"Enos lived ninety years and begat Cainan"**? There is a similar phrase in Genesis 11:12 where we read:

And Arphaxad lived five and thirty years, and begat Salah:

Like He did when speaking of Enos and Cainan in Genesis 5:9, God indicates here in Genesis 11:12 that **"Arphaxad lived five and thirty years and begat Salah."** Presumably, Salah was born to Arphaxad at age 35, just as Cainan presumably was born to Enos at age 90.

However, in Luke 3, the genealogical descent listed states that a different man named *Cainan* (who lived many years after the Cainan of Genesis 5) was in the blood line of Arphaxad. Luke 3:35-36 records the following information:

. . . Sala, which was the son of Cainan, which was the son of Arphaxad . . .

With the insertion of the name Cainan, Luke 3 clarifies that Sala was not an immediate son of Arphaxad.

The Bible is not contradicting itself. When we compare all these Scriptures, we discover that Salah could not have been the immediate son of Arphaxad. Therefore, we have additional evidence which assures us that the giving of the age of Enos when he begat Cainan (**"Enos lived ninety years and begat Cainan"**) does not indicate in any way that Cainan was an immediate son of Enos.

Isn't it interesting that, in order to develop the proof that the Cainan of Genesis 5 was not an immediate son of Enos, we needed to utilize information recorded in an entirely different part of the Bible -- in Luke 3. And isn't it interesting that the name Cainan in Luke 3:36 is the key word which demonstrates that the man named Cainan in Genesis 5 was not an immediate son of Enos. And amazingly, the Cainan named in Luke 3:36 lived thousands of years after the Cainan of Genesis 5.

What then could be God's purpose in telling us that Enos was 90 years old when he begat Cainan? There are at least two reasons why it may be that God has given us this notice.

The first reason is that God's wording of Genesis 5 assisted in keeping an understanding of the Calendars of the Bible secret until God wished to give us more insight. Throughout the history of the world, theologians and Bible scholars would ordinarily read this and logically and reasonably conclude that Cainan had to be an immediate son of Enos. Does not the Bible clearly say that Enos was 90 years old when he begat Cainan? But that would be a wrong conclusion concerning a timetable of the earth's existence.

> *Only in our day has God opened our minds to understand the principle of Calendar Patriarchs...*

Only in our day has God opened our minds to understand the principle of Calendar Patriarchs and has shown us how to tie together such passages as Genesis 5, Genesis 11, Exodus 6, and Luke 3 and other Scripture to obtain a correct understanding of the Biblical Calendar. And we are reminded that diligent examination of the whole Bible is essential to finding truth.

The second reason is that God is showing that the next Calendar Patriarch is truly of the same blood line as that of the previous Calendar Patriarch. This was especially important when a man lived more than 900 years. Where does the blood line of the next Calendar Patriarch enter into that of the previous Calendar Patriarch? In the case of Cainan, it was when Enos was 90 years of age.

Thus, we know that Enos was born in the year 235, and for the next 905 years, he was the Calendar Patriarch (Genesis 5:11). In the year 325 when Enos was 90 years of age, he became the father of a son. We do not know the name of this son. However, 815 years after the year 325 in the year 1140, the year that Enos died, this unnamed son became the father or the grandfather, or the great grandfather etc. (that is, the progenitor) of a man who was named Cainan. This son, Cainan, became the next Calendar Patriarch after Enos.

Thus, in the year 1140 (235 + 905) when Enos died at the age of 905, Cainan (born in the year 1140) became the next Calendar Patriarch. Enos had been the Calendar Patriarch for 905 years. He was followed by Cainan who became the next Calendar Patriarch during the 910 years of his life time (Genesis 5:14). Seventy years later, Cainan gave birth to a son who was the progenitor of a man named Mahalaleel (Genesis 5:12). Mahalaleel was born in the same year that Cainan died. That was the year that was 910 years after the year 1140 when Cainan was born. Thus the year 2050, the year in which Cainan died, became the year which began the Calendar Patriarchal period of Mahalaleel. His period would continue for the duration of his life time of 895 years (Genesis 5:17).

In similar fashion, Jared followed Mahalaleel, Enoch followed Jared, Methuselah followed Enoch, and Lamech followed Methuselah (Genesis 5:15-27).

However, when Lamech became the Calendar Patriarch, there was a change in the Calendar Patriarchal system. We are alerted to this by the language of Genesis 5:28-29:

And Lamech lived an hundred eighty and two years, and begat a son: and he called his name Noah, saying, this same shall comfort us concerning our work and toil of our hands, because of the ground which the LORD hath cursed.

By use of the phrase "called his name," God is assuring us that when Lamech was 182 years of age, he had a son and named him Noah. Noah was the immediate son of Lamech.

Why did God not continue the Calendar by naming a descendant of Lamech who would have been born the year Lamech died? The reason is that God's plan for the human race demanded a disruption! The complete destruction of the world by a universal flood would occur five years after Lamech died. Thus with the exception of Noah (and his three sons), all of the descendants of Lamech would have died in the flood.

Therefore, God continued the Calendar Patriarchal line from Lamech to his immediate son Noah. Thus the Calendar could continue through the time of the flood.

We have seen that it was the year 2050 when Mahalaleel was born. Jared was born 895 years later in the year 2945. Enoch was born 962 years later in the year 3907. Methuselah was born 365 years later in the year 4272. Lamech was born 969 years later in the year 5241 (Genesis 5:25-27). 182 years later in the year 5423, Noah was born as an immediate son of Lamech (Genesis 5:28-29).

Noah's father Lamech lived 595 years after the birth of Noah (Genesis 5:30) and died in the year 6018. Five years later when Noah had become 600 years of age, in the year 6023, the flood began.

Noah had become the Calendar Patriarch to carry the Calendar through the time of the flood. We read in Genesis 7:11:

In the six hundredth year of Noah's life, in the second month, the seventeenth day of the month, the same day were all the fountains

of the great deep broken up, and the windows of heaven were opened.

In summary, we have learned that the first chapter of Genesis gives us the information concerning the very beginning of time and the creation of the world. The fifth chapter of Genesis gives us the Calendar of time for the first 6,000 years of the history of the world.

From Noah to Abraham

Now we should look at the history of the world from the time of the flood to the time of Abraham who became the father of the nation of Israel. This calendar is recorded in the eleventh chapter of Genesis.

In Genesis 11:10-11 we read:

These are the generations of Shem: Shem was an hundred years old, and begat Arphaxad two years after the flood: and Shem lived after he begat Arphaxad five hundred years, and begat sons and daughters.

Verse 10 has a real problem within it. It tell us that Shem was one hundred years old two years after the flood. We will discover that to develop an accurate calendar, we must know when Shem was born. The phrase "after the flood" creates the problem.

Earlier in Genesis 7:11, we read that the flood began in the six hundredth year, in the second month, the seventeenth day of Noah's life. In Genesis 8:13-16, we learn that the flood was altogether ended, and Noah left the ark on the six hundredth and first year, the second month, the 27th day of the month. Thus the flood lasted a total of one year and ten days. Since the flood began in the year 6023, it therefore ended in the year 6024.

Therefore returning to the question of Genesis 11:10, was Shem 100 years old two years after 6023? Or was he 100 years old two years after 6024? If we are to develop an exact calendar, we must find a way to answer this question.

We search the Bible and find our answer to this puzzle in Genesis 9:28-29. There the Bible records:

And Noah lived after the flood three hundred and fifty years. And all the days of Noah were nine hundred and fifty years: and he died.

The identical phrase "after the flood" which we are puzzling over in Genesis 11:10 is found in Genesis 9, verse 28, as God is disclosing the death age of Noah. Remember Noah was 600 years old when the flood began and 601 years old when the flood ended. Yet in these verses, God informs us that Noah lived 350 years "after the flood" and died at the age of 950.

Therefore, we know that the phrase "after the flood" must be understood as "after the *beginning* of the flood." Noah was 600 years old at the beginning of the flood and died 350 years later at the age of 950. Three hundred and fifty years after the *beginning* of the flood, he died at the age of 950.

Returning to Genesis 11:10, we now are certain that we can understand that Shem was 100 years old two years after the beginning of the flood. Thus at the time Shem was 102 years of age, his father Noah would have been 602 years of age. Since two years after the beginning of the flood was the year 6025, Shem would have been born 100 years earlier, in the year 5925.

Thus, when Noah's father, who was named Lamech, died in the year 6018, the year 6018 ended the Calendar Patriarchal line of Lamech. However in the year 6018, Noah was already 595 years of age; so the next year would have been referenced to the 596th year of Noah's lifetime. Therefore when the flood began five years after the death of Lamech, the calendar was referenced to the 600th year of Noah. This 600th year of Noah was 6,023 years after creation.

Noah lived to be 950 years of age. In the year Noah died, the year 6373 (6023 + 350), Shem had become 448 years of age. (Remember we learned Shem was born in the year 5925. The year 6373 was 448 years later.) Therefore, the year after Noah died, the Calendar would have been referenced to the 449th year of Shem. Shem lived to be 600 years of age. He died in the year 6525.

We have just learned that, because of the Universal Flood, God could not continue the unfolding of the Calendar of history utilizing the Calendar Patriarchal system (the system in which one Calendar Patriarch died the same year that the next Calendar Patriarch was born).

For many years after the flood, there was a very similar situation to that which existed in the early years after the creation of Adam and Eve. At that earlier time in history, the first Calendar Patriarch for whom the Calendar was dated throughout his entire lifetime was Enos who was born the year Seth died.

Likewise, it was not until Shem died that, in the same year of his death, a baby was born who would be the next Calendar Patriarch throughout his entire lifetime. We learn that this was a man named Arphaxad. Now, we know from the language of Genesis Chapters 6 through 10 that Shem was the immediate son of Noah. But, when we study all that the Bible says concerning Arphaxad, we find no evidence that he was an immediate son of Shem. We do not find the phrase "called his name" in connection with his birth. Neither do we find any other evidence in the Bible that he was an immediate son of Shem. Therefore, we can be certain that he was the next Calendar Patriarch who was born the year Shem died. The ancestor of Arphaxad, who was required in order for Arphaxad to be the next Calendar Patriarch, penetrated the blood line of Shem when Shem was 100 years old.

As we have learned, the only people surviving the flood were Noah and his wife together with his three sons and their respective wives. Since Noah lived 350 years after the beginning of the flood which occurred in the year 6023, Noah would have died in the year 6373.

Since Shem lived 500 years after he begat the ancestor of Arphaxad in the year 6025, Shem would have died in the year 6525. And in the year 6525, a baby named Arphaxad was born who became the next Calendar Patriarch.

The calendar of history of Genesis 11 continues with the following sequence.

Calendar Patriarch	Year Born	Lifespan (and math)	Genesis 11 Reference
Arphaxad	6525	438 (35 + 403)	:12-13
Salah	6963	433 (30 + 403)	:14-15
Eber	7396	464 (34 + 430)	:16-17
Peleg	7860	239 (30 + 209)	:18-19
Reu	8099	239 (32 + 207)	:20-21
Serug	8338	230 (30 + 200)	:22-23
Nahor	8568	148 (29 + 119)	:24-25
Terah	8716	205	:32

With the birth of Terah, God again interrupted the Calendar Patriarch procedure. This is because an immediate son of Terah named Abram was to be the beginning of a new direction in the unfolding of God's salvation plan.

When Nahor died in the year 8716, the condition that had to be met was that the next Calendar Patriarch had to be in the blood line of Nahor and had to have been born in the year Nahor died. Terah met those qualifications and became the next Calendar Patriarch.

Twice before in the history of the world, God began with a single family to develop the timeline of history. God is showing us in His Word the Bible that the timeline of history is governed by the unfolding of His salvation plan. In both of these previous occasions, it was of necessity that the focus was upon a single family. The first occasion was at the beginning of time when only the family of Adam and Eve inhabited the earth. The second occasion was immediately after the Noachian flood when only the family of Noah inhabited the earth.

However, about 3,000 years has now passed since the Noachian flood, and the world has become increasingly populated. Unfortunately the same problem had come into existence that was the cause of the destruction of the world in the days of Noah. That problem was the increasing wickedness of the world. However, God had no plan in mind, at this juncture in history, to again destroy the world. Instead He isolated a single God-fearing family and continued the development of the timeline of history through this family. That family was the family of a man named Abram who was an immediate son of Terah.

Thus, the man Terah was the last individual at that time in history who fulfilled all the qualifications of a Calendar Patriarch. As noted above, he began his Patriarchal Calendar period in the year of his birth, 8716. The shift of the timeline of history from Terah as the last Calendar Patriarch into a new direction was not only made necessary because of the wickedness of the world, but it was also the plan of God to begin, at this point in history, the development of a <u>nation</u> to represent the kingdom of God on this earth.

> *That kingdom of God consists of each and every individual who becomes saved.*

The timeline of history has a goal; it has a focus. That goal or focus was the development of the kingdom of God. That kingdom of God consists of each and every individual who becomes saved. Those who become saved are made citizens of an eternal kingdom that will last forever. The kingdom of God, therefore is represented in this world by those who have become saved.

For the first approximately 9,000 years of the history of the world, the kingdom of God was represented by <u>individuals</u> who became saved. But it was God's intention to eventually develop a nation of people to be the external representation of the kingdom of God. It was within this special nation of people that God would further develop His timeline of history.

Thus, at the juncture in history when Terah was serving as the last of a series of calendar patriarchs, the mechanism to develop a nation which was to become the external representative of the kingdom of God was put into motion. This was done by God's selection of an immediate son of Terah, named Abram, to become the beginning of this special nation, the nation to which God gave the name "Israel" (Genesis 35:9-12).

The Bible gives ample evidence that Abram, whose name was later changed to Abraham (Genesis 17:5), was an immediate son of Terah. Fact is, we read in Genesis 11:31 that God called Abram out of the land of Ur of the Chaldees (another name for Babylon) to go to a far away land called Canaan. Abram immediately left Ur of the Chaldees, together with his wife Sarai, his nephew Lot and his aged father Terah to go to this new land.

The Bible reveals in Genesis 11:31-32 that they stopped in Haran where Abram's father died at the age of 205. Since Terah was born in the year 8716, his death year was the year 8921. The Bible also gives us information that Abram was 75 years of age at this time (Genesis 12:4).

From this time forward, the calendar of history that identifies with the unfolding of God's salvation plan is set forth in the Bible with sufficient citations so that by combining the Biblical information with the non-Biblical information (which can be shown to be very accurate), we are able to continue the calendar with complete precision all the way to our day.

We learned that Terah died in the year 8921. In the same year, Abram was 75. This was the year Abram came into the land of Canaan. We read in Genesis 21:5 that when Abram, now called Abraham, was 100 years old, Isaac was born to him and to his wife Sarah. (A year earlier, God had changed Sarai's name to Sarah, Genesis 17:15.) The year of Isaac's birth was 8946.

When Isaac was 60 years of age, he became the father of Jacob in the year 9006. When Jacob was 130 years of age, he came with his entire family into the land of Egypt (Genesis 47:9). That was the year 9136.

The people of Israel remained in Egypt exactly 430 years (Exodus 12:40-41). Therefore they came out of Egypt in the year 9566. Remember these dates are the years after the year "0" when God created the world.

The next Biblical citation pertaining to God's Calendar of History is in 1 Kings 6:1 where God records that it was 480 years after the year Israel came out of Egypt that the construction of the temple began. That was the year 10046. Here is what God says in 1 Kings 6:1:

> **And it came to pass in the four hundred and eightieth year after the children of Israel were come out of the land of Egypt, in the fourth year of Solomon's reign over Israel, in the month Zif, which is the second month, that he began to build the house of the LORD.**

Aligning the Biblical Calendar with Our Modern Calendar

As we continue our study of the Biblical Calendar, we should take time to align the Biblical calendar with our secular calendar.

During the Calendar Period of the development of the nation of Israel which extended over the last approximately fifteen hundred years of Old Testament history, God gave abundant detailed information concerning the passage of time. Thus we are able not only to know the overall length of that period of time, but we are also able to tie it to the New Testament Calendar making possible a continuous calendar from Creation to the present day. Therefore, as we continue this study, we should set forth several principles that make possible the harmonizing of our modern calendar with that of the Bible.

The first principle we must keep in mind is that the passage of time is governed by God's decrees. That is, God on the fourth day of Creation, created the magnificent celestial clock that is our solar system. Astronomers use that celestial timepiece to measure with great accuracy the length of a day, the number of days from one new moon to another, the time between eclipses and other celestial phenomena, and the number of days in any year. However it is God who determined that a year should equal a period of time of 365.2244 days and that the average time from one new moon to the next new moon is 29.53059 days.

Secondly, God has placed a great curiosity and interest concerning celestial phenomena such as new moons, eclipses, etc. in the minds of men. That, along with a God-given writing ability, has helped mankind to accurately correlate written historical data with the passage of time and even reference it to our modern calendar.

Thirdly, the Bible names kings that reigned over Israel or Judah and often the secular record makes reference to these same kings. Likewise the secular historical citations often make reference to heathen kings to which the Bible also makes reference.

Keeping this in mind, we can locate precise events, the dates of which are fixed by the secular record. These same events are recorded in the Bible, and if the time intervals between them are exactly the same as in the secular record, then the two calendars can be harmonized.

For example, five historical events are noted as on the following chart. The dates for these events are according to the secular record which has been coordinated with our modern calendar.

Historical Event	Modern Calendar/ Archaeological Year	Biblical Calendar Year (beginning with year zero)	Source
Joseph released from prison	1896 B.C.	9117	*Adam When?,** p. 98, Family Radio

Time Interval: 1896 B.C.-1447 B.C. (449 years)

Pharaoh died in the Red Sea	1447 B.C.	9566	*Adam When?,* p. 126, Family Radio

Time Interval: 1447 B.C.-853 B.C. (594 years)

Last year of King Ahab's reign	853 B.C.	10,160	*Handbook of Biblical Chronology,* Jack Finegan, Princeton Univer sity Press, 1964, p. 196

Time Interval: 853 B.C.-597 B.C. (256 years)

Zedekiah appointed king by Nebuchad- nezzar	597 B.C.	10,416	*Handbook of Biblical Chronology,* Jack Finegan, Princeton University Press, p. 205
Babylon was con- quered by the Medes and Persians	539 B.C.	10,4474	*Handbook of Biblical Chronology,* Jack Finegan, Princeton University Press, 1964, p. 212

* *Adam When?* may be obtained free of charge from Family Radio.

**THE BIBLICAL CALENDAR IS SYNCHRONIZED
WITH OUR MODERN CALENDAR**

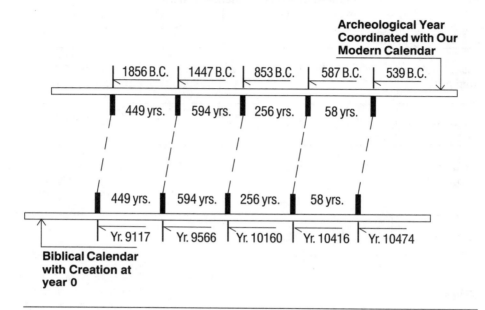

From the Biblical record, the time intervals between these five events are found to be identical to the secular record. Thus, we are able to tie the Biblical Calendar to our Modern Calendar. We see then that the Biblical Calendar year of 9117, based on a calendar beginning with the Creation year zero, meshes with our Modern Calendar year of 1896 B.C., and so on.

---

*Because we can thus harmonize the Biblical Calendar
with our modern calendar, we are enabled to set forth a Calendar
that goes all the way back to Creation.*

Because we can thus harmonize the Biblical Calendar with our modern calendar, we are enabled to set forth a Calendar that goes all the way back to Creation. We find that the Creation of this world occurred in the year 11013 B.C. The flood that came 6,023 years later thus occurred in the year 4990 B.C. (11,013-6,023). We can list with great accuracy many events recorded in the Bible. Important ones are as follows.

CALENDAR OF HISTORY

Event and Scripture Reference	Biblical Calendar Beginning with Creation at the Year "0"	Modern Calendar Harmonized with Biblical Calendar
Creation of Adam.	0	11013 B.C.
Birth of Seth. Adam was 130 when Seth was born (Genesis 5:6).	130	10883 B.C.
Birth of Enos. Seth was 105 when Enos was born (Genesis 5:6).	235	10778 B.C.
End of Enos's period, 905 years after his birth (Genesis 5:11), which is the year Cainan was born and his period began.	1140	9873 B.C.
End of Cainan's period, 910 years after his birth (Gen. 5:14). This is the year Mahalaleel was born and his period began.	2050	8963 B.C.
End of Mahalaleel's period, 895 years after his birth (Genesis 5:17). This is the year Jared was born and his period began.	2945	8068 B.C.
End of Jared's period, 962 years after his birth (Gen. 5:20). This is the year Enoch was born and his period began.	3907	7106 B.C.
End of Enoch's period, 365 years after his birth (Gen. 5:23). This is the year Methuselah was born and his period began.	4272	6741 B.C.
End of Methuselah's period, 969 years after his birth (Gen. 5:27). This is the year Lamech was born and his period began.	5241	5772 B.C.
Birth of Noah. Lamech was 182 when Noah was born (Genesis 5:28-29).	5423	5590 B.C.

Continued

CALENDAR OF HISTORY *Continued*

Event and Scripture Reference	Biblical Calendar Beginning with Creation at the Year "0"	Modern Calendar Harmonized with Biblical Calendar
The Flood. Noah was 600 when the Flood came (Genesis 7:6).	6023	4990 B.C.
Death of Shem, 502 years after the Flood (Genesis 11:10-11). This is the year Arphaxad was born and his period began.	6525	4488 B.C.
End of Arphaxad's period, 438 years after his birth (Genesis 11:12-13). This is the year Salah was born and his period began.	6963	4050 B.C.
End of Salah's period, 433 years after his birth (Gen. 11:14-15). This is the year Eber was born and his period began.	7396	3617 B.C.
End of Eber's period, 464 years after his birth (Genesis 11:16-17). This is the year Peleg was born and his period began.	7860	3153 B.C.

The tower of Babel must have occurreced between the dates 3153 B.C. and 2914 B.C. (Genesis 10:25)

Event and Scripture Reference	Biblical Calendar Beginning with Creation at the Year "0"	Modern Calendar Harmonized with Biblical Calendar
End of Peleg's period, 239 yrs. after his birth (Genesis 11:18-19). This is the year Reu was born and his period began.	8099	2914 B.C.
End of Reu's period, 239 years after his birth (Genesis 11:20-21). This is the year Serug was born and his period began.	8338	2675 B.C.
End of Serug's period, 230 years after his birth (Gen. 11:22-23). This is the year Nahor was born born and his period began.	8568	2445 B.C.
End of Nahor's period, 148 years after his birth (Genesis 11:24-25). This is the year Terah was born and his period began.	8716	2297 B.C.

Birth of Abram to Terah. Terah was 130 years old at the birth of Abram (Genesis 11:26, 32; 12:4).	8846	2167 B.C.
Circumcision of Abraham when he was 99 years of age (Genesis 17:24).	8945	2068 B.C.
Birth of Isaac. Abraham was 100 years old at the birth of Isaac (Genesis 21:5).	8946	2067 B.C.
Birth of Jacob. Isaac was 60 years old at the birth of Jacob (Genesis 25:26).	9006	2007 B.C.
Jacob enters Egypt at the age of 130. This is the year that begins the 430 years Israel was in Egypt (Genesis 47:9).	9136	1877 B.C.
Exodus of Israel from Egypt, 430 years after entrance (Genesis 12:40-41).	9566	1447 B.C.
The beginning of the building of the temple in the fourth year of Solomon (1 Kings 6:1).	10046	967 B.C.

Before we proceed with our study of the Bible's calendar of history, let us review what we have learned.

1. The development of God's salvation program is set forth in time. Every aspect of the unfolding of this marvelous plan has identification with time.

2. To record the time when previous events occurred in history requires some kind of a calendar. To anticipate future events in time also requires a calendar.

3. In a very decisive way, God teaches how the calendar was kept by showing how time was recorded during the 430-year period Israel was in Egypt. The method God uses is a system of calendar patriarchs. The calendar patriarchal system set forth that when the death age is given of a man who in his generation was the calendar patriarch, the next calendar patriarch was born in the same year the previous calendar patriarch died.

4. There are two exceptions to this rule. The first is that the usage of the phrase "called his name" always indicates that an immediate son is in view. The second exception is that if the Bible clearly sets forth other evidence that the son who was "begat" was an immediate son, even without the use of the phrase "called his name," then we must conclude that "begat" in this case is indicating an immediate son.

We have now developed from the Biblical information a precise Calendar of history that is integrated into our present secular calendar. We have discovered and compared many exact dates of notable events within these calendars. Now we should begin again at the beginning and witness in some detail the unfolding of God's salvation plan throughout the history of the world. We will begin at the creation date of 11,013 B.C.

11,013 B.C.

We have learned that the Bible teaches that about 13,000 years ago this world began. When we harmonize the calendar of the Bible with our modern calendar, we can know that the creation of the world occurred in the year 11,013 B.C. It was in this year that Almighty Eternal Infinite God spoke and, in a period of six literal days of 24 hours each, brought this whole universe into existence. He created it in all of its detail as a full-blown operating universe. Thus, when Adam, the first man, was created on the sixth day, he was instantly created with the appearance of age. He could have appeared to be 20 years old or 30 years old or any other adult age.

Likewise, when God created the universe, He instantly created it with an appearance of being many billions of years old. At the instance of creation, He created the light rays that brought the light from distant stars so they could be visible on earth.

On the fourth day of creation, God created the sun, the moon, the planets and the enormous number of galaxies of stars spread out in our gigantic universe. The sun, moon, and planets became a giant celestial clock to mark off days and years. We read in Genesis 1:14-19:

And God said, Let there be lights in the firmament of the heaven to divide the day from the night; and let them be for signs, and for seasons, and for days, and years: and let them be for lights in the firmament of the heaven to give light upon the earth: and it was so. And God made two great lights; the greater light to rule the day, and the lesser light to rule the night: he made the stars also. And God set them in the firmament of the heaven to give light upon the earth, and to rule over the day and over the night, and to divide the light from the darkness: and God saw that it was good. And the evening and the morning were the fourth day.

Thus, immediately at the time of the creation of this universe, all historical events became related to time. As we are learning in this study, the significant

Biblical events dealing with God's plan fit into a very precise and perfect time frame.

During the six literal 24-hour days of creation, God also instantly created all of the animals and biosphere. However, the crown of His creation was mankind who were created in the image and likeness of God. We read in Genesis 1:27:

So God created man in his own image, in the image of God created he him; male and female created he them.

Mankind was created to rule over this perfect universe and administer it entirely to the glory of the great and wonderful God who created it.

Because mankind was created in the image of and likeness of God, he became absolutely unique and the most significant part of the creation. First of all, he was created to exist forever even as God exists forever. True, in many ways his body was created in a fashion similar to the bodies of animals, and he was given physical life as animals and even insects have physical life. But, in addition, he was given a spirit essence (the Bible also calls this spirit essence a soul), which enabled him to think and act responsibly before God. He was created to love God and to obey Him perfectly.

However, as we learned in Chapter 2 of this study, which emphasized that the Bible is a law book, our first parents rebelled against God. And we must remember that in principle, the whole human race resided in Adam and Eve. Adam and Eve's rebellion was willful disobedience. They had been commanded not to eat of the forbidden fruit. However, they deliberately violated that command and *did* eat of the forbidden fruit. Thus they, as well as the whole human race, came under the wrath of God.

This introduced a serious problem. God had created a perfect universe which was to be ruled over by perfect rulers -- mankind. But when mankind became cursed by God, an impossible situation had developed. Now there existed a perfect earth ruled over by masters (mankind) who were in rebellion against God and who had become cursed by God.

To remedy this situation, God then cursed the creation itself. Thorns and thistles began to grow. Earthquakes, volcanoes, and hurricanes began to be seen. Many animals became carnivorous and some became poisonous. Illness and death were in evidence everywhere as both mankind and animals experienced physical death. This mighty change in the earth is spoken of in Romans 8:19-23:

For the earnest expectation of the creature waiteth for the manifestation of the sons of God. For the creature was made

subject to vanity, not willingly, but by reason of him who hath subjected the same in hope, because the creature itself also shall be delivered from the bondage of corruption into the glorious liberty of the children of God. For we know that the whole creation groaneth and travaileth in pain together until now. And not only they, but ourselves also, which have the firstfruits of the Spirit, even we ourselves groan within ourselves, waiting for the adoption, to wit, the redemption of our body.

The Scriptures indicate that this curse took place immediately following mankind's rebellion.

The Bible says in Genesis 3:17-19:

And unto Adam he said, Because thou hast hearkened unto the voice of thy wife, and hast eaten of the tree, of which I commanded thee, saying, Thou shalt not eat of it: cursed is the ground for thy sake; in sorrow shalt thou eat of it all the days of thy life; thorns also and thistles shall it bring forth to thee; and thou shalt eat the herb of the field; in the sweat of thy face shalt thou eat bread, till thou return unto the ground; for out of it wast thou taken: for dust thou art, and unto dust shalt thou return.

> *There will come a time in the future when this earth*
> *will be destroyed by fire...*

The citation of Romans 8:19-23 does offer a hope for this earth. There will come a time in the future when this earth will be destroyed by fire and then replaced with a perfect new heaven and new earth. We will look at this later in our study.

One other major event occurred when mankind fell into sin. The angel Lucifer (Genesis 3:1, Isaiah 14:12-17), who tempted Eve, **"the mother of all living"** (Genesis 3:20), had rebelled against God. But the angels, which are spirit beings, had been created by God to serve Him on behalf of mankind. We read in Hebrews 1:13-14:

But to which of the angels said he at any time, Sit on my right hand, until I make thine enemies thy footstool? Are they not all ministering spirits, sent forth to minister for them who shall be heirs of salvation?

Amazingly, Lucifer, though created a perfect spirit, somehow rebelled against God. He wanted to be like God. The Bible says in Isaiah 14:13-14:

For thou hast said in thine heart, I will ascend into heaven, I will exalt my throne above the stars of God: I will sit also upon the mount of the congregation, in the sides of the north: I will ascend above the heights of the clouds; I will be like the most High.

He saw his opportunity to rule. God had created mankind to be the ruler of this universe. If Lucifer could get mankind to obey him instead of God, then he, Lucifer, by right of conquest, would have become the ruler over mankind who in turn ruled over the earth.

And that is precisely what occurred. Our first parents, at the instigation of Lucifer who came to Eve in the form of a serpent, disobeyed God, and Lucifer (Satan) became ruler over the hearts of mankind. The Bible speaks of him as Satan, the devil, the dragon, the serpent, and the adversary.

That Satan rules over unsaved mankind is seen, for example, in 1 John 3:8 where God declared **"He that committeth sin is of the devil"** and in 1 John 3:10 where we read:

In this the children of God are manifest, and the children of the devil: whosoever doeth not righteousness is not of God, neither he that loveth not his brother.

This principle is also given to us in 1 John 3:12:

Not as Cain, who was of that wicked one, and slew his brother. And wherefore slew he him? Because his own works were evil, and his brother's righteous.

God further declares in John 8:44:

Ye are of your father the devil, and the lusts of your father ye will do. He was a murderer from the beginning, and abode not in the truth, because there is no truth in him. When he speaketh a lie, he speaketh of his own: for he is a liar, and the father of it.

In this study of the history of the world, we will learn that as God unfolds His salvation plan, it will be necessary that those persons whom Christ came to save must be taken out of the kingdom of Satan and brought into the kingdom of

God. As part of this task, it was necessary that Satan be vanquished and brought under the judgment of eternal damnation. Later in our study, we will learn how this was accomplished.

As we proceed down the timeline of history immediately after the beginning year of 11,013 B.C., at least three facts become abundantly evident. They are as follows.

1. Sin becomes prominently displayed.
2. A line of true believers are in evidence as time unfolds.
3. God continues to communicate with the human race.

We will briefly examine each of these three developments.

...sin became thoroughly imbedded within the human race...

The first fact we should note is the evidence that sin became thoroughly imbedded within the human race. The first two children born to Adam and Eve were sons. Cain was the firstborn. Abel was the second son. Both appeared to be quite religious in that both offered sacrifice to God (Genesis 4:3-4). Somehow Cain became aware that God rejected his sacrifice but accepted that of his younger brother Abel (Genesis 4:5).

We then learn that in envy, anger, and hatred, Cain murdered his brother Abel (Genesis 4:8). Clearly sin had become thoroughly entrenched in the human race.

Other evidences of man's tendency to sin are seen in Lamech, a descendant of Cain, marrying two wives (Genesis 4:19) and also desiring personal vengeance against another person (Genesis 4:23-24). From other Biblical information we know that both of these actions were contrary to God's law. Eventually, sin in the growing human race became so bad that God destroyed almost the entire human race. We will look at that dreadful event in a later chapter.

The second fact is that simultaneous with the development of sin in the human race, there was a line of worshipers of God in evidence, although that line was very small. We see this in two Biblical citations concerning righteous Abel. In Hebrews 11:4 we read:

By faith Abel offered unto God a more excellent sacrifice than Cain, by which he obtained witness that he was righteous, God testifying of his gifts: and by it he being dead yet speaketh.

God gives us further information in 1 John 3:12:

Not as Cain, who was of that wicked one, and slew his brother. And wherefore slew he him? Because his own works were evil, and his brother's righteous.

We note also the Bible's testimony concerning Enoch who was born about 4,000 years after the beginning of time (7106 B.C. to 6741 B.C.). God tells us in Genesis 5:23-24:

And all the days of Enoch were three hundred sixty and five years: and Enoch walked with God: and he was not; for God took him.

The line of true worshipers of God surfaced again in the life of Noah 6,000 years after creation. We read in Genesis 6:9:

These are the generations of Noah: Noah was a just man and perfect in his generations, and Noah walked with God.

The individuals we have just named were not typical of the world's population. For example, later we will discover that in the whole world of Noah's day, he and his family were the only true believers.

There is a third very important fact which should be noted that had everything to do with the unfolding of God's Gospel program for the world. You see, God spoke directly to Adam and Eve before they fell into sin. The Bible tells us in Genesis 2:16-17:

And the LORD God commanded the man, saying, Of every tree of the garden thou mayest freely eat: but of the tree of the knowledge of good and evil, thou shalt not eat of it: for in the day that thou eatest thereof thou shalt surely die.

However, the surprise is that God spoke directly to Adam and Eve even *after* they rebelled against God. We note that even though mankind had come under the wrath of God and had become spiritually dead so that God no longer spiritually energized him, God still had not abandoned the human race. Even after Cain murdered his brother Abel, God still spoke directly to Cain (Genesis 4:9-15).

This is a tremendously important fact. The essence, the driving force, the entire operation of God's salvation program is God Himself. If God had abandoned mankind at the time man sinned, there would be no salvation program.

There would be no hope for the world. Each and every human being, without any exception would end up paying the penalty of eternal damnation for his sins.

> *God is still speaking today to a rebellious world*
> *that is walking in the shoes of Adam and Cain.*

Thus, it becomes wonderful news that God still spoke to Adam and Cain after they both had committed such terrible sin in their lives, and all sin is terrible. This assures us that God is still speaking today to a rebellious world that is walking in the shoes of Adam and Cain.

In this connection one might ask, "How did God speak to Adam or Cain?" Furthermore, one could ask, "If God speaks to us today, how does He?"

We do know that for many thousands of years there was no written word. Until the Bible was completed, God communicated through visions (Genesis 15:1), or dreams (Genesis 41:1-25), or in an audible voice (Exodus 19:9-19, 20:19; Hebrews 12:25), or by having direct conversation with individuals (Exodus 32:7-Chapter 33). There were times that God did this having taken on the appearance of a human being (Genesis 18:1-3; Joshua 5:13-15). However, there came a time that God determined to preserve in written form all He would choose to tell mankind about Himself and His salvation plan. For example, we read that God dictated His words to the prophet Jeremiah. Today those words are in the Bible as the Book of Jeremiah.

God reveals in Jeremiah 36:1-3:

And it came to pass in the fourth year of Jehoiakim the son of Josiah king of Judah, that this word came unto Jeremiah from the LORD, saying, take thee a roll of a book, and write therein all the words that I have spoken unto thee against Israel, and against Judah, and against all the nations, from the day I spake unto thee, from the days of Josiah, even unto this day. It may be that the house of Judah will hear all the evil which I purpose to do unto them; that they may return every man from his evil way; that I may forgive their iniquity and their sin.

This is the way the Bible was written. We read in 2 Timothy 3:16a:

All scripture is given by inspiration of God . . .

Furthermore, we read in 2 Peter 1:21:

For the prophecy came not in old time by the will of man: but holy men of God spake as they were moved by the Holy Ghost.

However, once the Bible was completed in approximately A.D. 95, no further word has come from God. God assures us by His declaration in Revelation 22:18-19:

For I testify unto every man that heareth the words of the prophecy of this book, If any man shall add unto these things, God shall add unto him the plagues that are written in this book: and if any man shall take away from the words of the book of this prophecy, God shall take away his part out of the book of life, and out of the holy city, and from the things which are written in this book.

...it is the Bible and only the Bible, which is the Word of God, by which God speaks to us today.

Therefore, it is the Bible and only the Bible, which is the Word of God, by which God speaks to us today. Whenever we read a verse from the Bible, it is in essence the same as if we had just heard the voice of God speaking that verse. Therefore each and everyone of us should fear and tremble when we read verses of Holy Scripture. It is His Almighty Majesty, the King and Judge of all the earth, and Loving Redeemer of His people, who is speaking to us in a very personal way. We read in 2 Timothy 3:16-17:

All scripture is given by inspiration of God, and is profitable for doctrine, for reproof, for correction, for instruction in righteousness: that the man of God may be perfect, throughly furnished unto all good works.

It is true that for the first 9,500 years of the history of the world, no written Word of God existed. Nevertheless, mankind sufficiently heard from God so that he knew, for example, about sacrifices. We know this to be true because Cain and Abel both offered sacrifices (Genesis 4:3-4). Later on, Noah was given very specific instructions for the building of the ark, the huge boat that would provide safety for him and his family when God destroyed the whole world by water.

Moreover, there was a proclamation of an integral part of the Gospel even though there was no written Word. The Bible says that Enoch, who lived about 4,000 years after creation and about 2,000 years before the flood of Noah's day, preached the Gospel. In Jude 14-15, God gives us an excerpt from the message Enoch preached:

And Enoch also, the seventh from Adam, prophesied of these, saying, Behold, the Lord cometh with ten thousands of his saints, to execute judgment upon all, and to convince all that are ungodly among them of all their ungodly deeds which they have ungodly committed, and of all their hard speeches which ungodly sinners have spoken against him.

Noah, too, was a preacher. We read in 2 Peter 2:5:

And spared not the old world, but saved Noah the eighth person, a preacher of righteousness, bringing in the flood upon the world of the ungodly;

A significant fact to note as we view the unfolding of the Biblical timeline of history throughout the first 6,000 years is the phenomena that already, in those early years, God gave intimations of the future characteristics of His salvation program. We saw this when God provided animal skins to clothe Adam and Eve immediately after they sinned. This action pointed to the coming of the Lord Jesus Christ about 11,000 years later as the Lamb of God who by His death would cover the sins of those He came to save.

Remember that there were Enoch and Noah who warned that the sins of mankind would bring righteous judgment from God upon them.

The experience of Enoch, in that he lived 365 years and then went to heaven without dying, reveals another aspect of God's salvation program. We read in Genesis 5:22-24:

And Enoch walked with God after he begat Methuselah three hundred years, and begat sons and daughters: and all the days of Enoch were three hundred sixty and five years: and Enoch walked with God: and he was not; for God took him.

When God created time, He made each year to be 365.2422 days. Thus, a life of 365 years identifies with the passage of a year. When Jesus began to preach, He identified the preaching of the Gospel with the term **"acceptable year."** We read this in Luke 4:18-19:

> **The Spirit of the Lord is upon me, because he hath anointed me to preach the gospel to the poor; he hath sent me to heal the brokenhearted, to preach deliverance to the captives, and recovering of sight to the blind, to set at liberty them that are bruised, to preach the acceptable year of the Lord.**

...when the end of the world has come, there will be the rapture of the true believers.

Immediately following the time of the bringing of the Gospel to the world when the end of the world has come, there will be the rapture of the true believers. We read about this in 1 Thessalonians 4:16-17:

> **For the Lord himself shall descend from heaven with a shout, with the voice of the archangel, and with the trump of God: and the dead in Christ shall rise first: then we which are alive and remain shall be caught up together with them in the clouds, to meet the Lord in the air: and so shall we ever be with the Lord.**

Thus, in the life of Enoch, God at that early time in history demonstrated and prophesied in this unique manner His plan for the final unfolding of the Gospel. Enoch, a preacher whom God used to teach different characteristics of the Gospel, was raptured after the acceptable year.

God also intimated different aspects of His salvation program by the instruction He gave concerning the sacrifices (Genesis 4; Exodus; etc.). Each sacrifice pointed to the coming of the Lord Jesus who gave His life as a substitute sacrifice so that the justice of God could be satisfied and the sins of those whom God planned to save might be forgiven.

Already at the Beginning, We May See God's Prediction of the Future

We have been carefully examining the creation of the world together with the fall of mankind. This has enabled us to further understand the very beginnings of this tremendous plan of God that would demonstrate the magnificent glory of God as the Creator and Savior (Ephesians 1:9-10). It is a plan that will result in a great multitude of humans reigning with Christ forever.

We have also learned that God has a carefully developed timetable for the unfolding of His salvation plan. Because we are living very near the time of the end of that plan (as we will see as we continue to study), we can take note of some interesting facts that may be anticipating its finale.

We read in Isaiah 48:5:

I have even from the beginning declared it to thee; before it came to pass I shewed it thee: lest thou shouldest say, Mine idol hath done them, and my graven image, and my molten image, hath commanded them.

> *...from the very beginning of time, God discloses to us His grand plan of salvation...*

We see here that from the very beginning of time, God discloses to us His grand plan of salvation with the additional information that there would be a final judgment. This principle is also taught by the citation of Isaiah 46:9-10:

Remember the former things of old: for I am God, and there is none else; I am God, and there is none like me, declaring the end from the beginning, and from ancient times the things that are not yet done, saying, My counsel shall stand, and I will do all my pleasure:

Curiously, there is a very tiny intimation concerning the timing of the end of the world as we look at the date of Creation. We have seen that, according to the present calendar used in the world, Creation would have been 11,013 B.C. In actuality, later in our study we will learn that Christ in all probability was born in the year 7 B.C.

Did God allow those who designed our modern calendar to make a mistake of six years so that the creation date would be 11,013 B.C.? Remember 11,013 B.C. is based on the assumption that in A.D. 1, Christ was one year old. It might be altogether coincidental that the person who designed our calendar believed that Christ was born six years later than when He was actually born making the date of creation about 11,007 B.C. On the other hand the obtaining of the year 11,013 B.C. may have been guided by God so that in this number the timing of two great events in the unfolding of God's salvation plan are being predicted. Let's examine this idea.

Christ took on a human nature (that is, He was born) just a few years after 11,000 years had passed since creation. Evidence indicates that He is coming a second time just a few years past 13,000 years after creation. Thus the two numbers, 11 and 13, are very much in evidence as we view the whole timetable of God's salvation plan. Is it possible that, in the number 11,013, God, in a very veiled way, is prophesying the timing of the coming of Jesus as He comes to complete God's great plan of salvation? We will look at this further as we continue on in our study.

Here is a second intriguing concept. Cain murdered his brother Abel. Biblical evidence indicates that Abel was saved but Cain was not (Genesis 4:4b-5; Matthew 23:35; Hebrews 11:4; 12:24; 1 John 3:12; Jude 11). Afterwards, when Adam was 130 years old, his third son, Seth, was born. The name Seth means "appointed."

God tells us this in Genesis 4:25:

And Adam knew his wife again; and she bare a son, and called his name Seth: for God, said she, hath appointed me another seed instead of Abel, whom Cain slew.

Could it be that Eve saw in Seth a continuation of a Godly line of believers that had been cut off by Abel's death?

The words **"appointed"** and **"seed"** which are found in this verse assure us that Seth represents an important milestone in the unfolding of God's salvation plan. We have seen earlier that God uses past historical events to anticipate and represent future spiritual events. Thus we wonder if this is the situation with the birth of Seth. We note the following points.

1. Adam was 130 years of age when Seth was born.

2. Cain killed Abel, thus eliminating, for a time, any believers in the world who would be the physical seed of Adam.

3. Seth was appointed by God to be the **"seed"** to continue the line of believers.

Pondering these statements brings to our mind a very parallel situation that we examined in the book *The End of the Church Age and After* that began to occur precisely 13,000 years after the creation of Adam. We will develop these ideas later in this study, but as near as we can tell:

1. A.D. 1988 was exactly 13,000 years after creation. A.D. 1988 was the official beginning of the Great Tribulation which coincided with the end of the church age.

2. At the beginning of the Great Tribulation, the two witnesses spoken of in the Book of Revelation are killed (Revelation 11:7). Even as Cain murdered his brother Abel, so too, the local congregations spiritually murder their fellow church members who were faithful and obedient to God's commands. They spiritually murder them by driving them from, or silencing them in, the local churches and congregations (John 16:2).

3. However, even as God appointed a "seed" to follow the death of Abel, so too, God has appointed a seed that would follow the end of the church age. That "seed" are those who are the final harvest – those who are becoming saved during the time of the latter rain (Revelation 7:9).

It surely seems possible that at the very beginning of the salvation program, Christ was pointing to the end of the salvation program.

In similar fashion we might see the end of the world in the nature of the penalty imposed on Cain because he murdered his brother. Cain came under the judgment of God, and his banishment from the face of the earth (Genesis 4:9-15) could be a picture of the end-time churches coming under the wrath of God.

We should now summarize the most important points that were in evidence during the first 6,000 years of history.

1. Sin was greatly in evidence.

2. Mankind continued to be religious.

3. God continued to communicate with mankind even though sin abounded.

4. Only by the information the Bible gives us do we conclude that true believers were few and far between as there is very little reference to them.

5. True believers that did live during this period warned the world of the judgment of God as the consequence of sin.

6. As God has written in the Bible concerning this period of time, He seems to have revealed some of the major future aspects of His unfolding plan.

> *We are discovering that the Bible gives us*
> *the timeline of history that is identified altogether with the*
> *unfolding of God's salvation plan.*

We are discovering that the Bible gives us the timeline of history that is identified altogether with the unfolding of God's salvation plan. Because God's salvation plan is entirely related to mankind, it is mankind whom we must carefully examine.

As we continue our study of the history of the world, we must take time to understand who man is. How is he different from God? How is he like God? How is he different from animals? How is he like animals?

We will learn much about these questions as we look carefully at mankind.

1. What constituted his essence and nature when he was first created.

2. What changed when he fell into sin.

3. What changed when individuals became saved.

4. What happened to Jesus when He took on a human nature.

Now we should not lose sight of our main purpose as we study these important elements of history. That is that one day, God will bring everything together in one giant, grand conclusion.

Our source book for this study is the Bible. Only because the Bible is God's Word to us do we dare to offer the following understanding of mankind. Because each and every conclusion is derived from the Bible, and insofar as each conclusion can be determined to be harmonious with the whole Bible, may we believe that we have come to a correct Biblical understanding of man.

Our examination of mankind must begin at the very beginning because it was on the sixth day of this world's history that Adam was created. We will learn in our study that at that time, in principle, the whole human race was created.

Chapter 4
Mankind Was Created in the Image of God

We have learned that God has a very carefully developed timeline by which He has unfolded the history of the world. As we continue our study, we will increasingly find that the unfolding of the timeline of history is governed by the development of God's salvation plan. But God's salvation plan is intimately involved with mankind. Therefore, it is imperative that we know all that we can know about mankind. The only source that we can look to for this kind of truth is the Bible. This is so because the Bible is the only source in which God has set forth an accurate description of the nature of man whom God Himself has created. In this chapter, we will look very intently at the creation of the human race.

The first truth we discover about mankind is that he was created in the image, in the likeness of God. We read in Genesis 1:26-27:

> **And God said, Let us make man in our image, after our likeness: and let them have dominion over the fish of the sea, and over the fowl of the air, and over the cattle, and over all the earth, and over every creeping thing that creepeth upon the earth. So God created man in his own image, in the image of God created he him; male and female created he them.**

This is an exceedingly remarkable statement. Infinite God is the ever-present One who has been throughout eternity past and who spoke and brought this entire complex universe into existence. What can it mean that we are created in the image, in the likeness of God? Remarkably the same language is used when Adam's third son, Seth, was born. We read in Genesis 5:3:

> **And Adam lived an hundred and thirty years, and begat a son in his own likeness, after his image; and called his name Seth:**

All of us know what it means for a son to be in the "likeness" of his father. The father and the son may look alike, act alike, even think alike. Father and son may have the same desires, the same fears, the same interests. The son can be virtually a carbon copy of the father.

However, when God speaks of man being created in the likeness of God, we immediately realize that there are certain characteristics of God that can never be a part of man. God is from everlasting past, the ever-present One. Man has a beginning and no pre-existence. God is infinite in His power, in His knowledge, in His wisdom, in His presence. Man, in his physical being, has very limited power or knowledge or wisdom, and can be present in only one place at a time.

Yet there are very distinct similarities between God and man.

Yet there are very distinct similarities between God and man. The very fact that God wrote the Bible and man can read the Bible indicates great similarity. The fact that man can have some understanding of such concepts as love, hatred, joy, patience, mercy, grace, forgiveness, kindness, obedience, sorrow, etc. indicates a definite similarity between God and man.

As we examine Genesis 2:7, we will learn more about the similarity between God and man. There we read:

And the LORD God formed man of the dust of the ground, and breathed into his nostrils the breath of life; and man became a living soul.

This verse states that when God created man as a physical being, he was formed from the dust of the ground. This is almost identical language to that recorded in Genesis 2:19, where we read:

And out of the ground the LORD God formed every beast of the field, and every fowl of the air; and brought them unto Adam to see what he would call them: and whatsoever Adam called every living creature, that was the name thereof.

The word "dust" is added by God in Genesis 2:7 no doubt anticipating the curse that would come upon mankind at the time they would sin. Remember, *after* Adam sinned, God declared to him in Genesis 3:19:

In the sweat of thy face shalt thou eat bread, till thou return unto the ground; for out of it wast thou taken: for dust thou art, and unto dust shalt thou return.

Because the language given in Genesis 2:19 concerning the creation of animals is similar to that of the first part of Genesis 2:7 concerning the creation of man, we need to look first at the creation of animals.

The Creation of Animals

Animals were created as physical beings with the physical breath of life. The energy that God uses to keep them alive comes from two sources. One source is the food they eat and the water they drink. The second source is the oxygen they breathe. If deprived of these, they will die. The Bible speaks of the animals' creation in Genesis 2:19:

> **And out of the ground the LORD God formed every beast of the field, and every fowl of the air; and brought them unto Adam to see what he would call them: and whatsoever Adam called every living creature, that was the name thereof.**

Animals are formed from the ground in the sense that they totally identify with the elements found in the ground. All the minerals found in the earth are found in the bodies of animals. All of the food they eat comes from the ground. They return to the ground when they die. They were created in many shapes and sizes with varying degrees of animal intelligence. They in no sense have any spiritual nature. They are physically alive as long as they are able to breathe.

The Creation of Man

> *We must understand that the difference between man and animals is enormous.*

We must understand that the difference between man and animals is enormous. Of supreme importance is the fact that man is created in the image of God. Physically, there are similarities between man and animals. Many people therefore like to believe that mankind is a higher form of animal. If we did not have the Bible, this conclusion would appear to be quite true. In addition, if man were only an animal, then the Bible's teachings concerning sin, judgment, eternal damnation, mercy, etc. would be foolishness. This would be so because if we were but animals, albeit higher forms of animals, we, like any animal, would merely live out our lives and then die. That would be the whole story. We would never have to answer to God for our sins. We would never have to fear the wrath of God.

Unfortunately for those who would like to believe that humans are simply a higher form of animal, there is no truth in their conclusion. A human being is an entirely different creature from animals. Beyond the physical similarities of their physical bodies, man and animals bear little resemblance whatsoever.

Who or what man is cannot be learned in any way except by careful reading of the Bible. Fact is, the whole Bible is concerned with mankind. Thus, the unfolding of God's salvation program through history constantly focuses on mankind. True, by studying the Bible, we can also learn many things about animals, but the essential and all-important message of the Bible deals with you, me and the billions of people who live in this world.

> *Very quickly we will learn that each of us is a spiritual being.*

Because of the enormous importance of the teachings of the Bible that focus on human beings, and indeed, on you and on me, we are, in our study, going to spend some time trying to understand who we are. Very quickly we will learn that each of us is a spiritual being. Hopefully, as we go on, we will gain some understanding of the spiritual nature of man and how that spiritual essence impacts our relationship with God.

As we have learned, man was created with a physical body very similar to that of an animal. That is why, for example, animals can be used to test medicines that are being designed for human use. As it is with animals, all of the food we eat ultimately comes from the ground. When we die, our bodies return to the ground.

The major physical difference between man and animals is that man's brain is far more complex than that of an animal. God created man with a more complex brain because He created man also to be a spiritual being in the likeness of God? When God gave man a soul (or spirit essence), this wonderful act also impacted man's physical body so that particularly in his mind he became different from animals in that he could learn to read and write. He could understand to some degree such terms as love, joy, mercy, justice, etc. He could have the ability to design and build complex projects.

Man also would be able to communicate with God in prayer. He would understand that there is a God whom he must serve and to whom he must be accountable.

Human beings were created with a soul. (As we continue our study, we will learn more about the fact that the creation of man's soul has everything to do with his being created in the image of God.) Human beings were created with a physical body together with a soul. Whereas the animal is physically alive only as long as it breathes, what really makes humans physically alive is that their souls remain present in their bodies. We will examine this principle as we carefully look at Genesis 2:7. Remember, it declares:

> **And the LORD God formed man of the dust of the ground, and breathed into his nostrils the breath of life; and man became a living soul.**

We have learned from Genesis 2:7 that Adam was created with a physical body. But then this verse says **"and breathed into his nostrils the breath of life; and man became a living soul."** In this phrase, five words are especially significant. They are the Hebrew words "breathed" (*naphach*), "breath" (*neshamah*), "life" (*chayyim*), "living" (*chayyah*), and "soul" (*le nephesh*). We should examine each of these Hebrew words very carefully. As we do so, we will reaffirm that every word in the original language of the Bible is very important. In addition, we will learn that the Bible is its own dictionary. The Bible's usage of any word helps to define the meaning of that word.

"Breathed"

Let us first examine the word "breathed" (Hebrew *naphach*). We read that **"God breathed into his nostrils."** The Hebrew word that is translated "breathed" is found several times in the Bible. It is never used in connection with breath being given to animals. Thus, by the use of this word for "breathed," God is emphasizing a distinct difference between man and animals. It is significantly used in Ezekiel 37:9 where God describes the phenomenon of dry bones coming to life. There we read:

> **Then said he unto me, Prophesy unto the wind, prophesy, son of man, and say to the wind, Thus saith the Lord GOD; Come from the four winds, O breath, and breathe [*Hebrew naphach*] upon these slain, that they may live.**

This usage accords with the breathing of God in Genesis 2:7 where God is giving life to the dead body of Adam. It identifies with the statement of John 20:22 when God breathed on the disciples:

> **And when he had said this, he breathed on them and saith unto them, Receive ye the Holy Ghost.**

Christ's breathing on His disciples was a demonstration of one element of salvation: a spiritually dead soul becomes spiritually alive, indwelt by the Holy Ghost (also referred to in the Bible as the Holy Spirit, Luke 11:13). And so we see a direct parallel between the original creation of man when God created him perfect in the image of God and the spiritual re-creation of God's people when they receive a new, resurrected soul (John 3:3-8; 2 Corinthians 5:17; Ephesians 4:24; 1 John 3:9). (See Chapter 13, "What Must I Do to Become Saved?")

"Breath"

The next word found in Genesis 2:7 that we should examine is the word "breath." It is the Hebrew word "*neshamah.*" The word "*neshamah*" is never used in the Bible in connection with the breath of animals. The breath given to animals is the Hebrew word "*ruach*" which also can be translated "spirit" and is also used at times in speaking of the breath or spirit of mankind.

However, God's use of *neshamah* in Genesis 2:7 provides a total separation between animals and man. Thus, by the means of the two words "breathed" and "breath" as they are used in Genesis 2:7, God is teaching that mankind is totally unique. We are learning that this is describing how man became a spiritual being. It is by what God describes as His own breathing and breath that mankind was given a spirit essence (also called soul). This soul proved that mankind had become created in the likeness of God because in this soul, God in His Spirit entered into and identified with mankind. This provided not only the means by which God could bring God's energy into man so that mankind might will and work to God's good pleasure, but it also provided the means by which God Himself actually works in mankind. The presence of this soul in human beings sets them completely apart from animals. Animals were not created with a soul.

"Life"

The next word we should carefully examine is the word "life" (Hebrew *chayyim*). It is very closely related to the Hebrew words "*chay,*" "*chayah,*" and "*chayyah.*" All of these words express the concept of life or living. However, *chayyim* is a plural word. It should be translated as the plural word "lives." Thus, in Genesis 2:7, the phrase "breath of life" should be translated "breath of lives."

How are we to understand this odd phrase "breath of lives?" A search of the Bible reveals that it was used more than eighty times by God as He wrote the Bible. It is used as God speaks of a man's life, of an animal's life, and of God's life. We should look at examples of each of these three usages to determine more precisely what God is teaching by means of this plural word "*chayyim.*"

In Genesis 7:15 we read:

And they went in unto Noah into the ark, two and two of all flesh, wherein is the breath of <u>life</u>.

This verse is speaking of the unclean animals that were brought into Noah's ark. The phrase "breath of life" should be translated "breath of lives." How does this plural word "lives" fit in this context?

In Exodus 22:4 we read:

If the theft be certainly found in his hand <u>alive</u>, whether it be ox, or ass, or sheep; he shall restore double.

This verse is speaking of a single animal being alive; that is, having "lives." How can a single animal have "lives?"

In Numbers 16:33 we read:

They, and all that appertained to them, went down <u>alive</u> into the pit, and the earth closed upon them: and they perished from among the congregation.

This verse is speaking of unsaved men being alive; that is, having "lives." What can that mean?

In Psalm 21:4 we read:

He asked <u>life</u> of thee, and thou gavest it him, even length of days for ever and ever.

This verse is speaking of the one who becomes saved receiving "lives" forever. What can that mean?

These sample verses show us that the plural word "chayyim" applies to single animals, to unsaved people, and also to those who are saved. How can we harmonize all of these usages?

The answer is given, for example, in Psalm 36:9:

For with thee is the fountain of <u>life</u>: in thy light shall we see light.

In this verse, the phrase "the fountain of life" is actually "the fountain of lives." God is the fountain of lives. That is, He is the source of any and all life. He is the source of physical life for an animal. He is the source of physical life for mankind. He is the source of spiritual life given to man at Creation. He is the source of the eternal spiritual life given to the one who is saved.

God uses the plural word "lives" also because God is a plural being. In 1 Samuel 17:36 we read:

> **Thy servant slew both the lion and the bear: and this uncircumcised Philistine shall be as one of them, seeing he hath defied the armies of the living God.**

In the phrase "living God," both words "living" and "God" are plural. This verse could be translated "he hath defied the armies of the God of lives." That is, God reveals Himself as a plural being. The Bible declares that God is Triune, Father, Son, and Holy Spirit, and these three are one God (John 14:26; 1 John 5:7). He is the source of any and all life in this world. Life emanating from a plural being, God, therefore is spoken of as a plural word "lives." Life comes from God the Father, from God the Son, and from God the Holy Spirit. Therefore God, in many verses, employs the plural word "*chayyim*" (lives) when He speaks of life coming from God.

It is also a fact that many times the Bible uses a Hebrew word in the singular tense in indicating "life." This is very parallel to the teaching of the Bible that on the one hand, as God is speaking of Himself, He uses plural language like God (Hebrew *Elohim*, a plural word) such as in Genesis 1:26 where He says **"let us make man in our image."** But on the other hand, God insists there is only one God and uses such words as Lord, Christ, Jesus, etc. which are all singular words. The big principle we learn is that whether the physical life in animals, the physical life in man, the spiritual life (soul) given to man at Creation, or the spiritual life restored to those who have become saved, all life comes from God. He is the only source of life.

We should comment on two other verses. Psalm 52:5 declares:

> **God shall likewise destroy thee for ever, he shall take thee away, and pluck thee out of thy dwelling place, and root thee out of the land of the living. Selah.**

This world in which we live is the "land of the living." In this verse too, the word "living" is *chayyim* so that it could be translated "land of lives." In this world there exists both physical life and spiritual life. However, this verse also is indicating that those who are consigned to hell have been taken away from this "land of lives" and are being destroyed forever.

This truth is emphasized in connection with Jesus paying for the sins of those He came to save.

We read in Isaiah 53:8:

He was taken from prison and from judgment: and who shall declare his generation? for he was cut off out of the land of the living: for the transgression of my people was he stricken.

Again in this verse, the phrase "the land of the living" could be translated "the land of lives." Thus, Christ suffered the wrath of God by becoming like those who will be cast into hell forever.

"Living Being"

The next word we should examine is the word that is translated "living." The word "living" (Hebrew *chayyah*), is a noun that is used many times in the Old Testament. Frequently it is translated "life," or "living," or "living thing." Additionally. it is frequently translated as "beast." This comports with the concept that an animal has life or is a living thing as long as it has breath. Frequently the word "living" (*chayyah*) is used in association with the Hebrew noun *nephesh*. This is the way it is used in Genesis 2:7. There we find the Hebrew phrase *le nephesh chayyah*. The best translation of *chayyah* in this verse is "living being."

"For the Dead Body"

This brings us to the next word we should carefully examine. It is actually a Hebrew phrase *le nephesh*. The phrase *le nephesh* is the word "*nephesh*" connected with the Hebrew preposition "*le*." When the noun *nephesh* stands alone, as it does hundreds of times in the Bible, it is translated in a variety of ways such as "creature," "life," "soul," "person," etc. Fact is, the translators of the King James Bible simply translated the phrase *le nephesh* in Genesis 2:7 as "soul." [1] Thus, we see that the King James translation of Genesis 2:7 indicates that man became a living (*chayyah*) soul (*le nephesh*).

---

[1] This does not mean that the translators were less spiritually qualified or had less intellectual ability. We must keep in mind the principle of progressive revelation. Even now, when we are living in a time when God is opening the eyes of many to more and more truths of the Bible, we can expect that today God will give a more adequate understanding and better translation of various Bible phrases.

Additionally there are two verses that are written using the Hebrew *le khoi nephesh*. The word "*khoi*" means "any" or "every." In one of the verses, Numbers 19:11, the phrase "*le khoi nephesh*" is translated "of any man." This verse is speaking of "the dead body of any man," so in this verse, *le nephesh* is virtually giving the same meaning as the translation "for the dead body." Additionally, in Exodus 12:16, the Hebrew phrase "*le khoi nephesh*" is translated "which every man."

The Hebrew preposition *le* is found over 4,000 times in the Bible. It can be translated as "to," "toward," "with," "at," "for," or "of" depending on the context in which it is found. However, in connection with the word *nephesh*, it is found only thirteen times. One of those thirteen times is in the verse we are studying: Genesis 2:7. To help us understand the meaning of this phrase as it is used in Genesis 2:7, we must see how it is translated in the other twelve places in the Bible.

Of the thirteen times that the Hebrew phrase *le nephesh* is found in the Bible, in six of the occurrences, it is translated "for the dead," "by the dead," "by the dead body," or "of the dead body." These verses are Leviticus 19:28 and 21:1, and Numbers 5:2, 9:6, 9:7, and 9:10. In each instance, a human dead body is in view. For example, Numbers 9:10 records:

> **Speak unto the children of Israel, saying, If any man of you or of your posterity shall be unclean by reason <u>of a dead body</u>, or be in a journey afar off, yet he shall keep the passover unto the LORD.**

In three verses, *le nephesh* is translated "to the soul." These verses are Proverbs 13:19 and 16:24 and Lamentations 3:25. In another verse, Numbers 35:31, *le nephesh* is translated "for the life."

When we examine these usages of the phrase "*le nephesh*," it is evident that it can be translated in the sense of "for the dead body" or "to the soul" or "for the life." Therefore, we have options as we seek to translate "*le nephesh chayyah*" in Genesis 2:7. It could be translated in the sense of any of the following ways.

1. "man became *for the dead body* a living being."
2. "man became *to the soul* a living being."
3. "man became *to man* a living being."
4. "man became *for the life* a living being."

The first translation listed here is the most likely. In the first part of Genesis 2:7, God speaks about the physical creation of man's body: **"And the LORD God formed man of the dust of the ground."** As we learned, this is almost identical language to that which the Bible uses when speaking of the creation of animals as having been given physical life.

> *...we must remember that when a man's soul is separated from his body, he is physically dead.*

However, we must remember that when a man's soul is separated from his body, he is physically dead. He is a dead body. For example, when a true believer dies, his dead body is buried, but he in his soul existence goes to heaven to live and reign with Christ (2 Corinthians 5:6-9; Revelation 20:4). So it was -- only in reverse order -- when God created Adam. First there was the lifeless body of Adam which God had just created. Then He breathed the breath of life into that dead body. Suddenly Adam became both physically and spiritually alive because at that moment he was given a soul.

Therefore, Genesis 2:7 could likely be translated:

. . . God formed man of the dust of the ground, and breathed into his nostrils the breath of *lives*, and man became *for the dead body* a living *being*.

In whichever way Genesis 2:7 could best be translated, we can conclude that when God created man's body, he was neither physically or spiritually alive. It was only when God breathed the *breath of lives* into that dead body that man became both physically and spiritually alive.

Now, it may seem that the foregoing discussion has been highly technical and tedious. But we have shown examples that demonstrate that every word in the Bible has significance (Matthew 5:18), and these examples show how, in the usage of its words, the Bible explains itself and defines the terms it uses. This is a principle of Bible study that everyone should employ no matter what part of the Bible they are scrutinizing.

Man's Soul Impacted His Body

This soul or spiritual life, which became an integral part of mankind, and which was not given to animals, also greatly impacted mankind's physical body. The result was that when man was created, whatever desire he might have in his whole personality, he would want to do God's will. You will recall that, in our discussion about when mankind became a spiritual being, we pondered how God might have prepared for this by giving man, as a physical being, a far different brain than He gave to animals.

Incidentally, God links together the mind and the soul of man. For example, in Romans 7:22-25 we read:

For I delight in the law of God after the inward man: but I see another law in my members, warring against the law of my mind, and bringing me into captivity to the law of sin which is in my

members. O wretched man that I am! who shall deliver me from the body of this death? I thank God through Jesus Christ our Lord. So then with the mind I myself serve the law of God; but with the flesh the law of sin.

In this verse, the word "mind" is a synonym for "soul." It was in his "soul" or as a spiritual being that he was created in the image or likeness of God. It is possible that this exceedingly superior mind identified with a more complex brain because the more complex organ was required to enable his eternal soul to function properly. We have just learned that it was through his eternal soul that God energized him spiritually, and we will learn that God actually becomes a part of him.

Because God is eternal Spirit and man was created in His image, he was created a spiritual being with a physical body. Both man's soul and body were to live forever.

How Then Did Adam and Eve Fall Into Sin?

How then did Adam and Eve fall into sin? Fact is, in their soul which was created in the image of God, they could not sin. This is so because God cannot sin. We read in James 1:13 that God **"cannot be tempted with evil."** And in 1 John 3:9 we read:

Whosoever is born of God doth not commit sin; for his seed remaineth in him: and he cannot sin, because he is born of God.

These verses teach that God can never sin. Thus, when mankind was created as a spiritual being, in the likeness of God, he, too, could never sin even as God can never sin.

In His Body Mankind was Vulnerable

However, as a physical being, as a human with a body of flesh similar to that of an animal, we have a different matter. Let us understand this as we examine Biblical language that speaks about the life of a true believer. We have learned that a true believer has been given a resurrected soul (he is "born again" as we learn in John 3:3-8), in which he cannot sin (1 John 3:9). However in his flesh or physical body, the situation is altogether different. We read in Romans 7:5:

For when we were in the flesh, the motions of sins, which were by the law, did work in our members to bring forth fruit unto death.

Moreover, the Bible further states in Romans 7:22-24:

For I delight in the law of God after the inward man: but I see another law in my members, warring against the law of my mind, and bringing me into captivity to the law of sin which is in my members. O wretched man that I am! who shall deliver me from the body of this death?

These verses teach that sin, which is a transgression of God's law (James 2:9-10; 1 John 3:4), takes place in the true believer's body or flesh -- that part of him that was created out of the dust of the ground.

Likewise, when Adam and Eve were created, in their soul they would never sin -- but in their *bodies* they were vulnerable. This was so even though they were created perfectly sinless in their body as well as in their soul. Their body was the part of their personality that Satan attacked and was victorious. God had set up a testing arena which was the tree of the knowledge of good and evil. The fruit of this tree they were never to eat. They sinned by transgressing this command. The consequence of this sin was catastrophic. God had warned them that in the day they ate of this forbidden fruit, they would die. What could that have meant? At the moment of their sin, they did not die *physically*. They died *spiritually*. (Soon, we will go beyond our first parents and deal with what has happened to all of mankind. The sin of Adam has brought about the spiritual death of every human being! Adam's original sin has caused all of us to become spiritually dead at the moment of conception -- that moment when God creates the body and soul of a new human being!)

The Temptation Experienced by Jesus

Understanding the principle that it was in Adam and Eve's physical bodies that they were vulnerable to the possibility of sinning underscores why the temptation of Jesus by Satan was so awful. At His incarnation, Jesus took on a human nature which included a physical body. In this physical body, He could be tempted to do evil. Satan was after Him, constantly tempting Him (Matthew 16:1; 19:3; John 8:6; Luke 4:1-13; Satan even worked through the Pharisees, the scribes, etc.). Wonderfully, Jesus remained perfect, never falling into sin.

> *...it was in Adam and Eve's physical bodies that they were vulnerable to the possibility of sinning.*

On the other hand, our first parents had been given the Holy Spirit in that God had breathed into their physical bodies the breath or Spirit of God so that they had a spiritually perfect soul. But they also had a physical body that was identified with the dust of the earth. Because, in their soul, they were indwelt by God Himself, even as God cannot be tempted with evil, neither could they be tempted with evil in the soul part of their personality. Remember 1 John 3:9 where God speaks of the true believer who cannot sin because he has been born of God. It is only in his body that he can be tempted to sin. Even as Jesus was tempted with evil because He had taken on a human nature, so Adam and Eve in their human bodies could be tempted with evil.

It is truly remarkable that in order for Jesus to be the Savior, He had to go through the same experience as Adam. It is no wonder then that Romans 5:14 speaks of Adam as him **"who is the figure of Him that was to come."** Jesus, the "last Adam" (1 Corinthians 15:45), had to experience the same thing the first Adam did. Jesus took on a perfect sinless body, Adam was given a perfect sinless body when he was created. But unlike Adam, wonderfully, Jesus did not fall into sin when He was very severely tested.

Also remarkable is the fact that because God took on a human body in order to qualify to be the Savior, God will live throughout eternity future with a glorified spiritual body exactly as true believers will live forever with a glorified spiritual body (1 John 3:2).

Once again, we puzzle over what all this has to do with the Biblical Calendar of History. But if we remember that the Calendar of History is governed by the unfolding of God's *salvation* plan, then we can see that an indispensable part of our study must be the examination of the details of how mankind became so desperately in *need* of salvation. We will proceed to examine this further.

The Consequence of Man's Sin

When man sinned, he became spiritually dead. That is, God was no longer supplying spiritual energy to him. He was no longer dwelling in him. Man had become spiritually dead. However, he still retained an exceedingly superior mind which we call intelligence.

We thus can understand that when our soul is dead, our intelligence or ability to think does not disappear. Fact is, we still know that there is a God to whom we must be accountable. We still know that we are under the law of God.

We read in Romans 2:14-15:

For when the Gentiles, which have not the law, do by nature the things contained in the law, these, having not the law, are a law unto themselves: which shew the work of the law written in their hearts, their conscience also bearing witness, and their thoughts the mean while accusing or else excusing one another.

Every individual conceived in this world is not saved until God begins to supply spiritual energy to them.

Every individual who is conceived of their parents -- and most of them are born into this world -- is spiritually dead. All are descendants of Adam. Every one is sinful (Romans 3:23) and totally ruined by sin (Romans 5:12). The Bible terms our spiritually dead state as being "in Adam" (1 Corinthians 15:22). Every individual conceived in this world is not saved until God begins to supply spiritual energy to them. They are all spiritually dead, and they, in themselves can do nothing -- absolutely nothing -- to restore to themselves God's energy which has been lost (John 3:27; John 6:44, 65; John 15:5b; Romans 3:10-12).

An individual still can read and write and think and do many things that result from the fact that he was created in the image of God. However, in regards to his relationship to God, he is spiritually dead (1 Corinthians 1:18-20, 2:14). The Holy Spirit does not indwell him and does not energize him. He actually has become the enemy of God (Romans 5:10) so that he is under the wrath of God (John 3:36; Romans 1:18). Because he was created in the image of God and was originally indwelt by God, he therefore is entirely accountable to God. That is, at some time in his future eternal existence, he must be tried by God at God's Judgment Throne (2 Corinthians 5:10). This terrible event will occur when the end of the world comes (John 5:28-29; Revelation 20:11-15).

God had warned our first parents in Genesis 2:16-17:

And the LORD God commanded the man, saying, Of every tree of the garden thou mayest freely eat: but of the tree of the knowledge of good and evil, thou shalt not eat of it: for in the day that thou eatest thereof thou shalt surely die.

This command set the stage for the destruction of mankind and the necessity for God's Gospel plan of salvation (Romans 5:6-10; Ephesians 2:1-10).

Like a city that has abundant electricity and other sources of energy to energize it to make it a live city, so our first parents had received the breath of God's life and were enjoying to the highest degree the energizing presence of God Himself in their lives.

> *...they died spiritually, that is, the energizing presence of God that gave them spiritual life was cut off.*

But somehow perfect, sinless mankind rebelled against God. Eve, **"the mother of all living"** (Genesis 3:20), disobeyed God and ate of the forbidden fruit. Adam, too, followed the disobedient action of his wife and ate of the forbidden fruit. Suddenly, they died (Genesis 3:1-7). No, they did not die physically, but they died spiritually, that is, the energizing presence of God that gave them spiritual life was cut off. They became like a dead city that had suddenly had its sources of energy removed. Outwardly the city may still look magnificent. People may continue to live in it. But it is a doomed city that can only fall into decay and ruin.

God employs this analogy in Proverbs 25:28 where he likens an unsaved person to a city that is broken down. We read:

He that hath no rule over his own spirit is like a city that is broken down, and without walls.

This teaches us that without the energizing presence of God in our life we are dead in our sins (Ephesians 2:1-5). No wonder the Bible declares in Jeremiah 17:9:

The heart is deceitful above all things, and desperately wicked: who can know it?

The Bible speaks of this sad fact of man being cut off from God in many ways. For example in Psalm 37:9 God declares:

For evildoers shall be cut off: but those that wait upon the LORD, they shall inherit the earth.

And in verse 20 of the same Psalm the Bible states:

But the wicked shall perish, and the enemies of the LORD shall

be as the fat of lambs: they shall consume; into smoke shall they consume away.

This same horrible punishment was endured by the Lord Jesus Christ as He paid for the sins of those He came to save. Isaiah 53:10 informs us:

Yet it pleased the LORD to bruise him; he hath put him to grief: when thou shalt make his soul an offering for sin, he shall see his seed, he shall prolong his days, and the pleasure of the LORD shall prosper in his hand.

Unsaved mankind still retain their soul (or spirit essence). This gives the evil spirits, headed up by Satan, opportunity to rule very definitely over them. We read in Ephesians 2:2:

Wherein in time past ye walked according to the course of this world, according to the prince of the power of the air, the spirit that now worketh in the children of disobedience.

The word "worketh" in this verse is the Greek word "*energeo*" which is used to indicate that Satan energizes unsaved mankind even as the Holy Spirit energizes those who have become saved. We read in Philippians 2:12-13:

Wherefore, my beloved, as ye have always obeyed, not as in my presence only, but now much more in my absence, work out your own salvation with fear and trembling. For it is God which <u>worketh</u> in you both to will and to <u>do</u> of his good pleasure.

The word "worketh" and the word "do" in this verse are also the Greek word "*energeo*" from which we get the English word "energy." Thus, this verse is literally declaring that it is God who energizes those He saves to will and to energize of His good pleasure. That is, it is the saved individual's resurrected soul or the spiritual part of him that has been energized by God to do His will. God does this by actually becoming a part of the saved person's personality. This idea is also described in Ephesians 1:11 as we are taught that it is Christ **"who worketh** [*energizes*] **all things after the counsel of His own will."** This same truth is emphasized in Galatians 2:20:

I am crucified with Christ: nevertheless I live; yet not I, but Christ liveth in me: and the life which I now live in the flesh I

live by the faith of the Son of God, who loved me, and gave himself for me.

All Mankind was Included in Adam

In Genesis 2:16-17, God had decreed that in the day Adam ate of the forbidden fruit, he would surely die. But before we look more at what happened in the Garden of Eden, we should examine in detail the truth that within Adam, the whole human race was represented.

> *...within Adam, the whole human race was represented.*

Each and every human being, in principle, was in the loins or body of Adam. This principle is shown to us in a number of ways. In Hebrews 7:9-10 we read:

And as I may so say, Levi also, who receiveth tithes, payed tithes in Abraham. For he was yet in the loins of his father, when Melchisedec met him.

In this citation, God is teaching us that even though Levi would not be born until more than one hundred years after Abraham, nevertheless he was already in the loins or body of Abraham because he was in the blood line of Abraham. This is parallel to the concept that we who are living today were in a sense already in the bodies of, for example, our great, great grandparents. The whole human race in this sense was in the bodies of Adam and Eve because they were our first parents.

Moreover, we read in Romans 7:9:

For I was alive without the law once: but when the commandment came, sin revived, and I died.

Using himself as an example, Paul, under the inspiration of the Holy Spirit, is teaching that there was a time when he, and every human being, was spiritually alive in Adam before Adam sinned. That time long ago was the only time in the history of the world when there was no law. That time was the brief period between the day when Adam was created and the day when God gave him the command of Genesis 2:15-17:

And the LORD God took the man, and put him into the garden of Eden to dress it and to keep it. And the LORD God commanded the man, saying, Of every tree of the garden thou mayest freely eat: but of the tree of the knowledge of good and evil, thou shalt not eat of it: for in the day that thou eatest thereof thou shalt surely die.

Now we get a better understanding of another Bible verse, John 1:9, where we read:

That was the true Light, which lighteth every man that cometh into the world.

When God created Adam, in principle He created the whole human race. When God made Adam a spiritual being by breathing the breath of life into his nostrils, at that time every human being, in principle, was given a soul. At the beginning, before sin came, the soul of mankind was perfect. It was spiritually energized by God and in-filled by God. Thus, at the beginning, every human being who would ever live, in principle, was energized or "lighted" by Christ the Light of the World. Mankind was created in the likeness of God in that God's energizing presence in his life made him in many ways like God. Remember that every human being, in principle, was in the loins of Adam at the time Adam was created.

...the life that was originally given to mankind was conditional in that it demanded perfect obedience from them.

However, though man began as a perfect man in the likeness of God, God placed man in a very critical situation. If he were to rebel against God, the image of God within him would be ruined and distorted with no hope for ever being restored to his once-perfect condition.

In other words, the life that was originally given to mankind was conditional in that it demanded perfect obedience from them.

As we learned earlier, only God, in the person of Jesus Christ, taking on the nature and likeness of mankind and specifically taking upon Himself the sins of those whom the Father had given Him (John 17:1-2, 20-24), could rescue rebellious sinners from their seemingly irredeemable state (Romans 8:1-4; Philippians 2:6-8).

Therefore, when God moved Paul to write in Romans 7:9 that **"sin revived and I died,"** He is teaching what happens when any and every individual is conceived. He is conceived in sin (Psalm 51:5; 58:3). He comes under the commandment, the perfect Law of God, and the Law of God condemns him (Romans 7:11).

Thus, at the moment of conception, every individual has sin upon him -- he has spiritually died. Now he is urgently in need of salvation. His only hope is for God to rescue him from his desperately hopeless condition (Ephesians 2:12-17).

But that is the glorious theme of God's salvation plan -- unfolded throughout history -- that we are examining. God saves lost helpless sinners through the substitutionary sacrifice of Jesus Christ, the perfect God-Man.

God works His salvation in many in order that He might have a people for Himself and bring Himself ultimate glory throughout the eternal ages yet to come! How can this be? How can it be that any of us should be included in God's amazing salvation plan!

But make no mistake, this wonderful undertaking by Almighty God will be accomplished by His infinite power (Acts 15:14; Ephesians 1:9-10; Hebrews 12:2).

God as the Supreme Ruler of everything throughout eternity has established laws by which He governs all those over whom He rules. These laws must be perfectly obeyed by all who are subject to these laws. Those laws are set forth in God's law book, the Bible.

Remember, as we learned earlier in our study, that even God is subject to these laws of the Bible. That is why when God, in the person of the Lord Jesus Christ, took upon Himself the sins of those He planned to save, He, too, had to be judged by the laws written in God's law book, the Bible.

> *...when God, in the person of the Lord Jesus Christ,*
> *took upon Himself the sins of those He planned to save,*
> *He, too, had to be judged by the laws written in God's law book,*
> *the Bible.*

Since God Himself is subject to the laws of God, mankind, who was created in the image and likeness of God, is also subject to the laws of God. That is why at the end of time, every human who has not had his sins covered by the Lord Jesus must stand for trial before Christ who is also the Supreme Judge of the earth (Matthew 25:31-46; 2 Corinthians 5:10).

Thus, the all-important critical need in every human life at any time in history – and especially in our day when it appears that we are so near the end – has to do with his eternal destiny and whether or not Christ has become his sin-bearer.

Physical Death of Man

When Adam and Eve sinned, what caused them to eventually experience physical death? The same question can be asked concerning the death of animals following the fall of Adam and Eve into sin. Why did they begin to die?

> *...physical death was not in itself a part*
> *of the punishment for sin.*

Although it was a consequence, physical death was not in itself a part of the punishment for sin. We know this for certain because at the end of the world, there will be billions of people who have never died physically. Yet they will experience the full penalty of God for their sins by being cast into hell (2 Timothy 4:1; 1 Peter 4:5).

Physical death came to all creatures including humans because God cursed the ground following Adam's sin (Genesis 3:17-19). Thorns and thistles, earthquakes and hurricanes, poisonous and carnivorous animals, viruses and harmful bacteria, etc. became evident throughout the world. These in time were fatal to all physical creatures.

For thousands of years, mankind could attain life spans of more than 900 years. But as man's genetic makeup was assaulted by various life-threatening forces, a human's life expectancy gradually shrunk to that which is being experienced throughout the world in our day (Psalm 90:10).

Biblical Principles We Have Learned from Genesis 2:7

1. Animals and all creatures, exclusive of mankind, that have the physical breath of life, are alive or living, but they in no sense have spiritual life or are spiritual beings. They are dead when they stop breathing. Because they have no spiritual life, they have no continuing existence after death.

2. Mankind was created with a body similar in many ways to that of animals. Whereas an animal requires only breath to be physically alive, a man

requires a soul. Without a soul, man's body is physically dead (James 2:26). To have physical life, a human being has to have a soul as an integral part of his personality. At Creation, God breathed the breath of life into the dead body of Adam, and man became a living being. That is, he was given a soul and thus became both physically and spiritually alive. We see the opposite in a corpse. That corpse is a dead body without a soul.

3. We know absolutely that mankind was created with a body and with a soul. The Bible, in 2 Corinthians 5:7-8, indicates that those who walk with Christ as believers leave their bodies at the time of physical death. At the moment of physical death, their souls are brought to heaven where they live with Christ as spirit beings. At the end of the world, they come with Christ (1 Corinthians 15:42-44, 15:49-54; Revelation 19:14) and are united again with their bodies, their new resurrected spiritual bodies. (See also Philippians 1:21-24; Revelation 6:9, 20:4.) Psalm 115:17-18 indicates that when an unsaved person dies, his soul leaves his body. Because his soul was not saved, it cannot go into Heaven. Instead, it goes down into silence to await the resurrection of the last day. (See also Matthew 10:28; John 12:48.)

4. By virtue of the fact that Adam had been given a soul which was energized and occupied by God, he was created in the image of God. Because all mankind was created in Adam, every human being is also created in the image of God. In principle, each and every human, being the seed of Adam, was at Creation, in the body of Adam. This is so because all human beings descend from Adam. To say it another way, "we all inherit his genes." Every person has a soul which makes him a spiritual being, even as his body makes him a physical being. Mankind was not made in the image of God in his body because at Creation, God did not have a human nature. Later, Christ Jesus would take on a human nature.

5. In his soul, Adam could not sin because God cannot sin (James 1:13; 1 John 3:9). However, in his body, man was vulnerable (Romans 7:5, 7:22-23).

6. Thus, when Jesus took on a human nature (a physical body), He became vulnerable to sinning. For that reason, the Bible declares in Hebrews 4:15 that He was tempted (tested) in all points as we are. Praise God, He did not fall into sin!

7. When Adam sinned, even though he remained a spiritual being, his soul became spiritually dead because he was no longer energized by God. In

addition, his body became corrupted by sin. In other words, Adam's body also became "spiritually dead!" In his flesh, he could no longer please God (Romans 8:8). Adam remained physically alive, but he no longer had the capacity to measure up to God's standard of perfection (Matthew 5:48; Romans 3:23). His every thought, word and deed would be shot through with sin (Psalm 53:2-3; Isaiah 1:4-6, 64:6; Romans 7:18).

8. Before any man becomes saved, even though he is a physically-alive spiritual being, he is spiritually dead. Because of Adam's disobedience, and because all mankind were created in Adam, the infection of sin has become inherent in the whole human race. Hence every individual has become spiritually dead. This was Adam's condition the moment after he ate the forbidden fruit. Likewise every individual now has a spiritually-dead soul. This means he still is a spiritual being, but his soul is not energized or occupied by God. It can be energized and occupied by evil spirits headed up by Satan. He also has a body which is spiritually dead. His body lusts after sin (Romans 13:14), is the servant of sin (Romans 6:12,17), and hates any exposure of its evil deeds (John 3:20).

9. When a man becomes saved, he is made spiritually alive even though he still lives in a spiritually-dead body which is physically alive.

10. A man becomes spiritually alive in salvation when God spiritually breathes on that spiritually-dead person's soul so that this person is given a new soul. The Bible speaks of this as a resurrection (Colossians 3:1; Revelation 20:5-6), or as being born again (John 3:3-8), or as having been regenerated (Titus 3:5). His soul is once again energized by God, but his physical body remains spiritually dead because sin still reigns in his physical body.

11. Because Adam sinned, all mankind and all animals became subject to physical death because the whole creation was cursed. Even the source of physical energy (food, water, and oxygen) became increasingly contaminated, thus causing physical death.

12. At the end of time, the true believers, both those who are physically alive at that time and those who have physically died at any time in the more than 13,000 years of human history, will receive resurrected spiritual bodies in which they will be forever spiritually alive (Job 19:25-27; 1 Corinthians 6:14, 13:12, 15:12-13, 15:16-23, 15:35-57; 2 Corinthians 4:14, et al.). They will live eternally with Christ in the new heaven and new earth (2 Peter 3:13-14; Revelation 21:1-4). They, as a whole personality, that is, both in body and soul, will

again have become perfectly in the image of God. We know this because Christ also now has a body (a perfect spiritual body which He received as a requirement to become the Savior), and all the true believers will be like Christ at His coming (1 John 3:2).

13. At the end of time, all of the unsaved, both those who are physically alive at that time and those who have physically died at any time during the more than 13,000 previous years will be cast into Hell where they will exist under God's wrath with Satan and the fallen angels forever (Matthew 25:41, 46).

The Bible's Focus: God Saves Sinners

With the preceding principles in mind, we can now more clearly understand the grand panorama of how God imparts His salvation to an individual. Adam was created both as a physical being and as a spiritual being. He was a perfect individual created in the image and likeness of God. In his soul, he was spiritually energized by God Himself. Fact is, he was indwelt by God. Because both his soul and his body were an integral part of his personality, he, as a whole person, was completely obedient to God's laws. This perfect situation was conditional. As long as he remained perfectly obedient to God, he would be energized by God and be both physically and spiritually alive.

The moment he would disobey God, he would become spiritually dead (Genesis 2:17). That is, the energizing spiritual power of God would be taken from him, and God would no longer indwell him. Thus, when our first parents sinned after being tempted by Satan (the fallen angel Lucifer; Isaiah 14), they remained physically alive, but instantly they became spiritually dead. They were no longer spiritually energized by God.

Now, remember, in principle, every human being was in the loins (or body) of Adam. Therefore, what happened to him when he sinned is echoed in each and every human being that would ever come into this world. Every human being is conceived as a spiritually-dead individual and is under the wrath of God (Psalm 51:5; John 3:36; Ephesians 2:1-3). He is desperately in need of salvation.

When an individual becomes saved, the dreadful consequence of his sin is nullified. By nature, every human being before salvation is spiritually dead. However, because he has a soul, he is therefore still a spiritual being, even though he is spiritually dead. As a spiritual being created in the image of God, he is under the law of God and therefore eventually must stand trial for his sins. For certain, without God's salvation, he will be found guilty and receive the sentence of eternal damnation as payment for his sins.

But if by God's mercy, God is pleased to save him, God in the Person of Jesus Christ, becomes his Substitute. Jesus Christ bears the wrath of God in the place of the sinner. Jesus Christ takes the sinner's sins upon Himself, and God pours out His wrath -- equivalent to eternity in hell -- upon Jesus as punishment for those sins, and Jesus, because He is infinite God, fully endures the demand of God's law that every sin requires eternal damnation in Hell. Because of what Jesus Christ accomplished, the sins of all those God would mercifully choose to save are forgiven. For the true children of God, God rectifies the damage done in the Garden of Eden. He breathes the breath of the life of God into spiritually dead individuals. He washes away all their sins. The Bible says God remembers those sins no more (Isaiah 43:25). Thus, a physically-alive but spiritually-dead person again becomes spiritually alive. He again is indwelt by God and again is spiritually energized by God. The saved individual has become a "true believer" in that he trusts only and completely in God's work to have accomplished his salvation. He comes to understand that God's promise of salvation is firmly recorded in God's infallible Word the Bible (2 Timothy 1:12).

Because the demands of God's law for all of the newly-saved individual's sins, past, present, and future, have been satisfied by his Savior, Jesus Christ, the spiritual life that God breathes into him is <u>eternal</u>. It is not conditional in any sense. God has done all the work in the saved individual, and God takes an oath upon His own perfect faithfulness that His promise of eternal life for the true believer shall never fail (Hebrews 6:16-20).

> *...in no sense is the life conditional which God breathes into the newly-born again individual...*

To accommodate the changes effected by God's salvation in an individual (who was, both in soul and body, totally infected and corrupted by sin), God gives him a brand new soul. The Bible uses terms like "born again" or "raised with Christ" or "regenerated." The spiritual life that is given to a born again individual is eternal in character unlike the spiritual life which Adam and Eve were given when they were created. Their spiritual life could be lost by disobeying God. The individual that became saved has received eternal life because, Christ, their stand-in, perfectly obeyed God. As was noted above, in no sense is the life conditional which God breathes into the newly-born again individual. Therefore, when sinners become saved they are infinitely more blessed than Adam and Eve were before they sinned. True believers can never fall into spiritual death as did Adam. John 10:27-29 says:

My sheep hear my voice, and I know them, and they follow me: and I give unto them eternal life; and they shall never perish, neither shall any man pluck them out of my hand. My Father, which gave them me, is greater than all; and no man is able to pluck them out of my Father's hand.

Furthermore, saved man, within his new soul, has become alien to sin. We read in 1 John 3:9:

Whosoever is born of God doth not commit sin; for his seed remaineth in him: and he cannot sin, because he is born of God.

> *In his new resurrected soul, he never again can sin,*
> *but in his body, the potential to sin still exists.*

But we must also understand that this individual, who has become a new creature in Christ because of his new resurrected soul, still has a physical body. That body is still infected by sin. It is still in rebellion against God. Therefore, the true believer is subject to two opposing forces. In his new resurrected soul, he never again can sin, but in his body, the potential to sin still exists. Because in his new soul, he delights in the Word of God, he feels terrible when he sins. He is far happier when he is living obediently before God. Wonderfully, he is indwelt by God who works in him to will and to do of His good pleasure (Philippians 2:13). He, therefore, can constantly pray to God asking for help to keep him from sin (Hebrews 4:15-16). The Bible speaks of this as "growing in grace" (2 Peter 3:18).

In addition to all these amazing acts of God, He has also made provision for the eventual redemption of the sinful bodies of the saved. When Jesus returns at the end of time, every true believer will instantly receive an eternally-alive resurrected body (1 Corinthians 15:51-57). As an eternally-alive personality with a perfect body and soul, the true believer will live complete with Christ for evermore.

> *His attributes are exalted by His amazing plan*
> *for the salvation of rebellious sinners.*

It is impossible to comprehend the fullness and majesty of God in His infinite design, creation, love, goodness and truth (Romans 11:33)! His attributes are exalted by His amazing plan for the salvation of rebellious sinners (2 Timothy 1:8-10).

In this chapter we have spent considerable time trying to understand more clearly who we are. This is exceedingly important because the entire history of the world is focused on the Lord Jesus Christ who became like unto us in order that He might save sinners.

Hopefully we have learned some things about what it means that we were created in the image of God. We have learned something about what happens to an individual's personality when that person becomes saved. Hopefully, we should have a better understanding of why the timeline of history is so important. It puts on display the unfolding of God's salvation plan!

Now we should continue our pursuit of the wonders of God's Calendar of History by examining the next major milestone in the unfolding of God's magnificent salvation program.

Chapter 5
4990 B.C. The Flood

Six thousand years had passed since the year of creation. Mankind had slowly multiplied on the earth. Because man had been created with a perfect body, he began with no inherent birth defects. Therefore, the Bible discloses that during this period of history, life spans were exceedingly long. For example, Adam lived 930 years, Jared 962 years, and Methuselah 969 years (Genesis 5:5, 20, 27). However, the Biblical evidence suggests that the families of these long-lived individuals were no larger than at any other time in history. For example, Noah lived to be 950 years of age but bore only three children, Shem, Ham, and Japheth.

Almost 3,000 years after Noah, Terah the father of Abraham lived to be 205 years old. Yet he also bore just three sons: Abram, Nahor, and Haran (Genesis 11:27). Thus, the likelihood is that at the end of the first 6,000 years of this earth's existence, the population may have been on the order of one million persons. (What the population grew to be in these first 6,000 years is unimportant. This population speculation is suggested only to help us visualize the world situation at the time it had become about 6,000 years of age, the time at which the Noachian flood occurred.)

> *The year before us is 4990 B.C. It is supremely important because that year the earth suffered a cataclysmic judgment that has never been repeated.*

The year before us is 4990 B.C. It is supremely important because that year the earth suffered a cataclysmic judgment that has never been repeated. In Genesis 6:3-7, the Bible reports:

> **And the LORD said, My spirit shall not always strive with man, for that he also is flesh: yet his days shall be an hundred and twenty years. There were giants in the earth in those days; and also after that, when the sons of God came in unto the daughters of men, and they bare children to them, the same became mighty men which were of old, men of renown. And GOD saw that the wickedness of man was great in the earth, and that every imagination of the thoughts of his heart was only evil continually. And it repented the LORD that he had made man on the earth, and it**

grieved him at his heart. And the LORD said, I will destroy man whom I have created from the face of the earth; both man, and beast, and the creeping thing, and the fowls of the air; for it repenteth me that I have made them.

The judgment of the earth spoken of in verse 7 is the total devastation of the earth. We must carefully examine all that God has recorded in the Bible concerning this catastrophe that came to planet earth in 4990 B.C.

Immediately, we wonder about the phrase recorded in Genesis 6, verse 3, **"his days shall be 120 years."** What 120 years can this be? We know God is not speaking about an expected life span for individual humans. This is so because for the next 3,000 years, every death age given for any individual far exceeds 120 years. Furthermore, the only expected life span given in the Bible for anyone of the human race is found in Psalm 90:10:

The days of our years are threescore years and ten; and if by reason of strength they be fourscore years, yet is their strength labour and sorrow; for it is soon cut off, and we fly away.

Therefore, we can be certain that the 120 years does not identify in any way with the expected life spans of mankind at any time in history. But the 120 years does appear to relate to those living at the time this prophecy was given. That is, it seems to be a warning to the pre-flood people that in 120 years they would die under God's judgment. There is a huge likelihood that this 120 years given in Genesis 6:3 is the period of time between the giving of the warning and the time of the universal Flood. The Flood did occur in the year 4990 B.C. Thus, the prophecy of 120 years would have been given 120 years earlier in the year 5110 B.C.

The giving of this warning meant that for the next 120 years, Noah was engaged in two important tasks. One was that of building a huge boat (ark) which was to be at least 450 feet long, 75 feet wide, and 45 feet high with three decks (Genesis 6:15-16). The second task was to warn the peoples of the world of that day of the impending judgment they were facing.

We read in Hebrews 11:7:

By faith Noah, being warned of God of things not seen as yet, moved with fear, prepared an ark to the saving of his house; by the which he condemned the world, and became heir of the righteousness which is by faith.

In 1 Peter 3:19-20 the Bible declares:

By which also he went and preached unto the spirits in prison; Which sometime were disobedient, when once the longsuffering of God waited in the days of Noah, while the ark was a preparing, wherein few, that is, eight souls were saved by water.

> *For 120 years, the peoples of that world witnessed this preacher and his family building this huge boat on dry ground.*

Further, in 2 Peter 2:5 the Bible reports that God, **"spared not the old world, but saved Noah the eighth person, a preacher of righteousness, bringing in the flood upon the world of the ungodly."** For 120 years, the peoples of that world witnessed this preacher and his family building this huge boat on dry ground. We can speculate that they believed he was crazy, that he was completely and hopelessly out of his mind. Yet by his preaching and by his continuing action of building this huge vessel, he was constantly warning the world of that day that God's judgment was about to fall.

But then the 120 years came to an end. The building of the ark had been completed. Now every kind of animal and bird began to gather near the ark. And then for seven days, a male and a female of each of these animals and birds entered the ark. A few kinds of animals like sheep, goats, cows, doves, and pigeons were brought in as seven pairs of each kind. Certainly, we can assume that the people watched in astonishment. Yet no one except for the three sons of Noah, their wives, and Noah's own wife believed Noah's warning that judgment was about to fall. How could the world be destroyed by a flood of waters? Where would the water come from? But it did come. The Bible declares in Genesis 7:10-12:

And it came to pass after seven days, that the waters of the flood were upon the earth. In the six hundredth year of Noah's life, in the second month, the seventeenth day of the month, the same day were all the fountains of the great deep broken up, and the windows of heaven were opened. And the rain was upon the earth forty days and forty nights.

At the end of the seven days, all of the animals and the family of Noah were secure in the ark **"and the Lord shut him in"** (Genesis 7:16). And then the rain began to fall. For forty days and forty nights it rained. So much water inundated the earth, as the water poured out from great underground reservoirs as well as from the sky, that at the end of the forty days and forty nights, the highest mountains of that day were covered by water.[1] We read in Genesis 7:21-23:

> **And all flesh died that moved upon the earth, both of fowl, and of cattle, and of beast, and of every creeping thing that creepeth upon the earth, and every man: all in whose nostrils was the breath of life, of all that was in the dry land, died. And every living substance was destroyed which was upon the face of the ground, both man, and cattle, and the creeping things, and the fowl of the heaven; and they were destroyed from the earth: and Noah only remained alive, and they that were with him in the ark.**

Following the forty days and forty nights of rain, the waters began to recede. The land areas were thrust upward and the ocean basins were deepened (Psalm 104:5-9). Many animals were trapped in huge mud floes that later hardened into sedimentary rock. The great pressures that were generated caused their bones to fossilize. Today, the many fossils that are found give mute testimony to the reality of this gigantic Flood. They not only tell us that such a flood did occur, but they also give us some idea of the kinds of animals that existed on the earth during the 6,023 years from creation until the Flood.

> *Indeed, God very methodically and very deliberately had carried out his purposes.*

Indeed, God very methodically and very deliberately had carried out his purposes. For 120 years He had been warning the world through Noah, who was a preacher of righteousness (2 Peter 2:5), that judgment on the earth would come.

---

[1] We can speculate that in all probability, God guided our solar system in the direction of one of the deep space rain clouds that normally exist well away from our immediate planetary system (see *Adam When?*, pp. 182-186, 241-243). It would appear that it took forty days to pass through it. The evidence of this can be seen today as scientists find evidence of much water having been on our moon and on the planets of our solar system.

Not only did God tell the world *how* it would come, but we can understand by the citation of Genesis 6:3 (in which the 120-year warning is given), that in all likelihood, He told them *the year in which* it would come.

Another warning concerning God's coming wrath at the end of time was actually given much earlier than even the time of Noah. Remember we read about the preacher named Enoch who was born in the year 7106 B.C. In the New Testament Book of Jude, God tells us what he preached. We read in Jude 14-15:

> **And Enoch also, the seventh from Adam, prophesied of these, saying, Behold, the Lord cometh with ten thousands of his saints, To execute judgment upon all, and to convince all that are ungodly among them of all their ungodly deeds which they have ungodly committed, and of all their hard speeches which ungodly sinners have spoken against him.**

We will learn as we continue to study the Bible regarding the history of the world that even as God gave adequate warning of the terrible Flood of Noah's day, so, too, God has given adequate warning of the Judgment Day that in all likelihood, is coming very soon. These facts of past history are absolutely true and trustworthy. God has given us this information so that we can be put on notice that any warnings by God had better be listened to. God absolutely will bring to pass what He declares.

The Biblical Timeline After the Flood

More than a year passes. Noah and his family have been in the ark 370 days. They entered the ark on the seventeenth day of the second month of Noah's 600th year (Genesis 7:11). It appears that at that time in history a month was 30 days. We know this because we read in Genesis 8:3-4:

And the waters returned from off the earth continually: and after the end of the hundred and fifty days the waters were abated. And the ark rested in the seventh month, on the seventeenth day of the month, upon the mountains of Ararat.

God is indicating that there were 150 days from the 17th day of the second month, the day the Flood began, to the 17th day of the seventh month. One hundred fifty days thus equals five months of 30 days. While the year in actuality had to be the same length as our year, that is 365.2422 days, God does not tell us how they took care of this insofar as their calendars were concerned. Possibly every six years they observed a 13-month year. In our modern calendar, for example, every four years we add an extra day to keep as close as possible to the actual year of 365.2422 days.

In Genesis 8:14-16 we read:

And in the second month, on the seven and twentieth day of the month, was the earth dried. And God spake unto Noah, saying, Go forth of the ark, thou, and thy wife, and thy sons, and thy sons' wives with thee.

From this information we know that Noah was in the ark exactly 370 days. Later in our study, we will see the importance of the number 370.

But then the world began afresh. The only humans on the whole earth in the year 4989 B.C. were Noah, his wife, their three sons, and their sons' respective wives. The human race, as it were, began all over again.

Because of the great climatic changes that resulted from this giant Flood (see *Adam When?*, pp. 186-197), many of the animals became extinct. The only notice that we have of the previous existence of those species is in the fossil record. The birds and animals that are presently in the world survived and continued to propagate to the present day.

The Pre-Flood Spiritual Condition

We should now examine the spiritual condition of the world at the time this terrible Flood destroyed the earth. The first indication of the sinful condition of the world is given in Genesis 6:2 where we read:

That the sons of God saw the daughters of men that they were fair; and they took them wives of all which they chose.

The teaching of the Bible here in Genesis 6:2-4 has been misunderstood by many Bible teachers. Remember what God said in Romans 8:14:

For as many as are led by the Spirit of God, they are the sons of God.

The "sons of God" refers to the true believers. The "daughters of men" refers to the unsaved. The sin God is emphasizing is that of a true believer becoming unequally joined (that is married) to an unbeliever. Much later, God makes reference to this sinful practice as the Bible declares in 2 Corinthians 6:14:

Be ye not unequally yoked together with unbelievers: for what fellowship hath righteousness with unrighteousness? and what communion hath light with darkness?

The fact that there were many religious people in that day is suggested by the statement of Genesis 6:4 which indicated that the product of these mixed marriages were "mighty men, men of renown." We read there:

There were giants in the earth in those days; and also after that, when the sons of God came in unto the daughters of men, and they bare children to them, the same became mighty men which were of old, men of renown.

The phrase "men of renown" literally is "men of the name," that is, "men of the name of God." It appears that these were outstanding religious leaders who were identified with the name of God. They were also called "giants." The Hebrew word translated "giants" is the word "*nephilim.*" The word "*nephilim*" is a plural word probably signifying "fallen ones." It is derived from the Hebrew verb "*naphal*" which means "to fall."

...at that time, there were many reputable religious teachers and leaders, even as there are in our day.

Integrating the words "giants" (*nephilim*), mighty, and men of renown ("men of the name"), we can conclude that the Bible reveals that at that time, there were many reputable religious teachers and leaders, even as there are in our day. But these apparently spiritually important men who identified with the name of God had fallen. They were under the wrath of God. We know that this is so because they all perished in the judgment of the Flood.

Genesis 6:4 declares, **"There were giants [*nephilim*] in the earth in those days; and also after that . . . ."** The phrase "also after that" teaches us that the same spiritual condition that prevailed just before the Flood would continue after the Flood. As we continue to study the biblical calendar of history, we will learn that this sad condition of highly touted religious leaders who had spiritually fallen (becoming *nephilim*) did continue. Indeed, this sad condition is also everywhere present in our day at this time of history!

We have, therefore, learned that God's wrath that brought about the ruin of the whole earth by the waters of the Flood was not only upon the wicked who had little knowledge of God. Additionally, it was in a more particular way focused upon those who claimed a true relationship with God. Judgment came because of the wickedness of those who thought they were God's people, mighty men of the name. The focus was not first of all upon Cain's line which was the line of those who made no claim that they worshipped the God of the Bible. It was on those who claimed to be believers in Jehovah, the true God.

Nevertheless, God had in view the wickedness of all mankind. Genesis 6:5-7 reports:

And GOD saw that the wickedness of man was great in the earth, and that every imagination of the thoughts of his heart was only evil continually. And it repented the LORD that he had made man on the earth, and it grieved him at his heart. And the LORD said, I will destroy man whom I have created from the face of the earth; both man, and beast, and the creeping thing, and the fowls of the air; for it repenteth me that I have made them.

God repented and was grieved. Normally, the word "repentance" is identified with repentance from sin. The sinner repents by turning from sin. God cannot repent from sin because He has no sin and cannot sin. Actually, the context of Genesis 6 reveals the grief of God in that He must carry out His decree that rebellion against Him must be punished. The Hebrew word that is translated "repentance" is also translated "comfort" (see, for example, Psalm 23:4 and Isaiah 40:1-2). Therefore, it is an emotional word signifying God's grief over man's sin. God must carry out the demands of God's law which call for punishment of the sinner. God has no pleasure in the death of the wicked (Ezekiel 33:11).

No Surprise to the Remnant

Another fact that we should take note of is that while the whole world of that day was devastated, there was a remnant of people who were altogether protected from this terrible judgment.

We read in Genesis 6:8:

But Noah found grace in the eyes of the LORD.

The word "grace" indicates the gift of salvation (Ephesians 2:8). Noah and the other seven people on the ark were a tiny remnant of true believers. Later we will take note of the fact that at the end of the world, when the time of judgment has come, there also will be a remnant chosen by grace that will not come into judgment.

As we look carefully at this cataclysmic event that occurred about 7,000 years ago, we must recognize that God did not spring a surprise on the world of that day. Let us follow God's warnings to the people of that time.

We learned that Noah was a preacher (2 Peter 2:5), and that 120 years before the Flood, God told him that man's days would be 120 years. Genesis 6:3 records:

> **And the LORD said, My spirit shall not always strive with man, for that he also is flesh: yet his days shall be an hundred and twenty years.**

We learned earlier that these 120 years must be the time given to Noah to build this huge craft, called an ark in the Bible, whereby he, together with his family and representatives of all the animals of the world, would survive the monstrous Flood that would completely devastate the world. The construction, by Noah and his family, of this tremendous boat would have given him, as a "preacher of righteousness," ample opportunity to warn the world of the certainty and the timing of this terrible judgment of God. The drama would have become more intense as the world of that day witnessed the assembling together of the animals and the finishing touches put on the ark in accord with the timetable Noah preached.

And then God gave a timetable that revealed *the very day* that God's judgment would fall. Genesis 7:1-4 tells us:

> **And the LORD said unto Noah, Come thou and all thy house into the ark; for thee have I seen righteous before me in this generation. Of every clean beast thou shalt take to thee by sevens, the male and his female: and of beasts that are not clean by two, the male and his female. Of fowls also of the air by sevens, the male and the female; to keep seed alive upon the face of all the earth. For yet <u>seven days</u>, and I will cause it to rain upon the earth forty days and forty nights; and every living substance that I have made will I destroy from off the face of the earth.**

The whole world of that day had opportunity to witness what was occurring during these final seven days. And then the Bible declares in Genesis 7:11:

In the six hundredth year of Noah's life, in the second month, the seventeenth day of the month, the same day were all the fountains of the great deep broken up, and the windows of heaven were opened.

Verse 13 and verse 16 add:

In the selfsame day entered Noah, and Shem, and Ham, and Japheth, the sons of Noah, and Noah's wife, and the three wives of his sons with them, into the ark;

And they that went in, went in male and female of all flesh, as God had commanded him: and the LORD shut him in.

Surely, we must clearly recognize that this awful catastrophe should not have come as a surprise. One hundred twenty years earlier, the year of destruction was predicted. Furthermore, the building of the ark would have kept the warning of impending judgment before the eyes of the world. And finally, the very day of the Flood was announced. AND EVERYTHING TOOK PLACE PRECISELY AS IT HAD BEEN PROPHESIED.

This milestone, the year 4990 B.C. when God brought His judgment upon the world in the days of Noah, is of tremendous importance. One reason this is so is because the Bible uses it to point us to another worldwide judgment that must still take place. God speaks of a day when this whole world will be destroyed by fire. We read in 2 Peter 3:3-7, 10-13:

Knowing this first, that there shall come in the last days scoffers, walking after their own lusts, and saying, where is the promise of his coming? for since the fathers fell asleep, all things continue as they were from the beginning of the creation. For this they willingly are ignorant of, that by the word of God the heavens were of old, and the earth standing out of the water and in the water: whereby the world that then was, being overflowed with water, perished: but the heavens and the earth, which are now, by the same word are kept in store, reserved unto fire against the day of judgment and perdition of ungodly men.

But the day of the Lord will come as a thief in the night; in the which the heavens shall pass away with a great noise, and the elements shall melt with fervent heat, the earth also and the

**works that are therein shall be burned up. Seeing then that all
these things shall be dissolved, what manner of persons ought
ye to be in all holy conversation and godliness, Looking for and
hasting unto the coming of the day of God, wherein the heavens
being on fire shall be dissolved, and the elements shall melt
with fervent heat? Nevertheless we, according to his promise,
look for new heavens and a new earth, wherein dwelleth righteousness.**

This awful destruction will occur when time has come to an end, when
God's salvation program has been completed. When we come to the end of our
study of the Biblical calendar of history (remembering that this calendar is
governed by the unfolding of God's salvation plan), we will learn about many
parallels between the devastation of the world by the Flood of Noah's day and
the destruction of the universe at the end of time.

Suffice it to say now that all who perished in the universal Flood were
dumbfounded when the Flood came (Matthew 24:37-39). They were surprised
because none of them believed the Flood would really happen.

Today, we are near the end of time. At the coming of the Lord, those who
have not believed the warnings of impending judgment also will be surprised
because they have not believed the truth. That day will come upon them as a thief
in the night, and they, too, will perish (1 Thessalonians 5:1-5).

Before we leave the discussion of the Noachian Flood, we must take
note of an event that is just being reported in various scientific magazines. It is
an event we must look at very carefully because it definitely relates to this
study.

Pre-Flood Humans

Parts of the broken bodies of seven adult humans very recently were
found in a cave named Liang Bua. located 500 meters above sea level in Indonesia. In one case, the bones were almost sufficient for a complete skeleton. It
was that of a woman who was about 30 years of age. The skeletal remains
were not fossilized although the bones had a consistency that was described as
wet blotting paper, the result of age and the damp conditions.

> *The absolutely remarkable fact was that these were
> skeletal remains of people who at adulthood were only
> about three feet tall.*

The absolutely remarkable fact was that these were skeletal remains of people who at adulthood were only about three feet tall.

There was no evidence that these body parts were prepared for burial. That is, this cave did not in any way appear to be a burial site.

The bones were covered by many layers of water-deposited silt and clay with volcanic ash layers mixed with the other sediments.

Mixed in the sediment were many stone tools and bones of various animals. Some of the bones were charred suggesting that cooking was done in the cave.

Dating of the various datable objects gave dates that varied from 13,000 years to 95,000 years.

The evidence fits the conclusion that there was some kind of a massive disaster that suddenly killed all of the inhabitants of the cave, burying them under water-deposited sediment mixed with layers of volcanic ash.

Immediately we should ask a number of questions.

1. How could this cave be suddenly filled with water laden sediment when it exists 500 meters above sea level?

2. How did the volcanic ash layers get mixed in with the layers of sediment?

3. Who were these people who when full grown were only three feet tall?

4. What disaster was this that destroyed all the people in this cave?

The Bible Answers

Very significantly, the Bible can answer our questions. We will discover that this disaster identifies very well with the Biblical account of the Noachian flood that completely destroyed the world about 7,000 years ago. At the same time, it will also help us to further understand some of the language of the Bible.

The Flood of Noah's day is recorded by God in the sixth and seventh chapters of Genesis. The Biblical language we should particularly examine is that of Genesis 6:4 which speaks of giants.

Earlier in this study we learned that Genesis 6:4 reports that just before the flood of Noah's day, "**There were giants [Hebrew *nephilim*] in the earth in those days; and also after that.**" When we carefully studied this passage, we learned that spiritually it refers to the spiritual leaders of that day who had come under the wrath of God. That is they had become very sinful.

We also learned that the phrase "**and also after that**" emphasized that after the Flood, as men would again multiply upon the earth, the potential for spiritual leaders to fall would continue throughout the human race.

However, we must also look at this significant verse of Genesis 6:4 as a statement setting forth a historical physical fact. Therefore, we must carefully search the Bible to help us to know what we can about these words in their physical, historical teaching.

The only other place in the Bible where the Hebrew word "*nephilim*" can be found is in Numbers 13:33:

> **And there we saw the giants, the sons of Anak, which come of the giants [Hebrew nephilim]: and we were in our own sight as grasshoppers, and so we were in their sight.**

In this verse, God appears to use the word "giant" (Hebrew *nephilim*) to describe individuals of great physical stature. Indeed, in the early days of the nation of Israel literal, physical giants — men of great size — did live in the land of Israel.

This is attested to by several Biblical verses. For example, we read in Deuteronomy 2:10-11 and in Deuteronomy 2:20-21:

> **The Emims dwelt therein in times past, a people great, and many, and tall, as the Anakims; Which also were accounted giants, as the Anakims; but the Moabites call them Emims.**

> **That also was accounted a land of giants: giants dwelt therein in old time; and the Ammonites call them Zamzummims; A people great, and many, and tall, as the Anakims; but the LORD destroyed them before them; and they succeeded them, and dwelt in their stead:**

To give us an idea of the physical size of these giants God gives us two citations. In Deuteronomy 3:11 we read:

> **For only Og king of Bashan remained of the remnant of giants; behold, his bedstead was a bedstead of iron; is it not in Rabbath of the children of Ammon? nine cubits was the length thereof, and four cubits the breadth of it, after the cubit of a man.**

A bedstead 9 cubits in length and 4 cubits in width equals a bed 13½ feet long and 6 feet wide. Therefore, this king must have been more than 10 feet tall.

> *Therefore, this king must have been more than 10 feet tall.*

In 1 Samuel 17:4 we read of Goliath, the giant that David killed:

And there went out a champion out of the camp of the Philistines, named Goliath, of Gath, whose height was six cubits and a span.

Six cubits and a span is almost 10 feet in height. Goliath, too, was a huge man.

Thus, when God is speaking of giants He is speaking of very big people who were about twice as tall as, and therefore huge as compared with, the average person.

Incidentally, King Og and Goliath did not become giants because they lived in isolation on small island, or because they developed great size over a long period of each generation becoming bigger then the previous generation. God is simply teaching that as He controls the affairs of the world, He for His own purposes can cause babies to be born who will become far bigger (yes, even giants), than their parents.

For example, in the days of Goliath, the giant killed by David, the Bible appears to teach that there was only one family that was looked upon as giants. We read in 2 Samuel 21:18-22:

And it came to pass after this, that there was again a battle with the Philistines at Gob: then Sibbechai the Hushathite slew Saph, which was of the sons of the giant. And there was again a battle in Gob with the Philistines, where Elhanan the son of Jaareoregim, a Bethlehemite, slew the brother of Goliath the Gittite, the staff of whose spear was like a weaver's beam. And there was yet a battle in Gath, where was a man of great stature, that had on every hand six fingers, and on every foot six toes, four and twenty in number; and he also was born to the giant. And when he defied Israel, Jonathan the son of Shimea the brother of David slew him. These four were born to the giant in Gath, and fell by the hand of David, and by the hand of his servants.

A Giant is Nearly Twice as Tall as Average People

Moreover, the average height of people after the Flood was probably a little more than five feet. A man like Goliath was almost twice as tall and was called a giant. With this in mind, when we consider that before the Noachian Flood people three feet tall was possibly very common, then the people who came after the Flood and who were almost twice as tall, would be qualified to be called giants.

The question is, when we read Genesis 6:4 where God says, **"There were giants in the earth in those days; and also after that,"** is He speaking in the historical physical sense of men like Goliath or King Og? Or is God speaking of the whole post-flood human race whose average stature is more than five feet, and, therefore, qualify as giants when compared with humans whose average stature was probably three feet?

The King Og kind of giants became extinct and the Goliath giants appeared to be confined to one family whose sons were killed. Their families do not appear to be in view in the statement of Genesis 6:4. It definitely appears that if it were normal for Pre-flood people to average three feet in height, then the giants spoken of in Genesis 6:4 must refer to the Post-flood human race as being giants.

That brings us back to the archaeological discovery of the disaster that occurred in the Liang Bua cave in Indonesia. The finding of the bones of seven individuals which identify with humans who are three feet tall at maturity suggests very strongly that the pre-Noachian Flood population possibly consisted of small people.

Thus, when the Bible stipulates, **"There were giants in the earth in those days; and also after that,"** God must be implying that Noah and his sons were giants as compared with most pre-flood people. They were the only survivors of the flood. They were the progenitors of the whole human race following the Flood. And the human race following the flood on the average were much bigger than three feet tall. They, therefore, must have been considered to be giants as compared with the average pre-flood human. Only through the descendants of Noah could "giants" continue after the Flood.

This possible conclusion concerning the giants of Genesis 6:4 appears to receive strong support from this recent archaeological discovery in the Liang Bua cave in Indonesia. Fact is, it is the Bible that provides answers to the questions we raised earlier concerning this discovery. Let us utilize the Bible to provide the answers to our questions.

The Noachian Flood Provides The Answers

We have learned in this study that 7,000 years ago (4900 B.C.), the entire world was destroyed by the Noachian Flood. The Bible reports in Genesis 7:11-12 and Genesis 7:19-20:

In the six hundredth year of Noah's life, in the second month, the seventeenth day of the month, the same day were all the fountains of the great deep broken up, and the windows of heaven were opened. And the rain was upon the earth forty days and forty nights.

And the waters prevailed exceedingly upon the earth; and all the high hills, that were under the whole heaven, were covered. Fifteen cubits upward did the waters prevail; and the mountains were covered.

At that momentous time in history, about 7000 years ago, in a cave in Indonesia, now called the Liang Bua cave, a number of very small people lived. They possibly were typical of almost all of the people who were living anywhere in the world of that day.

Then disaster struck. In minutes the cave they were in filled with water and sediment. After 40 days the cave was hundreds of feet under water. It was a catastrophe a million times worse than any tsunami. The inhabitants in the cave together with every object in the cave were buried under layers of silt. The only people in the whole world that were still alive were those in the ark with Noah.

But! Have not we forgotten something? The dates of the objects in the cave showed an event that occurred 13,000 to 95,000 years ago. The Bible says the flood was about 7,000 years ago. How can these discrepancies be reconciled.

First of all, the fact that in this cave there were age differences of 13,000 to 95,000 years indicates there was a great amount of contamination of the specimens. Since all of the live objects in the cave died simultaneously, they should all show the same C14 age. The potential for contamination was very evident by the condition of the skeletal remains. It was reported that the bones had a consistency that was described as wet blotting paper, the result of age and damp conditions.

Moreover, the benchmark age was 12,000-13,000 years. This would result from testing objects that had the highest percentage of C14 isotopes. In this cave there was no apparent possibility of contaminating objects with excess C14. However, it is apparent the cave was ravaged by waters resulting from volcanic activity. Since the C14 isotope is formed by cosmic ray activity, underground water, unless fed by surface springs, would have little or no C14.

Therefore, if the cave was flooded by underground water as the fountains of the deep were broken up, water with little or no C14, the objects within the cave could readily show excessive age as they were contaminated by this underground water. Secondly, we should briefly consider the nature of C14 date testing.

Carbon — A Radioactive Timepiece

Natural carbon occurs in several isotopes, the most plentiful of which is C12. It is found especially as the carbon in carbon dioxide of the air which we breath and as the dissolved carbonates in ocean water, as well as carbon found in fossil fuels and sedimentary rock carbonates. While C12 is stable, the carbon isotope C14 disintegrates into C12 with a half life of 5,730 years. Wherever C12 is found in living organisms, C14 atoms can be found with it in about the same proportion as it occurs world wide, dissolved in the ocean, in living organisms, in the biosphere and in the CO_2 of the atmosphere.

At the moment of death of the living organism (tree, bone etc) the C14 atoms begin to disintegrate at a constant rate so that 5,730 years later only one half of the C14 atoms remain. Assuming that the C14 inventory at the time of the death of the organism was the same as it is at the time the organism is being tested, and assuming the C12 world wide inventory has not changed, it is possible to determine with some accuracy the age of the specimen being tested.

It must be remembered, however, that the C14 isotope is produced by the action of cosmic ray activity. Cosmic rays are formed from energy sources such as the sun, stars, and possibly super nova explosions. Thus, at the beginning of time (11,013 B.C.), when the light bearers were created there was little or no C14.

If we assume that ever since creation, C14 has been added to the worldwide inventory at a constant rate, then 6,000 years after creation there would have been less than half the amount of C14 in the world wide inventory than exists today.

Let us now suppose a specimen died 6,000 years after creation. During the 7,000 years following the death of this specimen, a little more than half of the C14 that was present in the specimen, when it died 7,000 years earlier, would have disintegrated. At the same time, the worldwide inventory of C14 would have more than doubled by the time this specimen was tested. Thus, if it were tested 7,000 years after it died, it would have less than 25% of the C14 that is present in the world at the time it was tested.

On the other hand, if the specimen that died 7,000 years ago is tested today, assuming the C14 worldwide inventory at the time of the death of the specimen was the same as it is today (which is not true), and assuming the world wide C12 inventory remained constant, the specimen would appear to be about 6,000 years older than it actually is.

This assumption of a constant worldwide inventory of C14 is the assumption that is made that resulted in a minimum C14 age of the objects in the Liang Bua cave to be 13,000 years. Therefore, we must understand that the actual age has to be about 6,000 years less than the 13,000 years reported. This is so because the world wide C14 inventory at the time of the cave disaster was on the order of less than half of what it is today.

Simply stated, because 7,000 years ago, the worldwide C14 inventory was much less than it is today, a specimen that died 7,000 years ago, today would show a C14 age of about 13,000 years.

This revised age of 13,000 years minus 6,000 years agrees perfectly with the date of the Noachian Flood which the Bible shows very conclusively to be 4990 B.C.

Thus, this disaster that occurred in the Liang Bua cave fits the Biblical account very closely and also assists us in understanding the Biblical account.

1. As we have learned, the time of this disaster fits the Biblical calendar of time of 4990 B.C.

2. The size of the humans within the cave agrees with the Biblical statement that "**There were giants in the earth in those days; and also after that.**" The post-Flood population beginning with Noah and his family are giants as compared with the pre-Flood population who on the average possibly would have been the size of the occupants of the Liang Bua cave.

3. A cave 500 meters about sea level obviously would have been filled with water and sediment if the flood waters covered the highest mountain.

4. The volcanic ash layered in the sediments agrees with the Biblical statement that "**the same day were all the fountains of the great deep broken up.**"

5. The finding of parts of broken bodies of seven humans scattered in the layers of sediment accords with a massive flood disaster.

It might be added that no scientist will accept this analysis unless they are ready to accept the Bible as the authoritative Word of God. On the other hand, without the Bible's help there is no possibility that any scientist will be able to come up with a rational and complete explanation for this very outstanding and unusual discovery of the disaster in the Liang Bua cave.

Leprechauns And Elves

Before we finish this analysis of the Liang Bua cave disaster we should take note of one additional thought. Repeatedly we hear fanciful stories of leprechauns and elves, and in Indonesia and Malay folklore of Ebu Gogo and Orang Pendek These mythical stories describing very small humans who apparently appear in many countries of the world. I believe these stories are developed because it would appear that at various times during the 7,000 years following the Flood, skeletal remains of pre-flood individuals who died in the Noachian flood were unearthed. Because of the tiny size of these individuals, fanciful imaginative stories were developed concerning them.

In other words the stories of elves and Ebu Gogo have a basis in fact. That fact is that from time to time the remains of the very small people who perished in the Noachian flood must have been unearthed. There is absolutely no reason to believe that any of these small people are alive today or at any time following the flood.

For additional information, the reader is invited to read the following:

"Archaeology and Age of a New Hominin from Flores in Eastern Indonesia." M. J. Morwood *et al.*, in *Nature*, Vol. 431, pages 1087-1091, October 28, 2004.

"A New Small-Bodied Hominin from the Late Pleistocene of Flores, Indonesia." P. Brown *et al.*, in *Nature*, Vol. 431, pages 1055-1061; October 28, 2004.

"The Littlest Human. "Kate Wong in *Scientific American*, February 2005, pages 56-65.

Adam When. Available free of charge from Family Radio. "Earth's Radiocarbon Timepiece," pages 160-186.

After the Flood

But now we should continue our study of the Biblical calendar of history. We must learn what happened to the world and its inhabitants immediately following the tremendous Flood of Noah's day.

Thus far, we have followed the timeline of history from the creation year of 11,013 B.C. to the Flood of Noah's day in 4990 B.C. We have learned that with the exception of Noah, his wife, and their three sons, together with their respective wives, the entire human race perished in the Flood.

Thus, even as God designed the human race in the beginning with one family, that of Adam, so, too, after the Flood, God began with one family, that of Noah. Shem, Ham, and Japheth, the three sons of Noah, became the progenitors of all the peoples of the world.

From the Biblical account we can know that the descendants of Noah settled in that part of the world that later became known as Babylon. We read in Genesis 11:1-8:

> **And the whole earth was of one language, and of one speech. And it came to pass, as they journeyed from the east, that they found a plain in the land of Shinar; and they dwelt there. And they said one to another, Go to, let us make brick, and burn them thoroughly. And they had brick for stone, and slime had they for morter. And they said, Go to, let us build us a city and a tower, whose top may reach unto heaven; and let us make us a name, lest we be scattered abroad upon the face of the whole earth. And the LORD came down to see the city and the tower, which the children of men builded. And the LORD said, Behold, the people is one, and they have all one language; and this they begin to do: and now nothing will be restrained from them, which they have imagined to do. Go to, let us go down, and there confound their language, that they may not understand one another's speech. So the LORD scattered them abroad from thence upon the face of all the earth: and they left off to build the city.**

> *God created man to serve Him. However, because of sin, mankind would rather serve himself.*

God created man to serve Him. However, because of sin, mankind would rather serve himself. Thus, as sin became greatly in evidence soon after the Flood, it showed that mankind was not serving God. Fact is, as Chapters 10 and 11 of Genesis set forth the development of the nations that began with the three sons of Noah, we find no Biblical record of anyone who became a true believer. This was a period of nearly 3,000 years that passed from the time of Noah to the time of a man named Abram who was born in the year 2167 B.C. What's more, even as we read Genesis 11:1-8 (quoted above), mankind believed they could find their own way to heaven. This will be further developed later in our study.

The Earth is Divided

In Genesis Chapters 10 and 11, God records two cataclysmic events that occurred probably about 2,000 years after the Flood. The first of these events is recorded in Genesis 10:25:

> **And unto Eber were born two sons: the name of one was Peleg; for in his days was the earth divided; and his brother's name was Joktan.**

An understanding of this simple citation is not developed in the Bible. However, the Scriptures do give accurate information concerning the dates of Peleg's life. Earlier in our study, we learned that Peleg was a calendar patriarch during his lifetime. He was born in the year 3153 B.C. and died in the year 2914 B.C.

However, in the year 3114 B.C., when Peleg was 39 years of age, a cataclysmic event must have occurred. To learn about this, we will look briefly at the secular evidence.

Scientists have long theorized that at a time in the world's history, there existed just one great continent instead of the various smaller continents that exist today. It can be shown, for example, that if the edge of the South American continent is pushed against the continent of Africa, a very close fit would result. Secular scientists conclude that perhaps 150 million years ago, there existed only one continent but over this eon of 150 million years, that original continent split and slowly moved over the ocean floor to produce the presently existing continents. The Biblical record of course makes the concept of 150 million years completely invalid. This continental split must have occurred in the days of Peleg because the Bible declares that **"in his days was the earth divided"** (Genesis 10:25).

An interesting time correlation is found in secular records in connection with the Maya civilization that existed hundreds of years ago in Central America. Dr. Howard LaFay wrote in National Geographic Magazine:

. . . the Maya practiced an astronomy so precise that their ancient calendar was as accurate as the one we employ today; they plotted the courses of celestial bodies, and to the awe of the faithful, their priests predicted both solar and lunar eclipses. They calculated the path of Venus–an elusive planet that is by turn a morning and evening star–with an error of only 14 seconds a year. The

Maya originated a complex system of writing and pioneered the mathematical concept of zero.[1]

The Maya produced square or rectangular elements called glyph blocks, which made up separate units of an inscription. These inscriptions were frequently calendars and were found on stelae and monumental buildings such as temples. Archaeologists have correlated the Maya calendar with our calendar to the extent that precise dates recorded in the Maya writings can be expressed in terms of our calendar. The curious thing is that these calendars frequently included a foundation date. (See also *Adam When?*, pp. 89, 91.)

Dr. George E. Stuart writes:

...the beginning of the Maya calendar [is] a date that most Mayanists agree corresponds to our own August 11, 3114 B.C. What, one can only wonder, was the high significance of that day, long before Maya history began? [2]

Archaeologists who study the ancient civilization of Maya puzzle about the date 3114 B.C., but the Bible gives the answer. Significantly, as we noted above, the Bible indicates Peleg's period was from 3153 B.C. to 2914 B.C., so that Peleg would have been 39 years of age in the year 3114 B.C., the beginning year of the Maya calendar. The Bible records that it was during Peleg's period that the earth was divided. The division of the continents occurred, therefore, in all likelihood, during Peleg's lifetime. Most people of that day would have gathered in one part of the huge continent that existed until the time of Peleg; however, some nomadic individuals such as the Maya would no doubt have lived in other parts of the original continent such as that part which became Central America. (See also *Adam When?*, pp. 89, 91.)

This was a gigantic event; the division of the original continent was equivalent to the beginning of time for these nomads! The awful event of part of the continent splitting off and moving across the ocean floor and the resultant mountain building must have been absolutely astounding and catastrophic to the progenitors of the Maya people. It is not surprising that in their calendar they used this event as a fixture for their foundation date. Even more so, it is not surprising that that date precisely equates with the Biblical statement that in the days of Peleg the earth was divided.

---

[1] Dr. Howard LaFay, "The Maya, Children of Time," in *National Geographic Magazine*, December, 1976, p. 729.

[2] Dr. George E. Stuart, "The Maya Riddle of the Glyphs," in *National Geographic Magazine*, December, 1976, p. 779.

The Earth's Language is Confused

But there was another very significant event which also probably occurred about the same time. Earlier we quoted Genesis 11:1-8. In that citation, God teaches that there was also another dramatic division. Remember we read that God declared in verse 7, **"let us go down, and there confound their language, that they may not understand one another's speech."**

But there existed an enormous problem in the world of that day.

Now God obviously was not finding fault with the speech of the people. The three sons of Noah, whom God saved from the universal Flood's destruction, all spoke the same language. But there existed an enormous problem in the world of that day. The problem was that of sin. As the population of the world grew, even as we have noted, mankind found strength in unity, so much so that they even thought that they could develop their own salvation program. They found in the world of their day a location that would eventually become the location of the nation of Babylon. They believed this location could be central to all the peoples of the world. There they built a great tower which would be the center point of worship as they designed their own religion.

This was the circumstance that God used to initiate the beginning of the various languages of the world. At the tower of Babel, God confused the one uniform language of that day so that it became many languages. Those who began to speak in the Chinese language moved in one direction, those who spoke Latin in another, etc.

This dramatic event probably would have produced the invention of writing. Before the confusion of the languages, the need to write was not nearly as great as when mankind suddenly discovered they could no longer understand each other. Significantly, the very earliest and most primitive writings according to the secular record date back to about 3200 B.C.-3000 B.C. Thus, there is an interesting correlation between the earth being divided in Peleg's generation (3153 B.C.-2914 B.C.), the advent of disparate languages, and the earliest beginning of writing. In all likelihood, these events occurred very close in time to each other.

Thus, a written record began to be produced beginning about 3000 B.C. In a number of instances, the secular record written during the period from 3000 B.C. to the time of Christ speaks of events also spoken of in the Bible. In each instance, however, whenever there appears to be a discrepancy between the two records, we can know that the Biblical record is the accurate record because it is the Word of God.

> *Only the Bible can be trusted concerning the truth of history including the history of these very early years.*

During the approximately 3,000 years that came immediately after the universal Flood, the Gospel was not altogether absent from the world. Even the secular archaeological evidence shows that there was an awareness of the God of the Bible as testified by ancient writings and petroglyphs depicting Creation or the Flood. However each and every one of these ancient accounts severely corrupted the true history of these dramatic historical events. Only the Bible can be trusted concerning the truth of history including the history of these very early years.

The archaeological evidences of ancient idol worship and sacrifices indicate that these people knew they were accountable to a Supreme Being. The evidences of sacrifices, even human sacrifices, give mute testimony to the fact that religion was not absent from them.

But all of this activity that was going on during the first 3,000 years after the Flood of 4990 B.C. did not produce many believers in the God of the Bible. True, we read in the Book of Job of a few believers who may have lived about 2,000 years before Christ. But aside from that one exception, the Bible speaks of only one household in which there were true believers, and moreover, even in that family, the father of the family, a man named Terah, served other gods (Joshua 24:2, 15).

Because mankind is created in the image of God, to some degree the laws of God are written on every person's heart. Thus, intuitively, these ancient peoples knew they had to come to be at peace with God. But they wanted their own religion through which they believed they could become accepted by God. We will learn in this study that the thinking of these ancient peoples was essentially no different from that of the peoples of our present day.

However, in spite of the natural tendency for mankind to design their own religion, God did have a salvation plan that would be unfolded and would proceed even though mankind continues in great rebellion against God.

> *...wickedness increases for a period of time and then God brings judgment.*

We observe (and the Bible records these historical events for our learning) that wickedness increases for a period of time and then God brings judgment. The result is the pouring out of God's wrath upon all of the human race except for a small remnant through whom God begins again to build a name for Himself.

Interestingly, we note that in each of these instances, the people upon whom God focuses our attention are the religious. As our study continues, the Bible will again bring this pattern to our attention. (See following chart.)

The Degeneration	The Focus	The Judgments	The New Beginning
Adam and Eve sin	Focus is on wanting to be "gods" or "wise"	Driven out of Garden of Eden	God begins again with Seth
(Gen. 3:1-7)	*(Gen. 3:6)*	*(Gen. 3:22-24)*	*(Gen. 4:25-26)*
Wickedness increases	Focus is on the "sons of God" and "men of renown"	The Flood	God begins again with Noah and his family as they were the only ones saved from the Flood
(Gen. 6:5)	*(Gen. 6:2-4)*	*(Gen. 7:17-23)*	*(Gen. 6:17-18, 7:23b, 8:20-9:3, 8:17)*
Wicknedness increases	Focus is on those who want to make a name for themselves and build a tower to "reach to heaven"	Confusion of languages	Beginning again with Abram and and builds a nation
(Gen. 11:6)	*(Gen. 11:4)*	*(Gen. 11:5-9)*	*(Gen. 12:1-3)*

Now we will look at the family of Terah who was the father of Abraham. It was through this family that God's salvation plan would continue to unfold.

2092 B.C. God Begins Again with Abraham

Terah lived in Ur of the Chaldees so we could identify him with very ancient Babylon. The words "Chaldees" and "Babylon" are virtually synonymous in the Bible. While Terah himself worshiped both the true God and false gods, his three sons, Abram, Nahor and Haran, appear to have been worshipers of the true God. It was with Abram (later God changed his name to Abraham) that God in a very definite way brought His plan of salvation into clearer focus. This focus was on a family and on a land. The family was that of Abram. The land was that of Canaan that was located hundreds of miles distant from Ur of the Chaldees.

In obedience to God's command, at the age of 75, in the year 2092 B.C., Abram, his wife Sarai, and his nephew Lot, arrived in the land of Canaan as total strangers. There God gave Abram promises that involved and structured the unfolding of God's salvation plan all the way to the end of the world. He would be the head, the beginning, of a special nation that would be formed to represent, in an external way, the kingdom of God. Later, it was called the nation of Israel.

Abram was called out of an unsaved heathen world. He was called by God to come out of the most visible representation of the nations of the world that had begun to form beginning about 1,000 years earlier. That nation was Babylon which was the only nation that existed prior to the tower of Babel (Genesis Chapter 11) and the division of the continents (Genesis 10:25). Great nations like Egypt and China came into existence following the tower of Babel.

> *...the world had again become as wicked as it was before the Flood.*

Abram's father, Terah, was an unbeliever. Furthermore, the Bible does not make us aware of any other individuals or peoples (except perhaps Abram's relatives in the small country of Haran, see Genesis 24:1-51; Genesis 28:1-7, 29:1-14) as having any interest in Jehovah God. This suggests very strongly to us that after the 3,000 years that had passed since the Flood, the world had again become as wicked as it was before the Flood. However, the fact that Abram and probably a few of his close relatives were true believers indicates that the Gospel was still in evidence in the world.

At the same time Abram was called out of Ur of the Chaldees (the country of Babylon), God designated a piece of land located on the shores of the Mediterranean Sea to be a physical, external representation of the kingdom of God. It was the land of Canaan that later was called the land of Israel or Palestine.

At the time Abram came to the land of Canaan, it was occupied by a number of small city nations, none of which served Jehovah God, the God of the Bible. The wickedness found in them was probably typical of the wickedness that could be found in all the nations of the world at that time in history.

As God developed the timeline of His salvation plan, the day would come when He would bring judgment on these nations in the land of Canaan. As we will learn later in our study, God would begin with judgment on the four cities of Sodom, Gomorrah, Admah, and Zeboim (Deuteronomy 29:23); then hundreds of years later, His judgment would fall on the rest of the cities of the land of Canaan. It was to this land of Canaan (also called the land of the Amorites) that God called Abram, and to which Abram, his wife Sarai and his nephew Lot came in the year 2092 B.C.

At the beginning of time, our first parents Adam and Eve (the only people existing in the world at that time) became central in God's timeline of history. As we have seen, slightly over 6,000 years later, Noah, his wife, and his three sons, together with their respective wives, became central in God's unfolding Salvation plan. They were the only people existing on planet earth because the rest of the human race had been completely destroyed by the Flood that began in 4990 B.C. Now in the year 2092 B.C., three people became central in God's unfolding salvation plan; but they are called out of a world that already was producing great ancient nations like Babylon, Egypt, and China!

God made great promises to Abram that anticipated Christ coming as the Savior about 2,000 years later. These promises also anticipated the fact that, as a result of Christ's coming, the Gospel would be sent into all of the nations of the world. For example, we read in Genesis 12:1-5:

> **Now the LORD had said unto Abram, Get thee out of thy country, and from thy kindred, and from thy father's house, unto a land that I will shew thee: <u>And I will make of thee a great nation, and I will bless thee, and make thy name great; and thou shalt be a blessing: And I will bless them that bless thee, and curse him that curseth thee: and in thee shall all families of the earth be blessed.</u> So Abram departed, as the LORD had spoken unto him; and Lot went with him: and Abram was seventy and five years old when he departed out of Haran. And Abram took Sarai his wife, and Lot his brother's son, and all their substance that they had gathered, and the souls that they had gotten in Haran; and they went forth to go into the land of Canaan; and into the land of Canaan they came.**

In obedience to God's command, Abram, together with his father Terah, had left Ur of the Chaldees and stopped in Haran on their way to the land of Canaan. In Haran, Terah died (at the age of 205 years). At that time, Abram was 75 years old, and his wife Sarai was 65 years of age.

Abram left Haran after his father's death and came into the land of Canaan in the year 2092 B.C. There God gave him additional promises which are recorded in Genesis 12:7:

And the LORD appeared unto Abram, and said, Unto thy seed will I give this land: and there builded he an altar unto the LORD, who appeared unto him.

This verse shows that God communicated with mankind very directly inasmuch as the Bible did not exist. God could take on the appearance of a human being and thus talk face to face with the one with whom He wished to communicate. It was possible that at other times He spoke to an individual in a dream or a vision or these individuals simply heard the audible voice of God.

As we have proven previously, today God speaks to mankind only by means of the Bible. Since every word and phrase in the Bible comes from the mouth of God, we can be certain when we are reading the Bible, that God Himself is speaking to us. Moreover, since the Bible is the whole law of God today, we should know far more about God's truth than individuals like Abram who lived before the Bible was written or before it was completed. What a marvelous blessing we enjoy today in that we have the entire Word of God!

Returning now to Abram, as we have indicated, the focus of God's developing salvation plan was on the physical land of Canaan to which Abram came in the year 2092 B.C. However, this physical land of Canaan was not to be the eternal inheritance which God had promised because the Bible clearly teaches that this world, of which the physical land of Canaan is a part, will be entirely destroyed by fire at the time Jesus comes again on the last day (2 Peter 3:10). The physical land of Canaan was used by God as a picture or visible representation of the eternal kingdom of God into which all true believers enter at the time they become saved.

At the end of time when this present universe is completely destroyed by fire, God will bring into existence a new heaven and a new earth.

At the end of time when this present universe is completely destroyed by fire, God will bring into existence a new heaven and a new earth. There all of those who have become saved, who have entered the kingdom of God, will live forever with the Lord Jesus Christ (2 Peter 3:13). That is the land represented or typified by the physical land of Canaan.

Thus, we see that when Abram and his family came into the land of Canaan in the year 2092 B.C., it was an exceedingly important milestone in the timeline of the unfolding of God's salvation plan. It was a dramatic picture of God's salvation plan. All who become saved, like Abram coming out of Babylon and coming into Canaan, are called out of this world, which is ruled over by Satan, and are transferred into the kingdom of God. The Bible spiritually calls this world Babylon and the kingdom of God is called the land of Canaan.

Later in our study, we will learn that all of the local churches at this present time are also "Babylon" (Revelation 18:1-5), because at this time, Satan is ruling in them.

And that brings us to the next important milestone in the unfolding of God's salvation plan. It is the year 2068 B.C.

2068 B.C. God Reiterates His Promise to Abraham

We have learned how important the year 2092 B.C. was in God's timeline of history. Abram, together with Sarai his wife, and his nephew Lot, had faithfully obeyed God's command to leave their home in Ur of the Chaldees and take up residency in the strange land of Canaan. Remember, God had given Abram and Sarai wonderful promises of a progeny that would be a blessing to every nation (Genesis 12:2-3). However, there was one huge problem. After living 24 years as a stranger in this foreign land of Canaan, Abram and Sarai were still childless. By this time Sarai had become 89 years of age and was well beyond the age of childbearing. Humanly speaking, there was no longer the possibility of Abram and Sarai becoming the progenitors of many people.

However, it was in that year 2068 B.C. that several very important events occurred.

1. God changed Abram's name to Abraham ("a father of many nations," Genesis 17:5), and He changed Sarai's name to Sarah ("princess," Genesis 17:15).

2. God appeared to Abraham and reiterated all of His promises concerning a multitudinous progeny that would inherit the land as an everlasting possession.

3. God promised Abraham and Sarah that one year later, Sarah would give birth to a son who was to be called Isaac (Genesis 17:19, 21; 21:1-3).

4. God utterly destroyed four cities, Sodom, Gomorrah, Admah, and Zeboim because of their wickedness (Genesis 19:24-25; Deuteronomy 29:23). Only Abraham's nephew Lot and Lot's two daughters were brought to safety.

5. God gave Abraham a sign that God's law (His covenant) would be carried out. The covenant decreed that through Isaac, all of God's promises would be fulfilled. The sign that God gave was that of circumcision of all males eight days old and older (Genesis 17:7-14). This sign became a picture of the nature of God's salvation plan. Even as the foreskin of the reproductive organ was to be cut off, so too, the sins of each one who would be eternally saved were to be cut off. The cutting off of the foreskin caused bleeding. So, too, in order for sins to be cut off, Christ as the Messiah shed His blood (that is, gave His life).

Thus, in the year 2068 B.C., a milestone was set in the timeline of history in that:

1. Abraham and Sarah's son Isaac, who would be born the following year, was a representative or picture of the Lord Jesus Christ. It is Christ who is the spiritual beginning and father of all who will live eternally as God's children.

2. All of those who are outside of God's salvation plan, typified by the destroyed cities of Sodom, Gomorrah, Admah, and Zeboim, are eternally under the wrath of God.

Exactly 2,100 years later, in A.D. 33, the Lord Jesus Christ bore the judgment and wrath of God on behalf of the peoples of every nation whom God, in the person of Christ, came to save. Christ paid the penalty for their sins in full so that they would become eternal children of God. At the same time, Christ's death and resurrection guaranteed that those who were not to be sons of Christ (saved by Christ), like those in the four cities upon which God's judgment fell, would in time be cast into hell. Only the sentence of spending an eternity in hell, under the judgment and wrath of God, would fully satisfy the demands of God's law for the payment required for the sins of the unsaved.

All of this was contemplated and anticipated by the events that took place in this notable year of 2068 B.C.

But now we shall go on to the next very important milestone in the unfolding of God's timeline of history, the year 2007 B.C.

2007 B.C. Jacob is Born

Sixty years have passed since Isaac was born in the year 2067 B.C. Twenty-three years earlier, Sarah had died. In the year 2007 B.C., Abraham had become 160 years old and would live fifteen years longer. Twenty years earlier than 2007 B.C., Isaac had married a relative of Abraham named Rebekah (Genesis 25:20, 26).

Incidentally, God's law at this time in history did not prohibit the marriage of close relatives. That law was given over 500 years later in the year 1446 B.C. In these earlier years, the need to marry close relatives was in evidence because of the scarcity of true believers. For example, Sarah was the half sister of Abraham (Genesis 20:12).

The year 2007 B.C. was propitious because it was the year Isaac and Rebekah were given their only children. Rebekah gave birth to twin sons, Esau and Jacob. Although Esau was the firstborn, God gave the salvation promises to Jacob. (See *The Fig Tree* available free of charge from Family Radio.) That is, the promises given to Abraham would be fulfilled in the line of the descendants of Jacob.

Moreover, we must keep in mind that events like the coming of Abraham into the land of Canaan, the birth of Isaac to Abraham and Sarah, and the birth of Jacob to Israel and Rebekah, although involving just a handful of people, were nevertheless, exceedingly important milestones in the unfolding of God's salvation plan. All of these events were laying the groundwork for, and pointing to, God's magnificent salvation program that eventually would involve millions of people throughout the whole world.

Significantly, the name Jacob means "supplanter." Esau as the firstborn would have normally received the special blessings that belonged to the firstborn. However, it was God's plan that the second born, Jacob, was to receive these special blessings. Thus, in that sense, Jacob supplanted Esau. In that sense also, Jacob became a picture or representative of all of those who become true believers. They, too, are sometimes called "Jacob" in the Bible (e.g., Jeremiah 10:16).

One of the reasons Jacob pictures true believers is that this earth, which presently is in the hands of the unsaved, will eventually become the eternal inheritance of the true believers. That is, the true believers supplant the unsaved as the final inheritors of the world. This will take place at the end of time when God will create new heavens and a new earth. This is the earth spoken of in Matthew 5:5 where God declares:

Blessed are the meek: for they shall inherit the earth.

It is the new heavens and new earth spoken of in 2 Peter 3:13:

Nevertheless we, according to his promise, look for new heavens and a new earth, wherein dwelleth righteousness.

Christ, too, at times, is typified by Jacob. When Jesus came as the Messiah, He supplanted Satan as the ruler of those whom God planned to save. Colossians 1:13 declares that those who have been saved have been taken out from under Satan's dominion and placed into Christ's kingdom. We read there:

Who hath delivered us from the power of darkness, and hath translated us into the kingdom of his dear Son.

Christ was typified by Jacob at times also because Jacob was the father of twelve sons who in turn became the heads of the twelve tribes of Israel (Genesis 49:28), which in turn became an external representation of the kingdom of God. Christ, typified by Jacob, became the eternal Father of all who are eternally citizens of the kingdom of God.

Fact is, when Jacob was 100 years of age, in the year 1907 B.C., he was given the name Israel (Genesis 32:28, 35:10). The name Israel means Prince of God. Eternally, it is Christ who is the Godly Prince (Isaiah 4:6). For that reason, the name Israel was assigned to the nation of the descendants of Abraham, Isaac, and Jacob -- the Jewish nation, the nation of Israel -- because that nation was externally a representation of the kingdom of God. Likewise, during the church age, the name Israel was assigned to the local congregations because during the church age each local congregation was an external representation of the kingdom of God. Later in our study, this will be further developed.

The year 2007 B.C., when Jacob was born, was a very significant year for other reasons. For example, exactly 1,000 years later, in the year 1007 B.C., David, another great type of Christ, ascended the throne to reign over Israel. Also, exactly 2,000 years after 2007 B.C. was the year 7 B.C., and in all likelihood, Jesus Christ was born in the year 7 B.C. In addition, exactly 4,000 years after 2007 B.C. was A.D. 1994. Later in our study, we will learn more about the great importance of A.D. 1994. We certainly can know that the year 2007 B.C. was a very significant milestone in the unfolding of God's salvation plan.

> *...there is no other accurate record in existence today that approaches the exquisite accuracy of the Bible's recording of these historical events.*

We might note that there is no other accurate record in existence today that approaches the exquisite accuracy of the Bible's recording of these historical events. Each of these milestone years is calculated solely from Biblical evidence. And we know that the Bible is God's Word, and therefore, is completely accurate. Moreover, these historical milestones are bound together by very significant time relationships which we will explore in a later chapter.

But now we should examine the next important milestone the Bible sets forth in the unfolding of God's salvation plan, which in turn governs all of history. That is the year 1899 B.C.

1899 B.C. Joseph is 17

As we have noted, Jacob, through whom God's salvation timeline flowed, eventually became the father of twelve sons. He also fathered one daughter. Each of these twelve sons became important names in the historical development of God's salvation program. They would become heads of the twelve tribes of Israel.

We should note that Esau, the twin brother of Jacob, also became a great nation. Esau, together with his uncle Ishmael (who was the son of Abraham by Hagar, the maid of Sarah), became the progenitors of the Arab nations. Now, Isaac the son of Abraham by Sarah, was the half-brother of Ishmael, and Esau was the twin brother of Jacob. Ishmael and Esau became enemies of Isaac and Jacob. This enmity continues today. Both the Jews and Arabs claim sonship from the line of Abraham to whom the promises of the land of Canaan were given.

Thus, both the Jews and Arabs lay claim to lands in the Middle East, and they continue to battle over them to this day! But, as we learned earlier, those promises were only pictures in which the physical land of Canaan was a type or representation of the kingdom of God. The true inheritors of the land of Canaan were neither the Jews nor the Arabs. It is the true believers, for whom Christ has become their Savior, who inherit the land! (See *The Fig Tree*, available free of charge from Family Radio.) These true children of God -- from all the nations of the world -- inherit the promise, the promise of a spiritual eternal land which the physical land of Canaan only represented (Galatians 3:29).

Returning now to the twelve sons of Jacob, we learn from the Bible that three of the sons, none of whom were the firstborn, became especially significant in the unfolding of God's salvation plan. Judah was the son through whom the salvation promises would flow (Genesis 49:10; Luke 3:33). Levi would head the tribe which would identify with the priests who would function as the spiritual rulers over the twelve tribes that later were, as a nation, called Israel.

The third son of Jacob that we note here who was of special Biblical importance was Joseph. Joseph was the next-to-the-last son born to Jacob. He is the only son whose birth year can be known for certain from the Biblical record. He was born in the year 1916 B.C. Even though it was not through him that God's salvation plan flowed, he was used by God as a type or picture or representative of the Lord Jesus Christ. By closely following the Biblical account of his lifetime, we can learn much about God's salvation plan.

With the exception of Genesis 38, all of the chapters beginning with Genesis Chapter 37 and continuing all the way through Chapters 48 and 50, record the experiences of Joseph. By means of the experiences of Joseph, God points to what are certainly the high points of the unfolding of the history of the world, namely, the first coming of Christ as Savior and ultimately, the second coming of Christ as Judge of all the earth.

In the year 1899 B.C., Joseph was 17 years of age. Father Jacob was 108 years of age. Forty-eight years earlier, at the age of 60 years, Jacob had received the blessed promise of God that the salvation promises to Abraham would flow through Jacob himself (Genesis 27:27-29; Genesis 28:3-4).

Earlier we noted that at the age of 100, Jacob's name was changed from Jacob to Israel. We noted Israel means "prince of God." Jacob also is presented to us in certain citations in the Bible as a picture or type of Christ who is the Prince of God. But remarkably, God puts the spotlight on Joseph, a son born to Jacob when he was 91 years of age (Genesis 37:2). Why did God do this? It is true that Jacob especially loved Joseph because he was a son of his old age (Genesis 37:3). Because of Jacob's special love for Joseph, Joseph's brothers hated him (Genesis 37:4). To make matters worse for Joseph, at the age of 17, he had two dreams that seemed to prophesy that the day would come when he would rule over his brothers and also over his father and mother (Genesis 37:5-11). This was the year 1899 B.C., a very important milestone in the unfolding of God's salvation plan. That this is a significant milestone is seen in the strange language of Genesis 37:1-2:

> **And Jacob dwelt in the land wherein his father was a stranger, in the land of Canaan. These are the generations of Jacob. Joseph, being seventeen years old, was feeding the flock with his brethren; and the lad was with the sons of Bilhah, and with the sons of Zilpah, his father's wives: and Joseph brought unto his father their evil report.**

Why would the generation of Jacob be focused on Joseph? Joseph was not the firstborn; neither was he in the blood line through which Christ would come. One reason must be that Joseph was an outstandingly significant and important type of Christ. God deliberately calls our attention to Joseph's being 17 years old as the beginning of all of Joseph's experiences. It is his life from that time forward that would embrace and anticipate the unfolding of God's plan of salvation. We will note a few highlights of the experiences of Joseph that show that through his experiences, he was a picture of Christ coming as Savior to pay the penalty for the sins of the true believers. Aspects of Joseph's life also point to Christ's coming at the end of the world to prepare this world for events that must occur just before the end of time.

> *Joseph was an outstandingly significant and important type of Christ.*

First, we take note that the number 17, when used in the Bible to signify something spiritual, usually points to heaven. It would appear that God gave us the information that Joseph is 17 years old in order to identify with Jesus Christ through whom all who become saved will go to heaven.

In the year 1877 B.C., Joseph had become 39 years of age. During the preceding 22 years of his life, he had experienced a great many trials and tribulations. An examination of each of these would show that his life was a historical parable. The true historical events of the life of Joseph were portraits of important spiritual events. Each of his experiences was pointing to the Lord Jesus Christ. For example:

1. He was rejected by his brothers (Genesis 37:4-5,8,18-28). Jesus was rejected by the nation of His birth, national Israel.

2. He was put into a pit (Genesis 37:24). Jesus suffered the wrath of God, hell, which is typified by a pit.

3. He was sold as a slave (Genesis 37:28). Christ was sold like a slave for 30 pieces of silver.

4. He remained faithful to God when tempted by Potiphar's wife (Genesis 39:10-12, 40:15). Christ remained faithful when tempted by Satan.

5. He came out of prison and became the highest ruler of the land, second only to Pharaoh (Genesis 41:14, 38-44). Christ, after

paying for the sins of those He came to save, became King of kings and Lord of lords.

6.   He saved his family from physical starvation (Genesis 45:7, 45:10-11, 47:12). Christ saved His spiritual family (those who become true believers) from spiritual death.

7.   The seven-year famine became a portrait of the Great Tribulation that comes just before Christ returns at the end of time (Acts 7:11; Matthew 24:21, 29).

In the timeline of history, Joseph, at the age of 30 (in 1886 B.C.), became second only to Pharaoh as ruler of Egypt (Genesis 41:39-44). There were to be seven years of bountiful harvest. This would be followed by seven years of great famine. Pharaoh had appointed Joseph to gather in the harvest during the seven years of plenty. He then was to rule over the distribution of this harvest during the following seven years of famine (Genesis 41:33-49, 53-57).

In the year 1877 B.C., already two years of famine had taken place (Genesis 45:6). This famine encompassed also the land of Canaan where Jacob, Joseph's father, was living with his family. Consequently, Jacob sent ten of his sons to buy grain, not knowing that the ruler of the distribution of the grain was his son and their brother Joseph. When that grain was used up, they came a second time, and on this second trip, Joseph revealed to them his identity. He was their younger brother who 22 years earlier had been sold as a slave because of their hatred toward him. The Biblical account of these experiences, ending with a reconciliation, are wonderfully fascinating. We can read about them in Genesis Chapters 42, 43, 44, and 45.

The result of this reconciliation of Joseph with his brothers brings us to the extremely important year 1877 B.C. We read in Genesis 45:6-9, 13:

> **For these two years hath the famine been in the land: and yet there are five years, in the which there shall neither be earing nor harvest. And God sent me before you to preserve you a posterity in the earth, and to save your lives by a great deliverance. So now it was not you that sent me hither, but God: and he hath made me a father to Pharaoh, and lord of all his house, and a ruler throughout all the land of Egypt. Haste ye, and go up to my father, and say unto him, Thus saith thy son Joseph, God hath made me lord of all Egypt: come down unto me, tarry not: . . .**

And ye shall tell my father of all my glory in Egypt, and of all that ye have seen; and ye shall haste and bring down my father hither.

Some of the significant words here are Joseph's commands to "come down unto me, tarry not" (verse 9) and "ye shall haste and bring down my father" (verse 13). This was an incredible command that Joseph, as a great type of Christ, was giving to Jacob his father. Jacob's predecessors, in obedience to God's command, had come into the land of Canaan even though they did not know what God intended to be their destination (Hebrews 11:8-9).

In the year 2092 B.C., grandfather Abraham had come into the land of Canaan. Abraham, Isaac, and Jacob had been given Canaan as an eternal possession (Genesis 17:8).

Moreover, we read about Jacob's father Isaac in Genesis Chapter 26, verses 2-3:

And the LORD appeared unto him, and said, Go <u>not</u> down into Egypt; dwell in the land which I shall tell thee of: Sojourn in this land, and I will be with thee, and will bless thee; for unto thee, and unto thy seed, I will give all these countries, and I will perform the oath which I sware unto Abraham thy father.

> *Joseph was commanding his father Jacob to leave the promised land to come to Egypt to live!*

For 215 years, the families of Abraham, Isaac and Jacob had dwelt in Canaan. But now Joseph was commanding his father Jacob to leave the promised land to come to Egypt to live! That Joseph was expressing God's desire for Jacob is seen in God's words to Jacob in Genesis 46:2-3:

And God spake unto Israel in the visions of the night, and said, Jacob, Jacob. And he said, Here am I. And he said, I am God, the God of thy father: fear not to go down into Egypt; for I will there make of thee a great nation.

That this was an extremely traumatic and awful command that Jacob was to obey is revealed in the words of Acts 7:11-15:

Now there came a dearth over all the land of Egypt and Chanaan, and great affliction: and our fathers found no sustenance. But

when Jacob heard that there was corn in Egypt, he sent out our fathers first. And at the second time Joseph was made known to his brethren; and Joseph's kindred was made known unto Pharaoh. Then sent Joseph, and called his father Jacob to him, and all his kindred, threescore and fifteen souls. So Jacob went down into Egypt, and died, he, and our fathers.

The words "great affliction" are the identical Greek words which are found in Matthew 24:21 where they are translated "Great Tribulation." It was a Great Tribulation for Jacob to leave the promised land of Canaan that had been given to Abraham, Isaac, and Jacob as an eternal inheritance. Had God's promises failed?

God's promises had not failed! His promises never fail! But the working out of God's promises sometimes is very complex. Therefore, it is necessary that we carefully study the Bible as we seek to gain insight into the plans of God. This is certainly true of this experience of Jacob as he is commanded to leave the promised land of Canaan.

We will discover that this terrible experience of Jacob leaving the land of Canaan and going into Egypt to escape the famine is of great importance in helping us to understand the Great Tribulation that the world will experience immediately before Christ returns at the end of time. Therefore, later in our study, we will return to Jacob and examine many aspects of his experience in great detail.

However, at this time, we shall continue on our journey through time. We will discover from the Bible that the next important milestone in the unfolding of God's salvation plan is the year 1447. B.C.

Chapter 6
1447 B.C. The Exodus

We have traveled the highway that is central to the main purpose and goal of the history of the world for about 9,500 years. To review, God, thus far, has used single families as He focuses on the unfolding of His purpose for the existence of this world. He began with the family of Adam and Eve who were the ancestors of each and every individual who would ever live on planet Earth (Genesis Chapters 1-5; 1 Corinthians 15:22, 45-47). Then, about 6,000 years after Adam and Eve, God again put the spotlight on a family, that of Noah (Genesis Chapters 5-11).

Then, about 3,000 years after the time of Noah, God placed another family in the position of continuing God's major plan and purpose for the entire world. That family consisted of a man named Abraham together with his wife Sarah and a nephew named Lot (Genesis Chapters 11-12). With this family as the centerpiece, God began the preparations to expand the focus of the earth's timeline. His plan was to develop a land and a nation instead of working through a single family. The land was the land of Canaan; the nation, Israel (Genesis Chapters 11-35). The land of Canaan was established as an external representation of the kingdom of God even as the nation which was to come from the family of Abraham had become an external representation of the kingdom of God.

Then, remember we learned from the Bible that to facilitate this important change from a family to a nation, God caused Abraham's grandson Jacob, and Jacob's family, to leave the promised land of Canaan and take up residency in the land of Egypt. That was in the year 1877 B.C. (Genesis Chapters 37-47).

But now, 430 years have passed since the family of Jacob came into Egypt to escape the famine. Seventeen years after they had come into Egypt, father Jacob had died in the year 1860 B.C. (Genesis 47:28). Fifty-four years later, in the year 1806 B.C., Joseph died at the age of 110 (Genesis 50:26).

One practical result of Jacob's family coming to Egypt was the protection of the bloodline of Abraham. Sons were born to the descendants of Abraham, and they needed wives. Except for the family of Abraham, all of the inhabitants of the land of Canaan were heathen. How were his grandsons and great grandsons to obtain wives who trusted the God of the Bible? Abraham, for example, worked very hard to obtain a godly wife for his son Isaac (Genesis Chapter 24). In the heathen world of that day, this was a difficult task. Through the marriage of Isaac and Rebekah, God gave Isaac twin sons, Esau and Jacob.

Esau married Canaanitish wives (Genesis 26:34-35, 28:6, 8). On the other hand, Jacob traveled hundreds of miles to the land of Haran to find a godly wife. Fact is, he ended up being married to four wives through whom God gave him twelve sons and one daughter (Genesis Chapters 28-29, 30:1-24, 35:16-18, 35:22-26). These sons also began to marry Canaanitish wives. The Bible records that one son of Jacob, named Simeon, married a Canaanite (Genesis 46:10), and Judah, another son of Jacob, also married a Canaanite (Genesis 38:2).

> *As God is planning the unfolding of His salvation program, it is clear that He planned to transition from a family to a nation.*

As God is planning the unfolding of His salvation program, it is clear that He planned to transition from a family to a nation. But how could this be done when the family is intermarrying with the heathen of the world? One thing was certain: down in the land of Egypt, this intermarrying would be very difficult. The family of Jacob was a shepherd family, and shepherds were an abomination to the Egyptians. We read in Genesis 46:34b:

. . . for every shepherd is an abomination unto the Egyptians.

Thus, one principle reason God brought the family of Jacob to Egypt was so that the unfolding of God's salvation program could transition from a family to a nation with little interference from other nations.

Year followed year. Finally, a Pharaoh began to reign who knew nothing about Joseph. Meanwhile, the family of Jacob was multiplying so rapidly that the Egyptians began to fear that the Israelites might attempt an overthrow of Egypt. To prevent this possibility, the Israelites were made slaves. At one point in time, the year 1527 B.C., when Moses was born, the reigning Pharaoh even decreed that all the Israelites' boy babies were to be killed. Indeed, the people who had been promised they would forever inherit the land of Canaan seemed inextricably trapped as slaves in Egypt. At the same time, the land of Canaan, which God had given to Abraham and his seed, was securely in the hands of wicked nations which had no knowledge of the God of the Bible.

But God had not abandoned this nation of Israel. In His divine mercy, He provided an individual named Moses to bring them out of Egypt (Exodus 3:6-10; Hebrews 11:24-28). By the year 1447 B.C., Israel had grown in size so that it numbered perhaps as many as two million people. We do know from the Biblical record that Israel had over 600,000 men who were twenty years old and older. Adding all the women and children could bring the total population to possibly two million (Numbers 1:45-46). Now the unfolding of the timeline of history would no longer be focused on a family. It would be focused on a nation. For the next 1,480 years, the nation of Israel was to be prominent in the unfolding of God's salvation plan.

God Sets the Stage for Israel's Departure From Egypt

> *Never before or since had a nation been presented to the world as a special people in the spectacular way in which the nation of Israel was.*

      How is a slave nation consisting of perhaps two million people to be delivered from a nation that had total control over them as slaves? Israel's enslavement set the stage for God's great announcement to the world that Israel was to become known as God's special people on earth. In the process of freeing them from their terrible enslavement, God would show His tremendous power and authority. God would send ten severe plagues upon Egypt the impact of which would ultimately leave Pharaoh with no choice but to expel the people of Israel out of his country (Exodus 3:19-20, 11:1, 12:39). Never before or since had a nation been presented to the world as a special people in the spectacular way in which the nation of Israel was. The drama that was to unfold as God prepared to free them from bondage to Egypt has never in the entire history of the world been equaled.

      To prepare for His announcement, God first of all raised up perhaps the greatest Pharaoh of all of Egypt's history. Because of the exquisite accuracy of the Biblical calendar, together with the available secular historical records, we can be certain this Pharaoh was Tuthmosis III. The secular record shows that he was such a mighty military king that the archeologists speak of him as the Napoleon of Egypt. The secular record disclosed that, in his lifetime as Pharaoh, he carried out seventeen successful military campaigns. The Bible describes him as a Pharaoh that had **"600 chosen chariots, and all the chariots of Egypt, and captains over every one of them"** (Exodus 14:7). The Bible further adds in Exodus 9:16:

      And in very deed for this cause have I raised thee up, for to shew in thee my power; and that my name may be declared throughout all the earth.

Thus, the stage is set for the great announcement of the power of God. On the one hand, there was this nation of slaves with no weapons of any kind. On the other hand, there was this despotic king of great military strength.

To further enhance the announcement, God gave this mighty Pharaoh an enormous determination to keep the nation of Israel in bondage. Even though again and again God commanded Pharaoh, **"Let my people go,"** the Bible repeatedly declares that God hardened Pharaoh's heart (Exodus Chapters 7-14). Thus, even though the land of Egypt was suffering increasing destruction by plague after plague falling upon Egypt, Pharaoh refused to let the nation of Israel leave.

We must understand that the Bible teaches that the heart of man is desperately wicked (Jeremiah 17:9). Mankind by nature is in complete rebellion against God and His commandments. The only reason unsaved mankind lives with any sense of decency and morality is because God to some degree restrains sin in the lives of individuals. Otherwise mankind would quickly destroy themselves and each other (Psalm 76:10). Thus, when God hardened Pharaoh's heart, we must understand that this means that God took away all restraint on sin in Pharaoh's life. Thus, in response to God's command to let Israel go free, Pharaoh absolutely refused to allow Israel to go.

> *The more sinful he becomes, the deeper*
> *he will go into sin.*

It might be noted that this is the essential nature of every human being. The more sinful he becomes, the deeper he will go into sin (2 Timothy 3:13). This is so even though he is destroying himself and others. This is true of the alcoholic, the sex pervert, the thief, and the murderer. The hardening of Pharaoh's heart is similar to the language of Romans Chapter 1. In that citation, God speaks of giving people up (verses 24 and 26) or giving people over (verse 28) to a reprobate mind. Romans 1 then names more than twenty gross sins which become abundantly evident in their lives. This is why mankind so desperately needs salvation. Only through the saving work of Jesus Christ can the power and enslavement to sin be broken (Romans 6:6-23; 1 John 3:8).

> *Only through the saving work of Jesus Christ*
> *can the power and enslavement to sin be broken.*

The Ten Plagues

Returning to the Pharaoh who refused to release Israel, this nation of slaves that God called **"my people,"** the Bible tells us that God brought a series of ten great plagues upon Egypt (Exodus Chapters 7-12). Each was preceded by a demand by God through Moses, God's prophet, to let God's people go free from Egypt. In each case, Moses warned Pharaoh that the plague was coming. In each case, except immediately after the tenth plague, Pharaoh still refused to free this nation of slaves.

God describes the purpose of this whole scenario of the ten plagues as being twofold. The first purpose was to teach succeeding generations the greatness of the God of the Bible. We read in Exodus 10:1-2:

> **And the LORD said unto Moses, Go in unto Pharaoh: for I have hardened his heart, and the heart of his servants, that I might shew these my signs before him: and that thou mayest tell in the ears of thy son, and of thy son's son, what things I have wrought in Egypt, and my signs which I have done among them; that ye may know how that I am the LORD.**

The second purpose was to declare to the world the mighty power of God. We read in Exodus 9:13-16:

> **And the LORD said unto Moses, Rise up early in the morning, and stand before Pharaoh, and say unto him, Thus saith the LORD God of the Hebrews, Let my people go, that they may serve me. For I will at this time send all my plagues upon thine heart, and upon thy servants, and upon thy people; that thou mayest know that there is none like me in all the earth. For now I will stretch out my hand, that I may smite thee and thy people with pestilence; and thou shalt be cut off from the earth. And in very deed for this cause have I raised thee up, for to shew in thee my power; and that my name may be declared throughout all the earth.**

The plagues were incredibly awesome. Each one demonstrated in an astounding way that God is the Creator and that God can and will accomplish whatsoever He threatens to perform. They also give abundant evidence that God is the Judge of all the earth and that His perfect justice will prevail (Genesis 18:25).

For example, as God brought the first plague upon Egypt, He declared to Pharaoh in Exodus 7:17-21:

Thus saith the LORD, In this thou shalt know that I am the LORD: behold, I will smite with the rod that is in mine hand upon the waters which are in the river, and they shall be turned to blood. And the fish that is in the river shall die, and the river shall stink; and the Egyptians shall loathe to drink of the water of the river. And the LORD spake unto Moses, Say unto Aaron, Take thy rod, and stretch out thine hand upon the waters of Egypt, upon their streams, upon their rivers, and upon their ponds, and upon all their pools of water, that they may become blood; and that there may be blood throughout all the land of Egypt, both in vessels of wood, and in vessels of stone. And Moses and Aaron did so, as the LORD commanded; and he lifted up the rod, and smote the waters that were in the river, in the sight of Pharaoh, and in the sight of his servants; and all the waters that were in the river were turned to blood. And the fish that was in the river died; and the river stank, and the Egyptians could not drink of the water of the river; and there was blood throughout all the land of Egypt.

For seven days (Exodus 7:25), the great Nile River was turned into a river of blood. How dreadful! God had created water to give life to plants, animals and mankind. But blood signified death and destruction. To change water into blood is an act of creation. Thus, in this first plague, God is demonstrating that He is both the Creator as well as the Judge of all the earth.

The second plague consisted of enormous quantities of frogs coming out of the river (Exodus 8:1-15). God is showing that, from a river devoid of life, He creates life.

The third plague was that of enormous quantities of lice in all the land. The Bible reports in Exodus 8:17:

And they did so; for Aaron stretched out his hand with his rod, and smote the dust of the earth, and it became lice in man, and in beast; all the dust of the land became lice throughout all the land of Egypt.

Thus, God demonstrated His enormous creative power over the insect world.

The fourth plague consisted of great swarms of flying insects that came **"into the house of Pharaoh, and into his servants' houses, and into all the land of Egypt: the land was corrupted by reason of the swarm"** (Exodus 8:24).

God added a further aspect of His power as He declared in Exodus 8:22-23:

> **And I will sever in that day the land of Goshen, in which my people dwell, that no swarms of flies shall be there; to the end thou mayest know that I am the LORD in the midst of the earth. And I will put a division between my people and thy people: to morrow shall this sign be.**

God not only can create insects, but He can control their behavior so that a land can be off-limits to them. Thus was the case with the area in which the Israelites lived. It was off-limits to these flying insects. Significantly, as God demonstrated His great power by means of these plagues, He made certain that there can be no mistake that all of them were totally under His control and could not be a result of an abnormal quirk in nature. Many of the plagues, while Egypt was devastated by them, did not touch Goshen, the land of the Hebrews.

Additionally, God frequently gave the precise day when the plague would hit Egypt and when the plague would be removed. For example, we read in Exodus 8:9 that Moses asked Pharaoh, at the time the plague of frogs was corrupting Egypt:

> **When shall I entreat for thee, and for thy servants, and for thy people, to destroy the frogs from thee and thy houses, that they may remain in the river only?**

Pharaoh's answer was "To morrow" (verse 10). Accordingly, Moses entreated the Lord that this might be the case. Then Exodus 8:13-14 records:

> **And the LORD did according to the word of Moses; and the frogs died out of the houses, out of the villages, and out of the fields. And they gathered them together upon heaps: and the land stank.**

In the fifth plague, God brought a serious pestilence on the cattle and other animals of the Egyptians. We read in Exodus 9:3, 6a:

> **Behold, the hand of the LORD is upon thy cattle which is in the field, upon the horses, upon the asses, upon the camels, upon the oxen, and upon the sheep: there shall be a very grievous murrain. And the LORD did that thing on the morrow, and all the cattle of Egypt died . . .**

Again, we read that nothing died of the people of Israel. Exodus 9:4, 6b
says:

> **And the LORD shall sever between the cattle of Israel and the cattle of Egypt: and there shall nothing die of all that is the children's of Israel...but of the cattle of the children of Israel died not one.**

> *God is showing His mighty power over disease, even as He has total authority over all of life.*

Again, God is showing His mighty power over disease, even as He has total authority over all of life (Deuteronomy 32:39).

The sixth plague demonstrated God's power over diseases afflicting mankind as well as animals.

We read in Exodus 9:8-9:

> **And the LORD said unto Moses and unto Aaron, Take to you handfuls of ashes of the furnace, and let Moses sprinkle it toward the heaven in the sight of Pharaoh. And it shall become small dust in all the land of Egypt, and shall be a boil breaking forth with blains upon man, and upon beast, throughout all the land of Egypt.**

In the seventh plague, God showed His mighty power over the elements of nature that produce storms.

We read in Exodus 9:18:

> **Behold, to morrow about this time I will cause it to rain a very grievous hail, such as hath not been in Egypt since the foundation thereof even until now.**

Once again, God demonstrated His complete control of this mighty storm as we read in Exodus 9:23-25:

> **And Moses stretched forth his rod toward heaven: and the LORD sent thunder and hail, and the fire ran along upon the ground; and the LORD rained hail upon the land of Egypt. So there was hail, and fire mingled with the hail, very grievous, such**

as there was none like it in all the land of Egypt since it became a nation. And the hail smote throughout all the land of Egypt all that was in the field, both man and beast; and the hail smote every herb of the field, and brake every tree of the field.

The eighth plague was that of locusts that devoured every green plant that had not been destroyed by the hail (Exodus 10:1-20).

The ninth plague was a time of thick darkness. We read in Exodus 10:22-23:

And Moses stretched forth his hand toward heaven; and there was a thick darkness in all the land of Egypt three days: they saw not one another, neither rose any from his place for three days: but all the children of Israel had light in their dwellings.

That thick darkness, like the other plagues, was a warning of future judgment upon the whole world. Christ is the light of the world (John 8:12). Darkness is the absence of light. This will be the awful condition that will prevail over all of the earth when every person at the end of the world will see Christ as Judge over all the earth (Revelation 6:12-17). Christ's appearance will signify that the Gospel of grace has come to an end. There is no longer any grace or mercy or possibility of salvation. How dreadful! The three days of total darkness signify that this is God's purpose (see Appendix on numbers). It will happen.

Yet there is light in the land of Israel. That is, the true believers are eternally secure in Christ who is the Light.

> *By means of these plagues, God is showing in stark reality that He will carry out all of the terrible consequences of sin and that He has the power to do so.*

What God is showing us in these ten plagues -- and we will examine the tenth plague in just a moment -- is the reality of Judgment Day. The people of Israel represent the fact that those who are truly saved will not experience His divine Judgment. Those who are rebelling against God's law (every unsaved person) will experience the awful wrath of God. By means of these plagues, God is showing in stark reality that He will carry out all of the terrible consequences of sin and that He has the power to do so (Psalm 78:43-53). Each of us should tremble as we read the Biblical account of these plagues.

As He protected Israel through the time of the plagues, God is demonstrating that those who have become genuine believers are always under God's care. Moreover, as the people of Israel were delivered from the bondage of Pharaoh and Egypt, so God delivers all those who become saved from sin's bondage.

The Death of the Firstborn

Egypt is frequently used in the Bible as a portrait or type identifying with those who are in bondage to sin. It is frequently used as a representation of the world that is ruled over by Satan. The world is chiefly occupied by those who are in bondage to sin. Those who are unsaved, that is, those who are in bondage to sin, have no ability to be freed from this enslavement. The same situation existed with Israel in Egypt. They were in bondage to a cruel king with no possibility of deliverance. The king of Egypt (Pharaoh) typified Satan who rules over the souls of the unsaved.[1] It is from Satan's kingdom that those who have become saved are set free. God speaks of this in Exodus 20:2:

> **I am the LORD thy God, which have brought thee out of the land of Egypt, out of the house of bondage.**

Every true believer spiritually has been rescued from Egypt where they spiritually were in bondage to sin and to Satan. To be set free from sin requires that a ransom be paid. That ransom is the death of the Firstborn, Jesus Christ. Christ is called the firstborn in Colossians 1:18 because He rose from the dead after paying for the sins of those He chose to save before the foundation of the world. Colossians 1:18 declares:

> **And he is the head of the body, the church: who is the beginning, the firstborn from the dead; that in all *things* he might have the preeminence.**

---

[1] Incidentally, in the year 1877 B.C., when Joseph, as second ruler in Egypt, commanded Jacob and his family to leave the land of Canaan and come to live in Egypt, the Pharaoh who ruled at the time of the famine was not a figure of Satan. He, in that instance, was a picture of God who rules the whole world. True, in the Bible, it is unusual to find the concept that Pharaoh would represent God. However, in this account of Joseph, and in at least one or two other passages, heathen kings were representative of God. This was true, for example, of King Ahasuerus in the Book of Esther in the Bible. The family of Jacob did not come into the land of Egypt as slaves but as shepherds to shepherd the cattle of the Egyptians. They were like the believers of today who are commanded to come out of the local churches to serve Christ (who was typified by Joseph) by being shepherds to the world (typified by the Egyptians). The chief trauma for Jacob was that he was commanded to leave the promised land -- the land of Canaan.

Christ, as the firstborn, who endured the wrath of God in the place of those who become true believers, who are also called firstborn (Exodus 13:13; Romans 8:29), was typified by all the firstborn of Egypt who were killed by God in the night just before the nation of Israel was freed from Egyptian bondage (Exodus 12:29-31).

> *Christ, as the firstborn, who endured the wrath of God in the place of those who become true believers, who are also called firstborn (Exodus 13:13; Romans 8:29), was typified by all the firstborn of Egypt who were killed by God.*

This is referred to by the citation of Isaiah 43:3:

For I am the LORD thy God, the Holy One of Israel, thy Saviour: I gave Egypt for thy ransom, Ethiopia and Seba for thee.

Ethiopia at times identifies with Egypt (see, for example, Isaiah 20:3-5). Seba was the eldest son of Cush (Genesis 10:7). Cush is the Hebrew word translated as Ethiopia. Isaiah 43:3 is referring to the fact that all the firstborn of Egypt were killed in order to typify that all true believers in Christ might be set free from spiritual bondage.

This brings us to the tenth and final plague that came upon Egypt as God is preparing the nation of Israel to come out of Egypt. We read in Exodus 4:22-23:

And thou shalt say unto Pharaoh, Thus saith the LORD, Israel is my son, even my firstborn: and I say unto thee, Let my son go, that he may serve me: and if thou refuse to let him go, behold, I will slay thy son, even thy firstborn.

> *The blood signified that Christ as the firstborn died for all those who are in the household of God.*

Significantly, the night God was to come into the homes of Egypt to kill all the firstborn, God had commanded the Israelites to kill a lamb and put the blood of the lamb on the doorposts of their homes. Then when God was killing all the firstborn of the land, He would see the blood and <u>pass</u> <u>over</u> the homes where the blood was placed on the doorposts. The blood signified that Christ as the firstborn died for all those who are in the household of God (Ephesians 2:13,17-19). Thus that night was the beginning of the "Passover" which was to be observed annually by Israel. It was pointing to Christ as the Passover Lamb who was killed (suffered the equivalent of eternal damnation) in order that all the true children of God would escape judgment and instead have atonement for their sin. The shed blood of Christ indicated His perfect substitutionary sacrifice on behalf of all those who become saved. The firstborn of the Israelites escaped the judgment of the tenth plague. Instead, the wrath of God came upon all the firstborn of Egypt which typified the judgment of God which will fall on all those who have no atonement for their sins. We read in Exodus 12:12-14:

> **For I will pass through the land of Egypt this night, and will smite all the firstborn in the land of Egypt, both man and beast; and against all the gods of Egypt I will execute judgment: I am the LORD. And the blood shall be to you for a token upon the houses where ye are: and when I see the blood, I will pass over you, and the plague shall not be upon you to destroy you, when I smite the land of Egypt. And this day shall be unto you for a memorial; and ye shall keep it a feast to the LORD throughout your generations; ye shall keep it a feast by an ordinance for ever.**

Interestingly, God prescribed the precise day and year this first Passover occurred at which time the nation of Israel actually departed from Egypt. God declared in Exodus 12:2-3, 12:6-11:

> **This month shall be unto you the beginning of months: it shall be the first month of the year to you. Speak ye unto all the congregation of Israel, saying, In the tenth day of this month they shall take to them every man a lamb, according to the house of their fathers, a lamb for an house:**
>
> **and ye shall keep it up until the fourteenth day of the same month: and the whole assembly of the congregation of Israel shall kill it in the evening. And they shall take of the blood, and strike it on the two side posts and on the upper door post of the houses, wherein they shall eat it. And they shall eat the flesh in that night, roast with fire, and unleavened bread; and with bitter herbs they shall eat it. Eat not of it raw, nor sodden at all with water, but roast**

with fire; his head with his legs, and with the purtenance thereof. And ye shall let nothing of it remain until the morning; and that which remaineth of it until the morning ye shall burn with fire. And thus shall ye eat it; with your loins girded, your shoes on your feet, and your staff in your hand; and ye shall eat it in haste: it is the LORD'S passover.

The day was the fourteenth day of the first month which was called Abib or Nisan. When Israel entered into the land of Canaan forty years later, they were instructed to observe this Passover annually (Exodus 12:25; 13:5). It was a ceremonial law that was pointing to the great day in A.D. 33 when Christ as the Passover Lamb was punished for the sins of all of those He came to save.

Let us now take another look at the biblical calendar. We can calculate, because of the exquisite accuracy of the great celestial clock which God put into place on the fourth day of creation, both the day of the week and the calendar day when the nation of Israel left Egypt. Moreover, the Bible teaches us that Israel left Egypt precisely 430 years to the very day after Jacob and his family had arrived in Egypt in the year 1877 B.C. (Exodus 12:40-41). Thus, we can know that it was the year 1447 B.C. when the nation of Israel departed from Egypt. Furthermore, we can know the calendar date and day of the month Jacob came into Egypt and the calendar date and day of the month of the Exodus. Our calculations show that the day Israel departed from Egypt was March 21, 1447 B.C. (according to our modern calendar). We may not know all the reasons why God has given us this precise historical information, but we do know it is altogether trustworthy information.

Curiously, the vernal equinox occurs in any year on or about March 21. On that date all over the world, the length of the nighttime is precisely equal to the length of the daytime. Each period is 12 hours in length. How interesting that this was the date Israel was set free from Egypt.

Though dates are interesting and may be of important significance, we do not want to lose our focus on the year 1447 B.C. It was a great milestone in the unfolding of the timeline of history. In this year, God thrust a nation, the nation of Israel, into great prominence as He unfolds His salvation plan. The Exodus from Egypt typifies God's salvation plan.

Israel Crosses the Red Sea

The rescue of the nation of Israel was not complete until a few weeks after they departed from Egypt. Israel had to traverse the Red Sea. Israel crossed the Red Sea safely by God's miraculous power as God provided a dry path through the Red Sea, heaping up the water so that it stood on either side (Exodus 14:21-22, 29; Psalm 78:13). However, when Pharaoh and his 600 chariots and armies attempted to follow Israel on the same dry path, Pharaoh and every one of his soldiers were drowned in the Red Sea (Exodus 14:23-28, 30). Miraculous!

Look at these amazing parallels!

Historical Subject	Spiritual Representation
Moses	Christ
Pharaoh and his armies	Satan and his angels
Nation of Israel	All those who become saved
Firstborn of Egypt who were killed	Christ as the Firstborn was was killed and became subject to the second death because the sin and guilt of those who would become saved was imputed to Him
Firstborn of Egypt who were killed	All those who are under God's wrath spending eternity in hell because they are in rebellion against Him
Passover lamb whose blood was placed on the door post	Christ who shed His blood (gave His life) as a substitute for all those who become true believers
Egypt	Satan's kingdom to which all people belong unless they have become saved
Red Sea	Hell, eternal damnation
The people of Israel passing through the Red Sea without harm	The true believers (because they are in Christ) going through hell without any spiritual harm
The destruction of Pharaoh and his armies in the Red Sea	Satan and all those over whom he rules ending up in hell forever

Observing these parallels, we learn that God is giving us a significant illustration of His salvation plan. These dramatic events have been recorded in the Bible to help all of those who read the Bible know much more about the mighty power of God. He demonstrates His power as He brings deliverance to those whom He chooses and as He brings His wrath upon those who arrogantly flaunt and disobey His laws.

We thus have learned that the year 1447 B.C. was an extremely important milestone in the unfolding of God's salvation plan. But now, as we proceed down the timeline of history, we will begin to look at several very important feast days that were to be observed by Old Testament Israel. We will discover how tremendously important these Old Testament feast days were as they anticipated and identified with the development of God's salvation plan throughout the New Testament era.

Laws Anticipating God's Salvation

When we were in that part of the timeline of history that featured Joseph, when God brought Jacob and his family into Egypt, we learned that God used Joseph to set forth patterns that identify with two all-important milestones of history. The first of these two great milestones was that of the first coming of Christ as Savior. The second all-important event was that of Christ coming at the end of the world, coming both as the Savior of all His true people and as the Judge of all the earth. We saw these tremendous events anticipated also as Israel went out of Egypt and as they went through the Red Sea.

Immediately after Israel went through the Red Sea, they came to Mount Sinai in the land of Arabia. While they were there, God gave them a great many laws that became an integral part of the Bible. Many of these laws were moral in nature in that they were instructions to the human race as to how mankind is to honor God and relate to their fellowman. For example, the Bible commands that the God of the Bible is the only God man should worship.

Furthermore, no likeness of God should be made. In addition, laws forbidding stealing, murder, and adultery were set forth. These kinds of laws were not given only to Israel when they were at Mount Sinai, but they are given throughout the Bible.

> *We are to recognize that Christ did all of the enormous work that is required for the salvation of an individual.*

Additionally, laws were given that were ceremonial in nature, that is, they were pointing to or representing some spiritual principle. For example, each and every seventh day was a Sabbath day during which no work of any kind was to be done. This ceremonial law was pointing to the divine principle that we cannot do any kind of work or put forth any kind of effort to merit the favor of God. We are to recognize that Christ did all of the enormous work that is required for the salvation of an individual. Likewise, there were ceremonial laws that involved sacrifices and burnt offerings. Each of these was pointing to the Lord Jesus Christ who is eternal God. But God's Law decreed that He must personally take on a human nature and sacrifice Himself as payment for the sins of those He came to save.

Included in the ceremonial laws were a number of laws setting forth feast days that were to be observed by national Israel. Those were especially significant because they definitely related to the unfolding of God's salvation plan. As we previously indicated, we should examine these because they help us to see elements of the timeline of history that have been worked out in exquisite detail from the beginning of time.

The feast days we will examine are the Passover, the Feast of Weeks (which is Pentecost), and the Feast of the First Day of the Seventh Month which, together with the Day of Atonement, is associated with the Jubilee.

The Passover Feast

If we could rank the feast days in order of importance, we would certainly place the observance of the Passover at the top of the list. We have learned that the Passover Feast was instituted at the time Israel left Egypt. We might remember that because the people of Israel obeyed the Lord's command and placed the blood of a lamb on their door posts, the Lord passed over them (Exodus 11:4-7; 12:28-29; Hebrews 11:28). At the time the Lord passed over Egypt, all of the firstborn of Egypt were killed because no blood was placed on the door posts of their homes.

These firstborn of Egypt represented all men who are under the wrath of God because of their sin. The blood of the lamb that was placed on the Israelites' doorposts represented Jesus as the Savior. He, as the Lamb of God, gave His life (shed His blood which was represented by the blood on the doorposts). He took the wrath of God upon Himself in order that the people He came to save might be spared the sentence of eternal spiritual death.

All those whom God saves are also sinful. They, too, deserve God's wrath (Ephesians 2:3). The wrath of God would justly fall upon them if Christ had not taken their sin upon Himself and endured the wrath of God for that sin in their place (1 Corinthians 5:7b; 2 Corinthians 5:21; 1 Peter 2:24; 3:18). He, therefore, became like the firstborn of Egypt who were killed. He became the firstborn in the sense that, on behalf of those He came to save, He experienced the second death which is eternal damnation (Revelation 21:8).

> *He had a beginning only because He arose from the second death.*

But Jesus did not remain eternally under the wrath of God. He did not stay dead. He rose again.

A further word of explanation is necessary. As the Savior, Jesus became someone of whom God can say He had a beginning by being born. Birth is essentially the beginning for each of us. But Jesus, of course, is eternal God from everlasting past who had no beginning. He is the ever-present One, the great I Am that I Am (Exodus 3:14). But after enduring the equivalent of eternity in hell on behalf of His people, He rose again. He revived (Romans 14:9) because He had satisfied the demands of God's law relating to the punishment for and absolution of His people's sins! It was as if He had in that sense a beginning! God speaks of Jesus as His only begotten Son (John 3:16). The word "begotten" implies that Jesus had a beginning. He had a beginning only because He arose from the second death.

Remember, to be eternally in hell is called **"the second death"** (Revelation 20:14). This is why the Bible says in Colossians 1:18:

> **And he is the head of the body, the church: who is the beginning, the firstborn from the dead; that in all *things* he might have the preeminence.**

Returning to the Passover, we read in Leviticus Chapter 23 of this special feast called the Passover that anticipated the wonderful fact that Jesus would be the firstborn from the dead. He, as the Lamb of God, would shed His blood, that is, give His life so that those He came to save would not suffer the eternal wrath of God.

Leviticus 23:5-6 says:

> **In the fourteenth day of the first month at even is the LORD'S passover. And on the fifteenth day of the same month is the feast of unleavened bread unto the LORD: seven days ye must eat unleavened bread.**

Speaking of the institution of the Passover, in the year 1447 B.C., God declared in Exodus 12:14:

And this day shall be unto you for a memorial; and ye shall keep it a feast to the LORD throughout your generations; ye shall keep it a feast by an ordinance for ever.

> *This Passover Feast anticipated and completely identified with the keystone, the centerpiece the very essence of the unfolding of God's salvation plan.*

This Passover Feast anticipated and completely identified with the keystone, the centerpiece, the very essence of the unfolding of God's salvation plan. God Himself in the person of the Lord Jesus Christ would provide a means by which God could have a great many human beings with Him throughout eternity future. But the human race was doomed because God's law decreed that the penalty for sin was eternal damnation, and the fallen human race was destined to experience that penalty.

With no exceptions, each and every human being throughout the history of the world are sinners. Only because Christ became the substitute, the stand-in, for those He chose to save, that is, He paid their penalty, could they live with Him throughout eternity future (John 15:16; Romans 5:19; 2 Corinthians 5:21; 2 Thessalonians 2:13; Hebrews 2:9-11; James 2:5).

Later, as we proceed down the timeline of history, we will learn that more than 1,400 years after Israel left Egypt, Christ fulfilled what this Passover Feast anticipated. In A.D. 33, Christ literally endured the wrath of God on behalf of those He came to save. On the very day the priests were in the temple killing the Passover lambs, Jesus, the ultimate Passover Lamb, was enduring the wrath of God as He hung on the cross.

The Passover day was to be observed on the fourteenth day of the first month of the Jewish calendar (Leviticus 23:5). The fourteenth day of that first month also became the first day of a seven-day period the Bible calls the Feast of Unleavened Bread.

We read in Deuteronomy 16:2-3:

Thou shalt therefore sacrifice the passover unto the LORD thy God, of the flock and the herd, in the place which the LORD shall choose to place his name there. Thou shalt eat no leavened bread

with it; seven days shalt thou eat unleavened bread therewith, even the bread of affliction; for thou camest forth out of the land of Egypt in haste: that thou mayest remember the day when thou camest forth out of the land of Egypt all the days of thy life.

The unleavened bread points to Christ, the Bread of Life. Those who become saved eat of the Living Bread and have their spiritual life sustained by the Pure Bread which is Christ (John 6:51). He declared **"I am that bread of life"** (John 6:48). We read in 1 Corinthians 5:7-8:

Purge out therefore the old leaven, that ye may be a new lump, as ye are unleavened. For even Christ our passover is sacrificed for us: Therefore let us keep the feast, not with old leaven, neither with the leaven of malice and wickedness; but with the unleavened bread of sincerity and truth.

The unleavened bread typifies that the power of sin, under which all are in bondage, is broken for the person who becomes saved.

The leaven (or yeast) which causes bread to ferment and thus to rise, in this setting, is a picture of sin. The unleavened bread typifies that the power of sin, under which all are in bondage, is broken for the person who becomes saved. That is, an individual who has become saved has spiritually experienced Christ as his Passover.

The Feast of Weeks

A second feast was instituted shortly after 1447 B.C. when Israel came out of Egypt. Among the many commands God gave to Moses, when Moses met with God on Mount Sinai, one order from God is recorded in Numbers 28:26:

Also in the day of the firstfruits, when ye bring a new meat offering unto the LORD, after your weeks be out, ye shall have an holy convocation; ye shall do no servile work.

This Feast of Firstfruits is called a "feast of weeks" in Deuteronomy 16:16 and a "feast of harvest" in Exodus 23:16. In the New Testament, this feast is called "Pentecost" (Acts 2:1). This feast was unusual because it followed the Passover Feast by a period of seven weeks plus one day (fifty days). The following is an outline of the Biblical teaching on this.

The command to observe this next feast day (which, as we have seen, was called the Feast of Firstfruits or the Feast of Weeks or the Feast of Harvest), ties this feast to the Feast of Unleavened Bread which began with the Passover. The rule was given that seven weeks after the first Sabbath after the Passover Day, the observance of this second feast was to occur (Leviticus 23:11-16; Joshua 5:10-11).

In A.D. 33, when Christ was crucified on Friday, Nisan 14 (Passover Day), the next day was Saturday the Sabbath. Saturday was the seventh day of the week and was, therefore, the Old Testament Sabbath day. Each week the seventh day was the Sabbath.

The Feast of Weeks was to be observed fifty days (seven weeks plus one day) after this Sabbath day following Passover. That is why the New Testament calls this feast day "Pentecost." The prefix "pente" signifies fifty. This fifty-day separation between a Sabbath day within the seven-day feast of unleavened bread and Pentecost tied the Passover very closely to Pentecost.

The Feast of Firstfruits or Weeks, or Pentecost, or Harvest, became a feast of great importance in the unfolding of God's salvation plan. It was on the very Day of Pentecost in A.D. 33 -- on that exact same day -- that God greatly implemented His grand plan of sending the Gospel into the world.

Remarkably, as we have already learned, on the very day the Passover lambs were killed in the temple, Jesus, as the Passover Lamb, was crucified. So, too, on the exact same day that the Jewish Feast of Firstfruits (Pentecost) was observed, the spiritual reality to which this feast pointed took place. Just as at the time national Israel celebrated the bringing in of the springtime harvest, which resulted from the seed that was planted after the observance of the Passover in that year, so the Feast of Firstfruits pointed to the harvest of saved people that would result from the sending forth of the Gospel into the world after the great event of Christ being crucified and then rising again.

The Feast of the Passover, first observed in 1447 B.C., anticipated and identified with the crucifixion of Christ in A.D. 33. In addition, we will see that the Feast of Harvest (or Firstfruits) anticipated and identified with the entire church age during which the world was harvested of those who became true believers. God used the local churches to send the Gospel into all the world so that the firstfruits of God's entire harvest could be brought into His Kingdom.

Very Occasionally a Translation Must be Corrected

The next feast day that we must examine is that of the Feast of the Seventh Month New Moon. However, before we will be able to understand the significance of this Feast more fully, we must make a few corrections in the English translation of the Bible. Of course, we would never attempt to make a correction of the original Hebrew of the Old Testament or the original Greek of the New Testament because those are the languages in which God wrote the Bible.

We absolutely would never desire to change what God Himself wrote.

We absolutely would never desire to change what God Himself wrote. But translators are not inspired by God, and therefore, their work is subject to correction if it can be shown that the original-language word of the Bible was not translated as carefully as it should have been.

For example, there are three distinctly different Hebrew words that are translated as our English word "trumpet." Yet, when we study the Biblical contexts in which these words are found, we learn that they each convey different spiritual meanings that are severely obscured when they are not carefully translated so that they remain three distinctly different words. We, therefore, must examine a few of these problem words before we can adequately continue our study of the Old Testament Feast days.

The Word "Trumpet"

There are three Hebrew words that are translated in our English language as the word "trumpet." They are *"taqoa,"* *"chatsotserah,"* and *"shophar."* The Hebrew word *"taqoa"* is used only once in the Bible (Ezekiel 7:14), and it comes from a root word *"taga"* which is ordinarily translated "to blow." Therefore, we cannot know what was blown or sounded in this verse where the Hebrew word *"taqoa"* is used.

The next Hebrew word is the word *"chatsotserah."* It refers to two silver trumpets that were musical instruments. This Hebrew word is always correctly translated as "trumpet." While these trumpets were normally sounded as musical instruments, occasionally, they were used to sound an alarm (Numbers 10:9). More significantly, they were sounded on the first day of each month (new moon) with the exception of the seventh month.

Numbers 10:10 declares:

Also in the day of your gladness, and in your solemn days, and in the beginnings of your months, ye shall blow with the trumpets over your burnt offerings, and over the sacrifices of your peace offerings; that they may be to you for a memorial before your God: I am the LORD your God.

We learn from this verse that the sounding of the silver trumpets was to remind Israel of the significance of the burnt offerings and peace offerings. In other words, they were blown on the first day of each month to remind Israel that their salvation was dependent upon the Messiah who would come and offer Himself as a burnt offering.

The third Hebrew word that is frequently translated as the word "trumpet" is the word "*shophar*." It is usually translated as our English word "trumpet," but additionally, in three instances, it is translated as "cornet."

The "*shophar*" was not a true musical instrument. It was a ram's horn that was used to give a loud blast of sound. It should never have been translated as "trumpet" or "cornet" because these incorrect translations seriously obscure the spiritual meaning that was conveyed by the blowing of the ram's horn. We will see this as we continue this study.

While we are making correction of the translation of Hebrew words, two other words should be examined very carefully. They are the Hebrew words "*teruah*" and "*yobel*."

The Hebrew word "*teruah*" is correctly translated in a number of ways, but also, upon occasion, it is translated altogether incorrectly. The Hebrew word "*teruah*" is used thirty-six times in the Bible. It is used at times of great joy or at the anticipation of great victory. For example, at the time the walls of Jericho fell, the priests gave a great shout (*teruah*), and the walls fell down flat (Joshua 6:20). At the time the ark was brought into Jerusalem, there was shouting (*teruah*) and the sound of many musical instruments (1 Chronicles 15:28). When the foundation of the temple was laid in Ezra's day, there was the shout (*teruah*) of joy (Ezra 3:13). Sometimes the anticipation of victory was on the part of the enemies of Israel as in Jeremiah 4:19, where God portrays the sorrow of Jeremiah as he hears **"the alarm [*teruah*] of war."** Jeremiah had been told by God that the enemy would be completely victorious.

"*Teruah*" is a Hebrew word that is also correctly translated as "jubilee." We read in Leviticus 25:9:

Then shalt thou cause the trumpet [Hebrew *shophar*, ram's horn]

of the jubilee [Hebrew *teruah*] to sound on the tenth day of the seventh month, in the day of atonement shall ye make the trumpet [Hebrew *shophar*, ram's horn] sound throughout all your land.

In two verses of the Bible, the Hebrew word "*teruah*" is incorrectly translated as "blowing of trumpets." In these verses, a more accurate translation would have been the word "jubilee" as was done in Leviticus 25:9 which is quoted above. These two verses are Numbers 29:1 and Leviticus 23:24.

In one additional verse, Numbers 31:6, the word "*teruah*" is translated as "blow" and would have been better translated as "of the alarm."

Before we harmonize these verses together, we must also examine the Hebrew word "*yobel*." The Hebrew word "*yobel*" should always be translated as "jubilee." While ordinarily this has been done by the translators, in one very significant place it is incorrectly translated "trumpet." Moreover, in a later chapter of the Bible, which we will carefully examine later in this study, it is repeatedly translated as "rams' horns."

The Feast of the Seventh Month New Moon[2]

With the above corrections in mind, we can now return to the feast days of the Old Testament. We began to examine the Feast of the Seventh Month new moon. There are verses that teach us the significance of this feast day.

Leviticus 23:24:

Speak unto the children of Israel, saying, In the seventh month, in the first *day* of the month, shall ye have a sabbath, a memorial of blowing of trumpets [Hebrew *teruah*, jubilee], an holy convocation.

Numbers 29:1:

And in the seventh month, on the first *day* of the month, ye shall have an holy convocation; ye shall do no servile work: it is a day of <u>blowing the trumpets</u> [Hebrew *teruah*, jubilee] unto you.

---

[2] Theologians frequently speak of this feast as the Feast of Trumpets. This is altogether an incorrect naming of this feast.

Psalm 81:3:

Blow up the trumpet [Hebrew *shophar*, ram's horn] in the new moon, in the time appointed, on our solemn feast day.

Remember it was the silver trumpets that were to be blown on the new moon days. Therefore, because it was the ram's horn that was blown on this new moon day mentioned in Psalm 81:3, this particular new moon day has to have occurred on the seventh month new moon which is also called a feast day in this verse.

Moreover, when we look ahead at the day of atonement, which was to be observed the tenth day of the seventh month, we will discover that the ram's horn was blown on that day as well, closely identifying the day of atonement with the word "jubilee" which is translated from the Hebrew word "*teruah*."

We read in Leviticus 25:9:

Then shalt thou cause [Hebrew *shophar*, ram's horn] the trumpet of the jubile [Hebrew *teruah*] to sound on the tenth *day* of the seventh month, in the day of atonement shall ye make the trumpet [Hebrew *shophar*, ram's horn] sound throughout all your land.

When we harmonize the verses we have been examining, we arrive at the following conclusions.

1. Except for the *seventh* month new moon, upon each month's new moon day, the silver trumpets were to be blown as a memorial of the burnt and peace offerings.

2. The seventh month new moon was a feast day on which the ram's horn was to be blown as a memorial of the jubilee.

3. On the *tenth day* of the seventh month, the ram's horn of the jubilee was to be sounded throughout the land. This was the Day of Atonement.

Thus, we discover that the first day (new moon day) of the seventh month, and the tenth day of the seventh month (the Day of Atonement), were closely identified with the Jubilee. Therefore, we should now carefully examine the Bible's teaching concerning the Jubilee. Why is it so closely linked to both the Feast of the Seventh Month New Moon and to the Day of Atonement? Let us first learn a bit more about the Day of Atonement.

The Day of Atonement

Nine days after the Feast of the Seventh Month New Moon, the Day of Atonement was to be observed. On this Day of Atonement, the high priest was to change from his glorious garments into simple linen clothing. After the temple was cleared of any other priests or occupants, and after offering suitable sacrifices, he was to enter into the Holy of Holies to sprinkle blood on the mercy seat which was the covering on the ark of the covenant. He would come into the Holy of Holies with burning incense so that the cloud from the incense would cover the mercy seat (Leviticus 16:2-29). Leviticus16:30-33 declares:

> **For on that day shall the priest make an atonement for you, to cleanse you, that ye may be clean from all your sins before the LORD. It shall be a sabbath of rest unto you, and ye shall afflict your souls, by a statute for ever. And the priest, whom he shall anoint, and whom he shall consecrate to minister in the priest's office in his father's stead, shall make the atonement, and shall put on the linen clothes, even the holy garments: and he shall make an atonement for the holy sanctuary, and he shall make an atonement for the tabernacle of the congregation, and for the altar, and he shall make an atonement for the priests, and for all the people of the congregation.**

A commentary on this holy activity that was carried out once a year on the Day of Atonement is recorded in Hebrews 9:11-12 where we read:

> **But Christ being come an high priest of good things to come, by a greater and more perfect tabernacle, not made with hands, that is to say, not of this building; neither by the blood of goats and calves, but by his own blood he entered in once into the holy place, having obtained eternal redemption for us.**

Thus, God teaches us that the Day of Atonement is completely focused on Christ as the Savior who was sacrificed in order to provide an eternal redemption for those He came to save. On this Day of Atonement, God commanded that while the high priest was making atonement for all of Israel, the Israelites were to afflict their souls.

Leviticus 16:29-31:

> **And this shall be a statute for ever unto you: that in the seventh**

month, on the tenth day of the month, ye shall afflict your souls, and do no work at all, whether it be one of your own country, or a stranger that sojourneth among you: for on that day shall the priest make an atonement for you, to cleanse you, that ye may be clean from all your sins before the LORD. It shall be a sabbath of rest unto you, and ye shall <u>afflict your souls</u>, by a statute for ever.

> *Why does God command Israel to afflict their souls?*

Why does God command Israel to afflict their souls? Should this not be a super happy day for true believers who were typified by the nation of Israel? What could be more wonderful than to know that sins were paid for?

The phrase "afflict your souls" is indeed to be understood as something very joyful. However, to understand its meaning, we must see that the Bible is its own dictionary. The term translated "afflict your souls" can be found in another part of the Bible. In Isaiah 58:3, 5 we read:

> **Wherefore have we fasted, say they, and thou seest not? wherefore have we <u>afflicted our soul</u>, and thou takest no knowledge? Behold, in the day of your fast ye find pleasure. . . . Is it such a fast that I have chosen? a day for a man to <u>afflict his soul</u>? . . .**

In this very revealing passage, God is connecting the "affliction of the soul" with "fasting." Therefore, on the Day of Atonement, when Israel was commanded to afflict their souls, Israel was to fast. But why were they to fast? What did that signify? The answer is given in Isaiah 58:6-7:

> **Is not this the fast that I have chosen? to loose the bands of wickedness, to undo the heavy burdens, and to let the oppressed go free, and that ye break every yoke? Is it not to deal thy bread to the hungry, and that thou bring the poor that are cast out to thy house? when thou seest the naked, that thou cover him; and that thou hide not thyself from thine own flesh?**

All of the phrases in these verses are metaphorically pointing to sending forth the Gospel. The unsaved are those in bondage to wickedness, are those under the burden of sin, who are spiritually hungry for the bread of life (who is

Christ Himself), who are spiritually naked, etc. God is teaching that the fasting God desires is that of sending forth the Gospel. He undoubtedly links fasting to sending forth the Gospel because the true believers are to deny themselves and follow Him (Jesus Christ) who came to bring the Gospel to the world (Luke 9:23).

Therefore, in a very hidden way, God tied the Day of Atonement to the true believers' glorious task of publishing the Gospel to the whole world. The command to Israel to afflict their souls on the Day of Atonement was pointing to the action of every true believer sending the Gospel into all the world – the Gospel that declares that Christ has made full atonement for the sins of all His true people.

> *Through Jesus Christ, people are set free from the tyranny of Satan and from their awful bondage to sin.*

We now can understand why God linked the Day of Atonement to the Jubilee. Remember we read in Leviticus 25:9 that the "*shophar*" (ram's horn) of the jubilee was to be sounded in the Day of Atonement. Remember that same verse also stipulated that the "*shophar*" (ram's horn) was to be sounded "throughout all your land."

The following verse, Leviticus 25:10, teaches that this proclamation, that was to be sounded throughout the land, was to be a proclamation of liberty. Liberty, of course, is the very heart of the Gospel. Through Jesus Christ, people are set free from the tyranny of Satan and from their awful bondage to sin. They escape the terrible wrath of God which all of us rightly deserve because of our sin. This proclamation of liberty is precisely what God's people proclaim as they send the Gospel into the world.

Remember, we have just learned from the Bible that "to afflict our souls" means to fast. To fast means to deny ourselves as we send the Gospel into the world. To send the Gospel into the world means to proclaim spiritual liberty throughout the land. The proclamation of spiritual liberty, which is the Gospel of salvation throughout the world, is completely identified with the Jubilee, proclaiming liberty throughout the land.

A significant emphasis on the word "jubilee" is recorded in Exodus Chapter 19. The setting is Mount Sinai on which Christ met with Moses to give him the law. The law of God identifies with God as the Judge of all the earth. Because of our transgression of God's law, that is, because of our sin, we cannot come to God. Only if the guilt of our sins has been removed can we freely come to Him. So God commanded Israel in Exodus 19:12-13:

And thou shalt set bounds unto the people round about, saying, Take heed to yourselves, that ye go not up into the mount, or touch the border of it: whosoever toucheth the mount shall be surely put to death: there shall not an hand touch it, but he shall surely be stoned, or shot through; whether it be beast or man, it shall not live: when the trumpet [Hebrew *yobel*, jubilee] soundeth long, they shall come up to the mount.

The message is very clear. Death, pointing to the second death (eternal damnation), awaits every human being because our sins have brought us completely under the wrath of God, despite the fact that God created us to live with Him.

> *...the Jubilee is a reference to publishing throughout the world the wonderful news that the time of liberty has come.*

But!!! look at the last part of verse 13. There we read, **"when the [jubilee] soundeth long, they shall come up to the mount."** Wonderfully, we see in this verse the very essence of the Gospel. Remember we are learning that the Jubilee is a reference to publishing throughout the world the wonderful news that the time of liberty has come. It is the most important of all liberties because it means to be set free from the tyranny of Satan and from the bondage of sin. It means to become free to eternally serve God as Savior and Lord. It means to have been set free from the penalty for sin that is demanded by the perfect law of God. It was a beautiful portrait showing that in the time of Jubilee, through Christ, a saved individual can come into the presence of God without fear of punishment.

When the Jubilee sounded, Israel could come to Mount Sinai from where God spoke to them. In like manner, forgiven human beings can come to Mount Zion and not be destroyed. Their sins have been paid for (Hebrews 12:18-24)! Genuine Christians have become free to come to God as their loving heavenly Father. Jubilee is a word that signifies all the blessings that flow from the Gospel of salvation.

Therefore, we can readily understand that Christ Himself is the very essence of the Jubilee. Even as Christ is the very essence of the Day of Atonement when the Jubilee was to be sounded, so we see Christ as the Jubilee who is to be proclaimed to the whole world.

We are beginning to understand the significance of the concept of the Jubilee. As we continue our study, we will learn how intimately the Jubilee concept is related to the timeline of history as God unfolds His salvation program. But the Bible has more to say about the Jubilee, and we must be certain that our present conclusions concerning it are in harmony with all that the Bible says about the Jubilee.

As we search the Bible, we discover that every fiftieth year beginning with the year 1407 B.C. is a Jubilee year. Therefore, we should now learn what the Bible says about each fiftieth year being a Jubilee year.

The Jubilee Year

When Israel came into the land of Canaan, they were to observe that first year as a Sabbath Year. God's Law for Israel given to Moses on Mount Sinai stated in Leviticus 25:2:

> **Speak unto the children of Israel, and say unto them, When ye come into the land which I give you, then shall the land keep a sabbath unto the LORD.**

Following this first seven years, they were to continue observing a Sabbath Year every six years until seven periods of seven years had elapsed. We read in Leviticus 25:8:

> **And thou shalt number seven sabbaths of years unto thee, seven times seven years; and the space of the seven sabbaths of years shall be unto thee forty and nine years.**

After these forty-nine years had occurred, the next year, which was the fiftieth year, was to be a Jubilee year. The Bible declares in Leviticus 25:10:

> **And ye shall hallow the fiftieth year, and proclaim liberty throughout all the land unto all the inhabitants thereof: it shall be a jubile unto you; and ye shall return every man unto his possession, and ye shall return every man unto his family.**

Thus, the Jubilee was a year in length. Moreover, as this verse indicates, it was a day when liberty was to be proclaimed throughout all the land.

Since the Jubilee Year was a year that came fifty years after Israel came into Canaan in the year 1407 B.C., the year 1357 B.C. was a Jubilee year.

Moreover, every fifty years thereafter would have been a Jubilee year. Thus, the years 1307 B.C., 1257 B.C., 1207 B.C., 1157 B.C., etc. through to 7 B.C. would have been Jubilee years. In the New Testament era, A.D. 1994 would also identify as a Jubilee year, since A.D. 1994 was exactly 40 x 50 years after 7 B.C. If the world would exist for another fifty years, the year A.D. 2044 would be the next Jubilee Year.

> In the New Testament era, A.D. 1994 would also identify as a Jubilee year, since A.D. 1994 was exactly 40 x 50 years after 7 B.C.

We thus far have learned a number of facts concerning the Feast of the Seventh Month New Moon, the Day of Atonement, and the Jubilee Year. We can summarize them as follows.

1. The first day of the seventh month was a feast day with a focus on being reminded of a "jubilee." Thus, it was a day in which special focus should be on the Jubilee Year.

2. The Day of Atonement identified altogether with the Lord Jesus Christ who, as the Savior, entered the Heavenly Holy of Holies with His own blood thus providing eternal forgiveness for all whom Christ came to save (Hebrews 9:24). On that day, the people of Israel were to afflict themselves which pointed to the sending forth of the Gospel of salvation (spiritual liberty) into all the world.

3. Beginning with the year 1407 B.C., every fiftieth year was designated as a Jubilee year. Thus both the years 7 B.C. and 1994 A.D. are Jubilee years.

4. Christ Himself was the very essence of the Jubilee. We will learn He was born in a Jubilee year (7 B.C.), in all likelihood on October 1, which was the Day of Atonement on which day the jubilee was to be sounded.

It is very curious that God gave strict commands concerning the timing and character of the Jubilee Year. Yet we do not read anywhere in the Bible that

Israel ever actually observed the Jubilee Year. However, when we see that the Jubilee Year had everything to do with sending the Gospel into the world, then we see that indeed it was an event that became an exceedingly important, integral part of the history of the world.

The key to our understanding of the Jubilee Year is in Luke 4:18-19:

> **The Spirit of the Lord is upon me, because he hath anointed me to preach the gospel to the poor; he hath sent me to heal the brokenhearted, to preach deliverance to the captives, and recovering of sight to the blind, to set at liberty them that are bruised, to preach the acceptable year of the Lord.**

The language that describes the "acceptable year'" is very parallel to the language that describes the "Jubilee Year." We read in Leviticus 25:10:

> **And ye shall hallow the fiftieth year, and proclaim liberty throughout all the land unto all the inhabitants thereof: it shall be a jubile unto you; and ye shall return every man unto his possession, and ye shall return every man unto his family.**

Both of these citations are focused on the concept of preaching deliverance or liberty. While the Luke 4 account does not mention the sending forth of the Gospel into all the world, we do know that this worldwide hearing of the Gospel is intimately identified with the language God sets forth in Luke 4:18-19. Thus, the teaching given concerning the "acceptable year" in fact is parallel to that given in connection with the "Jubilee Year" during which "liberty throughout all the land" was to be proclaimed.

We also know that the "acceptable year" was not a year that lasted 365 days. Actually, it encompassed the entire period that the Gospel was to go forth. Thus, we can also know, therefore, that the Jubilee Year, which would begin on one of the years in the fifty-year sequence established in Leviticus Chapter 25, would actually continue throughout the entire time that the Gospel was to be sent into the world.

> *Jesus is the very essence of the Jubilee, and as we shall learn, He was born in the Jubilee year of 7 B.C.*

Therefore, since Jesus is the very essence of the Jubilee, and as we shall learn, He was born in the Jubilee year of 7 B.C., we can know that His birth was the Biblical fulfillment of the principle of the Jubilee Year and could be considered the beginning of a Jubilee period. Later in our study, we will be able to show from the Biblical data that there is a good possibility that Jesus was born on the Day of Atonement, which we have learned is intimately focused on the Jubilee Year. In addition, we will learn that He was announced as the "Lamb of God" in A.D. 29, on the first day of the seventh month, which we have learned is also the day in the year that is intimately associated with the Jubilee Year.

Furthermore, we will learn that this first Jubilee period came to an end at the end of the church age. Following this, there was a brief period when no one was being saved. However, following this sad time, in the Jubilee Year A.D. 1994, a second Jubilee or Acceptable Year began. It will continue to the day that Christ returns on the clouds when every eye will see Him (Revelation 1:7). That will occur at the very end of the world.

We thus are learning, as we continue our study, the beautiful and cohesive fashion in which all of the language of the Bible fits into the unfolding of God's salvation program which alone governs the timeline of history.

Now we will continue going down the highway of time. The next significant milestone is the important year 1407 B.C.

1407 B.C. Israel Enters the Land of Canaan

Slowly, we are proceeding down the path of history. As we are proceeding, we are witnessing how God is showing us that the time line of history is the unfolding of His salvation plan.

We have now come to another milestone. It is the entrance of the nation of Israel into the land of Canaan. It was the same land that was abandoned by Jacob and his family 470 years earlier. But first we should learn that the Bible tells us that though Israel left Egypt in 1447 B.C., it was not until 1407 B.C. that the children of Israel reached their destination. God caused Israel to wander in the wilderness for these forty years. Earlier, when spying out the land, Israel had feared the heathen inhabitants of the land and had refused to go into the land as God had commanded them (Numbers Chapters 13 and 14; Hebrews 3:16-19). As a severe judgment upon the people, God delayed Israel's entrance into Canaan until all those who were at that time twenty years old and older died in the wilderness.

After Israel (Jacob's descendants) departed from Egypt in the year 1447 B.C., and as they began their wilderness journey, they first spent about a year at Mount Sinai which was located in the wilderness of Arabia. While they were there, several important events took place. The first event was the giving of a written law book to Israel. While they were encamped by Mount Sinai, Moses went high into the mountain to talk with God. God wrote on two tables of stone ten commandments that summarized how mankind was to relate to God and to their fellowman.

> *...even though for over 1500 years God would continue to add to the Bible, beginning in the year after Israel left Egypt, there was available to mankind a written record of many of God's laws.*

In addition, God gave Moses a great number of other commandments that were to be observed by Israel and which are presently part of the Bible. Fact is, before Moses died, forty years after leaving Egypt, God had given Moses all of the information contained in the first five books of our present Bible. God gave laws concerning those who were qualified to serve as priests and laws concerning burnt offerings and blood sacrifices which were to assist Israel in understanding something about the Messiah, the Lord Jesus Christ, who was coming to save sinners. Thus, even though for over 1500 years God would continue to add to the Bible, beginning in the year after Israel left Egypt, there was available to mankind a written record of many of God's laws.

Moreover, while camping at Mount Sinai, God caused a beautiful tabernacle to be built (Exodus Chapters 35-40). This was an external representation of the kingdom of God even as the nation of Israel had become an external representation of the Kingdom of God. In its design, many aspects of God's marvelous salvation program were anticipated. Fact is, it remained the chief worship center for more than 300 years after Israel came into the land of Canaan.

Within the tabernacle was the Holy of Holies. Within the Holy of Holies was the ark of the covenant with its golden cover called the mercy seat. Within the ark of the covenant were two tables of stone on which the ten commandments were written (Exodus 31:18, 34:27-28; Hebrews 9:4). Above the mercy seat were two cherubim with outstretched wings looking down on the mercy seat (Exodus 25:20, 37:9). The cherubim spiritually represented God as the Judge who looks upon the Law of God which was represented by the ten commandments.

But in between the judge (cherubim) and the law (ten commandments) was the mercy seat (the covering of the ark) which represented Christ as the Savior. For all of those whom Christ came to save, He took upon Himself the judgment of God. This wonderful fact was typified by the mercy seat which shielded the application of the law of God upon those who were saved. Thus, the full gaze of God the Judge was on Christ, the Mercy Seat.

> *In God's divine development of His salvation plan during the Old Testament time, the character of that salvation plan was veiled.*

In God's divine development of His salvation plan during the Old Testament time, the character of that salvation plan was veiled. It was faintly revealed by the multitude of ceremonial laws that were to be observed. It was also veiled in that the portrait of God's salvation plan, demonstrated by the cherubim and the ark of the covenant with its mercy seat, was located within the Holy of Holies. No one could look within the Holy of Holies except the high priest. And even he entered the Holy of Holies only once a year on the day of atonement to sprinkle blood on the mercy seat. However, he entered the Holy of Holies with burning incense so that, even to his eyes, the cherubim and the ark were obscured by the cloud of incense (see the Book of Hebrews in the Bible).

However, when Christ was on the cross, the great curtain that separated the Holy of Holies from the rest of the temple was torn open from top to bottom (Matthew 27:51). In this way, God demonstrated that His salvation plan was no longer hidden but was to be published to all of the world (see Hebrews Chapter 9). Indeed the Jubilee had come!

Another outstanding event continued to be observed during the forty years Israel was in the wilderness. It was the fact that God continually showed His presence with the nation of Israel in a most dramatic fashion. On each and every day, a cloud covered the tabernacle, and each and every night, this cloud appeared as fire. We read in Exodus 40:34-38:

> **Then a cloud covered the tent of the congregation, and the glory of the LORD filled the tabernacle. And Moses was not able to enter into the tent of the congregation, because the cloud abode thereon, and the glory of the LORD filled the tabernacle. And when the cloud was taken up from over the tabernacle, the children of Israel went onward in all their journeys: but if the cloud were not taken up, then they journeyed not till the day that it was taken up. For the cloud of the LORD was upon the tabernacle by day, and fire was on it by night, in the sight of all the house of Israel, throughout all their journeys.**

In the Bible, clouds and fire signify judgment. Thus, by this cloud and fire, God was constantly reminding Israel that, as humans created in the image of God, they were accountable to God. Therefore, as they experienced sin, they should know they were in deep trouble with God. Therefore, they should be constantly looking to God for His mercy and forgiveness.

God was constantly reminding Israel that, as humans created in the image of God, they were accountable to God.

This forty years in the wilderness is a portrait of our life in this world. Fact is, God continues this portrait in Revelation Chapter 12 where He portrays a woman in the wilderness. That woman represents the true believers in Christ especially as they live throughout the New Testament era (the one thousand two hundred sixty days of Revelation 12:6). Later, we will show how this 1260 days represents the whole New Testament era.

As we live in the wilderness of this world, we do not see a cloud or pillar of fire as a representation of the Law of God. But we do have the Bible. The Bible is a constant reminder to mankind that each and every one of us is accountable to God. There will be a Judgment Throne at the end of the world which every individual must face. Only if Jesus has become an individual's Savior will that person escape that awful trial which results in the unsaved being condemned to eternal damnation.

God also gave striking symbols that pointed to God as the Savior.

Even though God, by means of the fire and the cloud, primarily identified the reality of God as the Judge to whom someday each individual must answer, God also gave striking symbols that pointed to God as the Savior. For example, for forty years, God kept Israel in a hot, desolate wilderness where the scarcity of food and water were at times very great problems. To solve the food problem, God provided a food named "manna" which, on six mornings of each and every week, covered the ground. The manna was a representation of Christ who is the bread of life (John 6:47-51). Just as manna provided food to sustain life physically, so Christ as the Bread of Life provides eternal life to all who become saved.

Secondly, when water was not available, God provided water from a rock. This miraculous water represented the Gospel which comes from Jesus who was represented by the rock.

Unfortunately, even though the wandering nation of Israel, during their forty years in the wilderness, externally represented the Kingdom of God, the vast majority of the nation was not saved. As we mentioned earlier, the Bible discloses to us that virtually all of those who were twenty years or older when they left Egypt perished in the wilderness because of unbelief. We read this sad news in Hebrews 3:17-19:

> **But with whom was he grieved forty years? Was it not with them that had sinned, whose carcases fell in the wilderness? And to whom sware he that they should not enter into his rest, but to them that believed not? So we see that they could not enter in because of unbelief.**

And we read in Joshua 5:6:

> **For the children of Israel walked forty years in the wilderness, till all the people that were men of war, which came out of Egypt, were consumed, because they obeyed not the voice of the LORD: unto whom the LORD sware that he would not shew them the land, which the LORD sware unto their fathers that he would give us, a land that floweth with milk and honey.**

This is a huge lesson to all of us. We must never presume, just because we believe we are a Christian, or just because we have been baptized, or just because we are a faithful church member, or just because we live decent moral lives, that these actions mean that we are truly saved. The evidence of salvation is that we have an ongoing, intense desire to be obedient to all of God's commandments. That is, we are happiest when we are doing God's will.

One very important command God gave to Israel was the law that was concerned with the seventh day Sabbath. On the seventh day of each week, Israel was not to do any work of any kind. God in many Bible citations explained the importance of keeping this command. For example, in Exodus 31:13-15, God warned:

> **Speak thou also unto the children of Israel, saying, Verily my sabbaths ye shall keep: for it is a sign between me and you throughout your generations; that ye may know that I am the LORD that doth sanctify you. Ye shall keep the sabbath therefore; for it is holy unto you: every one that defileth it shall surely be put to death: for whosoever doeth any work therein,**

that soul shall be cut off from among his people. Six days may work be done; but in the seventh is the sabbath of rest, holy to the LORD: whosoever doeth any work in the sabbath day, he shall surely be put to death.

This command, like the commands concerning burnt offerings and blood sacrifices, was ceremonial in nature. That is, as Israel ceased from all work on each Sabbath Day, they were reminded that they were not to trust in any work that they did as a means to help them become saved.

The Bible teaches that all of the work required to save any individual was done entirely by Jesus. If, for example, a person believes he can become saved by accepting Jesus, or by praying a certain kind of prayer, or by being baptized in water, or by any other action *he* might perform, he becomes like someone who has done some work on the seventh day Sabbath. He, therefore, will be cut off by God. That is, he is still subject to eternal damnation.

Thus, the seventh day Sabbath command effectively is teaching that the work of salvation is 100% the work of God. Indeed, later in our study, we will discover that the principle hidden in the seventh day Sabbath, that all the work of salvation was done by Christ, has become greatly highlighted by God in our day as God's whole salvation program is nearing its end. We will find that the violation of the spiritual application of this ceremonial law is one of the most serious sins of the church age.

But now we should return to Israel in the wilderness. After wandering for forty years in the wilderness, God finally prepared Israel to go into the promised land, the land of Canaan. Before they crossed the Jordan River into the land of Canaan, Moses, under the inspiration of God, gave them instructions concerning certain truths the nation of Israel were to keep in mind. They are truths that each of us whom Christ saves are to keep in mind because each word applies to us just as well as them. For example, in Deuteronomy 6:14-15 God warned:

Ye shall not go after other gods, of the gods of the people which are round about you; (For the LORD thy God is a jealous God among you) lest the anger of the LORD thy God be kindled against thee, and destroy thee from off the face of the earth.

In Deuteronomy 7:7-8, God declared to them:

The LORD did not set his love upon you, nor choose you, because ye were more in number than any people; for ye were the fewest of all people: But because the LORD loved you, and

because he would keep the oath which he had sworn unto your fathers, hath the LORD brought you out with a mighty hand, and redeemed you out of the house of bondmen, from the hand of Pharaoh king of Egypt.

In Deuteronomy 6:6-7, God instructed:

And these words, which I command thee this day, shall be in thine heart: And thou shalt teach them diligently unto thy children, and shalt talk of them when thou sittest in thine house, and when thou walkest by the way, and when thou liest down, and when thou risest up.

These truths are typical of many given to ancient Israel as well as to all of us today.

The Crossing of the Jordan River

And so God brought Israel to the Jordan River to cross over into the land of Canaan. It had been exactly forty years and three days since they left Egypt. Moses had died a few weeks earlier, and their new leader was a man named Joshua. On March 25, 1407 B.C., four days before the celebration of the Passover, God miraculously parted the rain-swollen waters of the Jordan River, and Israel crossed over on dry ground. They finally were in the promised land.

> *The details of the entrance into Canaan are very significant in showing God's salvation plan which He had been unfolding.*

The details of the entrance into Canaan are very significant in showing God's salvation plan which He had been unfolding. The time was the spring of the year (actually, March 25) when the Jordan River, which had to be crossed, was at flood stage. Therefore, it was a formidable barrier that a nation of perhaps two million people must cross.

This gave opportunity to God to demonstrate in a wonderful way the glorious salvation plan which was the object of the whole history of the world. Remember that the land of Canaan, which more than six hundred years earlier had been given to Abraham, was a picture or representation of the kingdom of God which true believers enter into when they become saved.

The swollen Jordan River was a picture or representation of hell or the eternal damnation that is the penalty that must be paid by all of mankind as a result of their sins. The nation of Israel was a picture or representation of those who become saved. We must remember that before God can forgive sins and bring anyone into the kingdom of God, the penalty God's law demands as payment for our sins must be made. Therefore, to illustrate how this payment was to be made on behalf of those whom God brings into the kingdom of God, God performed a great miracle in connection with this entrance of Israel into the land of Canaan.

First of all, God separated from Israel the priests who carried the ark of the covenant. Remember, this ark was the golden box normally kept hidden in the Holy of Holies of the tabernacle and which represented Jesus as the Savior.

In Joshua 3:3-4 the Bible records:

And they commanded the people, saying, When ye see the ark of the covenant of the LORD your God, and the priests the Levites bearing it, then ye shall remove from your place, and go after it. Yet there shall be a space between you and it, about two thousand cubits by measure: come not near unto it, that ye may know the way by which ye must go: for ye have not passed this way heretofore.

In Joshua 3:15-16 we read:

And as they that bare the ark were come unto Jordan, and the feet of the priests that bare the ark were dipped in the brim of the water, (for Jordan overfloweth all his banks all the time of harvest,) that the waters which came down from above stood and rose up upon an heap very far from the city Adam, that is beside Zaretan: and those that came down toward the sea of the plain, even the salt sea, failed, and were cut off: and the people passed over right against Jericho.

The truly saved person, as it were, has gone through an eternity of hell and come out on the other end with the penalty for sin completely, totally paid!

The priests with the ark remained on the dry river bed of the Jordan River until all of Israel had crossed over into the land of Canaan on dry ground. The spiritual lesson being taught is that Christ, typified by the ark in the river, endured the wrath of God on behalf of those whom God saves. The truly saved person, as it were, has gone through an eternity of hell and come out on the other end with the penalty for sin completely, totally paid!

Once those sins were paid for, Christ, too, came out of hell, as typified by the language of Joshua 4:18:

> **And it came to pass, when the priests that bare the ark of the covenant of the LORD were come up out of the midst of Jordan, and the soles of the priests' feet were lifted up unto the dry land, that the waters of Jordan returned unto their place, and flowed over all his banks, as they did before.**

To further point to God's salvation program, twelve stones from the dry land were placed in the bottom of the river before the ark came out of the river. This typified the fact that those whom Christ came to save, if it had not been for His paying for their sins, they personally should have spent an eternity in hell paying for their sins.

Additionally, another twelve stones were taken out of the bottom of the river, and they were erected as a monument on the Canaan side of the river. The setting up of these twelve stones typified that all of those who have become saved were saved from enduring the eternal wrath of God.

The miraculous crossing of the Jordan River took place in the year 1407 B.C., exactly 1,400 years before Christ was born, in the year 7 B.C., and exactly 1,440 years inclusive from A.D. 33 when Christ actually did endure hell as payment for the sins of all His true eternal people.

It also occurred precisely 3,400 years before A.D. 1994 when Christ came as the Jubilee to announce to the world that through Christ, sinners can be set at liberty from their sins. Indeed, we can see that the year 1407 B.C. was an important milestone in the development of the Calendar of history.

The following table summarizes the spiritual significance of the numbers "1,400," "1,440" and "3,400." *

---

* See Chapter 8 of this study for a more detailed study of God's use of numbers in the Bible.

Number	Spiritual Significance
Since ... 2	signifies those who are caretakers of the Gospel
7	signifies perfect completeness
10	signifies completeness
12	signifies fullness
17	signifies heaven
Therefore ... $1,400 = 2 \times 7 \times 10 \times 10$	conveys the information that in the perfect completeness of God's timetable for the believers, Christ was born
$1,440 = 12 \times 12 \times 10$	conveys the information that in the complete fullness of time, Christ came as the Savior
$3,400 = 2 \times 100 \times 17$	conveys the information that believers, in the completion of time, would still become saved, that is, they would become identified with heaven

Israel Faces the Wicked Cities of Canaan

More than 700 years earlier, in the year 2092 B.C., God had given the land of Canaan to Abraham. As near as we can tell, the land at that time had relatively few inhabitants within it. But after 700 years, the land of Canaan had many walled cities within it, and the population was greatly increased.

These cities had become extremely wicked, and it was God's plan to destroy them because of their wickedness. We can remember how, at a much earlier time in history, God destroyed the whole world which had become exceedingly wicked. This was by means of the Flood of Noah's day. We might also remember how, in the days of Abraham, God destroyed Sodom, Gomorrah, Admah, and Zeboim because of their wickedness. Just forty years earlier than the year 1407 B.C., God had destroyed the Egyptian armies in the Red Sea because of their wickedness. And we have learned that even all the men of Israel, because of their wickedness, died during the forty years that Israel was in the wilderness as they journeyed to the land of Canaan.

> *God's plan was to use the men of Israel to be the executioners.*

Now, it was the wicked cities of Canaan which were about to be destroyed because of their wickedness. But this time it is different. God's plan was to use the men of Israel to be the executioners. In Deuteronomy 7:23-24 we read:

> **But the LORD thy God shall deliver them unto thee, and shall destroy them with a mighty destruction, until they be destroyed. And he shall deliver their kings into thine hand, and thou shalt destroy their name from under heaven: there shall no man be able to stand before thee, until thou have destroyed them.**

God also commanded in Deuteronomy 12:2-3:

> **Ye shall utterly destroy all the places, wherein the nations which ye shall possess served their gods, upon the high mountains, and upon the hills, and under every green tree: and ye shall overthrow their altars, and break their pillars, and burn their groves with fire; and ye shall hew down the graven images of their gods, and destroy the names of them out of that place.**

God further commanded in Deuteronomy 9:4-5:

> **Speak not thou in thine heart, after that the LORD thy God hath cast them out from before thee, saying, For my righteousness the LORD hath brought me in to possess this land: but for the wickedness of these nations the LORD doth drive them out from before thee. Not for thy righteousness, or for the uprightness of thine heart, dost thou go to possess their land: but for the wickedness of these nations the LORD thy God doth drive them out from before thee, and that he may perform the word which the LORD sware unto thy fathers, Abraham, Isaac, and Jacob.**

Please note that in verse 5, God is indicating His faithfulness to the promises He had made more than 700 years earlier to Abraham, Isaac, and

Jacob. Those promises included the statement that the whole land of Canaan had been given to the descendants of Abraham, Isaac, and Jacob as an eternal possession.

Because Israel was not altogether obedient to the commands of God concerning the destruction of the wicked and concerning the commands not to worship any of the heathen gods, Israel, in turn, experienced many chastisements from God. God sets forth His rule on this matter in Deuteronomy 8:5:

Thou shalt also consider in thine heart, that, as a man chasteneth his son, so the LORD thy God chasteneth thee.

Therefore, looking ahead for a moment, during the 360 years following Israel's return to the land of Canaan, Israel experienced many periods of oppression by enemies in the land. Each time, the Lord delivered them, but repeatedly, they disobeyed God so that repeatedly God brought an enemy upon them to oppress them.

However, in spite of these recurring difficulties, many of the cities were destroyed by Israel, and God divided the entire land of Canaan to the nation of Israel, giving each of the tribes of Israel a portion of the land.

We Can Understand All of the Killing

The Bible record of the conquest of Canaan by Israel appears to us to be altogether alien to the Gospel of love and peace that is the true nature of God's salvation plan. We read about God commanding that entire cities were to be destroyed. When God commanded, for example, in Deuteronomy 20:16-17, **"thou shalt save alive nothing that breatheth but thou shalt utterly destroy them,"** we are appalled. Would a good, loving God give that command? Surely, we must be misunderstanding what the Bible is teaching.

> *The Bible record of the conquest of Canaan by Israel appears to us to be altogether alien to the Gospel of love and peace that is the true nature of God's salvation plan.*

Fact is, we are not misunderstanding what the Bible is saying. But we must read these statements in the light of the whole message of the Bible. An understanding of the conquest of Canaan and the complete destruction of its cities by the nation of Israel requires that we understand God's entire program for the world. We must go back to the very beginning of time at which time God created this world. At the very beginning of time, God created a perfect earth. God gave the earth to mankind. We read in Psalm 115:16:

The heaven, even the heavens, are the LORD'S: but the earth hath he given to the children of men.

Man's task was to rule over this world. In Genesis 1:26, we read:

And God said, Let us make man in our image, after our likeness: and let them have dominion over the fish of the sea, and over the fowl of the air, and over the cattle, and over all the earth, and over every creeping thing that creepeth upon the earth.

Mankind and all of the universe were perfect at the time of creation. God indicates in Genesis 1:31:

And God saw every thing that he had made, and, behold, it was very good. And the evening and the morning were the sixth day.

Disaster Strikes

But then disaster struck. Some of the angels which had been created by God as ministering spirits (Hebrews 1:14), that is, they were created to humbly serve God, rebelled against God. They were under the leadership of an angel called Lucifer (Isaiah 14:12) who somehow fell into the sin of pride. In his pride, he wanted to be like God. In this way, both he and all who acknowledged him as their king would become the rulers and owners of this beautiful world that God had created.

> *Beginning with our first parents, Adam and Eve,*
> *the whole human race came under bondage to Lucifer*
> *(who is also called Satan).*

We cannot understand how this could happen, but we know it did happen. Beginning with our first parents, Adam and Eve, the whole human race came under bondage to Lucifer (who is also called Satan). Consequently mankind, who had been created by God to rule over this earth, became cursed by God because of their rebellion against God. God, therefore, also cursed this beautiful world so that it no longer was a perfect creation.

We read in Romans 8:20-22:

For the creature was made subject to vanity, not willingly, but by reason of him who hath subjected the same in hope, because the creature itself also shall be delivered from the bondage of corruption into the glorious liberty of the children of God. For we know that the whole creation groaneth and travaileth in pain together until now.

All of the foregoing events set the stage for the unfolding of God's salvation plan. This plan called for several very important events to take place. We can briefly outline them as follows.

1. Satan, who became prince of this world (John 12:31; 14:30; 16:11), had to be destroyed.

2. The wicked people, which included every human being, hadtobelegally judged and be sent to Hell as punishment for their rebellion.

3. Some of the people of the world had been chosen by God to live eternally as God's servants. They had to have their sins paid for so that God's perfect justice would be perfectly served without these individuals being required to be personally sent into eternal damnation.

4. The world, which had been claimed by Satan and the wicked people of the world, had to be taken from them and given to those who had been chosen by God to be His righteous servants forever.

5. Thus, the wicked owners of the world had to be destroyed.

Psalm 37:9, 20 declares:

For evildoers shall be cut off: but those that wait upon the LORD, they shall inherit the earth. . . . But the wicked shall perish, and the enemies of the LORD shall be as the fat of lambs: they shall consume; into smoke shall they consume away.

Psalm 104:35 declares:

Let the sinners be consumed out of the earth, and let the wicked be no more. Bless thou the LORD, O my soul. Praise ye the LORD.

6.   Once the wicked are destroyed, the world is to be given to the people who had become the righteous servants of God.

Psalm 37:9, 11, 29, and 34 informs us:

For evildoers shall be cut off: but those that wait upon the LORD, they shall inherit the earth. . . . But the meek shall inherit the earth; and shall delight themselves in the abundance of peace. . . . The righteous shall inherit the land, and dwell therein for ever. . . . Wait on the LORD, and keep his way, and he shall exalt thee to inherit the land: when the wicked are cut off, thou shalt see it.

7.   The earth will not begin as an eternal inheritance to God's people in its present sin-cursed condition. Instead it will become a new earth, that is, it will become so eternally perfect that it will actually become an integral part of heaven itself.

We read in 2 Peter 3:13:

Nevertheless we, according to his promise, look for new heavens and a new earth, wherein dwelleth righteousness.

The Land of Canaan Portrays the World

Keeping the above principles in mind permits us to understand the conquest of the cities of Canaan. Remember the land of Canaan had been given to the family of Abraham as an eternal inheritance. God had promised Abraham in Genesis 17:8:

And I will give unto thee, and to thy seed after thee, the land wherein thou art a stranger, all the land of Canaan, for an everlasting possession; and I will be their God.

When Israel was ready to come into the land of Canaan, this promise was reiterated to Moses as he viewed the land. We read in Deuteronomy 34:1-4:

And Moses went up from the plains of Moab unto the mountain of Nebo, to the top of Pisgah, that is over against Jericho. And the LORD shewed him all the land of Gilead, unto Dan, and all Naphtali, and the land of Ephraim, and Manasseh, and all the land of Judah, unto the utmost sea, and the south, and the plain of the valley of Jericho, the city of palm trees, unto Zoar. And the LORD said unto him, This is the land which I sware unto Abraham, unto Isaac, and unto Jacob, saying, I will give it unto thy seed: I have caused thee to see it with thine eyes, but thou shalt not go over thither.

In this historical situation, the land of Canaan is a portrait or type of the world that has become the possession of the wicked of the world and which must be restored to the people of God. In that sense, therefore, it is also a picture of the kingdom of God into which every genuine believer enters when he has become saved. Remember the kingdom of God consists of every true believer who will eternally occupy the new heaven and the new earth.

> *It was Christ who endured the wrath of God on behalf of all the people God had chosen to become saved.*

The work of restoring the world to the perfect service of God was to be done entirely by Christ who, as God Himself, was fully qualified to accomplish every aspect of that work. It was Christ who endured the wrath of God on behalf of all the people God had chosen to become saved. It is Christ who gave Satan a death blow that insures that Satan and all the wicked angels and men who follow him will be cast into hell forever (1 John 3:8). Thus, it was Christ who rescued this world from the possession of Satan and will give it as the new heaven and new earth to those who were made righteous by God's salvation plan (1 Corinthians 15:22-28).

To clearly illustrate that Christ was in charge of the destruction of the cities of Canaan, we read a very interesting account in Joshua 5:13-15:

And it came to pass, when Joshua was by Jericho, that he lifted up his eyes and looked, and, behold, there stood a man over against him with his sword drawn in his hand: and Joshua went unto him, and said unto him, Art thou for us, or for our adversaries? And he said, Nay; <u>but as captain of the host of the</u>

LORD am I now come. And Joshua fell on his face to the earth, and did worship, and said unto him,What saith my lord unto his servant? And the captain of the LORD'S host said unto Joshua, Loose thy shoe from off thy foot; for the place whereon thou standest is holy. And Joshua did so.

This captain was Christ Himself who for a brief period of time took on the appearance of a man so He could speak with Joshua. The drawn sword represented the Word of God which will condemn the wicked on the last day (Revelation 19:11-21). It is the law of God that condemns the sinner and calls for the penalty of eternal damnation. Mankind, being created in God's image, were created to live forever. However, if any sin is committed by any individual, he must stand for judgment at the end of time so that he can be legally found guilty of breaking God's law, and therefore, legally be sentenced to eternal damnation.

> *To illustrate the certainty, the awfulness, the severity*
> *of eternal damnation as a consequence of sin, God frequently*
> *used physical death as an illustration.*

To illustrate the certainty, the awfulness, the severity of eternal damnation as a consequence of sin, God frequently used physical death as an illustration. We have spoken before of the destruction of the entire world in the days of Noah. Nothing in the entire world with the breath of life escaped physical death at that time. Nothing, that is, except for those who had found refuge in the huge vessel that God had commanded Noah to build. These eight individuals were the only people in the whole world of that day who truly wanted to obey God's commands. They were a vivid illustration of those who have truly become saved, the evidence being their delight in obeying all of God's commandments. This dreadful event is carefully recorded in the Bible so that all mankind can know the certainty of God's wrath upon sin. Remember sin is disobeying the laws of God which are set forth in the Bible (1 John 3:4).

While the Flood of Noah's day was by far the most universal judgment that took place in history, many other judgments are recorded in the Bible so that we cannot miss the truth that sin will bring God's judgment. You will remember that God, by fire and brimstone, totally destroyed the four cities Sodom, Gomorrah, Admah, and Zeboim in the days of Abraham (Genesis 19; Deuteronomy 29:23). Only three individuals escaped that awful conflagration, an illustration that showed that sin will eventuate in God's bringing judgment.

Sometimes in the Bible, we read that God directly caused physical death and destruction. At other times, God used individuals or whole nations to bring death and destruction. All were means to demonstrate the terrible nature of the final judgment that shall come upon the whole world on the last day of this world's existence.

Thus, it was God who used the Israelites to bring death to the wicked people of the land of Canaan. Later, God used Babylon to bring destruction upon the wicked of Judah. Physical death is always horrible to contemplate. But, in each instance, it is pointing to the certainty of a death far more horrible. It is what the Bible calls the second death. And the second death is to be eternally damned to hell as a consequence of our sins (Revelation 20:14; 21:8). Only as a sinner is truly in Christ can there be escape from death's sting (1 Corinthians 15:51-57; Philippians 1:21; Revelation 2:11).

How Terrible Is Punishment For Sin

The Bible repeatedly speaks of the punishment of eternal damnation. But the problem is that we can only read about it. No one can describe how super awful it is because no one has been there.

In the parable of the rich man and Lazarus (Luke 16:23-25, 28), Jesus characterized hell as a place of torments and flame. Throughout the Bible, God uses dramatic language such as hell being a lake of fire (Revelation 19:20, 20:10, 15, 21:8), a place of weeping and gnashing of teeth (Matthew 8:12), a place where the smoke of their torment never ends (Isaiah 34:10; Revelation 14:11), but no one can testify that they had been there and that now they can testify concerning its horrors.

Therefore, God has done at least two things as He speaks of this awful punishment in the Bible. One thing He has done is to use dreadful language in describing the horrors of hell. One might read such passages as Deuteronomy 28:15-68 or Leviticus Chapter 26 to get some understanding of the awfulness of eternal damnation.

> *How can God convince us that eternal damnation,*
> *which every unsaved person will absolutely experience, is as*
> *terrible, as awful, as horrible as it really is?*

Even more vividly, God has had people, who were under the wrath of God, ruthlessly killed. This killing could have been accomplished directly by the action of God as in the case of Sodom or Gomorrah, or it could have been done by the action of men who were under the command of God. In either case, we are horrified that this should happen! And that is just the point of all of this.

How can God convince us that eternal damnation, which every unsaved person will absolutely experience, is as terrible, as awful, as horrible as it really is? To be killed by strangling, by beheading, or even by being burned alive is terribly repulsive to our senses. But it is nothing when compared with the experience of eternal damnation. Whether a person dies of a lingering painful disease or by the action of his fellowman, it is a bad and tragic experience, but it is nothing compared to the awfulness and reality of eternal damnation.

Thus, God programmed and recorded the conquest of the land of Canaan so that we humans might take notice of the terrible predicament we are in because of our sins.

> *God programmed and recorded the conquest of the land of Canaan so that we humans might take notice of the terrible predicament we are in because of our sins.*

Returning to the conquest of the land of Canaan, it is important to note that not all the people in Canaan were to be destroyed. God had decreed in Deuteronomy 20:10-11:

> **When thou comest nigh unto a city to fight against it, then proclaim peace unto it. And it shall be, if it make thee answer of peace, and open unto thee, then it shall be, that all the people that is found therein shall be tributaries unto thee, and they shall serve thee.**

This parallels the situation that occurs as God's true people bring the Gospel to the world. We read in 2 Corinthians 2:15-16:

> **For we are unto God a sweet savour of Christ, in them that are saved, and in them that perish: to the one we are the savour of death unto death; and to the other the savour of life unto life. And who is sufficient for these things?**

This explains why Rahab (who comes into view in our upcoming discussion on Jericho) and all that were in the house with her (that is, all those who were of like mind) were saved, whereas the rest of the city of Jericho was destroyed (see following discussion). This also explains why a very important city of Canaan named Gibeon was not destroyed (Joshua Chapter 9).

Jericho Destroyed

And that brings us to the destruction of Jericho. It was the first city encountered by Israel at the time they had crossed the Jordan River and had arrived in the land of Canaan. In one sense, Jericho represented all of the cities of the land of Canaan. Remember the entire land of Canaan at the time of Abraham had been given to Israel, and now Israel was in the land to receive it back.

Jericho was perhaps the oldest city of Canaan. It was well protected by a great wall around it. The destruction of Jericho would, in a sense, represent the destruction of all of the cities of Canaan, which in turn typified the judgment of God upon all of the world. The saving of Rahab (Joshua 6:22-23, 25) paralleled the saving of the city of Gibeon which in turn typified the salvation of all true believers throughout the world.

While, in one sense, Jericho was representative of all the cities of Canaan, in actuality, its destruction was pointing altogether to yet another extremely important aspect of God's salvation plan. There was another very important truth hidden in the account of the destruction of Jericho. This hidden truth is like a wonderful golden nugget waiting to be discovered. One of the reasons it remained hidden was because Bible translators incorrectly translated some very significant words in the sixth chapter of Joshua in which we find the account of the destruction of Jericho.

Incorrect Translation

What is not seen in the King James Bible is that a number of verses have been incorrectly translated. These verses have one or more key words that in the Bible narrative superficially do not appear to fit. These words are the Hebrew word "*shophar*" which should always be translated "**ram's horn.**"

The second is "*yobel*" which should always be translated "**jubilee.**"

The third word is "*teruah*" which can be translated "**shout**" as was done in this Biblical account, or it can be translated "**jubile**" as was done in Leviticus 25:9. "*Teruah*" is a word that is frequently used in the context where jubilee is in view.

The first verse we should look at is Joshua 6:4 which declares:

And seven priests shall bear before the ark seven trumpets of rams' horns: and the seventh day ye shall compass the city seven times, and the priests shall blow with the trumpets.

In actuality, the Hebrew words used in this verse should not have been translated **"seven trumpets of rams' horns."** It should have been translated, "**seven rams' horns of the jubilees**."

What did the Jubilee have to do with the
destruction of Jericho?

We can understand the difficulty the translators faced. What did the Jubilee have to do with the destruction of Jericho? The Jubilee was the time when liberty was to be proclaimed. Every first day of each seventh month was to be a memorial of the Jubilee. The Day of Atonement -- the tenth day of the month -- was identified with the Jubilee, and every fiftieth year was to be a Jubilee.

But what did these notices of the Jubilee have to do with the destruction of Jericho? Moreover, the word "**jubilee**," as it is written in Joshua 6:4, is a plural word. In no place in the Bible except in Joshua is the word "**jubilee**" a plural word. Indeed, the translators must have struggled with this chapter!

Joshua 6:5 gave the same difficulties. In the King James Bible, we read:

And it shall come to pass, that when they make a long blast with the ram's horn, and when ye hear the sound of the trumpet, all the people shall shout with a great shout; and the wall of the city shall fall down flat, and the people shall ascend up every man straight before him.

In actuality, the phrase **"long blast with the ram's horn"** should have been translated "**horn of jubilee**."

Joshua 6:8 and 6:13 are equally incorrectly translated. In each verse, the phrase **"seven trumpets of rams' horns"** should have been translated "**seven rams' horns of the jubilees**." Having learned this does not make the understanding of the Bible easier. What does this signify that the priests bearing the ark are marching around the walls of Jericho blowing on seven rams' horns of the jubilees?

Does proper translation assist us in our understanding of this historical event?

We will discover that the plural word **"jubilees"** will greatly assist us in our understanding of the destruction of Jericho.

More Spiritual Truth is Revealed

Do you recall that Jericho is called the **"city of palm trees?"** This is noted both in Deuteronomy 34:3 and in 2 Chronicles 28:15. Moreover, in Psalm 92:12a we read:

The righteous shall flourish like the palm tree: . . .

Furthermore, the word **"walls,"** which certainly is important in this Jericho narrative, is spoken of as walls of salvation in Isaiah 26:1 and Isaiah 60:18. Isaiah 26:1 reads:

In that day shall this song be sung in the land of Judah; we have a strong city; salvation will God appoint for walls and bulwarks.

And Isaiah 60:18 reads:

Violence shall no more be heard in thy land, wasting nor destruction within thy borders; but thou shalt call thy walls Salvation, and thy gates Praise.

Moreover, the city of Jericho was a city in the land of Canaan. Canaan was the promised land that externally represented the kingdom of God.

> *Jericho was a city that represented true believers who are citizens of the kingdom of God.*

What are we learning? We are learning that Jericho was a city that represented true believers who are citizens of the kingdom of God. But Jericho is being destroyed. Only Rahab the harlot and those who were with her in her house, which was located on the wall of Jericho, would escape. How can we understand this?

Question: What was going to follow once Jericho was destroyed? Answer: The conquest of the land of Canaan would begin. Remember we just learned that the conquest of Canaan typified the sending forth of the Gospel into all the world.

Remember 2 Corinthians 2:15-16:

For we are unto God a sweet savour of Christ, in them that are saved, and in them that perish: to the one we are the savour of death unto death; and to the other the savour of life unto life. And who is sufficient for these things?

Those who resist the Gospel end up under eternal damnation just as those who resisted Israel's conquest of the land of Canaan were destroyed. Those who believed the Gospel were those who had been given eternal life, just as those in the land of Canaan who came under service to the God of Israel (the city of Gibeon, for example), had their lives spared. But Christ first had to go to the cross to pay for sins before the double-edged message of the Gospel would be sent into all the world.

And something else had to happen.

For almost 1500 years, the nation of Israel was the keeper of the vineyard (Matthew 21:33-45). That is, they were the divine institution appointed by God to be the custodian, the caretaker, of the Gospel. They represented the spiritual City of God. In them were the righteous who grew like palm trees. They were surrounded by walls of salvation. But then Christ came. The Jubilee began to sound. We will learn that Jesus was born in 7 B.C., a Jubilee year. He was announced on a Jubilee day. Remember, the first day of the seventh month in A.D. 29 was to be memorial of the Jubilee.

But before the program of worldwide evangelization could begin, God had to shift the task from national Israel to the church age. The walls surrounding Jericho, depicting any salvation found in the nation of Israel, had to be removed. No longer would God use the temple or the Jewish synagogues in the task of proclaiming the true Gospel. Effectively, the nation of Israel was spiritually destroyed. It was destroyed except for those who were typified by Rahab. They are the true believers like Mary and Martha and the saved disciples who lived right at the end of the period of national Israel. These individuals became the beginning of the church age.

Now we understand that the Jubilee was sounding, but the walls did not fall until the great shout, the "*teruah*." Once they fell, Israel was ready to go on in its conquest of Canaan.

Once God was finished with the nation of Israel as the representative of the Gospel, the year of Jubilee -- the entire church age -- commenced.

Two Jubilees

But remember, we learned that in connection with the conquering of

Jericho, the word "**jubilee**" was a plural word. That meant that there was a second Jubilee in view. What could that mean?

As we go on in this study, we will learn that, most likely, in A.D. 1988, the church age came to an end. That terrible end was immediately followed by about a half hour of silence from heaven (Revelation 8:1). That is, the end of the church age was the end of the first Jubilee. The first Jubilee in principle had begun when Christ was born. In reality, it identified with the wonderful task of sending the Gospel into the world that had been assigned to the local congregations throughout the church age.

But then there was a second Jubilee. It began as the latter rain. It identified with the sending of the true Gospel throughout the world by individuals outside of the local congregations. For 1955 years, from A.D. 33 to A.D. 1988, the local churches were represented by Jericho, the city of palm trees, surrounded by walls of salvation. But before this second Jubilee could begin, this Jericho of the local congregations had to have its walls fall. The Holy Spirit had to leave the divine institution of the local congregations. The city of the palm trees had to come under the judgment of God. The Rahabs -- the true believers -- within the city had to come out. Only then, the final conquest of the land of Canaan -- the final sending forth of the Gospel -- could begin. Only then could the beautiful promise of Isaiah 11:11-12 come to pass:

And it shall come to pass in that day, that the Lord shall set his hand again the second time to recover the remnant of his people, which shall be left, from Assyria, and from Egypt, and from Pathros, and from Cush, and from Elam, and from Shinar, and from Hamath, and from the islands of the sea. And he shall set up an ensign for the nations, and shall assemble the outcasts of Israel, and gather together the dispersed of Judah from the four corners of the earth.

> *...the destruction of the city of Jericho was a great historical parable.*

Thus, we have learned that the destruction of the city of Jericho was a great historical parable. It truly was physically and literally destroyed as described in the Bible. But the detail of its destruction was like a huge parable pointing to, first, the end of national Israel as God's divine institution for externally representing the kingdom of God, and second, the end of the local churches being the external representative of the kingdom of God. The end of national Israel being used in that capacity was followed by the Jubilee of the church age. The end of the church age was followed by the Jubilee of the latter rain and the final ingathering of the elect by the sending forth of the Gospel by individuals outside the local churches.

We should note one other significant fact: the "teruah," that is, the loud shout of the Jubilee, sounded after the armies of Israel had marched around Jericho's walls thirteen times. We cannot help but see that the last Jubilee period -- the period of the latter rain -- begins a few years (2,300 days, Daniel 8:13-14), after the end of the church age. We will see that, most likely, the church age ended in the 13,000th year of the history of the world (A.D. 1988). That is when the local churches were abandoned by God, so that they were no longer being used of God to bring the Gospel of salvation to the world. But now, the final conquest is underway!

Now we should leave Jericho and continue down the highway of time as Israel begins to live in the promised land, the land of Canaan.

1047 B.C.

We are learning that God has recorded in the Bible many historical events which are portraits or illustrations of significant aspects of God's salvation plan.

The Old and the New Testaments of the Bible are in actuality one Testament or "Covenant." The word "testament" and the word "covenant" are synonyms. Since the Bible is the law of God, the words "testament" and "covenant" are also synonyms for the phrase "law of God." [3] That is why the Ten Commandments are called the "Covenant" (Exodus 34:28).

The Old Covenant, which is the Old Testament, has recorded within it a great many historical events. These events are illustrations of aspects of the reality of God's salvation plan as it was to be worked out throughout the New Testament era. The New Testament of the Bible describes how Jesus actually did come to be the Savior as a fulfillment of these Old Testament illustrations. The New Testament describes how the Gospel was sent into all of the world. It describes the end of the church age which would coincide with the beginning of God's final judgment upon the world; and it describes in some detail the actual

---

[3] Occasionally, the Bible uses the word "covenant" when it is speaking of an agreement between two individuals (1 Samuel 18:3; Matthew 26:15). Actually, the Bible, the law of God, is an agreement within the Godhead on behalf of the human race. That is why those who sin are called "covenant-breakers" (Isaiah 24:5; Romans 1:31).

return of Christ and the end of the world. Woven into the fabric of both the Old Testament and especially into the New Testament are copious references to the sinfulness of mankind, the righteousness of God, and the desperate need of mankind to have a Savior. In turn, the Bible gives much information to show that God Himself, in the person of the Lord Jesus Christ, is that Savior.

In this study, as we have been traveling down the timeline of history, we have already examined a number of these historical events, these illustrations of aspects of God's salvation plan. We learned, for example, that Abram's entrance into the land of Canaan represented the true believers coming into the kingdom of God. We learned that God's rescue of the nation of Israel from Egyptian bondage was an illustration of those who become saved, being set free from the bondage of sin and of Satan.

Now we will look at that part of God's timeline of history that was the 360-year period following 1407 B.C. (the year that Israel entered the land of Canaan). The experience of Israel during this period of time can be summed up in a few words. Israel would rebel against God, and God would send an oppressor. The oppressor could be any one of the nations that Israel had not obediently destroyed. Then, as Israel cried to God for help, God would send a deliverer. Fact is, during these 360 years, seventeen different individuals were raised up to provide deliverance for them.

However, as time went on, wickedness became increasingly apparent until, finally, we sadly read the indictment in Judges 17:6 and in Judges 21:25, where God says:

> **In those days *there was* no king in Israel: every man did *that which was* right in his own eyes.**

...we should be impressed by the remarkable mercy and forgiveness of God and His perfect faithfulness to fulfill His program of salvation.

As we are proceeding down the Biblical timeline of history, we should be impressed by the remarkable mercy and forgiveness of God and His perfect faithfulness to fulfill His program of salvation. We must realize that the Bible is primarily focused on those who are actively involved in the Gospel program God has planned for the world. Yet, as God describes in the Bible His experiences with those who are especially under God's care, we wonder how He can countenance their conduct which is so often completely rebellious.

As we read the pages of the Bible, we learn much, on the one hand, about the righteousness, the holiness, the mercy, the grace, the patience, the faithfulness, the integrity, the power, the authority, the love, the tenderness, and the kindness of God. On the other hand, we learn much about the pride, the weakness, the untruthfulness, and the rebellion against God which characterize mankind. The Bible is a book every human should ponder, should meditate upon, should listen to most carefully, should be thankful for. Every human should rejoice that God has made it available!

Therefore, as we read about the experiences of Israel during the forty years in the wilderness or during the 360-year period of the judges, or as we read anything else in the Bible, we can anticipate a great learning experience for us in our day. This is true because God is the same yesterday, today, and forever (Hebrews 13:8).

One additional thought could be inserted at this time. We should never presume upon God. We should never play games with God. We should never look upon Him as an equal. We should always remember He is the royal Majesty, King of kings, Almighty Creator, and Judge of all the earth. Therefore, as we approach the Bible, as we contemplate any sinful action, as we speak of God or His Word, the Bible, we should tremble before Him (Isaiah 66:2; James 2:19).

Shiloh

Very near the end of the period from 1407 B.C. to 1047 B.C., a dreadful event happened to Israel that became a picture or illustration of the end of the church age, a time that would not come until about 3,000 years later in history. We might recall that when Israel was in the wilderness on their way from Egypt to the land of Canaan, God instructed them to build a beautiful tent called a tabernacle. The tabernacle was effectively a holy shrine that identified in a very special way with God Himself.

In this tent was the room called the holy of holies in which was placed the ark of the covenant. That ark was a beautiful golden box in which were kept the Ten Commandments, which were written by the finger of God on stone tables (Exodus 31:18). Above the ark were two golden cherubim that represented God as the Judge of all the earth. The covering of the ark was called the "mercy seat." It was a golden lid that represented Christ as the Savior who alone provides a covering of the sins of His true people.

The holy of holies was separated from the main part of the tabernacle by a great veil or curtain which was never to be opened except on the day of atonement. On that day, the high priest opened the curtain in order to sprinkle blood on the mercy seat. However, his vision of the ark, the mercy seat, and the cherubim was obscured. When he opened the curtain, he was to carry a pan of burning incense so that the smoke from the burning incense, to a degree, hid these things in the holy of holies from his view.

The tabernacle was permanently placed in a city named Shiloh after Israel began to occupy the land of Canaan in the year 1407 B.C. (Joshua 18:1). The name Shiloh was a significant name because it was a name that God applied to Himself.

In Genesis 49:10 we read:

The sceptre shall not depart from Judah, nor a lawgiver from between his feet, until Shiloh come; and unto him shall the gathering of the people be.

In this prophetic verse, the name Shiloh, which is possibly derived from a Hebrew word signifying "rest" or "tranquility," can be speaking only of the Lord Jesus Christ who would come as the Savior (Matthew 1:20-21; Luke 2:11; John 17:2, 24). Therefore, it was altogether fitting that the city in which the tabernacle was placed would have the name Shiloh. This city, until the year 1068 B.C., was the most holy city in the land of Israel.

In the year 1068 B.C., however, everything changed for the worse. During the previous forty years (1108 B.C.-1068 B.C.), the high priest Eli was also the individual appointed by God to be the Judge of the people of Israel (1 Samuel 4:18). Eli appointed his two sons, Hophni and Phineas, to officiate in the tabernacle in Shiloh (1 Samuel 1:3). Unfortunately, these two men lived very wicked lives (1 Samuel 2:12-25), and Eli, himself, became, to some degree, a part of that wickedness (1 Samuel 2:27-29). Therefore, a situation developed under the watchful eye of God (and we must remember that nothing ever happens without God having full knowledge of all that is taking place), that precipitated utter disaster for Israel.

We read in 1 Samuel 4:1-2 that Israel went to war against the Philistines, and four thousand of the Israelites were killed. God was putting Israel to the test. The number forty is frequently used in the Bible to signify testing (see Chapter 8). At this juncture in Israel's history, the number forty is featured twice. It was the fortieth year of Eli's rule over Israel, and 4000 (40 times 100) Israelites were destroyed in battle with the Philistines. From the Biblical information, we can calculate that the year was 1068 B.C.

What should Israel have done in the face of this defeat? They should have cried to God for His mercy. The priests, as well as the people, should have seen their sinful ways and turned from them (1 Samuel 2:27-30; 4:3). But Israel failed the test. They had a brilliant idea (so they thought). They took the ark of the covenant out of the tabernacle in Shiloh and brought it to the battle field! They truly believed that the ark represented God. With God being present with them, they would surely defeat the Philistines (1 Samuel 4:3). Actually, their conduct was dreadfully sinful. The ark was never to be taken from the Holy of Holies unless God decreed that this was to happen.

Therefore, great judgment from God came to Israel. The ark was captured by the Philistines and moved to the Philistine cities of Ashdod, Gath, and Ekron (1 Samuel 5:1, 8 and 10). The two Israelite priests, Hophi and Phineas, were killed; 30,000 Israelites were killed in battle; and Eli, the high priest, died of a broken neck. The number three spiritually signifies purpose; the number 10,000, completeness (see Chapter 8). The 30,000 men who were killed in battle effectively signified that it was God's complete purpose that Israel be severely punished for desecrating the tabernacle in Shiloh. Never before in the history of Israel had such a disaster struck Israel. It was like God had departed from Israel (1 Samuel 4:21-22). It was the ultimate tragedy.

Because the ark was no longer in the Holy of Holies, the tabernacle in Shiloh no longer served as a holy shrine. After almost 400 years, the tabernacle effectively was destroyed because now it was a tabernacle without the ark of the covenant within it. It was like the house of God without God being present. Because the tabernacle was no longer God's house, the city of Shiloh, in a certain sense, was a city without God. And because the city of Shiloh was without God, the nation of Israel, in a sense, was without God. This terrible event was a picture pointing to our time in history. Today, God has departed from all the local congregations throughout the world (see *The End of the Church Age and After*, available free of charge from Family Radio).

God uses the tabernacle to demonstrate salvation. In the tabernacle, God met sinners to give them atonement and forgiveness of their sins. Likewise, in God's spiritual tabernacle, Christ Himself, God gives mercy to those He saves. Christ keeps the law of God perfectly in their place so their sins can be forgiven (Exodus 25: 21-22; Hebrews 9:1-15, 19-26). But God also uses the tabernacle to represent the local congregations during the church age. We read in Isaiah 54:2-3:

Enlarge the place of thy tent, and let them stretch forth the curtains of thine habitations: spare not, lengthen thy cords, and strengthen thy stakes; for thou shalt break forth on the right hand and on the left; and thy seed shall inherit the Gentiles, and make the desolate cities to be inhabited.

The word "Gentiles" in this verse is speaking of the nation that would hear the Gospel and become saved. The work of the New Testament churches was to send the Gospel, the message of salvation in Christ, into all the world. Therefore, the local New Testament congregations were typified by the tabernacle that was in Shiloh. Moreover, even as the ark of the covenant was in the tabernacle, so, too, God was in the local congregations applying the Word of God to the lives of all those whom He saved. Thus, the spiritual tabernacle was steadily increasing in size, the cords were lengthened and the stakes were strengthened.

> *...the local New Testament congregations were typified by the tabernacle that was in Shiloh.*

But then disaster struck the local congregations even as disaster struck the tabernacle in Shiloh. God departed from the local congregations just as the ark was removed from the tabernacle. In Jeremiah 10:20-21 we read:

> **My tabernacle is spoiled, and all my cords are broken: my children are gone forth of me, and they are not: there is none to stretch forth my tent any more, and to set up my curtains. For the pastors are become brutish, and have not sought the LORD: therefore they shall not prosper, and all their flocks shall be scattered.**

These verses can be speaking only of the end of the church age. This theme is further emphasized by the language of Jeremiah 7:14:

> **Therefore will I do unto this house, which is called by my name, wherein ye trust, and unto the place which I gave to you and to your fathers, as I have done to Shiloh.**

Jeremiah was speaking long after the tabernacle of Moses and Joshua and Eli's day had disappeared. During Jeremiah's day, the tabernacle had been replaced by the temple. Thus, these words could be speaking only of our day.

> *The "house called by my name" had become the entity in which the people trusted. That is, their trust was in the external church itself.*

In Jeremiah 7:14, God is particularly calling attention to a grievous sin of the local congregations which existed during the New Testament church age. The trust of the people was not in Christ and the Bible. The "house called by my name" had become the entity in which the people trusted. That is, their trust was in the external church itself. Their trust was in a set of creeds or in the consensus of a group of like-minded people. It was in whatever the pastor or leader said or taught. The people's trust was not in Christ alone, nor was it fortified by a thorough individual examination of God's Word, the Bible. Truly, there has never been a church that could save anyone.

So much for a brief look at the disaster that struck Shiloh. But let us look again at our Biblical timeline of history. It is noteworthy that in the same year (2068 B.C.) in which Abraham was circumcised, the city of Sodom together with three other cities were totally destroyed by God because of their great wickedness. Significantly, God links the destruction of Sodom to the end of the world, and particularly to the end of the church age, when God's judgment came upon the local congregations. (Later we will learn that this judgment most likely began in A.D. 1988.)

There are Biblical references that tie the destruction of Sodom to God's judgment falling on the local congregations at the beginning of the Great Tribulation (Luke 17:28-32; Revelation 11:8).

    2068 B.C.:   Destruction of Sodom
    +1988 A.D.: Beginning of judgment on all local congregations
    4056

Curiously, the number of years inclusively (4,056) from the destruction of Sodom in 2068 B.C. to A.D. 1988, when the Great Tribulation in all likelihood began, breaks down into very significant prime numbers. The number 4,056 can be factored as follows:

$$4,056 = 2 \times 2 \times 2 \times 3 \times 13 \times 3$$

For much more detailed full information on how God uses numbers, see Chapter 8. But for now, as we consider the number 4,056, we might note the following.

- The number "2" signifies those who are assigned by God to bring the Gospel.
- The number "3" signifies the purpose of God.
- The number "13" signifies super fullness.

Spiritually, we could therefore conclude that it was God's purpose that national Israel (which began in the year 2068 B.C., when Abraham was circumcised and Sodom was destroyed), and the local churches (which began at Pentecost in A.D. 33), both of which were mandated by God to be the caretakers of the Gospel, would be finished in the super fullness of time. (See more about A.D. 1988 in the next paragraph.)

We also note that the circumcision of Abraham (Genesis 17:23-26) which officially marked the beginning of the nation of Israel was related in a very curious way to what happened in Shiloh. Abraham was circumcised in the year 2068 B.C. It was in the year 1068 B.C. that this tragic end of Shiloh occurred. It is striking that, between 2068 B.C. and 1068 B.C., there are precisely 1,000 years. What is even more interesting and possibly significant is that the end of the church age most likely occurred in the year A.D. 1988. This is precisely 13,000 years after the year 11013 B.C. when God began the world and created our first parents, Adam and Eve. Could this be coincidental?

We can also point out that the ark of the covenant, when it was captured by the Philistines, remained in their country for seven months (1 Samuel 6:1). There are definite parallels having to do with the Great Tribulation to be considered. The tribulation that Jacob endured when he was commanded to leave the land of Canaan in the year 1877 B.C. lasted seven years. The tribulation the nation of Judah endured, when it was humiliated by the Assyrians and Babylonians from 609 B.C. to 539 B.C., lasted 70 years. We have seen previously that these two periods typify the Great Tribulation. So now also we see that when the ark was taken from Shiloh, it was outside of Israel for seven months. Surely we can see the parallels between these three events as God links them together by the number "7."

The construction of the tabernacle began in the year 1447 B.C. which was the year Israel was freed from Egypt. It came to its end, as we have seen, in the year 1068 B.C. or 379 years later. Seven months later, it was returned to Israel. This would have been very late in the year 1068 B.C. or very early in the year 1067 B.C. Exactly 100 years later, in the year 967 B.C., the building of the temple, which replaced the tabernacle, was begun by King Solomon. Exactly 380 years later, in the year 587 B.C., the temple was destroyed by the armies of Babylon.

We have learned that the tabernacle was a picture of many from the nations of the world who would become true believers during the church age. The same is true of the temple that Solomon built. We cannot help but marvel that God allowed the tabernacle to stand for 379 years; and that He also allowed the temple built by Solomon to exist from the beginning of its construction to the end of its existence for almost exactly the identical period -- 380 years.

We should comment that all this is not surprising. The unfolding of God's timetable of His Gospel program for the world is not at all capricious or haphazard. God is the Grand Designer, and He has set up carefully and perfectly-planned patterns. When we look at God's design of the universe, whether we are looking at the structure of chemical elements or the petals of a daisy, we see that everything follows a distinct pattern. We will learn that, all the way to the end of time, a definite pattern will be clearly seen.

We Want a King

After Israel had been in the land of Canaan almost 360 years, they had another complaint against God. They wanted a king like all the other nations. Therefore, in the year 1047 B.C., God gave them their first king. He was a tall impressive individual named Saul. God the Holy Spirit came into Saul's personality to qualify him to be what a king over a political nation should be. This was necessary because such political national structure was wholly new to Israel. Saul came from a farm. There was no palace, no royal government, etc. Saul was selected by God as a man with whom the people would be pleased.

To give spiritual counsel to the king as well as to the people, God provided prophets. Because the Bible was still only partly completed, and because copies of the written Word had to be handwritten, and because God was still writing the Bible, those prophets, who were true believers, at times would receive messages directly from God. This was a great assistance to the kings who would eventually rule over Israel.

King Saul, however, was not a saved man. He was not always willing to obey God. Therefore, after a 40-year reign, in the year 1007 B.C., Saul was killed in battle and was replaced by a king who dearly loved God and whom God loved. His name was David, who at the age of 30, ascended the throne.

Under the reign of David, Israel greatly prospered because it was altogether under the blessing of God. David ascended the throne in the year 1007 B.C., exactly 1,000 years before Christ (who was typified by David) was born. 1007 B.C. is exactly 3,000 years before the second Jubilee began in A.D. 1994.

Do we recognize the precision of God's timeline of salvation?

$$
\begin{array}{r}
1007 \\
+ \quad 1994 \\
- \quad\quad 1 \\
\hline
3000
\end{array}
$$

David not only ruled well, but also was used by God to write some of the Bible. That is, God spoke through David. In our Bibles, in the Book of the Psalms, often the notation is made "A Psalm of David" to indicate that the words of that psalm were written by God utilizing David as the scribe.

David as a youth had been a shepherd boy. Now, as a mature adult, he was ruling over the kingdom of Israel which became a very significant kingdom in that time of history (1 Chronicles 17:8). God unfolded His salvation plan using the rule of David over Israel as a type or representation, and as an anticipation, of Jesus Christ who rules over the eternal Kingdom of God. Jesus spoke of Himself as **"the good Shepherd . . . I lay down my life for the sheep"** (John 10:14-15). After reigning for 36 years, King David made one of his sons, named Solomon, co-regent with him. This was the year 971 B.C. Four years later, King David died, and Solomon continued as king of Israel for an additional 36 years.

King David had a passionate desire to build a magnificent permanent temple to replace the tabernacle Moses had constructed in the wilderness. Therefore, a great amount of preparation had already been done for the building of this temple by the time David died (1 Chronicles Chapters 17 and 22). Immediately upon David's death, the foundation of the temple was laid by his son Solomon. That year, which was the year 967 B.C., was an important milestone in the highway of time. Fact is, the Bible reports in 1 Kings 6:1:

> **And it came to pass in the four hundred and eightieth year after the children of Israel were come out of the land of Egypt, in the fourth year of Solomon's reign over Israel, in the month Zif, which is the second month, that he began to build the house of the LORD.**

This citation is of great help to us in constructing the biblical calendar of history because it assures us that 480 years after 1447 B.C., the year Israel was set free from Egypt, was Solomon's fourth year as King. Thus, 1447 B.C. minus 480 years brings us to the year 967 B.C. as the fourth year of Solomon's reign. Therefore, the first year of Solomon's reign was four years earlier than 967 B.C. It was the year 971 B.C.

> *Both Jerusalem and the temple became very prominent in the Bible as types or portraits of the eternal kingdom of God.*

The temple, like the city Jerusalem where the temple was located, became an external representation of the kingdom of God. Both Jerusalem and the temple became very prominent in the Bible as types or portraits of the eternal kingdom of God.

During Solomon's reign of 40 years (four years of which he was co-regent with his father David), the kingdom of Israel became the most notable kingdom of the world at that time in history. God gave King Solomon wisdom and riches and honor above any subsequent king who ruled in Israel (2 Chronicles 1:12; 9:22). Solomon was a true believer who also was used by God as a means of expanding God's Law Book, the Bible. Much of the wisdom of Solomon is recorded in the Book of Proverbs.

A Major Change

Solomon did have one serious fault. Mainly for political purpose, he had 700 wives and 300 concubines. This strengthened his position in the political world of that day, but it also provided for his downfall. In his old age, probably to please some of his foreign wives, he worshiped heathen gods. The Bible gives little detail about this sin, but God's Word does use Solomon's idolatry as the reason God made a major change in the nation of Israel which, in turn, made a major change in the external representation of the kingdom of God (1 Kings Chapter 11).

Chapter 7
931 B.C. The Divided Kingdom

Major change occurred when King Solomon died in the year 931 B.C. As we have just learned, God brought judgment upon the nation Israel as a result of Solomon's sin. This judgment took the form of a split in the Kingdom. Much tragedy and grief would follow in subsequent years. We read in 1 Kings 11:9-12:

And the LORD was angry with Solomon, because his heart was turned from the LORD God of Israel, which had appeared unto him twice, and had commanded him concerning this thing, that he should not go after other gods: but he kept not that which the LORD commanded. Wherefore the LORD said unto Solomon, Forasmuch as this is done of thee, and thou hast not kept my covenant and my statutes, which I have commanded thee, I will surely rend the kingdom from thee, and will give it to thy servant. Notwithstanding in thy days I will not do it for David thy father's sake: but I will rend it out of the hand of thy son.

Ten of the twelve tribes were taken away from Solomon's son Rehoboam who followed Solomon as the next king ruling from Jerusalem. Those ten tribes, located north of Jerusalem, were given by God to a man named Jeroboam (1 Kings 11:31). Thus, beginning in the year 931 B.C., Israel became two independent Kingdoms. One was named Judah with its capital in Jerusalem. It now only consisted of the two tribes, Judah and Benjamin (2 Chronicles Chapters 10 and 11). The other which consisted of ten tribes was called Israel, and its capital city eventually became Samaria. From the year 931 B.C. and after, both the nation of Judah and the nation of Israel became external representatives of the Kingdom of God.

The kingdom of Israel was ruled by a total of twenty different kings, none of whom were in King David's blood line. Moreover, none of them gave evidence of a saved relationship with God. The kingdom of Judah was ruled by twenty monarchs also. Some of them obeyed the Lord, but others led the people of Judah to sin. Nevertheless, God continued to minister to both the nations of Israel and Judah by sending prophets to them who gave them His warnings and His counsel.

Many of the prophetic books of the Bible, like the books of Isaiah, Jeremiah, Ezekiel and Amos, etc., were written by God speaking through these prophets to warn Israel and Judah of the judgment of God that would fall upon these nations if they did not turn from their wicked ways.

However, these same prophecies and warnings are especially directed against the spiritual Israel of our day which consists of the local congregations located throughout the world. Thus, God tolerated the kingdom of Judah and the kingdom of Israel so that, using them as examples, He could bring His warnings to the church world and also to the secular world that exists in our day.

This is the key to studying the Bible. Each historical event is written so that readers throughout the history of the world can make personal spiritual application to their own situation. In the historical setting, we can witness God's reaction to sin and the unfolding of His salvation plan, and therefore, we can be more insistently warned of the extreme peril we are in if we disobey God. That is why we read in 2 Timothy 3:16:

All scripture is given by inspiration of God, and is profitable for doctrine, for reproof, for correction, for instruction in righteousness:

How wonderful it is that God uses His word, the Bible to correct His people so that they may serve the Lord more faithfully!

Jonah

It was during this time that a most significant event took place. It is recorded in the Bible in the Book of Jonah. Jonah was a prophet of Israel during the time that Jeroboam II was king over Israel (2 Kings 14:25). The Bible shows us that this king ruled over Israel from 792 B.C. to 751 B.C.

At this time in history, the most powerful kingdom in that part of the world was Assyria. Fact is, in the year 709 B.C., Assyria completely destroyed Israel. Jonah was given a command by God to go to the very powerful, very wicked capital city of Assyria, a city called Nineveh, with the message that it was God's intention to destroy it because of its great wickedness. We read in Jonah 1:2 and 3:2-4:

Arise, go to Nineveh, that great city, and cry against it; for their wickedness is come up before me. Arise, go unto Nineveh, that great city, and preach unto it the preaching that I bid thee. So Jonah arose, and went unto Nineveh, according to the word of the LORD. Now Nineveh was an exceeding great city of three days' journey. And Jonah began to enter into the city a day's journey, and he cried, and said, Yet forty days, and Nineveh shall be overthrown.

The first time Jonah heard God's command, he refused to obey. Possibly we can understand his reluctance. Assyria was the enemy of Israel. Would not Israel greatly benefit if this mighty Assyrian city was destroyed? So Jonah disobeyed God's command and took a ship bound for a far away city named Tarshish. His intent was to flee from the presence of the Lord. He went down into the ship and fell fast asleep.

Jonah Chapter 1 goes on to record that a great storm arose, and the ship was about to sink. Jonah recognized that the storm was a result of his disobedience and, to save the ship, he counseled the sailors to throw him into the sea. They did so. The sea became calm, and Jonah was swallowed by a whale.

> *Amazingly, the whole city of more than 120,000 people, together with its king, repented and cried to God for mercy.*

Jonah Chapters 2 and 3 continue the account. After three days and nights in the whale's belly (see also Matthew 12:40), Jonah was cast out alive upon the land. He then dutifully preached to the Ninevites that, because of their wickedness, in forty days, God was going to destroy them. Amazingly, the whole city of more than 120,000 people, together with its king, repented and cried to God for mercy. The king decreed in Jonah 3:8-9:

> **But let man and beast be covered with sackcloth, and cry mightily unto God: yea, let them turn every one from his evil way, and from the violence that is in their hands. Who can tell if God will turn and repent, and turn away from his fierce anger, that we perish not?**

Because the whole city repented, God did not destroy Nineveh, even as God stipulated in Jeremiah 18:7-8:

> **At what instant I shall speak concerning a nation, and concerning a kingdom, to pluck up, and to pull down, and to destroy it; if that nation, against whom I have pronounced, turn from their evil, I will repent of the evil that I thought to do unto them.**

The fact is we can know that this whole city became saved because we read in Matthew 12:41:

> **The men of Nineveh shall rise in judgment with this generation,**

and shall condemn it: because they repented at the preaching of Jonas; and, behold, a greater than Jonas is here.

In this study, we have already made reference to this event both in the Preface and in Chapter 1. Because of the enormously significant truths given in this account, we must examine it in greater detail.

Looking for the Spiritual Meaning

The Book of Jonah is a true historical account that is teaching tremendously significant spiritual truths. The following is a summary of some of the major truths taught in this book.

Historical Fact	Spiritual Application
Ship going to Tarshish (Jonah 1:3) Isaiah 60:9, **"Surely the isles shall wait for me, and the ships of Tarshish first, to bring thy sons from far, their silver and their gold with them, unto the name of the LORD thy God, and to the Holy One of Israel, because he hath glorified thee."**	Picture of churches throughout the church age, going into all the world with the Gospel.
Jonah went down into the ship and was fast asleep (Jonah 1:5).	Jonah represents churches which, at the end of the church age, are spiritually dead.
Jonah fleeing from the presence of God (Jonah 1:3–1:10; 4:2) (Actually, this is literally impossible, Psalm 139:7-12)	Churches at the end of the church age no longer having God present with them in the sense that He is no longer saving anyone as the local churches minister the Gospel
Ship ready to sink (Jonah 1:4)	Churches at the end of the church age are spiritually destroyed. They no longer are used of God in His program of bringing people into the kingdom of God.
Tarshish (Jonah 1:3; 4:2)	The whole world from which, throughout the church age, true believers have come

Continued

Historical Fact	Spiritual Application
Jonah thrown into the sea (Jonah 1:12, 15)	Jonah now represents Christ who experienced eternal damnation on behalf of those He came to save.
Sailors who were saved from shipwreck because Jonah was thrown into the sea (Jonah 1:15-16)	Those saved because Christ endured hell on their behalf
Nineveh (Jonah 1:2, 3:2, 7-8; 4:11	The entire wicked world
120,000 (Jonah 4:11)	Complete fullness of all those in the world who become saved during the last part of the Great Tribulation
Jonah preaching to Nineveh (Jonah 3:3-4)	All those who, as ambassadors of Christ, are warning the world that the end of the world is almost here
They did not know their left hand from their right hand (Jonah 4:11) (See Deuteronomy 28:14 and Joshua 23:6)	Those in the world who have never known the commands of the Bible (they are altogether ignorant of the Bible's teachings.
Much cattle (Jonah 4:11)	The entire creation, which will become the New Heavens and the New Earth (This is parallel to the experience of the true believers who will receive a new resurrected body)
Forty days (Jonah 3:4)	The time of the end (This is a test for those who hear today's warning that the year A.D. 2011 could be the year in which the world ends. Will they react like the people of Nineveh who became saved or will they react like the world of Noah's day who remained in rebellion against God when they were given a timetable of 120 years before destruction?

The people of Nineveh knew nothing about Biblical truths.

This extremely insightful historical parable is teaching both a most awful and a most wonderful lesson. God continually came to the nation of Israel by means of prophets which taught the Israelites many Biblical truths. But Israel continued to rebel against God and eventually were destroyed. The people of Nineveh knew nothing about Biblical truths. No prophets of God had ever come to them. Even when Jonah preached as a lone prophet to a great city of more than 120,000 people, their knowledge of Bible truth would have been minuscule.

God had warned Israel, for example, in 1 Kings 14:15:

For the LORD shall smite Israel, as a reed is shaken in the water, and he shall root up Israel out of this good land, which he gave to their fathers, and shall scatter them beyond the river, because they have made their groves, provoking the LORD to anger.

The groves spoken of in this verse identify with the worship of false gods. Because Israel did not listen to those warnings of God, they were totally destroyed by the Assyrian nation in the year 709 B.C. We read in 2 Kings 17:14, 18:

Notwithstanding they would not hear, but hardened their necks, like to the neck of their fathers, that did not believe in the LORD their God. Therefore the LORD was very angry with Israel, and removed them out of his sight: there was none left but the tribe of Judah only.

The same situation prevails in the world in our day. On the one hand, there are all of the local congregations that have been taught from the Bible for many years. Presently they are being warned that God's wrath is upon them because they are not nearly as faithful to the Bible as they should be. Their members are trusting in their denomination, or their pastor, or their creedal confessions, or their water baptism, or their church membership as the guarantee of their salvation. But they are not trusting the Bible as the ultimate authority. The proof of this is the fact that they are not repenting of wrong doctrines they hold. Nor are they obeying God's command to leave the churches. Because God has come to the local churches as the Judge of all the earth to prepare those who are not true believers to stand before the Judgment Throne, the genuine believers must get out of the local churches. (See *The End of the Church Age and After* and *Wheat and Tares*, available free of charge from Family Radio.)

In spite of the ready availability of the Bible, most of those in the churches and in the world will remain in rebellion against God. Like Matthew 24:37-38 declares:

But as the days of Noe were, so shall also the coming of the Son of man be. For as in the days that were before the flood they were eating and drinking, marrying and giving in marriage, until the day that Noe entered into the ark.

Those remaining in the local churches and most of the people of the world will give no heed to the warning that the end of the world is almost here. They will remain in complete denial to the truth that they must very soon stand before the Judgment Throne of God.

However, there is wonderful news. In a world of more than six billion people, most of the people know little or nothing about the Bible. They are typified by the wicked citizens of Nineveh. The Bible assures us that a great multitude of these will become saved (Revelation 7:9-14). Even as the spiritually ignorant Ninevites became saved when God warned of impending destruction, so it could well be that most of the great multitude that are spoken of in Revelation 7:9 will also come from the billions of spiritually ignorant peoples of the world. How wonderful! It is glorious that salvation does not depend in anyway upon knowledge of Bible truths. It is magnificent to know that all that is required is that the individuals God intends to save be under the hearing of the Bible.

> *...many of those who are the last to hear the Gospel will become God's people, but many who had been the first to hear the Gospel will be cast away because they had never become saved.*

In this connection, we might keep in mind the teaching of Luke 13:25-30 where God reveals that those who have had first opportunity to be God's people will be last. But those who are the last to be given the opportunity to hear the Gospel will be first. That is, many of those who are the last to hear the Gospel will become God's people, but many who had been the first to hear the Gospel will be cast away because they had never become saved. Here is what Luke 13: 25-30 says:

When once the master of the house is risen up, and hath shut to the door, and ye begin to stand without, and to knock at the door, saying, Lord, Lord, open unto us; and he shall answer and say unto you, I know you not whence ye are: then shall ye begin to say,

We have eaten and drunk in thy presence, and thou hast taught in our streets. But he shall say, I tell you, I know you not whence ye are; depart from me, all ye workers of iniquity. There shall be weeping and gnashing of teeth, when ye shall see Abraham, and Isaac, and Jacob, and all the prophets, in the kingdom of God, and you yourselves thrust out. And they shall come from the east, and from the west, and from the north, and from the south, and shall sit down in the kingdom of God. And, behold, there are last which shall be first, and there are first which shall be last.

I am afraid that these verses are teaching that, in our day, those in the churches, to a high degree, are the first who shall be last; whereas those who heretofore were taught nothing from the Bible are the last who shall be first.

Incidentally, we must remember that when God reached into Nineveh and saved 120,000 people, it did not mean that Nineveh would continue as a city of saved people. The situation is analogous to God who, for His own glory and purpose, reaches into a family clan and saves one or two individuals, even though the rest of that family clan remains altogether in rebellion against God.

Likewise, the saving of these 120,000 did not signify in any way that any of the rest of the nation of Assyria who lived outside of the city of Nineveh, or that any of the following generations of people who would live there, would also become saved.

> *As we approach the end of time, we can know that wickedness all over the world will increase and the wicked will be brought into judgment.*

As we speak of the wickedness of Nineveh, who we learned identify with the enormous wickedness of our world today, it would be well to recognize that, at this time of Great Tribulation, God is not only preparing the peoples in the local churches for their time of trial at the Judgment Throne of God, but God is also preparing for judgment those who are not a part of local churches. This is so even though a great multitude which no man can number will become saved, even as the 120,000 citizens of ancient Nineveh became saved. As we approach the end of time, we can know that wickedness all over the world will increase and the wicked will be brought into judgment. To understand this, we should examine for a moment the Bible's statement about God's judgment upon the unsaved world at large.

Unsaved Mankind is Desperately Wicked

We do not normally realize that any individual who is not saved is tremendously wicked. But the Bible tells us in Jeremiah 17:9:

The heart is deceitful above all things, and desperately wicked: who can know it?

In Matthew 15:19, the Bible adds:

For out of the heart proceed evil thoughts, murders, adulteries, fornications, thefts, false witness, blasphemies.

We read these verses and know that they are true. However, there have always been people who, though they pay no attention to the Bible, do live decent moral lives. Think, for example, of a mother's love for her children. Surely we cannot detect terrible wickedness in the lives of such kindly, loving, generous, law-abiding individuals. Nevertheless, we know that the Bible is true in all that it teaches. But how can the indictment of these verses be correct?

God Restrains Wickedness in the Lives of the Unsaved

When we search the Bible for an answer to this puzzle, we find at least two answers. The first answer is that God restrains sin in the lives of people (Psalm 76:10). God gives us an example of this in Genesis Chapter 20. There we read of a heathen king named Abimelech who had an opportunity to sin against Sarah, the wife of Abraham. However, he did not commit this sin. God explained in Genesis 20:6 why Abimelech did not commit this sin:

I also withheld thee from sinning against me; therefore suffered I thee not to touch her.

The lesson we learn from this is that God restrains mankind from being as sinful as they are by nature. Obviously, since the heart of man is as wicked as God declares it is, mankind would soon completely destroy themselves if God allowed all mankind to live as wickedly as they are by nature.

> *...any wickedness, however slight in our eyes,*
> *is grievous wickedness against God.*

It is also true that any wickedness, however slight in our eyes, is grievous wickedness against God. Therefore, anyone who refuses to live altogether like a true believer is, in God's sight, exceedingly wicked.

God Gives People Up To Sin

In any case, the Bible does speak of a time when God gives people up to gross sin. To give people up to sin is another way of saying that God's restraint on sin is completely removed. In Romans Chapter 1, more than twenty gross sins are named. These sins are named immediately after God emphasizes, in three of these verses, that the peoples of the world have been given up to commit terrible sin (Romans 1:24, 26, 28). In addition, the curious and surely dramatic truth displayed in this chapter is in connection with the first sin that is named. In Romans 1:21-23, God first explains:

> **Because that, when they knew God, they glorified him not as God, neither were thankful; but became vain in their imaginations, and their foolish heart was darkened. Professing themselves to be wise, they became fools, and changed the glory of the uncorruptible God into an image made like to corruptible man, and to birds, and fourfooted beasts, and creeping things.**

These verses express the continuing rebellion of mankind who set up their own man-made religions and gospels. They, with their own sinful minds, believed they were wise while they lived for their own glory rather than for the glory of God.

Following this are verses 24 through 28 which detail the first of more than twenty sins that will be named after this first sin. In these verses we read:

> **Wherefore <u>God also gave them up</u> to uncleanness through the lusts of their own hearts, to dishonour their own bodies between themselves: who changed the truth of God into a lie, and worshipped and served the creature more than the Creator, who is blessed for ever. Amen. For this cause <u>God gave them up</u> unto vile affections: for even their women did change the natural use into that which is against nature: and likewise also the men, leaving the natural use of the woman, burned in their lust one toward another; men with men working that which is unseemly, and receiving in themselves that recompence of their error which was meet. And even as they did not like to retain God in their**

knowledge, <u>God gave them over</u> to a reprobate mind, to do those things which are not convenient.

The startling and shocking thing about the sin of lesbianism and homosexuality named in these verses is that never in New Testament history has this sin been in evidence like it is in our day. There are those who try to argue that, at the time Rome ruled the known world, this kind of sin was very prevalent. While any kind of sin is always present in any group of people, the Bible's own testimony assures us that this kind of sin was not prevalent in that Roman era. Ancient Rome ruled over many countries including Greece and the lands of Israel. Read in 1 Corinthians 5:1 of a member of the church in Corinth who was apparently living adulterously with his father's wife. In that connection, 1 Corinthians 5:1 declares:

It is reported commonly that there is fornication among you, and such fornication as is not so much as named among the Gentiles, that one should have his father's wife.

We are astonished to recognize that it is at our time in history that the sin of homosexuality has taken off like a skyrocket!

The Gentiles named in this verse would have been the Greeks of Corinth, a city over which the Romans ruled at that time. Surely the sin named in this verse is far less heinous and perverted than the sin of homosexuality or the enormous sexual depravity that is occurring in our day. We are astonished to recognize that it is at our time in history that the sin of homosexuality has taken off like a skyrocket! A generation ago, this sin was still regarded as an awful perversion, a sin far more despicable than fornication or adultery. But today, the "gay" lifestyle is increasingly regarded as merely another accepted way of people living together. Not only are a far greater number of people openly living in this sin, but increasingly, the general public is accepting it as a lifestyle that is not necessarily sinful at all.

But God is not fooled. He declares three times in these verses of Romans 1:24-28 that He has given people up to this sin. This explains why it is multiplying so rapidly and why people so blindly are accepting it as a non-sin.

...when God removes His restraint on sin on a worldwide basis, as is evidenced by this homosexual issue today, it means that Judgment Day must be close.

The ominous fact is that when God removes His restraint on sin on a worldwide basis, as is evidenced by this homosexual issue today, it means that Judgment Day must be close. Even as God has removed Himself from the local congregations so that they can easily increasingly rebel against the Law of God, so too, God is removing Himself from restraining sin in the lives of the unsaved of the world. We can only conclude that God is preparing the whole world for His return at which time each and every unsaved person must stand for judgment.

Truly, we can thank God that, at this same perilous time in the earth's history, God is still saving people.

But now we should return to our journey down the timeline of history as we continue to witness the unfolding of God's magnificent salvation plan.

709 B.C. The End of The Ten Tribes

Traveling down the Biblical highway of time has brought us to the year 709 B.C. In the year 709 B.C., disaster struck the ten tribes of Israel, whose capital was Samaria. Because of Israel's constant rebellion against God, after 222 years of existence as a nation, they were completely destroyed by the nation of Assyria.

Incidentally, virtually every commentary on the Bible will give a date of 722 B.C. as the year the nation of Israel was destroyed by the Assyrians, but that conclusion is based on very incomplete archaeological evidence. That date forces the conclusion that the Biblical record or the Biblical writing has errors. (See Thiele, *The Mysterious Numbers of the Hebrew Kings*, pages 118-154.) And that conclusion, that the Bible is in error, is an outstanding demonstration of the low opinion a great number of theologians and Bible teachers have concerning the infallibility of the Bible. See *The Perfect Harmony of the Hebrew Kings* (available free of charge from Family Radio) to learn that when the Bible is understood to be the perfect authority, then the archaeological evidence, though incomplete, does not in any way contradict the Bible. We can be certain that 709 B.C. is the correct date and not 722 B.C.

Then the remnants from Israel joined with the nation of Judah with its capital at Jerusalem. The Bible is very clear as to why Israel was destroyed. We read in 2 Kings 17:7-8:

For so it was, that the children of Israel had sinned against the LORD their God, which had brought them up out of the land of Egypt, from under the hand of Pharaoh king of Egypt, and had feared other gods, and walked in the statutes of the heathen, whom the LORD cast out from before the children of Israel, and

of the kings of Israel, which they had made.

The Bible continues to detail their sins and then declares how God had warned them. 2 Kings 17:13 declares:

Yet the LORD testified against Israel, and against Judah, by all the prophets, and by all the seers, saying, Turn ye from your evil ways, and keep my commandments and my statutes, according to all the law which I commanded your fathers, and which I sent to you by my servants the prophets.

However, Israel did not listen to the prophets of God. They continued in all of their sins. Finally, God declares in 2 Kings 17:18:

Therefore the LORD was very angry with Israel, and removed them out of his sight: there was none left but the tribe of Judah only.

Thus, in the year 709 B.C., Israel, which for 222 years had been an external representation of the kingdom of God, ceased to be a nation. The spotlight of the Gospel will now be pointing at the remaining nation, Judah. This will bring us to the year 609 B.C., the next important milestone in the unfolding drama of God's salvation program.

609 B.C. Disaster Comes to Judah

In the year 709 B.C., a king reigned over Judah who was one of the most God-fearing kings who ever ruled over Judah. His name was Hezekiah, and the Bible has many wonderful things to say about him. During the reign of Hezekiah (715-686 B.C.), Judah experienced great blessings from God.

Unfortunately, however, Hezekiah was followed on the throne by his son Manasseh. Manasseh reigned a long time (697-642 B.C.). During the first eleven years as a young man he reigned as co-regent with his father. When his father, Hezekiah, died, he continued to reign for an additional 44 years. But he proved to be an exceedingly wicked ruler. The consequences of his evil rule were catastrophic for the nation of Judah. We read in 2 Kings 21:11-14:

Because Manasseh king of Judah hath done these abominations, and hath done wickedly above all that the Amorites did, which were before him, and hath made Judah also to sin with his idols:

Therefore thus saith the LORD God of Israel, Behold, I am bringing such evil upon Jerusalem and Judah, that whosoever heareth of it, both his ears shall tingle. And I will stretch over Jerusalem the line of Samaria, and the plummet of the house of Ahab: and I will wipe Jerusalem as a man wipeth a dish, wiping it, and turning it upside down. And I will forsake the remnant of mine inheritance, and deliver them into the hand of their enemies; and they shall become a prey and a spoil to all their enemies.

God is fully capable of bringing to pass any prediction He makes.

Would God punish Judah in such terrible fashion? Indeed, God never gives idle warnings. God is fully capable of bringing to pass any prediction He makes.

But then it looked like the horrendous prediction of doom upon Judah would not happen. Manasseh died, and his son Amon, who was also wicked like his father, reigned for two years and was killed by his servants. The eight-year old son of Amon, a child named Josiah, became king. Josiah proved to be the most obedient, God-fearing king who ever sat on the throne of Israel or Judah.

The Bible declares in 2 Kings 23:25:

And like unto him was there no king before him, that turned to the LORD with all his heart, and with all his soul, and with all his might, according to all the law of Moses; neither after him arose there any like him.

Surely a new era had dawned for the nation of Judah. With such a marvelous kingk they should be set for a long period of enjoying God's blessings.

But God has a timetable for the unfolding of His Gospel plan. We know that this is so because, as we discover the precise way in which God's timeline unfolds, we are finding that God is following a very precise plan. Each element of that plan interlocks with each other in a way that could never happen if God were developing the plan simply depending on how things were going at any time in history.

This is dramatically seen in the situation with Josiah. Judah finally has the finest king they have ever had. Because he began to reign at the young age of eight years, he could conceivably reign for 50 or 60 years. Judah could be guided into a more blessed relationship with God than they ever had before experienced.

But that did not fit God's plan. Even though Josiah excelled spiritually, God declared in 2 Kings 23:26-27:

Notwithstanding the LORD turned not from the fierceness of his great wrath, wherewith his anger was kindled against Judah, because of all the provocations that Manasseh had provoked him withal. And the LORD said, I will remove Judah also out of my sight, as I have removed Israel, and will cast off this city Jerusalem which I have chosen, and the house of which I said, My name shall be there.

The prophecy of God's wrath coming upon Judah had to mesh precisely with God's plan.

Likewise, we must understand that, today, there still exist churches that believe they are altogether faithful to God. Therefore, somehow they believe they are not included in God's judgment falling upon the local congregations.

God's time plan cannot be changed. We have come to the end of the church age, and God's divine process of judgment is already at work in each and every local congregation.* Therefore, even as a wonderful and faithful king like Josiah could not stop God's timetable of judgment, so too, a pastor who believes he is altogether faithful to the Bible cannot stop the present timetable of God's judgment.

Moreover, as we shall learn later in this study, even though Josiah excelled spiritually, the rot of spiritual rebellion permeated Judah. Later we will look at many verses in the Bible that detail this spiritual rottenous.

Thus, disaster came upon Judah exactly one hundred years after the ten tribes of Israel had been destroyed by Assyria. In the year 609 B.C., when Josiah was only 39 years of age, he was killed in battle. Upon his death, Judah lost its independence. First it became subject to the rule of Egypt and then after a few years, it became a servant of Babylon. During the next 23 years inclusively, three sons and one grandson of Josiah each in turn reigned over Judah. But all four of these final kings were vassals of Egypt or of Babylon. Thus, the year 587 B.C. became the next important milestone in the unfolding of God's salvation plan.

587 B.C. Jerusalem is Destroyed

We are proceeding down the timeline of history and have come to a year of great significance. It is the year that the kingdom of Judah was completely

---

* For much more Biblical information on this very serious subject, the reader is invited to send for the books *The End of the Church Age and After* and *Wheat and Tares*, available free of charge from Family Radio.

destroyed by Nebuchadnezzar the king of Babylon. Jerusalem, together with the magnificent temple Solomon had built, was destroyed. A high percentage of the people of Judah were killed and many were taken captive.

Earlier in our study, we learned that this terrible time in the history of the nation of Judah was actually anticipated by the much earlier experiences of the patriarch Jacob. Do you recall that, in the year 1877 B.C,. he was commanded by God to leave the land of Canaan and go to Egypt?

The destruction of Jerusalem by Babylon in the year 587 B.C. was a parallel situation in that Israel was commanded to leave the land of Canaan and go to live in the land of Babylon. The consequence of this change in authority ended up with the complete destruction of Judah inasmuch as the last king of Judah, a king named Zedekiah, rebelled against the king of Babylon.

We read in 2 Kings 24:19-20:

And he did that which was evil in the sight of the LORD, according to all that Jehoiakim had done. For through the anger of the LORD it came to pass in Jerusalem and Judah, until he had cast them out from his presence, that Zedekiah rebelled against the king of Babylon.

We must remember, God was in control of the events that were taking place. It was His plan that Judah would come under the authority of Babylon. We read, for example, in Jeremiah 38:17-18:

Then said Jeremiah unto Zedekiah, Thus saith the LORD, the God of hosts, the God of Israel; If thou wilt assuredly go forth unto the king of Babylon's princes, then thy soul shall live, and this city shall not be burned with fire; and thou shalt live, and thine house: but if thou wilt not go forth to the king of Babylon's princes, then shall this city be given into the hand of the Chaldeans, and they shall burn it with fire, and thou shalt not escape out of their hand.

The above verses, together with a great many others that could be cited, show that God placed the kingdom of Judah under the authority of Babylon. This was done because of the continuing wickedness of Judah.

The final result of this placing of Judah under the authority of Babylon was the utter destruction of Jerusalem.

The final result of this placing of Judah under the authority of Babylon was the utter destruction of Jerusalem. The great tribulation Judah was enduring began officially in the year 609 B.C. when King Josiah was killed in battle. Three months later his son Jehoahaz was removed from the throne by the king of Egypt (2 Kings 23:31-34). The oppression of Judah by Egypt and Babylon would continue for seventy years until the year 539 B.C. when the Jews could be allowed to return from Babylon to Jerusalem. The year 609 B.C. was 322 years after Judah began as a nation.

Remember that we learned that this seventy-year period was divided into two parts. The first part was the twenty-two-year period (23 years inclusive) from 609 B.C. The second part was the period continuing from 587 B.C. to 539 B.C.

In a real sense we could say that God was finished with Judah in the year 609 B.C. The remaining four kings were all under the authority of heathen nations so that, in principle, God had left Judah and had as it were turned over the rulership of Judah first to Egypt and finally to Babylon. Babylon in turn finally destroyed the nation of Judah. The Bible gives us the exact day of the year when this occurred. We read in Jeremiah 39:2:

And in the eleventh year of Zedekiah, in the fourth month, the ninth day of the month, the city was broken up.

This tragic event was not by any means the end of God's salvation program in the world. The events that were literally happening at that time in history were a portrait or an anticipation of God's plan for the time of the Great Tribulation of our day. While Jerusalem had become the scene of horror and destruction beginning in 609 B.C., in Babylon the true believers were being protected by God. They were a portrait or an anticipation of all the true believers who are living during the second part of the present Great Tribulation.

We read in Jeremiah 29:4-7:

Thus saith the LORD of hosts, the God of Israel, unto all that are carried away captives, whom I have caused to be carried away from Jerusalem unto Babylon; Build ye houses, and dwell in them; and plant gardens, and eat the fruit of them; take ye wives, and beget sons and daughters; and take wives for your sons, and give your daughters to husbands, that they may bear sons and daughters; that ye may be increased there, and not diminished. And seek the peace of the city whither I have caused you to be carried away captives, and pray unto the LORD for it: for in the peace thereof shall ye have peace.

These verses altogether identify with God's present program as He sends the Gospel through the world during this present time of the latter rain and the end of the world harvest.

It is curious and perhaps very significant the way God has woven into the fabric of the histories of the two nations Israel and Judah, and also during the church age, two numbers that signify judgment. They are the numbers 23 and 37. We will tentatively develop this concept a bit further, although later, in Chapter 8, some of these conclusions will be repeated.

Twenty-Three Kings

Remember that both of these two nations had 20 monarchs who ruled during their existence. Moreover, both of these nations had their earliest beginning when Saul became the first king. He ruled over the twelve tribes of Israel as did King David and as did King Solomon who followed him. Upon Solomon's death, two of these tribes became the nation of Judah, and ten of the tribes became the nation of Israel. Therefore, in a real sense, the nation of Israel, which consisted of the 10 tribes, had a total of 20 plus 3 = 23 monarchs rule over them. Likewise in a real sense the nation of Judah which consisted of two tribes had 20 + 3 monarchs rule over them. Thus, both nations were tied into the number 23 which signifies judgment. And significantly, both nations ended under the judgment of God.

> *Thus, both nations were tied into the number 23 which signifies judgment.*

Moreover, the nation of Israel existed as an independent nation from 931 B.C. until 709 B.C. when they were destroyed by the nation of Assyria. 931 - 709 = 222 years that they existed as a nation. Significantly, the number 222 is the product of 2 x 3 x 37. As Chapter 8 shows, the number 2 identifies with those who are caretakers of the Bible; the number 3 signifies God's purpose; and the number 37 God's judgment.

Thus, we see hidden within the 222 years of the history of Israel that it was God's purpose (No. 3) that eventually those who were made caretakers of the Bible (No. 2) would come into judgment (No. 37).

Likewise, the nation of Judah was an independent nation from 931 B.C. until 609 B.C. 931 - 609 = 322 years. The number 322 breaks down into 2 x 7 x 23. As Chapter 8 shows, the number 7 signifies perfect completeness. Thus, we see hidden within the 322 years of the history of Judah that God's people (No. 2) would perfectly completely (No. 7) eventually come under God's judgment (No. 23).

Later we will learn that the duration of the church age extended from A.D. 33 to A.D. 1988 (1988 - 33 = 1955 years). The number 1955 breaks down into 5 x 17 x 23. From Chapter 8 we learn that the number five signifies God's salvation or judgment, and the number 17 signifies heaven. Therefore, we will learn that during the church age, which lasted 1955 years, God's salvation program (No. 5) brought people to heaven (No. 17), but the church age would end in judgment (No. 23).

It is also curious and perhaps significant that the history of the twelve tribes of Israel, which began in the year 1047 B.C. when Saul was made king, ended in the year 587 B.C. when Babylon destroyed the temple and Jerusalem. 1047 - 587 = 460 years. The number 460 breaks down into the significant numbers 10 x 2 x 23. Since the number 10 signifies completeness, we again get the message that those who were believers (No. 2) would be under God's complete (No.10) judgment (No. 23).

Amazingly, another significant number is also woven into the history of Israel. As previously noted the twelve tribes became a nation in the year 1047 B.C. In the year 609 B.C. King Josiah was killed in battle, and, for the remaining 23 years inclusive, the kings of Judah were altogether controlled by Egypt and Babylon. Therefore Judah ceased to exist as an independent nation in the year 609 B.C. Thus the year 609 B.C., in a sense, was the year of the end of Judah, although it was the year 587 B.C. that they no longer had a land or a temple that belonged to them.

It is also remarkable to note the time interval from the destruction of Sodom and Gomorrah, which took place in the year 2067 B.C., and the destruction of Judah in 587 B.C. 2067 - 587 = 1480. The number 1480 breaks down into the significant numbers 10 x 2 x 2 x 37, thus indicating that even as Sodom and Gomorrah came into judgment, so the body of believers (No.2) came into complete (No.10) judgment (No.37).

> *...beginning with Abraham and until Christ came, the nation of Israel was the centerpiece of God's salvation plan.*

We must keep in mind that, beginning with Abraham and until Christ came, the nation of Israel was the centerpiece of God's salvation plan. By examining these time relationships, we are learning that their time location in history was not erratic, haphazard, or capricious. There existed a well-defined time plan. Israel was raised up by God to be an external representation of the kingdom of God. However, as we count the number of kings that ruled over them or review the time durations of their existence, we learn very clearly that, even though they, in many ways, were a special people of God, this did not protect them from judgment. Fact is, they became a prime example that however holy and righteous we may think we have become, we are still under the wrath of God, if we have not become saved. This was dramatically illustrated by the eventual destruction of both Israel and Judah after Israel became divided, as well as by the local congregations of the church age that also eventually came under the wrath of God.

There are more time relationships relating to the nations of Israel and Judah. We can take note, for example, that David ascended the throne in the Jubilee year of 1007 B.C. Exactly 1000 years later in the Jubilee year, Christ was born. David, as the physical king of physical Israel, typified Christ who is the spiritual King who rules spiritually forever over the spiritual kingdom of God that consists of all true believers in Christ.

Again we might take note of the fact that David ascended the throne of Israel in the year 1007 B.C. Exactly 1,040 inclusive years later, in the year A.D. 33, Christ arose from the dead. The number 1,040 breaks down into the significant numbers 2 x 2 x 2 x 13 x 10. Spiritually, this can signify that in the super fullness of God's timetable (No.13), the complete (No.10) number of the believers (No.2) will become saved.

> *We have taken time in our study of the unfolding of the timeline of history to show that God has a very methodical, carefully worked out plan for His salvation program.*

We have taken time in our study of the unfolding of the timeline of history to show that God has a very methodical, carefully worked out plan for His salvation program. This plan is carefully structured so that nothing happens capriciously or in some erratic fashion. This is why God declares in Galatians 4:4-5:

> **But when the fulness of the time was come, God sent forth his Son, made of a woman, made under the law, to redeem them that were under the law, that we might receive the adoption of sons.**

The term fullness of time indicates there was a precise time in history when Jesus was to be crucified. This fact is also emphasized by the language of Luke 9:51 and John 13:1. We read in Luke 9:51:

And it came to pass, when the time was come that he should be received up, he stedfastly set his face to go to Jerusalem.

And God says in John 13:1:

Now before the feast of the passover, when Jesus knew that his hour was come that he should depart out of this world unto the Father, having loved his own which were in the world, he loved them unto the end.

We, therefore, can be assured, as we progress down the timeline of history and finally come to the end of time, we will learn that the closing events of the history of the world must fit into a very well-developed pattern of time pre-prepared and pre-ordained by God.

This brings us to the next important milestone as God unfolded His Gospel program for the world. That was the year 539 B.C. which was precisely seventy years after Judah was placed under heathen rule in the year 609 B.C.

539 B.C. Babylon Conquered

In the year 539 B.C., Babylon was conquered by the Media-Persian ruler Darius who is also called Cyrus in the Bible. (He is the Cyrus of archaeological history who ruled from 559 B.C. to 529 B.C.) This event is recorded in the Book of Daniel. Following the conquering of Babylon, King Cyrus made a decree that the Jews could return to Jerusalem and rebuild the temple. For the next 500 years, however, Israel, which again consisted of 12 tribes, would not be an independent nation. They were under the rule of the Media-Persian empire or under Roman rule. Finally, in A.D. 70, Jerusalem was destroyed by the Romans, and they ceased to be a nation amongst the nations of the world. During these closing years of the history of Old Testament Israel, they continued to be an external representation of the kingdom of God, but the light of the Gospel was very dim in the world.

There is one more significant milestone noted in the Old Testament we should take note of, that is, the year 391 B.C. It is a significant milestone because it appears to be the last Biblical record of God interrelating with Old Testament Israel.

391 B.C. The Last Old Testament Word From God

What could be significant about the year 391 B.C.? Let us explore that question for a moment. As a part of the Bible, we find the Book of Esther. This book details experiences of the nation of Israel about 140 years after the auspicious year of 539 B.C., when the Jews were permitted to return from Babylon and go to Jerusalem.

The Book of Esther, like the Book of Jonah, is a historical parable. That is, it is a true historical narrative placed in the Bible to illustrate spiritual truth. The chief characters and what they spiritually represent are as follows.

King Ahasuerus	Almighty God
Provinces ruled over by King Ahasuerus	All the kingdoms of the world
Queen Vashti	Nation of Israel
Queen Esther	All true believers headed up by Christ
Mordecai	The Holy Spirit
Haman	Satan
Haman's ten sons	Satan as also represented by the ten horns of Revelation

Simply outlined, the narrative begins with Queen Vashti disobeying the king and, therefore, being replaced by Queen Esther. This points to the nation of Israel, who. in the Old Testament, was spiritually married to God, being replaced by the New Testament true believers who become the bride of Christ. In this historical parable, Esther therefore represents:

1. The New Testament true believers who are married to Christ.

2. Christ Himself as the head of the true believers.
   Christ represents the true believers because He took upon Himself their sins.

Included in the Media-Persian kingdom of King Ahasuerus were the Jews who lived in the capital city, Shushan, which was located east of Babylon, as well as in many of the other 127 provinces. Esther and Mordecai were Jews.

The wicked Haman who was very highly placed in the Kingdom managed to get permission to kill all the Jews, which, unbeknownst to the king, would include Queen Esther. Haman cast the lot (like throwing dice) to determine which day the annihilation of the Jews would take place. The answer was the thirteenth day of the twelfth month of the twelfth year (Esther 3:7; 9:1), of the reign of King Ahasuerus.

Queen Esther, at the risk of her own life, pleaded for the Jews and received permission from the king that allowed the Jews to fight against Haman's ten sons and all the enemies of the Jews. The king also had Haman executed because he had plotted to have Esther killed.

Therefore, on the appointed day, the Jews were completely victorious over their enemies and the ten sons of Haman were hanged.

This historical victory by the king's command was thereafter annually celebrated by the Jewish nation as the feast of Purim, a word signifying the casting of the lot (Hebrew *"pur"*).

This historical parable is definitely pointing to the end of the world when Satan and all the unsaved will be cast into the second death, eternal damnation. It also gives very valuable information relating to the calendar of history.

When Did King Ahasuerus Reign

Which Persian king of history was the Ahasuerus of the Book of Esther? We must know this in order to place the events recorded in the Book of Esther in their proper place in the timeline of history. This information will guide us to the very significant year in which the Old Testament was completed by God.

Surprisingly, the common theological thinking is that this Ahasuerus was King Xerxes who reigned from 486 B.C.-465 B.C. This conclusion, that it was this king, is made with no evidence to support it except for what is found in typical statements that emphasize that he was a self-indulgent tyrant. Obviously, this statement is indicating that no substantial information has been found that links Xerxes to King Ahasuerus of the Book of Esther.

There is, however, at least some information that can help to identify which king of Persian history was the Ahasuerus of the Book of Esther. If we can with any certainty discover which king of secular history was king Ahasuerus, we should also be helped in our calendar of history. We should spend a bit of time to try to discover which Persian king Ahasuerus could have been.

First, we must realize the name "Ahasuerus" was probably a title, much like the word "Pharaoh" was a title used by Egyptian kings. This is strongly suggested when we examine two other words recorded in the Bible. These are the words "prince" and "lieutenants."

The Hebrew word "Ahasuerus" is transliterated in our alphabet as "achashwerosh." A very similar word, "achashdarpan" is translated as "prince" (Daniel 6:1-7). Additionally, the word "achashdarpenin" is translated as "lieutenants" in Esther 3:12, 8:9, and 9:3.

It is easy to see the similarity of these three words.

a cha sh werosh	Ahasuerus
a cha sh darpan	prince
a cha sh dar penin	lieutenants

Since the second and third words signify the titles "prince" and "lieutenant," it is easy to see the likelihood that the first word also signifies a title. Since Ahasuerus was a king even as Pharaoh (a title) was king of Egypt, we strongly suspect that just as the word "Pharaoh" is equivalent to "king," so too, the word "Ahasuerus" is equivalent to "king."

Given this clue, what could be another name for Ahasuerus? The Septuagint, a Greek translation of the Old Testament, translates the word "Ahaseres" as Artaxerxes. Josephus, a Jewish historian who lived about the time of Christ, also emphasizes that Ahasuerus was Artaxerxes. Of course we cannot trust the Septuagint and Josephus as we do the Bible. Their conclusions, however, do reflect the common opinion of about 2,000 years ago.

Their conclusions also agree with the testimony of the Bible. In Ezra 4:6, 11, we read:

And in the reign of Ahasuerus, in the beginning of his reign, wrote they unto him an accusation against the inhabitants of Judah and Jerusalem. This is the copy of the letter that they sent unto him, even unto Artaxerxes the king; Thy servants the men on this side the river, and at such a time.

The context shows that Ahasuerus and Artaxerxes are names for the same king.

Furthermore, King Ahasuerus/Artaxerxes of Ezra Chapter 4 was a king who ruled between the time of the rule of Cyrus (559-529 B.C.), and the rule of Darius I (522-485 B.C.) (Ezra 4:24). The two kings who ruled in this time interval were Cambyses (529-522 B.C.) and Smerdis (522 B.C.). Therefore, either of these two kings would have carried the title Ahasuerus/Artaxerxes spoken of in Ezra 4:6-23.

We should look carefully for other kings who bore the name Artaxerxes. The secular record shows us the reigns of the following Persian kings.*

Cyrus	559-529 B.C.
Cambyses	529-522 B.C.
Smerdis	522 B.C.
Darius I	522-485 B.C.
Xerxes I	486-465 B.C.
Artaxerxes I	465-424 B.C.
Xerxes II	424-423 B.C.
Darius II	423-404 B.C.
Artaxerxes II	404-358 B.C.

In this list of kings, there are two who are named Artaxerxes. The first is Artaxerxes I who reigned from the year 465 B.C. to the year 424 B.C. He is the Artaxerxes spoken of in Ezra 7:1 who gave Ezra permission, in the year 458 B.C., to teach the law in Jerusalem. We read in Ezra 7:12, 25:

> **Artaxerxes, king of kings, unto Ezra the priest, a scribe of the law of the God of heaven, perfect peace, and at such a time. . . . And thou, Ezra, after the wisdom of thy God, that *is* in thine hand, set magistrates and judges, which may judge all the people that are beyond the river, all such as know the laws of thy God; and teach ye them that know them not.**

He is the Artaxerxes who, in the year 445 B.C., gave Nehemiah permission to rebuild the walls of Jerusalem (Nehemiah 2:1-8).

Moreover, the archaeological record which relates to the Book of Nehemiah identifies a number of the individuals named in the Book of Nehemiah.

---

* *Encyclopaedia Britannica*, Vol. 17, 1959, pp. 554, 555.

These are Hanini (Nehemiah 7:2), Sanballat (Nehemiah 2:10), Johanan (Nehemiah 12:22), and Geshem, the Arabian (Nehemiah 6:1). But in the archaeological record, no identification with any of the names in the Book of Esther have been found. Thus, it strongly appears that the Artaxerxes of the Book of Nehemiah was a different Artaxerxes than that of the Book of Esther.

The other Artaxerxes in the list of the kings is Artaxerxes II who reigned from 404 B.C. to 358 B.C. He in all probability must be King Ahasuerus of the Book of Esther. His long reign together with his reputation fits him well. The *Encyclopaedia Britannica* (1959 Edition, Vol. 17, pg. 555), makes the comment, "Artaxerxes I and Artaxerxes II, so far from being gloomy despots, were good-natured potentates, but weak, capricious and readily accessible to personal influences." This quotation very well identifies Artaxerxes II with Ahasuerus of the Book of Esther. We read in the Bible about his lavish feasting and his accessibility to the desires of wicked Haman.

Another reason might be advanced as to why Artaxerxes II is King Ahasuerus of the Book of Esther. It was his long reign. We see a direct parallel in the Book of Esther to that which is reported in Genesis concerning the Pharaoh who appointed Joseph Prime Minister. Remember that Joseph, at the age of 30, in the year 1886 B.C., became second in command to the Egyptian Pharaoh. We read in Genesis 41:41-44:

And Pharaoh said unto Joseph, See, I have set thee over all the land of Egypt. And Pharaoh took off his ring from his hand, and put it upon Joseph's hand, and arrayed him in vestures of fine linen, and put a gold chain about his neck; and he made him to ride in the second chariot which he had; and they cried before him, Bow the knee: and he made him ruler over all the land of Egypt. And Pharaoh said unto Joseph, I am Pharaoh, and without thee shall no man lift up his hand or foot in all the land of Egypt.

Please note the parallel language in the Book of Esther 10:3:

For Mordecai the Jew was next unto king Ahasuerus, and great among the Jews, and accepted of the multitude of his brethren, seeking the wealth of his people, and speaking peace to all his seed.

We now should take note of the results of this arrangement in which a heathen king began using a Jewish person as second in command. The Pharaoh of Joseph's day was Sesostris III who reigned from 1888 B.C. to 1850 B.C., a long reign of 38 years. Artaxerxes II reigned from 404 B.C. to 358 B.C., a long reign of 46 years.

Furthermore, the events recorded in Nehemiah and Ezra were greatly spiritual in nature, while those in the Book of Esther are far different in their spiritual content. Reading these Biblical books gives virtually no possibility of the same Persian king ruling. All of the evidence points to the fact that the only Artaxerxes who could identify with the Book of Esther has to be Artaxerxes II who reigned from 404 B.C. to 358 B.C.

Returning to the Book of Esther, we read that the victory of the Jews over their enemies, which included the hanging of the ten sons of Haman, occurred on the thirteenth day of the twelfth month of the twelfth year of the king's reign. Since we have learned that the first year of King Ahasuerus was 404 B.C., his twelfth year was 392 B.C. However, the twelfth month of his twelfth year would have been approximately March of 391 B.C.

The year 391 B.C. becomes an extremely significant milestone in the unfolding of God's salvation plan.

We read in Esther 9:32:

And the decree of Esther confirmed these matters of Purim; and it was written in the book.

Obviously, the book referred to in this verse is the Bible. This is so because it is in the Bible that we find the historical record of the beginning of the feast of Purim.

We know of no other writings in the Old Testament that were written at a later date than 391 B.C. Thus, we can be certain that God ended the writing of the Old Testament in the year 391 B.C., at the time the Book of Esther was finished. Later in our study, we will discover that it was in the year 8 B.C. that God again began to bring new revelation that would become the New Testament of the Bible.

There is another very interesting fact that presents itself in this account of the Book of Esther. As we have noted, the victory of Esther and the Jews over Haman and all of the enemies of the Jews is a dramatic portrait of the end of the world. At that time Satan (typified by Haman and his ten sons), will be cast into hell. At the same time, all the enemies of Christ (typified by the wicked people who wanted the Jews killed) will also be cast into hell.

The number twelve signifies fullness. Thus, the twelfth year and the twelfth month emphasize that, in the fullness of time, Christ will end the world. Could it be that the thirteenth day signifies the end of 13,000 years? We will learn that precisely 13,000 years after creation, the Great Tribulation did begin and that set into motion the closing events of the history of the world. Indeed, the year 391 B.C. appears to be a significant milestone as God unfolds His salvation program throughout time.

The last notice of God's reporting in the Old Testament is this small Book of Esther. It is there that we find the last Old Testament Word from God. This came in the year 391 B.C. during the twelfth month of the twelfth year of the reign of the Media-Persian King Artaxerxes II. The citation is found in Esther 9:32:

And the decree of Esther confirmed these matters of Purim; and it was written in the book.

The only book that can be in view is the Bible. It is in the Bible that these matters were written. Significantly, the number of years between 391 B.C., when God last spoke in the Old Testament day, until A.D. 2011, when God will again in all likelihood speak as He comes with the voice of the chief messenger (I Thessalonians 4:16), equals 391 + 2,011 - 1 = 2,401 years. The number 2,401 breaks down into 7 x 7 x 7 x 7. How interesting!

Moreover, we will discover that it was in the year 7 B.C. that Christ, in all likelihood, was born. Significantly, the number of years from 391 B.C. to 7 B.C. equals 384 years. Also very significantly, the number 384 breaks down into 3 x 2^7 or 3 x 2 x 2 x 2 x 2 x 2 x 2 x 2. In the next chapter, we will learn the possible significance of these numbers.

Fact is, from time to time we have indicated that there could be important spiritual significance to certain time intervals that have occurred as God has unfolded His salvation plan. Therefore, before we continue down the highway of time, we should carefully address the question of God's use of numbers in the Bible. This we will do as we continue our study.

Chapter 8
The Numbers In The Bible

As we are proceeding with our study of the unfolding of the timeline of history, we constantly are making reference to numbers that God has recorded in the Bible. These numbers are placed in the Bible by God and, therefore, are to be very seriously considered. That is, we must not gloss over them as if they have little or no importance. Therefore, before we continue our study we should pause to learn how God uses numbers in the Bible. Given the spiritual principle that we are to compare spiritual things with spiritual (I Corinthians 2:13), and given the fact that the whole Bible and all that it declares is an integral part of the spiritual message, we know we must search the Bible to discover how God uses numbers.*

> *These numbers are placed in the Bible by God and, therefore, are to be very seriously considered.*

Moreover, we must carefully consider God's use of numbers in the Bible because it is the numbers in the Biblical text that have especially given cause to a mistrust of the Bible. For example, there is probably no other body of Biblical citations that has done more to seem to invalidate the authority of the Bible than those pertaining to the duration of the reigns of the Hebrew kings.

We read, for example, in one citation (2 Kings 8:26), that Ahaziah was 22 years old when he began to reign. Yet in another citation (2 Chronicles 22:2), we read that he was 42 years old when he began to reign.

Or, for example, we read in 1 Samuel 13:1 that Saul was apparently one year old when he began to reign. Many more of these kinds of apparent errors can be cited in connection with the reigns of these kings.

The result of these apparent contradictions and errors is that a great many theologians have concluded that the numbers of the Bible are not accurate;

---

* We must be careful not to confuse an activity called "numerology" with the study of the numbers of the Bible. Numerology has to do with assigning number values to the Hebrew or Greek letters and adding together the number values of Bible words in an attempt to arrive at a hidden Bible message. Numerology has no Biblical validation and is not related in any sense to anything written in this book.

they are not to be trusted. They have concluded that perhaps they are not accurate, not because they are not accurate in the original manuscript, but perhaps a scribe made an error in transcribing a later copy.

In any case, these apparent errors associated with the numbers of the Bible are very obvious and, therefore, they conclude that we cannot trust any numbers of the Bible.

> *After all, numbers are words and the whole Bible consists of words. If some words of the Bible are not to be trusted, then how can we trust any words of the Bible?*

This conclusion concerning the apparent inaccuracies of the numbers of the Bible destroys the authority of the whole Bible. If the ancient copies, from which we obtain our present Bible, are inaccurate insofar as the numbers of the Bible are concerned, then how can they be trusted concerning any part of the Bible? After all, numbers are words and the whole Bible consists of words. If some words of the Bible are not to be trusted, then how can we trust any words of the Bible? We thus can understand why so many Bible scholars do not trust the Bible. They like what they read when it pleases them, but a passage that does not please them can easily be set aside in their minds as having no binding authority.

Unfortunately, this undercurrent of mistrust is far more in place than we might think. So many preachers and teachers of the Bible stress that the Bible is the infallible, inerrant Word of God, yet in practice, they subject themselves to the authority of the Bible only when it appears to agree with the theological ideas that they themselves or their church hold. But when the Bible appears to disagree with their theological position, the Biblical citation in question is disregarded or modified in their thinking so that it does agree with their theological position.

This kind of conduct is often consciously or unconsciously fostered and encouraged because they at some time in their studies have read commentaries that suggest the possibility of scribal error, particularly in connection with the numbers of the Bible.

There are no errors or real contradictions in the Bible. The whole Bible in the original languages is completely trustworthy. This includes every word whether it is a number or some other word.

The only errors that may be found will be those resulting from faulty translation into our present languages or because inferior Greek texts were used in translating the New Testament. Wonderfully, the King James translation has used the correct Greek copies.

For example, in connection with the apparent contradiction of Ahaziah being 22 years of age (2 Kings 8:26) and also 42 years of age (2 Chronicles 22:2), when he began to reign, the solution is that in the first instance, God is teaching that he was indeed 22 years old when he began to reign. In the second citation, God is teaching that he began to reign 42 years after the kingly dynasty of Omri, of whom Ahaziah was a descendant, began. (For a full discussion of these apparent discrepancies, the reader is invited to obtain free of charge the book *The Perfect Harmony of the Hebrew Kings* from Family Radio.)

> *Each and every word, even each letter of each word, in the original languages was precisely what God desired.*

We must bear in mind that the Bible was crafted by God. Each and every word, even each letter of each word, in the original languages was precisely what God desired. Because He is God, He could have designed the Bible so that any six-year-old child could clearly understand each and every teaching that God wished mankind to understand.

But God purposely wrote the Bible so that it would be difficult to discover many truths of the Bible. Jesus declares in Mark 4:11-12:

> **And he said unto them, Unto you it is given to know the mystery of the kingdom of God: but unto them that are without, all these things are done in parables: That seeing they may see, and not perceive; and hearing they may hear, and not understand; lest at any time they should be converted, and their sins should be forgiven them.**

In Proverbs 25:2, He further declares:

> **It is the glory of God to conceal a thing: but the honour of kings is to search out a matter.**

God declares in 1 Corinthians 2:11-14:

> **For what man knoweth the things of a man, save the spirit of man which is in him? Even so the things of God knoweth no man, but the Spirit of God. Now we have received, not the spirit of the world, but the spirit which is of God; that we might know the**

things that are freely given to us of God. Which things also we speak, not in the words which man's wisdom teacheth, but which the Hold Ghost teacheth; comparing spiritual things with spiritual. But the natural man receiveth not the things of the Spirit of God: for they are foolishness unto him: neither can he know them, because they are spiritually descerned.

> *God purposely wrote the Bible to foster unbelief in the hearts of those who do not want the salvation of the Bible.*

As we examine these citations, we begin to understand that God purposely wrote the Bible to foster unbelief in the hearts of those who do not want the salvation of the Bible. For them, the Bible appears to contain errors, contradictions, and many things that apparently have no relationship to truth.

This, I believe, is the reason that the numbers that relate to the chronology of the kings of Judah and Israel appear so frequently to be in error.

But when we adopt Biblical principles, namely, that we are to trust that every word in the Bible in the original languages is God-breathed, that we are to compare Scripture with Scripture, and that we are to pray for wisdom, asking that the Holy Spirit will lead us into truth, these supposed errors and contradictions will be eliminated. If they are not eliminated, it means that we must patiently wait upon God because ultimately they will be eliminated. This is so simply because the Bible is the Word of God.

Emphasis must be made once more: In trying to understand a difficult passage, we must never countenance the thought that perhaps a word of a phrase has been accidentally or purposely altered by a scribe in transcribing from one copy to another. We can rest assured that not only did holy men of God speak as God the Holy Spirit moved them (2 Peter 1:21), but also God protected His Word so that it would be available in its pure form to succeeding generations.

We must keep in mind that numbers are words and therefore should be studied and defined like any word in the Bible. That is, if we wish to know the meaning of a word, we should locate that word wherever it can be found in the original language of the Bible. By examining the context of each place it is used ordinarily it is possible to know the meaning of that word as it is used in the Bible. Thus, for example, we can learn from the Bible that the word "grace" may be defined as "God's free gift of salvation." Occasionally, some help in understanding a word used in the Bible may come from a non-Biblical source. However, the ideal source should be the Bible.

Frequently, words have more than one meaning. The Hebrew word "*yam*," for example, is translated as the word "sea" and as the word "west" in addition to several other ways, depending upon the context.

Frequently, words can be understood in a literal physical manner and also to signify spiritual truth. For example, the word "lamb" can refer to an animal, the offspring of a sheep, but it can also refer to Jesus as the Lamb of God who was offered to take away our sins.

We must remember numbers are words and the same rules apply to numbers that apply to words. We, therefore, discover that a number can be understood in various ways. Following are the most common ways the Bible uses numbers.

1. Numbers can be used to measure the passage of time. For example, Israel was in Egypt for 430 years (Exodus 12:40).

2. Numbers can be used to describe how many people, objects, things etc., are being spoken of. Thus, we read that their were eight souls on the ark (1 Peter 3:20).

3. Numbers can be used to describe the size of an object. For example, the ark was 300 cubits long and 50 cubits wide (Genesis 6:15).

4. Numbers can have a literal, physical application and at the same time also a spiritual or symbolical application. For example, we read in John 21:11 of 153 fish that were caught. This was the literal number that were caught but the number 153 also has a definite spiritual application, as we shall presently learn.

    At times the spiritual application will be readily seen and at times it may be hidden from our understanding.

5. In some instances, in a particular context a number may have only a spiritual or symbolical meaning.

    For example, Jesus was asked the question in Matthew 18:21:

Then came Peter to him, and said, Lord, how oft shall my brother sin against me, and I forgive him? till seven times?

And Jesus answered in the next verse:

Jesus saith unto him, I say not unto thee, Until seven times: but, Until seventy times seven.

Seventy times seven equals four hundred and ninety. Was Jesus teaching that when we have forgiven someone 490 times we can then stop forgiving that person? We know that the number 490 is not being used in that fashion because the rest of the chapter teaches that we are to forgive each other as Christ has forgiven us. We know that Christ does not just forgive 490 of our sins but He forgives all of the sins of those for whom He died.

> *The numbers 70 and 7 are conveying the spiritual truth that our forgiving is to be completely perfect which means we are never to stop forgiving.*

Therefore, we must understand the numbers 70 x 7 in this context are conveying the truth that there is to be no limit to the number of sins we are to forgive of each other. The numbers 70 and 7 are conveying the spiritual truth that our forgiving is to be completely perfect which means we are never to stop forgiving.

Another illustration is recorded in Psalm 105:8, where God declares:

He hath remembered his covenant for ever, the word which he commanded to a thousand generations.

The translators incorrectly translated the Hebrew word for "generation" as a plural word. However, in the original Hebrew, it is a singular word. Thus, the verse should read "the word which He commanded to a **thousand generation.**" But that does not make any apparent sense. What kind of a generation is a thousand generation? Only when we realize that the number 1,000 can spiritually mean that which is complete does the meaning of the verse become clear. God's commands are to a complete generation. The generation that God has in mind based on the context in which this phrase is found are all the peoples of the earth. Psalm 105, verse 7, shows this:

He is the LORD our God: his judgments are in all the earth.

Likewise, when we read Revelation 20:2-7 we learn that Satan was bound for a thousand years. But when we carefully study everything in the Bible that relates to the binding of Satan, we learn that 1,000 years covers the whole period of time from A.D. 33 to A.D. 1988. This obviously is a much larger period of time than a literal 1,000 years. Therefore, even as was the situation in Psalm 105 the "one thousand" is a synonym for the word "complete" or "completeness." Satan was bound for the completeness (1,000 years) of God's timetable for his binding.

6. Frequently large numbers can be broken down to smaller significant numbers to expose the spiritual significance of the larger number.

Two outstanding examples can be given. In John Chapter 21 God by means of a historical parable describes all of those who will become saved during the latter rain. This is the time when there will be the final salvation period during which all those who are to become saved will become saved. It occurs during the second part of the Great Tribulation which will immediately precede the end of the world. God describes these who are to be saved as 153 fish that were caught in a net that did not break and which were brought to land without the use of a ship. The number 153 equals 3 x 3 x 17. Presently we will learn that the number three signifies God's will or purpose and the number 17, if it has spiritual meaning, signifies "heaven." Therefore, the 153 fish signify that it is the purpose (No. 3) of God to bring to heaven (No. 17) all of those who are to be saved during the Great Tribulation.

Similarly, in Acts 27:37 God speaks of 276 individuals who were aboard a ship that was totally wrecked in a severe storm. However, all 276 people were saved. The number 276 breaks down into the numbers 12 x 23 or the number 3 x 2 x 2 x 23. Spiritually it can be shown that the destroyed ship represents the end of the church age. The number 276 spiritually represents that it was God's purpose (No. 3) that those who are to continue to bring the Gospel (No. 2) would be rescued from the judgment (23) that destroyed the ship (the local churches).

As we study the Bible, we occasionally notice that in the recording of certain historical events a number appears to be featured. This is true, for example, in connection with the accounts of the crucifixion of our Savior. Remember there were three crosses, three denials by Peter, three apostles with Him in the Garden of Gethsemane, three times Jesus prayed in the Garden, the announcement on the cross "Jesus of Nazareth King of the Jews" was in three languages, three groups of men, the chief priests, the elders, and all the council wanted Him killed (Matthew 26:59, etc.). Included are some larger numbers that feature the number three. For example, thirty pieces of silver were paid to betray

Him and there was three hours of darkness, from the sixth to the ninth hour (Matthew 27:45).

Numbers May Convey Spiritual Truth

Is the development of all of these events that were done and recorded so that the number three is repeatedly in view accidental or incidental? Or is God, by the use of the number three, conveying a great spiritual message that every thing that happened in connection with the crucifixion of Jesus was altogether in accordance with God's purpose or God's will.

Similarly, we find the number 23 featured in places in the Bible where the judgment of God is definitely in view. For example in Daniel 8:14 God teaches that the sanctuary and the host would be trodden under foot 2,300 days. In I Corinthians 10:10 God speaks of a plague that killed 23,000 individuals in one day. That this is focusing on the number 23 as a number of judgment can be quickly understood because in Numbers 25:9 the Bible records that there were 24,000 killed in the plague. There is no contradiction between these two accounts. It is obvious that of the total number of 24,000 killed in the plague, 23,000 were killed in one day and that means that an additional 1,000 were killed in a second day. However, God is particularly associating the number 23 with His judgment on sin. We thus learn that the number 23 can convey the spiritual meaning of God's judgment or God's wrath.

If we look at many numbers of the Bible, therefore, we can see that they may be conveying spiritual truth as well as teaching simple numerical value.

The number 2 is used frequently to describe those who bring the Gospel. Jesus sent the 70 out "two and two" (Luke 10:1). Revelation Chapter 11 describes the two witnesses who were killed and then again stood on their feet to bring the Gospel. In Acts Chapter 13 Paul and Barnabas were sent out together as first missionaries. Thus, if the number 2 has symbolical or spiritual meaning, it would identify with those who are to bring the Gospel or who are the caretakers of the Bible.

The number 4 identifies with the whole world. The Bible speaks of north, south, east, and west. Or it speaks of four winds (Matthew 24:31), or four corners of the land (Ezekiel 7:2). Thus, if the number 4 has any symbolical or spiritual meaning, it would identify with universality or worldwide.

But the number 4 is also used to convey universality in the sense of going all the way to the end. For example, Jesus waited until Lazarus was dead four days before he was raised (John 11:15-17). King Jehu's dynasty was allowed to continue through four kings (2 Kings 10:30). Israel came out of Egypt in the fourth generation after being afflicted 400 years. (Genesis 15:13-16).

Abraham bought a burial ground for his wife Sarah for 400 shekels (Genesis 23:15) because she represents all true believers all the way to the end of time who expect to receive with Sarah their resurrected bodies. In all of these instances the use of the number four is to indicate to the extremity or end of time even as it is used to point to the ends of the world which would be worldwide.

The number 5 very frequently identifies with salvation or judgment. Christ had to experience judgment to bring salvation so we are not surprised that both judgment and salvation identify with the number 5. The number 5 is used both as ½ which is .5 and as 5 or 50 or 500 or 5,000, etc. We immediately think of the temple tax which was .5 shekel, or of the 5,000 who were fed by Jesus, or of the 5 wise and 5 foolish virgins etc. Thus, if the number 5 has any symbolical or spiritual meaning it would be that of salvation or judgment.

If the number 6 has any symbolical or spiritual meaning it probably should identify with work. Jesus worked six days to create the universe. The number 666 of Revelation 13:18 identifies with the unsaved who essentially are working to get right with God.

The number 7 is used throughout the Bible in the sense of a completed cycle (seven days, seven years) or in the sense of perfect completeness. For example, earlier we looked at forgiveness to be 70 x 7 times.

The number 9 is 3 x 3. Therefore, symbolically or spiritually it should signify "purpose."

The number 10 like the number 100, or 1,000 or 10,000 etc. signifies completeness. The Bible speaks of 10 coins, 100 sheep, 1,000 years, 1,000 generations, etc. Thus, if it has any symbolical or spiritual meaning, it should be that of "completeness."

The number 11 is frequently used in the Bible to convey the idea of defective fullness. For example, there were 12 tribes (actually 13 tribes) of Israel, but after David pridefully numbered Israel, God speaks of 11 tribes (I Kings 11:31-32). When the Apostle Judas took his own life after he betrayed Jesus, there were left eleven apostles. Immediately another apostle was chosen to bring the total back up to twelve. There are eleven millenniums from creation to the first coming of Christ. But His coming is not complete (in that sense defective) until He comes on the last day to finish all of His work that He has planned for mankind and this world.

The number 12 is used frequently to signify the fulness of whatever is in view. There were 12 tribes, 12 apostles, the holy city is spoken of as 12,000 furlongs by 12,000 furlongs by 12,000 furlongs (Revelation 21:16), etc. Thus, if the number 12 has any symbolical or spiritual meaning it should be the fulness of whatever is in view. The numbers 7, 10, and 12, are, therefore, very similar to each other in signifying spiritual truth.

The number 13 symbolically or spiritually signifies super fulness. Ordinarily the Bible speaks of twelve apostles but in actuality there were thirteen. The thirteenth was the Apostle Paul who insisted under the inspiration of the Holy Spirit that he met all of the qualifications of the original twelve (1 Corinthians 15:8-9; 2 Corinthians 12:11-12). The Bible ordinarily speaks of twelve tribes of Israel but in actuality there were thirteen. The universe has existed for slightly more than 13,000 years. Thus, if the number 13 has any symbolical or spiritual meaning it identifies with "super fulness."

Curiously, we see this concept identified with the age of the earth. We have learned that the Old Testament era from creation to the birth of Christ is almost exactly 11,000 years (11,006 years). We also can easily misunderstand the opening verses of Revelation Chapter 20 which speak of Satan being bound for a thousand years after which the end of the world would come. Eleven thousand years plus one thousand years equals the number twelve thousand years which symbolically identifies with complete fulness of time. But the New Testament era is about two thousand years. Therefore, the total time is very close to 13,000 years (13,023 years to be exact). And thus we see again the concept of super fulness identified with the number 13.

The number 17 is found in several places that identify with heaven. For example Jacob during the last 17 years of his life lived under the complete safety of Joseph who was a portrait or type of Christ at the time he was used of God to save his family from starvation. (Genesis 17:48). Jeremiah paid 17 shekels for a piece of land in Israel as a sign that God would again bring Israel into the land, the land signifying the eternal Kingdom of God. (Jeremiah 32:9). Thus, if the number seventeen has any symbolical or spiritual meaning it would be that of "heaven."

The number 37 like the number 23 signifies God's judgment. Noah was in the ark for a total of 370 days at the time God's judgment came on the earth. The army of Sennacherib that was destroyed by God in one night numbered 185,000. 185,000 equals 5 x 37 x 1,000.

The number 666 which is the number assigned to the unsaved who are under the judgment of God, when broken down to significant numbers, is 3 x 6 x 37. Thus, if the number 37 has any symbolical or spiritual meaning it would be "judgment."

The number 40 is used repeatedly in the Bible to signify testing. Moses was forty days on Mount Sinai. Israel failed the test of his absence and made the golden calf. Israel was 40 years in the wilderness. They failed the test because almost none of them became saved. Jesus was tested 40 days and forty nights by Satan. Wonderfully He did not fail the test. Thus, if the number 40 has any symbolical or spiritual meaning it would be that of testing.

The number 43 surfaces from time to time. For example, Israel was in Egypt for 430 years. The end of the 430 years brought judgment upon Egypt but freedom (a picture of salvation to Israel). Thus, if the number 43 has any spiritual or symbolical meaning it would be like the number 5, judgment or salvation.

The following is a summary of probable meanings of the numbers set forth above.

No.	Symbolical or Spiritual Meaning
2	Caretaker of the Bible
3	God's purpose
4	Universality or to the end
5	Salvation or judgment
6	Work
7	Perfect completeness
9	Purpose
10	Completeness
11	Defective fullness
12	Fullness
13	Super fullness
17	Heaven
23	Judgment
37	Judgment
43	Judgment or salvation

These comments about God's usage of numbers do not in any way insist that this, then, is the basis of recognizing the high possibility that the year A.D. 2011 may indeed be the year of the end of the world. If it were true that not a single number in the Bible conveyed any spiritual truth, the conclusions set forth in this study identifying with the unfolding of God's salvation plan would not change at all.

However, it is true that as we understand God's use of numbers in the Bible we do have increased evidence that the timeline of history we have projected to the year 2011 A.D. has a great possibility of being correct.

> *...the numbers God has used in the Bible can have spiritual value; that is, they can be used of God to teach spiritual truth.*

Now that we have learned that the numbers God has used in the Bible can have spiritual value; that is, they can be used of God to teach spiritual truth, we shall also learn that in the Calendar of history major milestones are separated from each other in such a way that spiritual truth shines forth.

For example, Israel was in the wilderness 40 years from the year 1447 B.C. to 1407 B.C. As we learned the number 40 spiritually signifies testing.

In Deuteronomy 8:2 we read:

And thou shalt remember all the way which the LORD thy God led thee these forty years in the wilderness, to humble thee, and to prove thee, to know what was in thine heart, whether thou wouldest keep his commandments, or no.

This verse clearly teaches that the 40 years Israel was in the wilderness was to test them. By this verse we are assured that the duration of a time period set forth in God's Gospel Calendar can be used to emphasize spiritual truth.

Again, the Bible teaches that Abraham was 75 years of age when he came into the land of Canaan and that he died at the age of 175 years (Genesis 25:7). We have learned that the land of Canaan symbolically represents the eternal kingdom of God. We have also learned that the number 100 or 1,000 can spiritually signify completeness. Additionally, we know from the Bible that Abraham represents all of those who are true believers (Galatians 3:29). Thus, the 100 year period from the year 2092 B.C. when Abraham entered the land of Canaan until the year 1992 B.C. when Abraham died, signifies the completeness of eternal life for all those who become saved.

Fact is, God has structured the unfolding of His salvation plan so that as we discover the calendar of history, we find two major principles to be in place:

1.   The Gospel milestones in the unfolding of history are not in any sense haphazard, or at random.

2.   Frequently the time duration between significant milestones convey important spiritual truth.

We should test these principles. We shall do so by listing a number of the significant milestones and then checking to discover if there is any possibility of spiritual meaning to the time segment between various milestones.

Time Intervals Can Convey Spiritual Truth

The following is a list of some of the milestones we have already uncovered as we have been unfolding the timeline of history. Additionally, there are listed three milestones we will come to as we later continue in our progress through time all the way to the end of time.

1. 2092 B.C.	Abraham arrives in the promised land, Canaan, which externally typifies the kingdom of God.	
2. 2067 B.C.	Sodom and Gomorrah completely destroyed.	
3. 1877 B.C.	Jacob and his family commanded to leave the promised land, Canaan, and go to live in Egypt.	
4. 1447 B.C.	Israel as a nation leaves Egypt at the time that God's judgment falls on Egypt so that all of the firstborn are killed.	
5. 1407 B.C.	Israel crosses the Jordan River and enters Canaan which externally typifies the kingdom of God.	
6. 1047 B.C.	Israel becomes a monarchy.	
7. 1007 B.C.	David becomes king of Israel.	
8. 931 B.C.	Kingdom of 12 tribes divided into two kingdoms Judah 2 tribes) and Israel (10 tribes).	
9. 709 B.C.	Israel destroyed by the Assyrians.	
10. 609 B.C.	Beginning of great tribulation for Judah at which time Judah loses its independence becoming first a vassal of Egypt and then a vassal of Babylon.	
11. 587 B.C.	Judah and Jerusalem destroyed by Babylon. All remaining Jews commanded to leave Judea and live in Babylon.	
12. 539 B.C.	Babylon conquered by the Medes and Persians.	
13. 391 B.C.	Last writing of the Old Testament.	
14. 7 B.C.	Jesus born. Beginning year of first Jubilee period.	
15. A.D. 29	Jesus announced as Lamb of God.	
16. A.D. 33	Jesus crucified. Church age begins.	
17. A.D. 1988	Church age ended. Beginning year of the Great Tribulation.	
18. A.D. 1994	Beginning year of second Jubilee period.	
19. A.D. 2011	Probable end of world.	

The milestones set forth above did not occur in a random or haphazard manner. It can be shown that they are interrelated with each other in a definite pattern. We can see this pattern when we break down the intervals between these various events into their significant numbers. Remember we learned that numbers can have spiritual meaning.

Two numbers will always signify judgment if they are used in a spiritual or symbolical way. They are the numbers 23 and 37. Additionally there are two numbers that either may, depending upon the context, signify judgment or salvation. They are the numbers 5 and 43. Surprisingly a great number of the time intervals between these important milestones feature these numbers of judgment.

For example, in the year 2092 B.C. Abraham came into the promised land of Canaan. It was the land that externally represented the Kingdom of God. Yet 215 years later in the year 1877 B.C. his grandson Jacob was commanded to leave the land of Canaan and go to Egypt. This was a portrait of God abandoning the external representation of the Kingdom of God in this illustration the land of Canaan, to Satan. The number 215 can be factored or broken down into the significant numbers 5 x 43 = 215.

Again, for example, in the year 2067 B.C. Sodom was destroyed, and in the year 587 B.C. Judah was destroyed. Judah is linked to Sodom by the language of Ezekiel 16:46-48 where we read of Judah:

And thine elder sister is Samaria, she and her daughters that dwell at thy left hand: and thy younger sister, that dwelleth at thy right hand, is Sodom and her daughters. Yet hast thou not walked after their ways, nor done after their abominations: but, as if that were a very little thing, thou wast corrupted more than they in all thy ways. As I live, saith the Lord GOD, Sodom thy sister hath not done, she nor her daughters, as thou hast done, thou and thy daughters.

Samaria which was the capital of the ten tribes (Israel) is called the older sister and Sodom is called the younger sister. These three, Judah, Israel, and Sodom, are linked together in that they came into destruction because of their wickedness. They are also linked together by the significant numbers into which the time intervals between the dates of Sodom's destruction and Judah's destruction are broken down into significant numbers.

The time interval between Sodom's destruction in 2067 B.C. and Judah's in 587 B.C. equals 1,480 years. The number 1,480 can be broken down to the significant numbers 4 x 10 x 37 or 2 x 4 x 5 x 37 or 2 x 2 x 2 x 5 x 37. Spiritually, the number 1,480 can thus be understood that in the end (No. 4) of these nations there will be complete (No. 10) destruction (No. 37). Or in the end (No. 4) Judah which was the caretaker of the Bible (No. 2) comes under the judgment of God (No. 5 and No. 37). Or it could be understood to say that it is God's purpose (three 2s) that Judah which had been the caretaker of the Bible (Nos. 2 x 2 x 2) would be brought under judgment (No. 5 and No. 37).

In similar fashion, we should take note of the following time intervals that also feature God's judgment that came upon Israel as a twelve tribe nation or upon Israel and upon Judah after they were divided into two nations. Please note that repeatedly the numbers of judgment, 23, 37, and 43, come into view.

1. Year 1877 B.C.	Jacob commanded to leave the promised land to live in Egypt. Year 587 B.C. Judah commanded to leave Jerusalem to live in Babylon. 1 877 - 587 = 1 290 = 3 x 10 x 43
2. Year 1447 B.C.	First born of Egypt killed and Israel delivered from captivity. Year 33 A.D. = Christ as the first born killed to provide deliverance to those who are to become saved. 1,447 plus 33 = 1,480 yrs incl = 2 x 2 x 10 x 37
3. Year 1047 B.C.	12 tribes of Israel become a monarchy. Year 587 B.C. Israel ceases to be a monarchy. Jerusalem is destroyed. 1,047 - 587 = 460 = 10 x 2 x 23
4. Year 931 B.C.	Israel becomes two nations. One is called Judah. One is called Israel. Year 709 B.C. Nation of Israel destroyed by Assyria. 931 - 709 = 222 yrs. 222 = 2 x 3 x 37
5. Year 609 B.C.	Nation of Judah becomes a servant first of Egypt, then of Babylon. Seventy year tribulation period begins in year 609 B.C. 931 -609 = 322 yrs. 322= 2 x 7 x 23
6. Year 587 B.C.	Judah destroyed by Babylonians. 931 - 587 = 344 yrs. 344 = 2 x 2 x 2 x 43

When we project the Biblical milestones into the future we are discovering that three years come into great prominence. They are the years:

A.D. 1988.	End of the church age. Beginning of the Great Tribulation.

A.D. 1994.   Beginning of second Jubilee.

A.D. 2011.   End of the world.

When we examine time intervals that link these dates to earlier significant dates, we take note of the following.

1. In the year 587 B.C. Judah which in the Old Testament externally typified the kingdom of God was ruling in Judea while the true believers which were driven out of Judea and Jerusalem were to pray for Babylon and seek its spiritual welfare. We read in Jeremiah 29:4, 5, and 7:

Thus saith the LORD of hosts, the God of Israel, unto all that are carried away captives, whom I have caused to be carried away from Jerusalem unto Babylon; Build ye houses, and dwell in them; and plant gardens, and eat the fruit of them; And seek the peace of the city whither I have caused you to be carried away captives, and pray unto the LORD for it: for in the peace thereof shall ye have peace.

Likewise, in A.D. 1994, the second Jubilee began during which throughout the world a great multitude are being saved. This is true even though the churches remain under great tribulation. They remain under the rule of Satan so that no one is saved within them.

Remember there is no year 0. Therefore, to determine the number of years from an Old Testament date to a New Testament date the years are added together and one year is subtracted. Thus, when we add 587 B.C. to A.D. 1,994, we obtain 587 + 1994 - 1 = 2,580 years. The number 2,580 breaks down into the significant numbers 3 x 2 x 10 x 43 or 3 x 4 x 5 x 43 or 12 x 5 x 43.

Please note that the number 43 which can signify both salvation and judgment is featured. In the year 1994 A.D., indeed, judgment continues on the local churches while salvation begins again throughout the world outside of the churches.

2. In A.D. 33, the church age began. In the year 1,988 A.D. the church age came to an end. 1988 - 33 = 1,955. The number 1,955 breaks down into the significant numbers 5 x 17 x 23. The number 17 signifies heaven. The number 23 judgment. Thus, these significant numbers corroborate the statement of 2 Corinthians 2:15-16:

For we are unto God a sweet savour of Christ, in them that are saved, and in them that perish: To the one we are the savour of death unto death; and to the other the savour of life unto life. And who is sufficient for these things?

3. The interval of time between the year 1,988 A.D. when the Great Tribulation likely began and the year 2,011 which probably is the year of the end of the world is 23 years. 2,011 - 1,988 = 23.

4. The year Christ experienced the judgment of God on behalf of all of those he came to save was A.D. 33. The year that God will judge the unsaved and sentence them to eternal perdition is probably A.D. 2011, which is the end of the world. 2,011 - 33 = 1,978 years. 1978 factors into 2 x 23 x 43.

5. We will discover that the first part of the Great Tribulation period is 2,300 days. 2,300 = 100 x 23.

6. The time from creation to the flood that destroyed the world in Noah's day was 6000 plus 23 years.

7. The time from the flood to 33 A.D. when Christ came under judgment for our sins was 5,000 + 23 years inclusive.

8. The time from creation in the years 11013 B.C. until the end of the world in 2011 A.D. equals 13,000 plus 23 years.

Significantly, in each and every one of the important time intervals listed above the time interval has one or more of the four numbers that are frequently associated with judgment.

Significantly, in each and every one of the important time intervals listed above the time interval has one or more of the four numbers that are frequently associated with judgment. Remember those numbers, are 5, 23, 37, and 43. The time periods listed occurred in past history and therefore have actually taken place. However, we cannot help but notice how similar the projected time periods ending with the A.D. years 1988, 1994 or 2011 are to the actual time periods of past history. Is all of this coincidental or is it an indication of God's carefully preplanned program for the unfolding of God's Gospel program?

We must remember none of the years shown above are developed in an effort to make, for example, these numbers signifying judgment to become evident. Each and every one of the years of the past that are shown or those that are projected in the future have been set forth with no regard or concern for the spiritual or symbolical meaning of any of the resulting time periods.

To say it another way, if it were true that not a single number in the Bible conveyed any spiritual truth, the conclusions set forth in this study identifying with the unfolding of God's salvation plan would not change at all.

The time periods shown above as well as elsewhere in this study do emphasize that we can know that the unfolding of God's salvation plan is not at all in a haphazard, random, capricious manner. They clearly demonstrate that the unfolding of history was carefully preplanned and structured by God. Moreover it indicates that the numbers in the Bible are extremely important if we are to have any understanding of the timing of the history of the world all the way from the beginning of time to the end of the world.

> *The same God who gave us the Bible also set up the laws that govern the movement of planets and stars. These laws are expressed as numbers that were carefully designed by God.*

If secular scientists paid no attention to numbers as they attempted travel to the moon or to the planet Mars they could never achieve any success. The same God who gave us the Bible also set up the laws that govern the movement of planets and stars. These laws are expressed as numbers that were carefully designed by God. Likewise the history of the world as it relates to the unfolding of God's salvation plan is expressed by numbers that have been carefully included in the Bible text.

It might be noted that there are many other indicators of the careful preplanned character of the unfolding of God's salvation program in which the numbers of judgment (23, 37, 43) are not featured. A few examples should be given.

1. Abraham, of whom all believers in Jesus Christ are spiritually called the seed (Galatians 3:29), was circumcised in the year 2068 B.C. (Genesis Chapter 17). At that time God's salvation promises were re-emphasized. Exactly 2,100 years later in A.D. 33, the certainty of those promises is seen as Jesus literally endures the wrath of

God to fulfill those promises. The number 2100 breaks down into the very significant numbers 3 x 7 x 100.

2. Abraham was 75 years of age when he came into the promised land, the land of Canaan. He died at the age of 175 having lived 100 years in the land of Canaan. Thus, God emphasized the principle that believers live in the kingdom of God for the completeness (No. 100) of God's plan which is eternally.

3. The last written entry was made into the Old Testament part of the Bible in the year 391 B.C. We will discover that it was the year 7 B.C. that Jesus was born. He is the very Word of God. That is, from the year 11013 B.C. until 391 B.C. Holy men of God spoke as God the Holy Spirit moved them.

But in 7 B.C. Christ who is the very Word of God appeared in the flesh. We read in John 1:14:

And the Word was made flesh, and dwelt among us, (and we beheld his glory, the glory as of the only begotten of the Father,) full of grace and truth.

It surely seems very significant that the duration of time between 391 B.C. and 7 B.C. is 384 years. Amazingly the number 384 breaks down into 3 x 2^7 or 3 x 2 x 2 x 2 x 2 x 2 x 2 x 2. We have learned that the purpose or will of God is frequently signified by the number 3. We have also learned that the No. 2 spiritually can signify the care taking of the Word of God. We also have learned that the number 7 signifies complete perfection. Please note that the 384 has the number 2 multiplied seven times. Thus, in the number 384 = 3 x 2 x 2 x 2 x 2 x 2 x 2 x 2 we find these three very significant numbers. It was God's purpose that the Word who is the Lord Jesus would finally come in the flesh as the caretaker of the Gospel, indeed the very essence of the Gospel (No. 2), in the complete perfection of God's timetable (7 No. 2s).

It is also quite amazing to learn that there exists a very significant relationship between the years 391 B.C. and A.D. 2011, which is the probable end of the world. We do know that at the end of the world Christ will again speak very literally as He comes with a shout, with the voice of the chief messenger who can only be Christ Himself. We read in 1 Thessalonians 4:16:

For the Lord himself shall descend from heaven with a shout, with

the voice of the archangel, and with the trump of God: and the dead in Christ shall rise first:

As indicated above the word "archangel" is improperly translated. Christ is not an angel. He is the messenger of the covenant (Malachi 3:1).

Moreover, at the end of time, Christ will be speaking as the judge of the earth, as all of the unsaved are brought into judgment.

Significantly, the period of time between 391 B.C. and A.D. 2011 equals 2,401 years. 391 B.C. + A.D. 2011 = 2,402 - 1 = 2,401 years. Amazingly, the number 2,401 breaks down into 7 x 7 x 7 x 7. Thus, two very important numbers are featured, the numbers 7 and 4. The number 7 indicates perfect completeness. The number 4 (four 7s), we have learned speaks of the end or the utmost extremity. Indeed, Christ will have spoken in complete perfection at the end of this world.

Many more examples showing the unfolding of God's salvation plan could be given. A few additional are indicated on the time chart set forth at the end of this book.

While we are speaking of numbers we might also take note of the number of times events are interrelated by the No. 1,000. We should note the following.

1. Jacob, the father of the twelve tribes of Israel, was born in the year 2007 B.C. Exactly 2,000 years later in the year 7 B.C., Jesus was born who is the eternal King of Israel.

2. In the year 1007 B.C. David, a great type of Jesus became king of Israel. Exactly 1,000 years later in 7 B.C., Jesus the eternal King of Israel was born.

3. The year 7 B.C. signaled the beginning of the first Jubilee (the proclamation of the Gospel to the world). Exactly 2,000 years later, in A.D. 1994, the second Jubilee began as God began his final program of saving, **"a great multitude which no man can number"** (Revelation 7:9) during the time of the Great Tribulation.

4. Creation occurred in the year 11,013 B.C. On the first day of creaation God said **"Let there be light"**(Genesis 1:3). This declaration anticipated the fact that the light of the Gospel would go into all of the world. Exactly 13,000 years later, the year 1988 A.D. identifies with the end of the church age and the beginning of the Great Tribulation. During the first part of the Great Tribulation there would

be the half hour of silence (Revelation 8:1). Immediately following this half hour of silence the second Jubilee period began which will probably end 17 years later in A.D. 2011.

> *It is indeed curious and possibly significant that many milestones found on the timeline of history ending with the year 2011 A.D., are very interesting and possibly are very important helps in further tying the whole program of history together.*

It is indeed curious and possibly significant that many milestones found on the timeline of history ending with the year 2011 A.D., are very interesting and possibly are very important helps in further tying the whole program of history together. For example, we will discover that the probable duration of the Great Tribulation will be 23 years. The fact that the number 23 signifies judgment fits exceedingly well. Likewise we will discover that 2,300 days is the time duration of the first part of the Great Tribulation when there was the half hour of silence from heaven (Revelation 8:1).

Likewise we will find that the seventeen year period of the final harvest that takes place during the second part of the tribulation fits perfectly in as much as it is during these 17 years that there is a great multitude which no man can number which are being saved (Revelation 7:9-14).

Curiously, as we have already noted, the precise 1,955 years of the church age factors into the significant numbers 5 x 17 x 23 = 1,955. The effect of bringing the Gospel to the world is stated in 2 Corinthians 2:15-16:

For we are unto God a sweet savour of Christ, in them that are saved, and in them that perish: To the one we are the savour of death unto death; and to the other the savour of life unto life. And who is sufficient for these things?

The Gospel which is the law of God both damns people to the eternal wrath of God and saves people by providing eternal life. This is illustrated in the numbers 5 x 17 x 23 = 1,955. Remember the No. 5 signifies both judgment and salvation, the number 17 signifies heaven which is the result of salvation, and the number 23 signifies judgment.

Earlier we also commented that there were 1,978 years from the cross to the probable end of the world. Remember the number 1,978 factors into 2 x 23 x 43. Earlier we learned that the number two signifies those who are caretakers of the Bible. We also have learned that the number 23 signifies God's judgment. Furthermore the number 43 can signify salvation or judgment. Therefore, we can see in the number 1,978 that at the end of time those who have been caretakers of the Bible will end under God's eternal salvation or under eternal judgment.

We must be impressed by God's use of the numbers of the Bible.

We must be impressed by God's use of the numbers of the Bible. Let it be emphasized again that no date or milestone in the timeline of history that we have set forth in this study has been prompted by any desire whatsoever to develop number relationships that may have spiritual or symbolical meanings. The calendar of history that has been set forth in this study is based solely on Biblical information without any regard for the spiritual meaning that may be inherent in the numbers that result.

However, it cannot be coincidental or accidental that the number patterns that the Bible reveals are so beautifully interrelated.

However, it cannot be coincidental or accidental that the number patterns that the Bible reveals are so beautifully interrelated. They surely should further encourage us that God's timetable of history is indeed almost to an end.

We have spent a little time learning how accurate and how important God's use of numbers is. Before we continue down the highway of time, we should also take a moment to emphasize another aspect of Bible prophecy that is frequently grossly misunderstood. It is God's use of parables.

Christ Spoke in Parables

We have been continuing our journey through time as it is viewed in the light of the unfolding of God's grand salvation plan. Repeatedly, we have indicated that historical events recorded in the Bible were pictures or portraits of some aspect of God's salvation plan. We actually can think of the Old Testament as a picture gallery, with each picture representing some aspect of God's salvation plan.

We should, therefore, pause for a moment to show the solid Biblical basis for understanding the Bible in this way.

> *The extremely important principle that must be kept in mind as we search the Bible for any kind of truth is that Christ spoke in parables.*

The extremely important principle that must be kept in mind as we search the Bible for any kind of truth is that Christ spoke in parables. We read in Mark 4:11:

> **And he said unto them, Unto you it is given to know the mystery of the kingdom of God: but unto them that are without, all these things are done in parables:**

Jesus added in Mark 4:34

> **"But without a parable spake He not unto them. . ."**

The principle that Jesus, the author of the Bible, spoke in parables cannot be too strongly emphasized. Only by a clear understanding of this principle can a large part of the Bible be understood. Jesus explained why He wrote in parables. We read in Mark 4:9-12:

> **And he said unto them, He that hath ears to hear, let him hear. And when he was alone, they that were about him with the twelve asked of him the parable. And he said unto them, Unto you it is given to know the mystery of the kingdom of God: but unto them that are without, all these things are done in parables: that seeing they may see, and not perceive; and hearing they may hear, and not understand; lest at any time they should be converted, and their sins should be forgiven them.**

God is explaining to us that He purposely wrote the Bible so that those who are without the kingdom of God, those who have not been given spiritual ears to hear, those whom God does not intend to convert because they are not chosen of God to salvation, will remain completely ignorant of many of the truths of the

Bible. To assure this, God has written much of the Bible as historical parables which those who have not been given spiritual ears cannot understand. They can understand the historical reality of the Biblical statement, but they cannot understand the spiritual message that is hidden within the statement.

> *For example, the nation of Israel was given the ceremonial laws which are all like parables*

For example, the nation of Israel was given the ceremonial laws which are all like parables or metaphors. The observance of these laws should have pointed them to the coming Messiah (Christ) to save them. They, however, looked only at the physical observance of these laws as the key to their salvation. Thus, for example, they rigorously offered burnt offerings and kept the seventh day Sabbath. But they perished because of their unbelief (Romans 9:31-33). They did not at all see the spiritual Gospel hidden within those laws.

Amazingly, we find that most churches have adopted a man-designed hermeneutic (method of Bible interpretation) that blocks them from understanding many portions of the Bible.* Their hermeneutic is altogether contrary to the Biblical teaching that Christ spoke in parables about which we are reading in Mark Chapter 4. It blocks them from understanding such great truths as the end of the church age, the Great Tribulation, the latter rain, etc. Their false hermeneutic virtually forces them to remain in their local congregations under the judgment of God. It is indeed remarkable that so many theologians and Bible teachers are trusting in an un-Biblical, man-made method of Bible interpretation that locks them out of the kingdom of God.

Because these theologians and church leaders have implicit trust in the man-made method of Biblical interpretation which they have been taught in the seminary where they attended they are convinced that the method of Bible interpretation taught in this book is heresy. Therefore, they also warn their followers that this is so. Thus, entire congregations remain in spiritual darkness. It is absolutely imperative that we never try to understand the Bible through the filter of any man-made principles. To do so effectively removes God as the supreme and only authority who rules over His Word, the Bible.

A parable simply stated is an earthly story with a heavenly or spiritual meaning. It is like a metaphor or a simile.

---

* For a full discussion of this, the reader is invited to obtain a free copy of "Wheat and Tares" available from Family Radio.

> *A parable simply stated is an earthly story with a heavenly or spiritual meaning.*

Because Jesus identifies Himself completely as the Word of God and indeed is God Himself, we, therefore, would expect that when God wrote the Bible, He constantly would use parables. That is, He would hide important spiritual truth in stories or in historical events. We see this, for example, in God's utilization of the ceremonial laws to point to spiritual truth. For example, the burnt offerings, the blood sacrifices of the Old Testament were physical earthly activities pointing to or illustrating the spiritual truth of Jesus enduring the fires of hell, of shedding His blood (that is, giving His life) that sinners might be saved.

Thus, He was announced by John the Baptist as the Lamb of God. Jesus, of course, was literally not a lamb; but He was the fulfilment of the ceremonial activity that was pointed to or represented by the Passover lamb as well as by the various burnt offerings, or blood sacrifices in which lambs were sacrificed.

Likewise, we read in Isaiah 14:4 where God is apparently speaking of the king of Babylon, and He says:

That thou shalt take up this proverb against the king of Babylon, and say, How hath the oppressor ceased! the golden city ceased!

However, if we continue to read this chapter, we discover God is not speaking of any historical king of Babylon. Instead, He is speaking of Satan. The citation of Isaiah 14 shows this as it continues in verses 12-15:

How art thou fallen from heaven, O Lucifer, son of the morning! how art thou cut down to the ground, which didst weaken the nations! For thou hast said in thine heart, I will ascend into heaven, I will exalt my throne above the stars of God: I will sit also upon the mount of the congregation, in the sides of the north: I will ascend above the heights of the clouds; I will be like the most High. Yet thou shalt be brought down to hell, to the sides of the pit.

God is speaking of Lucifer, who is also called Satan, as the king of Babylon because, in the Bible, the nation of Babylon externally represented all of the kingdoms of this world who are ruled over by Satan. Therefore, Satan is externally typified or represented by the king of Babylon.

Because Christ spoke in parables and is, Himself, the Word of God, we can understand why this kind of presentation of truth is found here in Isaiah Chapter 14. Once we understand this principle, that God constantly utilized parables or metaphors or similes, much truth can be discovered in the Bible that otherwise would remain hidden.

Parables and The Book of Jeremiah

The Book of Jeremiah is a much larger example of Jesus speaking in parables. When we read it carefully, we will know that while most of this prophetic book is using the names of Old Testament nations, people, and cities, in actuality, it is pointing to the spiritual reality of the unfolding of God's salvation plan that identifies with the time of the Great Tribulation that ends with the return of Christ and the end of the world.

For example, when we carefully examine Chapter 25 of the Book of Jeremiah, we will find the language that assures us that we are on the path of truth. In Jeremiah 25:2-5, we read that God is addressing Judah and Jerusalem, warning them to turn from their evil ways so that they could dwell in the land for ever and ever. We read:

> **The which Jeremiah the prophet spake unto all the people of Judah, and to all the inhabitants of Jerusalem, saying, From the thirteenth year of Josiah the son of Amon king of Judah, even unto this day, that is the three and twentieth year, the word of the LORD hath come unto me, and I have spoken unto you, rising early and speaking; but ye have not hearkened. And the LORD hath sent unto you all his servants the prophets, rising early and sending them; but ye have not hearkened, nor inclined your ear to hear. They said, Turn ye again now every one from his evil way, and from the evil of your doings, and dwell <u>in the land</u> that the LORD hath given unto you and to your fathers <u>for ever and ever.</u>**

The phrase in verse 5, **"land . . . for ever and ever,"** is an immediate clue that God is using parabolic language. The Bible is absolutely clear that this earth in its entirety will be destroyed by fire when Jesus returns at the end of the world (2 Peter Chapter 3). Thus, the phrase **"the land . . . for ever and ever"** must be understood to be the kingdom of God which the true believers occupy eternally. Eternally, the location of the kingdom of God will be in the New Heavens and the New Earth. Thus, by use of this statement, God is warning the reader to look for the deeper spiritual meanings in the Jeremiah Chapter 25 message to Judah and Jerusalem.

Verses 11 and 12 of Jeremiah further illustrate the principle that Christ spoke in parables. These verses say:

And this whole land shall be a desolation, and an astonishment; and these nations shall serve the king of Babylon seventy years. And it shall come to pass, when seventy years are accomplished, that I will punish the king of Babylon, and that nation, saith the LORD, for their iniquity, and the land of the Chaldeans, and will make it perpetual desolations.

In these verses, God uses the phrase **"perpetual desolations."** The Hebrew word translated **"perpetual"** is a word that signifies "eternal." Thus, this phrase could be translated "eternal desolations." Immediately we sense this verse is speaking about eternity future after this world has been destroyed.

But these verses indicate this everlasting desolation of the king of Babylon (also called the land of the Chaldees), was to begin at the end of 70 years.

Because everlasting desolation is to begin at the end of this world's existence we wonder how the time of 70 years fits in. We have learned that historically, this 70-year period began in the year 609 B.C., the year Israel's last good king, King Josiah died in battle. This 70-year period was the time of tribulation that followed the time of his death. During this 70-year period, first Egypt, and then Babylon, ruled in Judea and Jerusalem. However, in the year 539 B.C., Babylon was conquered by the Medes and Persians.

> *...we are to look for the spiritual or Gospel application even though God is using actual literal historical names and events to illustrate and represent the Gospel application.*

But following the year 539 B.C., Babylon was not eternally desolated. The city of Babylon was still existing 200 years later, during the days of Alexander the Great. Thus, the prophecy of Jeremiah 25:11-12 which speaks of everlasting desolation immediately following a period of 70 years must be understood metaphorically. We must recognize God is using parabolic or metaphorical language. That is, we are to look for the spiritual or Gospel application even though God is using actual literal historical names and events to illustrate and represent the Gospel application.

Let us look at a few more verses in Jeremiah 25 before we outline the spiritual application being portrayed in this chapter.

The next verse is Jeremiah 25:13 which reports:

And I will bring upon that land all my words which I have pronounced against it, even all that is written in this book, which Jeremiah hath prophesied <u>against all the nations.</u>

This verse says something very remarkable. It is teaching that all the information that God has given the prophet Jeremiah to write in this Book of Jeremiah is prophesied against all the nations. That is, the Book of Jeremiah is not concerned with a few nations, it is concerned with all the nations of the world. That we have correctly understood this is evidenced by a further disclosure in verse 26 of this chapter. There we read, after God has named many kingdoms that were in existence at the time Jeremiah is writing:

And all the kings of the north, far and near, one with another, <u>and all the kingdoms of the world, which are upon the face of the earth:</u> and the king of Sheshach shall drink after them.

The phrase "**all the kingdoms of the world, which are upon the face of the earth**" assures us that God is speaking of the entire world. It is the entire world that will be under judgment when Christ returns at the end of the world.

> *The spiritual Gospel focus of the whole Book of Jeremiah was on the worldwide events that would occur as the world came to an end*

Now we can understand why God said in verse 12 that Babylon would end up in everlasting desolation. Now we can understand why verse 5 spoke of Israel dwelling in the land for ever and ever. God has written the Book of Jeremiah in the context of nations and historical events that were occurring in Jeremiah's day. But the spiritual Gospel focus of the whole Book of Jeremiah was on the world-wide events that would occur as the world came to an end.

Therefore, with a few exceptions, we discover as we carefully analyze anything and everything we read in the Book of Jeremiah, the message is ultimately focused on the spiritual events occurring in our day, during which we have come so close to the end of the world.

We now can know that references to Jerusalem, Judah, Israel, Canaan, the temple, etc., which existed during the time of the Old Testament, externally represented the kingdom of God. However, in our day, it has been the local churches that have externally represented the kingdom of God. Therefore, the local churches are called Jerusalem, Judaea, the temple, etc. Thus, the local churches of our day are being warned by the prophecies and warnings set forth in the Book of Jeremiah.

As we indicated earlier, we might think of the Old Testament particularly, and to some degree also the New Testament, as a series of picture galleries. These true historical events recorded in the Bible are word pictures designed by God to illustrate important spiritual principles and future events that would take place as God unfolded His salvation plan.

As we are now learning, we must realize that most of what we read in the Book of Jeremiah is speaking of the churches and the world that exist today. Thus, it is of particular importance to us today. The experiences of Judah, Babylon etc. reported in the Book of Jeremiah are as fully relevant to us today as any New Testament book. Fact is, they are as fully relevant as today's newspaper. The following principles should be kept in mind.

1. Babylon, Chaldea, Sheshach are all synonyms that are speaking of Satan and his kingdom, which includes all of the unsaved of the world.

2. Egypt, Assyria, Philistines, etc., are also referring to the kingdom of Satan.

3. Judah, Israel, Jerusalem, Tyre, Zidon are normally referring to the local churches of our day although in certain instances these names may refer to the eternal body of true believers.

4. Edom, Esau, Bozra, Esau, Mt. Seir are names referring to the unsaved within the local congregations.

Because the Book of Jeremiah clearly teaches that the revelations given to Jeremiah definitely apply to the whole world of our day we may expect the same is true of the other prophetic books of the Bible such as Isaiah, Ezekiel, Hosea, Joel, etc. We will see this as we look at representative verses in the Bible that address the issue of the Great Tribulation which the church and the world is now experiencing.

As we continue our study, we will look at many additional verses of the Bible that we can understand once we have learned the principle that Christ spoke in parables. Because He is identified as the Word of God (John Chapter 1), we will understand that these verses were written as parables or metaphors.

Now, however, we shall return to the unfolding of God's timeline of history as we examine the next great milestone, the birth of Jesus.

Chapter 9
7 B.C. Christ's Birth
and Ministry

We have been traveling down the highway of time which is governed by the unfolding of God's salvation plan, and His plan has been unfolding for well over 10,000 years. The last milestone we examined was the year 391 B.C. which, in all likelihood was the last year of the Old Testament era in which God broke the silence between heaven and earth.

For the next approximately 400 years, there is no Biblical record that can be identified with the unfolding of the timeline of God's program of salvation. It is not until 8 B.C. that once more God begins to speak. It is the time in God's Gospel program for God in the person of the Lord Jesus Christ to take on a human nature and physically as the Son of God and the Son of man endure the wrath of God on behalf of all those individuals whom God throughout time had committed Himself to save. The birth date and the date of His crucifixion must be the most important milestones in the unfolding of God's salvation plan. For the previous eleven thousand years every event in one way or another was pointing to this awesome event of God taking on a human nature and actually suffering the wrath of God on behalf of all of those He came to save.

Therefore, we should search the Bible to discover what we can concerning the timing of these extraordinary events.

Curiously, God has not given easily understood information concerning an exact day, month or year in which Jesus was born. We wonder why this is so in view of the fact that God has given so many other dates as He has unfolded His Gospel timeline. At this time in our understanding of the Bible we can only speculate why He may have done it this way.

We do know that Christ's coming on a certain day and certain month and certain year was all carefully pre-arranged. The Bible tells us that Christ came in the fullness of time (Galatians 4:4).

Significantly, God gave considerable information that relates to the time of Jesus' birth. Fact is, there is so much of this related information we can almost be certain we can know His birth date. Indeed, it may have been God's purpose that only by a careful study of this related information would we learn the date of Christ's birth. We should spend a little time to assemble this information because it will prove to be very helpful as we continue to unfold the timeline of God's salvation program.

At the time Jesus was born Israel was under the rule of the Roman government. However, Israel was permitted to have their own puppet king. He was a wicked old king named Herod. We know from trustworthy secular records that Herod died in April of 4 B.C.

We know from the Biblical record that there were Magi to whom God had announced Christ's birth by placing a miraculous star in the sky. When these Magi searched their holy books to try to discover the significance of this unusual star, they eventually would have read in Numbers 24:17:

> **I shall see him, but not now: I shall behold him, but not nigh: there shall come a Star out of Jacob, and a Sceptre shall rise out of Israel, and shall smite the corners of Moab, and destroy all the children of Sheth.**

At that time in history there was in Persia a second level ruling party called Magian. In all likelihood, the Magi who saw the star were from Persia. Remember, Babylon defeated Judah and in turn, the Media-Persian nation defeated Babylon. Therefore, the libraries of Judah could easily have ended up in Persia.

In any event, because the Magi saw this miraculous star, they believed a great king must have been born in Jerusalem, the capital city of Israel. They therefore eventually came to Jerusalem to pay homage to this King who was predicted in the holy book of Israel.

They arrived in Jerusalem and enquired concerning this baby king. Wicked Herod who would not for a moment want the possibility of another king ruling over Israel, inquired diligently of the Magi about when the star had appeared.

In Matthew 2:7 we read:

> **Then Herod, when he had privily called the wise men, enquired of them diligently what time the star appeared.**

Certainly, considerable time had gone by because it was a huge undertaking for the Magi to make all of the preparations and assemble all of the personnel necessary to make the long trip from Persia to Jerusalem.

The theologians in Herod's court reported that the Bible prophesied that a king, the Messiah, was to be born in Bethlehem (Micah 5:2). The Magi therefore went on their way to Bethlehem and the star which they had seen in the east went before them and stood over the house where Jesus was living with Joseph and Mary (Matthew 2:9-11). Thus, the star was a miraculous star, only a few hundred feet high in the sky. If it were higher than that, it could not stand over one house.

Herod had wanted the Magi to come back to Jerusalem and report to him if they found this child King (Matthew 2:8). But the Magi were warned by God not to return to Jerusalem. Therefore, they went home another way (Matthew 2:12).

But now comes important information. We read in the Bible that Herod in great anger gave the command that all of the children in Bethlehem were to be killed, **"from two years old and under, according to the time which he had diligently enquired of the wise men [Magi]"** (Matthew 2:16).

Thus, God has given us a time reference. We can know that the star must have appeared about two years earlier because in his effort to kill Jesus, Herod killed all the two year olds in Bethlehem according to the time the Magi had given him. Therefore, we may assume, as did Herod, that Jesus was born about two years before the Magi spoke to Herod. Since Herod was still living prior to April of 4 B.C., it meant that Jesus had to have been born at least two years earlier; that is, two years prior to April of 4 B.C. Remember, Herod died in April of 4 B.C.

Presently, we will look at Biblical evidence that indicates Jesus had to have been born late in September or early in October. Therefore, Jesus would then have had to have been born in 7 B.C. because if He were born in September of 6 B.C. Jesus would have been only one and a half years old when he was visited by the Magi. Therefore, Jesus must have been born in September or October of 7 B.C.

> *...the very essence of the Jubilee year resides in Christ through whom liberty can be proclaimed to the world.*

The year 7 B.C. was a very significant year. Earlier we learned that it was a Jubilee year. We also learned that the very essence of the Jubilee year resides in Christ through whom liberty can be proclaimed to the world.

In Which Month Was Jesus Born

But what about the month of the year? What can we learn? In Luke 1:35-36, God records the messenger from heaven giving Mary the news of her impending conception:

And the angel answered and said unto her, The Holy Ghost shall come upon thee, and the power of the Highest shall overshadow thee: therefore also that holy thing which shall be born of thee

shall be called the Son of God. And, behold, thy cousin Elisabeth, she hath also conceived a son in her old age: and this is the sixth month with her, who was called barren.

These verses suggest that Jesus was conceived about five to six months after John the Baptist was conceived in the womb of his mother Elisabeth. Since the ordinary period of pregnancy is about nine months, the conception of John the Baptist would, therefore, have been fourteen to fifteen months before the birth of Jesus. Thus, if we can determine when John the Baptist was conceived, we would also have a fairly good idea when Jesus was born. In Luke 1:5 we read:

There was in the days of Herod, the king of Judea, a certain priest named Zacharias, of the course of Abia: and his wife was of the daughters of Aaron, and her name was Elisabeth.

Zacharias was the father of John the Baptist, and in this verse, we learn that in his priestly duties he was of the course of Abia. We, therefore, must search the Bible to learn what we can about the course of Abia (Hebrew *Abijah*).

In 1 Chronicles 24, we learn that the divisions of the priests were twenty four, that is, the priesthood was divided into twenty four courses. In verse 10, we read, **"The seventh to Hakkoz, the eighth to Abijah."** Thus, Zacharias being of the course of Abia or Abijah served in the eighth course. These courses followed one another throughout the twelve months of the Jewish calendar. Since there were twenty-four courses in all, two courses would have served in each month with the eighth course ending its service at the end of the fourth month.

That we might understand this correctly, God has given us information concerning the armed services in 1 Chronicles 27. They were divided into twelve courses of 24,000 men in each course. Each course was assigned to one month's service. Thus, we read for example in 1 Chronicles 27:5:

The third captain of the host for the <u>third</u> <u>month</u> was Benaiah the son of Jehoiada, a chief priest: and in his course were twenty and four thousand.

This verse teaches that the third course served the third month. Thus, we are quite sure that in similar fashion the eighth course of the twenty-four of the priesthood, that of Abijah, would have ended at the end of the fourth month of the Jewish calendar.

Returning to Zacharias, we read in Luke 1:23-24:

And it came to pass, that, as soon as the days of his ministration were accomplished, he departed to his own house. And after those days his wife Elisabeth conceived, and hid herself five months,

This verse suggests that the conception of John the Baptist occurred shortly after the fourth month of the Hebrew calendar. The course of Abia was finished, as we have learned, at the end of the fourth month. From Luke 1:36 we learned that it was in the sixth month of Elisabeth's pregnancy that Mary was told that she would be of child of the Holy Spirit. Therefore, the conception of Jesus by the Holy Spirit probably took place about six months after the end of the fourth month which ended Zacharias' temple assignment. The conception of Jesus, therefore, would have been close to the end of the tenth month or early in the eleventh month of the Jewish calendar.

If Jesus were born in 7 B.C., John the Baptist would have been conceived in 8 B.C. According to the Jewish calendar the end of the tenth month in 8 B.C. was December 28 of our modern calendar. Thus, the birth of Christ would have been nine months later which would have been very late in September or very early in October of 7 B.C.

We can analyze Christ's birth date in a slightly different way. The last day of the fourth month in 8 B.C. was July 5. This was the date Zacharias left the temple. It thus means that Elisabeth conceived John the Baptist probably as early as July 15. Thus John the Baptist would have been born about nine months later or about April 15, 7 B.C. We know it was a full term birth because Luke 1:57 records:

Now Elisabeth's <u>full</u> time came that she should be delivered; and she brought forth a son.

We also know that Mary spent about three months with Elisabeth for we read in Luke 1:56, **"And Mary abode with her about three months, and returned unto her own house."** We surely can assume that Mary stayed with Elisabeth until her son John was born.

Remember we read in Luke 1:35-36 that the angel informed Mary that Elisabeth had conceived and this was her sixth month. The Bible then records in Luke 1:38-39:

And Mary said, Behold the handmaid of the Lord; be it unto me according to thy word. And the angel departed from her. And Mary arose in those days, and went into the hill country with haste, into a city of Juda.

Assuming it took about two weeks to arrive in Elisabeth's house, it meant that Mary was about three and a half months pregnant when she left Elisabeth at the time John was born. As we learned earlier, the birth of John was about April 15. Thus, it appears Mary would have left Elisabeth about April 15. Therefore, Jesus would have been born about five and a half months later than April 15 or about October 1.

In any case, we know that the information concerning such things as the course of Abia, the sixth month of Elisabeth's pregnancy, and the three months visit of Mary with Elisabeth has been carefully placed in the Bible for a purpose. That purpose focuses on the date of Jesus' birth. For certain it means that Jesus had to have been born very close to October 1 in the year 7 B.C.

When we calculate the date of the day of atonement in 7 B.C., we discover it was October 1, a date that appears to fit perfectly with our present conclusion that Jesus was born about October 1. With all of the forgoing evidence, may we assume that Jesus was born on the day of atonement? Let us look at a bit more evidence that shows that this is a very logical assumption.

In Daniel 9:25-27, God presents to us the seventy weeks that focus on the coming of Jesus. Verse 25 of Daniel 9 declares:

Know therefore and understand, *that* from the going forth of the commandment to restore and to build Jerusalem unto the Messiah the Prince *shall be* seven weeks, and threescore and two weeks: the street shall be built again, and the wall, even in troublous times.

Earlier in our study we learned that seven weeks of years is the time between Jubilee years. Thus, this first seven weeks are to be understood as a Jubilee period. The year 458 B.C. is the year in which Ezra was commanded by the king of the Medes and Persians to re-establish the law of God in Jerusalem (Ezra 7:8-26). Spiritually, it is the believers, to whom God gives the desire to keep the law, who are the Jerusalem that is being built. The year immediately following 458 B.C. was the year 457 B.C., which was a Jubilee year. Thus, this first seven weeks would begin immediately following the year 458 B.C. This Jubilee period covered the years 457 B.C. to 407 B.C. (See *The Seventy Weeks of Daniel 9*, available free of charge from Family Radio.)

But could there be an additional meaning? Note again the language, from the time **"from the going forth of the commandment to restore and to build Jerusalem unto the Messiah the Prince *shall be* seven weeks."** Is this a veiled reference to the fact that Jesus would come in a Jubilee year? We learned earlier that Jesus is the essence of the Jubilee year. He is totally identified with the Jubilee. Remember, too, that the year 7 B.C. was a Jubilee year.

> *Jesus, the very essence of the Jubilee, is to be published throughout the world.*

Earlier in our study we learned that the day of atonement identified with the Jubilee year. It was on that day the Jews were to afflict themselves which we understand was pointing to the fact that they were to bring the Gospel in that the Jubilee was to be sounded. That is, Jesus, the very essence of the Jubilee, is to be published throughout the world. We wonder, was this the import of the information noted in Luke 2:16-17 concerning the shepherds? The Bible declares:

And they came with haste, and found Mary, and Joseph, and the babe lying in a manger. And when they had seen it, they made known abroad the saying which was told them concerning this child.

The shepherds surely symbolize all true believers. Surely on the day of the birth of Jesus the Jubilee, the Lord Jesus, was being proclaimed throughout the land.

Indeed, it appears that all of the circumstantial evidence points to Jesus as the very essence of the Jubilee being born on the day of atonement in the Jubilee year of 7 B.C.

More Information about 7 B.C.

The year 7 B.C. is very uniquely related to many other important milestones in the unfolding of the history of God's salvation program. For example, note the following.

- Isaac the son of Abraham who typified Jesus in many ways was born in the year 1967 B.C. 1,967- 7 = 1,960. That is exactly 1960 years after the birth of Isaac Jesus was born. Curiously the number 1,960 breaks down into the significant numbers 4 x 7 x 7 x 10. The number 4 signifies universality. Jesus is the only Savior in the entire world.
  The number 7 signifies perfect completeness.
  The number ten signifies completeness. Thus God ties the birth of

Isaac to the birth of Jesus by the number 1,960 which can be understood to say that Jesus is the completely perfect Savior for the whole world.

- Jacob was born in 2007 B.C. Exactly 2,000 years later, Jesus was born.

- Israel left Egypt in the year 1447 B.C.
1,447 - 7 = 1,440 years.
1,440 = 10 x 12 x 12.
The number 12 signifies fullness.
Thus, God ties the time of deliverance from Egypt to the birth of Jesus indicating that in the complete fullness of time the Deliverer will come.

- Israel entered the land of Canaan in the year 1407 B.C.
1,407 - 7 = 1,400.

  Thus, God ties the entrance of Israel into the land of Canaan which signifies salvation by the number 2 x 7 x 10 x10. The number 2 signifies those who as caretakers of the Bible are to bring the Gospel. God therefore, by the passage of 1,400 years, is teaching that in the perfect completeness of time, the believers will be able to proclaim that entrance into the kingdom of God is possible.

- David ascended the throne in the year 1007 B.C.
1,007 - 7 = 1,000 years.
Thus, God is signifying in the completeness of time, the King would come to rule over His people. Remember Jesus answered Pilate's question **"Art thou a king"** by saying, **"To this end I was born"** (John 18:37).

All of the above calendar milestones are definitely taught in the Bible. Therefore, we can see how God has not laid out an erratic time program for the unfolding of His Gospel program. Rather it is very carefully and harmoniously structured so that even in the pattern of times there is great harmony. We are reminded that God created flowers, etc., so that there is beauty in the exact arrangement of the petals in that flower. It is the same God who has pre-arranged His salvation program so that there is beautiful harmony in the timing of each event.

A.D. 29. Jesus is Announced

The next important milestone in the unfolding of God's salvation program is the occasion when Jesus officially began His work. This was at the time He was announced as the Lamb of God that takes away the sin of the world. That is, He in all the world is the only one who can take away sin.

Immediately, we will ask the question. Does the Bible tell us the precise time of this important announcement? To assist us God wrote in Luke 3:1-3:

> **Now in the fifteenth year of the reign of Tiberius Caesar, Pontius Pilate being governor of Judea, and Herod being tetrarch of Galilee, and his brother Philip tetrarch of Ituraea and of the region of Trachonitis, and Lysanias the tetrarch of Abilene, Annas and Caiaphas being the high priests, the word of God came unto John the son of Zacharias in the wilderness. And he came into all the country about Jordan, preaching the baptism of repentance for the remission of sins;**

This verse gives us an historical time reference. According to accurate secular historical information, the first year of the reign of Tiberius Caesar was A.D. 15. Therefore, his fifteenth year would have been A.D. 29.

We wonder if, at this important milestone in the unfolding of God's salvation program, there is any other information that shows the importance of this time in Biblical history. For example, can we know the day of the year this momentous event occurred? And was that day an important day for any additional reason?

We can know the precise day this great announcement was made and we will discover it was a very special day.

To find an answer to these questions we must look at a very curious citation written in Daniel 12:12. There we read:

> **Blessed is he that waiteth, and cometh to the thousand three hundred and five and thirty days.**

Because this verse is written in a book of the Bible that has much to say about end time events, for years I have tried to relate this verse and its reference to 1,335 days to the timing of the end. However, no matter how I tried, I was unsuccessful in relating it in any meaningful way with the end of time.

Truth concerning this verse began to dawn when I started to wonder if these verses related to the first coming of Christ. Could it be the word "he" in this verse is a reference to Jesus Himself? He would be the blessed one. He would be the one who must wait to come.

Why must Christ wait to come? Couldn't He have come whenever He decided to come?

Why must Christ wait to come? Couldn't He have come whenever He decided to come? The answer is No! As we have learned, God has a very carefully planned timetable for all of history. This timetable is tied very securely to God's salvation plan. The coming of Christ is the greatest event in this salvation plan, but His coming had to fit precisely into this timetable. Therefore, Jesus had to wait for the exact time when this timetable called for Him to come. That is why Galatians 4: 4-5, which we looked at earlier, indicates that Jesus came in the **fullness of time.**

What then is the period of 1,335 days for which he must wait to come? Examining the 1,335 days in the light of what we know concerning the timetable of Christ's first coming, it is not difficult to see the possibility that the 1,335 days identifies in some way with His coming to be crucified.

In our study of Daniel 9:27 (see *The Seventy Weeks of Daniel 9*, available free of charge from Family Radio), we learned that the time from the baptism of Jesus to the cross was approximately three and a half years. We learned that it was at Jesus' baptism that He officially began His work as the Messiah and that sacrifice and offering ceased in the middle of a week of seven years. We learned that the only time sacrifices ended was at the cross when Jesus sacrificed Himself for our sins. If the middle of the week meant precisely three and a half years, then that equals 1,279 days. Three and a half years equals 3½ x 365.25 days, which equals 1,278 days. But 1,278 days is short of 1335 days. Could it be that the middle of the week was an approximation? But then the Bible would have said **"about the middle of the week."**

Then I remembered that Jesus had one more task to do that distinctly related to the atonement. It was a task was an absolutely important part of God's salvation plan. That task was the sending of the Holy Spirit. It was God's plan that the Holy Spirit, who is God Himself, must begin His activity of applying the Word of God, the Bible, to the lives of those whom God planned to save. Unless this was done, no one could become saved.

Jesus spoke of this, indicating that He Himself would take care of this matter as soon as He returned to heaven. We read in John 16:7-8:

Nevertheless I tell you the truth; It is expedient for you that I go away: for if I go not away, the Comforter will not come unto you; but if I depart, I will send him unto you. And when he is come, he will reprove the world of sin, and of righteousness, and of judgment:

The Holy Spirit was poured out at Pentecost in A.D. 33. We read about this in Acts 2, wherein God discloses that in that day, about 3,000 were saved. Pentecost was about fifty days after the cross. Fifty days added to an exact three and one half years (1,278 days), gives us a span of time equal to 1,328 days. This is only seven days less than 1,335 days. Daniel 9:27, which speaks of the Messiah being cut off, does not appear to be insisting on an exact three and a half years, which would be 1,328 days. It would appear that given the fact that 1,328 days is so close to 1,335 days, we have discovered what God had in mind with the 1,335 days. However, by studying the Bible more carefully we will find the three and one half years are a very exact time.

If we start with the 1,335 days prophesied in Daniel 12:12, we can reconstruct the timing of events that preceded Pentecost. The last fifty days of the 1,335 days was the period from the Saturday of the crucifixion to Pentecost. Six days earlier than this was the Sunday we call Palm Sunday. On this day the time of the atonement was officially announced as having come. Jesus came into Jerusalem and was proclaimed a King. This precipitated all of the required events that brought Christ to the cross a few days later. Such actions as the evidences of the hatred of the Pharisees and the betrayal by Judas brought to reality Christ's crucifixion. Therefore, the Sunday we call Palm Sunday and the crucifixion are inseparably connected.

Moreover, we read in Exodus 12:3 that on the tenth day of Nisan, the Passover lamb was to be selected. It was to be killed on Nisan 14. In A.D. 33, when Jesus became the Passover Lamb, the tenth day of Nisan began at sundown on Sunday and continued until sundown on Monday. In Mark 11:9-11, God identifies Palm Sunday with the tenth day of Nisan, which began at sundown on Sunday.

And they that went before, and they that followed, cried, saying, Hosanna; Blessed is he that cometh in the name of the Lord: Blessed be the kingdom of our father David, that cometh in the name of the Lord: Hosanna in the highest. And Jesus entered into Jerusalem, and into the temple: and when he had looked round about upon all things, and now the <u>eventide was come</u>, he went out unto Bethany with the twelve.

Please note that the activities of Palm Sunday came to a close in the evening, thus tying the day to Nisan 10 when the Passover lamb was selected. Therefore, Palm Sunday is intimately identified with the cross in that it was the day when Jesus effectively announced that the atonement was at hand. The Passover lamb that was to be killed had been selected.

If we now recognize that Palm Sunday occurred exactly three and a half years after Jesus was baptized, the timetable is as follows.

1. Jesus' baptism to Palm Sunday	3½ years	1,298	days
2. Palm Sunday to cross		5	days
3. Cross to Saturday in tomb		1	day
4. Saturday of crucifixion to Pentecost		50	days
		1,334	days or
		1,335	days, inclusive

When we include both the day of Christ's baptism and the day of Pentecost, we end up with precisely 1,335 days.

This 1,335 days is the exact number prophesied in Daniel 12:12. To the very day, this prophecy was fulfilled.

When we examine the 1,335 days we can pinpoint that period on the calendar. The end of it is on Pentecost in A.D. 33. In an examination of the Jewish calendar for A.D. 33, we find that Pentecost was May 21. We know that this is an accurate date because of the great amount of Biblical evidence that points to A.D. 33 as the year of the cross. When we examine the Jewish calendar for A.D. 33, we find that the timing of the Passover of A.D. 33 agrees perfectly with the Biblical information that identifies with the timing of the Passover.

Therefore, we can be quite certain that Pentecost occurred on May 21, A.D. 33. But what date in A.D. 29 A.D. exactly 1,335 days earlier than this? It would be interesting to know if Jesus was baptized on any kind of special day insofar as new moons or other feast days are concerned.

According to astronomical calculation we can discover that in A.D. 29, when Jesus was baptized, that the date of His baptism was September 25.

The computation of the 1,335 days of Jesus' ministry works out as follows.

Number of Days in Calendar	Number of Days Toward 1335 Days
Three years: 9/25/29 to 9/24/32 (3 x 365.2422) = 1,095.7266	1,096
Sept. 25-Sept. 30 incl. (A.D. 32)	6
October 31 (A.D. 32)	31
November 30 (A.D. 32)	30
December 31 (A.D. 32)	31
January 31 (A.D. 33)	31
February 28 (A.D. 33)	28
March 31 (A.D. 33)	31
April 30 (A.D. 33)	30
May 1-May 21 incl. (A.D. 33)	21
	1,335

Please note that six days are included for September. This is because the day of the baptism of Jesus, which was September 25, was also a day identified with Jesus' work on earth, which began with His baptism. Also, the 21st day of May (A.D. 33), is included because that was the date when Jesus sent the Comforter who is the Holy Spirit. Therefore, the period of time from September 25, A.D. 29 to May 21, A.D. 33, inclusive, equals 1,335 days.

Interestingly, September 25, A.D. 29, is a very special date. This is because September 25 is Tishri 1, and Tishri 1 is the date of the first day of the seventh month. Concerning this day, we read in Leviticus 23:23-25:

And the LORD spake unto Moses, saying, Speak unto the children of Israel, saying, In the seventh month, in the first day of the month, shall ye have a sabbath, a memorial of a Jubilee an holy convocation. Ye shall do no servile work therein: but ye shall offer an offering made by fire unto the LORD.

We can be absolutely certain that it was on this special day of the first day of the seventh month in A.D. 29 that Jesus was baptized. We can be absolutely certain because God had prophesied hundreds of years earlier in

Daniel 12:12 that, **"Blessed is he** [*the Messiah*] **that waiteth, and cometh to the thousand three hundred and five and thirty days."** How precisely the Bible gives information!

The Hebrew word in Daniel 12:12 that is translated "cometh" in the King James Bible is used very interestingly in another place. The word "cometh" used in Daniel 12:12 is the Hebrew word "*naga*." The same word "*naga*" is translated "touch" more than ninety times in such phrases as **"the soul that toucheth any unclean thing"** or **"a hand touched me."** But this same word "*naga*" is also translated "come" in a few places. One of these places is extremely interesting because it is used in connection with the observance of feast days. This citation is Ezra 3:1, where we read:

> **And when the seventh month was <u>come,</u> and the children of Israel were in the cities, the people gathered themselves together as one man to Jerusalem**.

The word "come" is the Hebrew "*naga*" even as it is in Daniel 12:2. In Ezra 3:6 God adds the words:

> **From the first day of the seventh month began they to offer burnt offerings unto the LORD. But the foundation of the temple of the LORD was not yet laid.**

These verses historically relate the experiences of Israel in Ezra's day. Spiritually, they must point to Jesus Who laid the foundation of the spiritual temple -- the whole body of true believers -- by going to the cross. The historical event recorded in Ezra 3 is, therefore, a portrait pointing to the baptism and announcement of Jesus as the Lamb that would take away the sins of the world. Both in Ezra 3 and in Daniel 12:12 God is focusing on Tishri 1 which is the first day of the seventh month. Three and one half years later, the foundation of the temple would be laid by Jesus experiencing God's wrath.

Since the word "come" used in both Ezra 3 and Daniel 12:12 ordinarily signifies "touch," we can know that Daniel 12:12 is teaching that Christ as the blessed one had to wait for the fulness of God's timetable before He could come to, or be in touch with, the 1335 days, which was the period of time when Jesus did all of His work as Savior. It began on the feast of Tishri 1 in A.D. 29 and ended 1,335 days later on May 21, A.D. 33, when the Holy Spirit was given at Pentecost. How beautiful and harmonious is the Word of God! How trustworthy are all the prophecies and numbers of the Bible!

As we learned earlier, the Bible speaks of two Jubilee periods. The first began with the birth of Jesus in the Jubilee year 7 B.C. Later we will learn that the second Jubilee period began in A.D. 1994, which was also a Jubilee year. Later in our study we will examine the second Jubilee period very carefully.

However, the baptism of Jesus in A.D. 29 was intimately identified with the first Jubilee. Remember we learned that at the time Jesus was born, the Bible especially calls attention to two important events that identify with the nature of the Jubilee, i.e., the proclamation of liberty to the world. The first was the heavenly host that appeared to the shepherds, announcing the birth of Christ (Luke 2:9-14). The second was the activity of the shepherds as they told the world all that they had seen and heard (Luke 2:17).

Moreover, we learned that in all likelihood, Jesus was born on the day of atonement in the year 7 B.C., a Jubilee year. Remember we learned also that the day of atonement is identified with the Jubilee.

We have now come to the first day of the seventh month in A.D. 29. As we have learned, this feast day was also identified with the Jubilee. Thus, we are not surprised that on that day in A.D. 29, two great announcements were made that by means of the Bible have been published all over the world.

The first was the announcement by John the Baptist **"Behold the lamb of God which taketh away the sin of the world"** (John 1:29).

The second was the announcement from heaven. We read in Mark 1:9-11:

> **And it came to pass in those days, that Jesus came from Nazareth of Galilee, and was baptized of John in Jordan. And straightway coming up out of the water, he saw the heavens opened, and the Spirit like a dove descending upon him: And there came a voice from heaven, saying, Thou art my beloved Son, in whom I am well pleased**.

In both John 1:29 and in Mark 1:9-11 we see the reason why Jesus was baptized and announced on the Holy Day of the first day of the seventh month. It was the day that we received an enormous reminder that the Jubilee year has come.

How precisely God has knit together the unfolding of His Gospel plan!

How Old was Jesus when He was Baptized?

We have arrived at the conclusion that Jesus was in all likelihood born on October 1, 7 B.C. and that He was announced on September 25, A.D. 29. Thus, Jesus would have been six days short of being thirty five years of age when He was announced and baptized. Is that possible? Doesn't the Bible say He was 30 years old when He was baptized? Let us examine this question.

In Luke 3:23 we read:

And Jesus himself began to be about thirty years of age, being (as was supposed) the son of Joseph, which was the son of Heli,

Very literally the first phrase should read. **"And Jesus Himself was about thirty years beginning"** etc. That is, it took about thirty years of preparation before Jesus would officially begin His work as Messiah. Did the preparation begin with His birth or did it begin at another time?

Since we know from other very clear evidence we have derived from the Bible that He actually was almost thirty five years of age at the time of His announcement and baptism, we wonder why God focuses on the number thirty. True, God carefully inserted the word **"about"** to assure us He was not actually thirty. Being thirty four years of age at this time certainly does not disagree with the statement **"about thirty."**

Several reasons may be advanced why God features the number 30. Four will be suggested.

1. The about 30 years may be identified with the call out of Egypt. We read in Matthew 2:13-15:

And when they were departed, behold, the angel of the Lord appeareth to Joseph in a dream, saying, Arise, and take the young child and his mother, and flee into Egypt, and be thou there until I bring thee word: for Herod will seek the young child to destroy him. When he arose, he took the young child and his mother by night, and departed into Egypt: And was there until the death of Herod: that it might be fulfilled which was spoken of the Lord by the prophet, saying, Out of Egypt have I called my son.

Jesus would have been a few years old when his family returned from Egypt. Thus it would have been very close to thirty years later that He officially began His ministry. This is the most likely solution to the puzzle of the **"about thirty years"** phrase. It was about 30 years after He was called out Egypt. Remember that the Bible says **"Out of Egypt I have called My Son"** (Matthew 2:15).

2. The number 30 symbolically signifies complete purpose of God. This would emphasize that it was God's complete purpose that Jesus was ready to officially begin His work as the Messiah now that He had been announced and baptized.

3. Joseph of the Old Testament, who was a picture or type of Jesus was thirty years old when He became Prime Minister of Egypt and began the activity that would save his family from starvation. The term "about thirty" might thus show identification between Jesus and Joseph.

4. David, also a type of Christ, ascended the throne of Israel when he was 30 years old. The term "about thirty" might thus show identification between Jesus and David.

But now we should look at the next very important milestone in the unfolding of God's salvation plan. It is the crucifixion of Jesus.

A.D. 33. Christ is Crucified

We have come a long way on the highway of time. All along the way, there have been important milestones that were focusing on this stupendous event of God Himself in the person of the Lord Jesus Christ becoming our Savior. We already have learned much about His birth at which time the wonderful proclamation throughout the land had begun because the Jubilee, Jesus Christ, had come. Remember the shepherds spread abroad what they had heard and seen. And then came the reminders of the Jubilee as Jesus was announced both by John the Baptist and by the voice from heaven.

But now we have come to the great year, A.D. 33. It was the year that the whole world and the whole creation unknowingly had been waiting for. How can we be sure that this auspicious year was A.D. 33 and not some other year?

Remember this year was anchored as the year A.D. 33 when we analyzed the 1,335 days of Daniel 12. It is locked into A.D. 33 because in the study of the seventy weeks of Daniel 9 (see *The Seventy Weeks of Daniel 9*, available free of charge from Family Radio), we learned that it was the year A.D. 33 that sacrifices and offerings ceased. All of the previous sacrifices of the past eleven thousand years were fulfilled and ended when Christ was sacrificed as He went to the cross.

There is another cogent reason why A.D. 33 had to be the year of the crucifixion. The Bible is very clear that Christ was crucified on Friday. The year in which He was crucified had to be a year when Nisan 14, the delegated Passover date, fell on a Friday.

We must remember that each year Nisan 14 could identify with a different day of the week. For example in A.D. 32, Nisan 14 would have come on Tuesday. In A.D. 34, Nisan 14 the Passover date would have come on

Monday. But the Bible tells us that when Jesus was crucified it was Friday. Remember when Jesus' body was placed in the tomb it was the day before the Sabbath. We read in Mark 15:42-45:

> **And now when the even was come, because it was the preparation, that is, <u>the day before the sabbath</u>, Joseph of Arimathaea, an honourable counsellor, which also waited for the kingdom of God, came, and went in boldly unto Pilate, and craved the body of Jesus. And Pilate marvelled if he were already dead: and calling unto him the centurion, he asked him whether he had been any while dead. And when he knew it of the centurion, he gave the body to Joseph.**

Had Christ not been punished for our sins there would be no salvation for anyone.

We, therefore, can be assured for many reasons that our Lord was crucified in the year 33 A.D. This is the year and occasion that is super important. Had Christ not been punished for our sins there would be no Salvation for anyone. No event in the entire history of the world can stand in the shadow of this climatic event. The impact of what happened at the cross identifies with each and every human being who ever had inhabited planet earth. On the one hand, Christ in His atonement guaranteed the salvation of all those whom God had chosen from the foundation of the earth to become saved. But on the other hand, the fact that Christ suffered the equivalent of eternal damnation on behalf of those He came to save also guaranteed that every person who does not become saved must himself, as payment for his sins, bear the wrath of God, which is eternal damnation.

True, there are a great many Bible teachers and theologians who teach that because Christ physically suffered the death of crucifixion, He therefore, by this intense physical suffering, has covered and atoned for each and every sin that was ever committed by any human being. They, therefore, believe the physical beating and the other mistreatment he endured when He was crucified must have been super awful. This kind of totally un-Biblical conclusion has produced movies such as the recent "Passion of Christ" movie.

When Christ was crucified, He suffered physical pain just as the two thieves hanging on crosses next to Him experienced. But the physical pain He endured did not in any way pay for our sins. When Jesus was still very much alive

He said, **"It is finished"** (John 19:30).

What was finished? How could anything be finished if He were still physically alive? What was finished was payment for sin. For whose sins? For the sins of those who had been elected by God to become saved.

How could the payment be "finished" if He was still physically alive? The payment was fully paid because the payment was the fact that beginning in the Garden of Gethsemane and until Jesus said **"It is finished,"** He had been under the punishment of God. This is why already in the Garden of Gethsemane, before He endured any physical suffering, the sweat was already pouring from His body like great drops of blood.

That is why the cry was wrenched from His lips, **"My God, My God, why hast thou forsaken me"** (Matthew 27:46). We do know that God's law demanded eternal damnation as the payment for any and every sin. Therefore, in order for Christ to free His elect from the sentence of eternal damnation it meant that God's wrath that God poured out upon the Lord Jesus Christ had to be equal to the penalty of eternal damnation that each and every one of God's elected people must endure.

So it was a horrendous suffering Christ endured. Only because He was, and never ceased to be, God, could God so intensify the punishment that in the hours from the Garden of Gethsemane until Christ's words **"It is finished,"** the whole penalty was paid.

However, as we noted earlier, this terrible experience of Jesus in which God's law concerning payment for sin had been fully satisfied also impacted every human being who never does become saved. The fact that Jesus met and fulfilled all the demands of the law guarantees that each and every person who never does become saved must on his own behalf bear the punishment of eternal damnation as payment for his own sins.

This is why the unfolding of history in terms of the rise and fall of civilizations, or of nations or of any other aspect of human existence is entirely unimportant. It is unimportant because when its all over and the world has come to an end the only thing that is important is "Do I spend eternity future in Hell under the awful wrath of God?" Or is it possible that I will spend eternity future with Christ in the New Heaven and the New Earth? There is no third solution. It is one or the other. It is heaven or hell.

Pentecost

Returning now to the propitious year 33 A.D. there is another great event that took place as God unfolds the time line of history. When we were following the time line of history in the Old Testament we noted that one of the important ceremonial feast days was the feast of weeks. It was also called the feast of harvest or feast of first fruits. It was a very important time when portions of the early spring harvest were brought to the temple.

> *It was on this day that there is evidence that a great shift had taken place insofar as the unfolding of God's salvation plan was concerned.*

We learned that this feast day was observed in the New Testament as Pentecost. It was called Pentecost from the Greek word "*pence*" which we translate as "fifty." It was a day that came fifty days after the Sabbath following the Passover. It was on this day that there is evidence that a great shift had taken place insofar as the unfolding of God's salvation plan was concerned.

Remember that when Israel came out of Egypt the external representation of the Kingdom of God was shifted from an individual family to the nation of Israel. At that time in history, God gave further pictures to illustrate the character and nature of the kingdom of God. For example, the land of Canaan which had been given to the nation of Israel also became an external representation of the kingdom of God.

Moreover, God additionally focused on Jerusalem and the temple in Jerusalem and the nation of Israel and the land Judea to externally represent the kingdom of God. Thus, even when Christ came, such entities as the temple, Jerusalem, and the nation of Israel, etc., were still to be regarded as the external representation of the kingdom of God.

But then when Christ was hanging on the cross the veil of the temple was rent. As we noted earlier in our study the huge curtain that hid from the eyes of mankind the Holy of Holies was opened. It was effectively a great announcement that God was finished using Judea or Jerusalem or national Israel or the temple to be an external representation of the Kingdom of God.

Jesus had told the disciples that when He went back to heaven He would send or pour out the Holy Spirit who would convict the world of sin, righteousness, and judgment (John 16:7-8). In other words, there was a new era dawning.

The evidence of this new era which was the central focus of the unfolding of God's salvation plan can be clearly seen on that day of Pentecost in 33 A.D. Jesus, the perfect preacher had been preaching for three and a half years. Very few people became saved. Yet on that Pentecost Sunday about 3,000 became saved (Acts 2:41). It was the beginning of the church age whereby local congregations would come into existence all over the world.

These local congregations as divine institutions, carefully designed by God, Himself, would now externally represent the kingdom of God. The land of Canaan, Judea, Jerusalem, the temple would no longer typify or externally represent the kingdom of God. Fact is, the local congregations would be spoken of as the temple, or Jerusalem, or Judea, or the house of God because they now had become the external representation of the kingdom of God.

> *Within these local churches two kinds of people could be found.*

Within these local churches two kinds of people could be found. There were those who truly had become saved so that already they were eternal citizens of the kingdom of God. God speaks of them in the Bible as Jerusalem above (Galatians 4:26). They are spoken about in the Bible as "wheat" (Matthew 13). They are the eternal church which Christ came to build, against which the gates of hell cannot prevail.

On the other hand, there were many in the local churches who believed they had become truly saved, who gave substantial outward evidence of having become saved. But they were not saved. They were still under the wrath of God. They are spoken of in the Bible as Jerusalem which is now (Galatians 4). They are called "weeds" of "tares" in the Bible (Matthew 13). They were actually trusting in their church or their Pastor or in some spiritual work they had done. They did not understand that the entire work of salvation was God's work. They had not received from God a brand new resurrected soul in which God would energize them and God Himself would work in them to will and to do of His good pleasure.

These local churches would rise and fall through out the time of the church age. Some would become so apostate that they would disappear. Some would become so overrun with false Gospels that finally Satan as an angel of light (2 Corinthians 11:14), would be ruling within them.

Again and again God would raise up new local congregations. Thus as a whole the local congregations carried out the task God had assigned to them. That task was to send the Gospel into all the world.

Because **"faith *cometh* by hearing, and hearing by the word of God"** (Romans 10:17), wherever the Bible could be read, God would save people. Therefore, in the churches in which encouragement was given to read the Bible, God's salvation program for the world continued. This was in spite of the fact that many wrong doctrines were taught in most of these churches. How wonderful that it was not the church or the pastor who saved anyone.

The year A.D. 33, when Christ was crucified and when the church age began, also interrelated with many other significant milestones in the time line of history. For example, we might recall that in the year 2092 B.C., Abraham, together with his wife Sarah and his nephew Lot, arrived in the promised land, the land of Canaan, which externally represented the kingdom of God.

Now $2,092 + 33 = 2,125$ years inclusive. That is, 2,125 years after coming to the promised land the kingdom of God is forever secured. That is so because Christ rose from the grave proving that the sins of those He came to save had been paid for.

Curiously the number 2,125 breaks into some very significant numbers.

$2,092 + 33 = 2,125$ inclusive years.

2,125 is the product of 5 x 5 x 5 x 17.

The number 5 can signify salvation or judgment. The number 3 (there are 3 fives) signifies God's purpose. The number 17 signifies heaven. Thus the number 2,125 in a sense teach that the land of Canaan and the resurrection of Jesus symbolize God's purpose of salvation is to bring people to heaven. This is another brief example of how the milestones of God's salvation history are tied together in a very definite pattern.

Chapter 10
The Church Age

We are in the process of unfolding the time line of the history of the world. We have found that, that time line is governed by God's salvation program for the world as it is revealed in God's Holy Book, the Bible. We have come to that period which we will call the "Church Age."

Actually, when, earlier in our study, we looked at Pentecost as it occurred in A.D. 33, at which time the Holy Spirit was poured out, we were standing at the beginning of the church age. That day officially marked the beginning of the church age.

By the term "Church Age," we are speaking of the period in God's unfolding history of the world, during which He would be utilizing a divine institution consisting of local congregations or local churches to evangelize the world.

The official beginning of the church age coincided with the end of the long period of time during which the nation of Israel was officially the external representative of the Kingdom of God on this earth. The nation of Israel with its headquarters in Jerusalem had become so wicked that even though the Messiah Himself (the Lord Jesus) was physically present in their midst they refused to recognize Him as their Savior. Fact is, they hated Him so intensely that they finally killed Him (Acts 2:36).

Jesus said of the Jews in John 8:44, **"Ye are of your father the devil."** Jesus ministered for many months in cities such as Chorazin and Capernaum, which were located by the Sea of Galilee. Yet Jesus observed in Luke 10:13-15:

> **Woe unto thee, Chorazin! woe unto thee, Bethsaida! for if the mighty works had been done in Tyre and Sidon, which have been done in you, they had a great while ago repented, sitting in sackcloth and ashes. But it shall be more tolerable for Tyre and Sidon at the judgment, than for you. And thou, Capernaum, which art exalted to heaven, shalt be thrust down to hell.**

> *...during Jesus' ministry very, very few became saved.*

Thus, during Jesus' ministry very, very few became saved.

However, it was God's plan that this was the time that God would shift from using the nation of Israel as God's special people, to the utilization of local congregations as the external representative of the Kingdom of God.

Thus, seven weeks after the resurrection of Jesus, God began the Church Age. Remember we earlier learned that on the Pentecost afternoon in the year A.D. 33, about 3,000 individuals were saved. For the next 1,955 years this church age would continue. During the church age the nature and structure of the local congregations were carefully designed by God. They were to have as church overseers (elders and deacons), men who met very stringent spiritual qualifications (1 Timothy 3). The people who attended these churches were to be under the rule of these elders. Thus, they were to have membership in these congregations (1 Corinthians 5, 1 Peter 5:1-5).

The task of each congregation was to assist in the sending forth the Gospel into the world. As they carried out this task they started additional churches wherever a few people became believers. These mission churches in turn would send missionaries out to establish additional churches. Thus, by the end of the church age, local congregations are to be found all over the world. Those who believed they had become saved became members of one of these local congregations.

> *God, however, designed the local churches*
> *as a divine institution that could effectively teach the Gospel*
> *in spite of these obvious shortcomings.*

For the greatest part of the church age the printing press did not exist. It was invented about 500 years ago, but the church age existed for more than 1,900 years of time. Thus, for about 1,400 years all copies of the Bible were hand written. Therefore they were quite rare and most people were illiterate. God, however, designed the local churches as a divine institution that could effectively teach the Gospel in spite of these obvious shortcomings. God established the local churches in such a way that the church members could be taught the Scriptures by pastors and elders who had access to a handwritten copy of the Bible and who were able to read it.

Even after the invention of the printing press, during most of the remaining years of the church age, a copy of the Bible was not readily available to many people of the world and many people still lived with the problem of illiteracy.

New Testament Ceremonial Laws

To assist with the understanding of the Gospel message God also gave the local churches two ceremonial laws. The observance of these ceremonial laws did not initiate salvation or in any way guarantee salvation. They were given to assist individuals in understanding the nature of salvation. There was no spiritual power in the observance of these ceremonial laws.

The first ceremonial law was the act of water baptism. The purpose of water baptism was to show that even as water washes away the physical dirt on us, so the Gospel, which is the spiritual water, is required to wash our sins away.

> *The second ceremonial law that was given was that of the communion service.*

The second ceremonial law that was given was that of the communion service. The bread and the wine which were eaten in this ceremony were foods that contributed to our physical life. Thus, they were symbols that reminded us that we receive spiritual strength and life from the fact that Christ gave His life, that is, His body was broken and His blood was shed (He gave His life), that we might have life.

The Lord's Supper, as the communion service was frequently called, also was pointing to the completion of our salvation when spiritually we will be called to the marriage supper of the Lamb who of course is Jesus (Revelation 19:9). The Bible teaches us that spiritually, the true believers are the bride of Christ. These ceremonial acts were to be carried out under the supervision of the church overseers.

The underlying spiritual power of the church age was the fact that God Himself was present whenever two or three or more people were gathered together in Christ's name. God was present as the Holy Spirit not only in the lives of the true believers but also to apply the preached Word of God to the lives of those whom God planned to save. Therefore, even though the preaching was often very faulty, God still saved people as long as those that He planned to save were hearing the words from the Bible. The principle taught in Romans 10:17, **"faith cometh by hearing and hearing by the Word of God,"** continually was a fundamental principle that God utilized to cause the local churches to grow.

This was in sharp contrast to the spiritual conditions that prevailed at the time the nation of Israel was coming to its end as the external representation of the Kingdom of God. At that time Jesus preached perfect sermons but virtually no one was saved. This was the situation because at that time, God the Holy Spirit was not applying the perfectly preached Word of God to any hearer's life so that they might become saved.

Moreover, during the church age, Satan, the great enemy of Christ, was restricted by God from interfering with God's desire to save those that He wished to save as they heard the Word of God.

Satan Impacts the Local Congregations

> *Satan, however, as the enemy of Christ*
> *was still able to seriously affect the local congregations*
> *throughout the time of the church age.*

Satan, however, as the enemy of Christ was still able to seriously affect the local congregations throughout the time of the church age. He did so by bringing into the congregations individuals who were convinced they were saved but in fact were not saved. Because they were convinced they were saved they tried very hard to live the way a truly saved person should live. Therefore they were virtually indistinguishable from the true believers within the congregation. Because no church overseers could know with certainty the true spiritual condition of any individual, they could easily give membership to those who outwardly appeared to be saved but actually were not saved. They were still under the authority of Satan.

Very frequently these unsaved individuals were pastors, elders, or deacons who had the spiritual oversight of the congregations. Thus, even though Christ was officially the King of the New Testament churches, in effect, Satan to a high degree ruled in those churches. This is spoken of in 2 Corinthians 11:14-15:

And no marvel; for Satan himself is transformed into an angel of light. Therefore it is no great thing if his ministers also be transformed as the ministers of righteousness; whose end shall be according to their works.

This is also the teaching of Matthew 13:24-25:

Another parable put he forth unto them, saying, The kingdom of heaven is likened unto a man which sowed good seed in his field:

But while men slept, his enemy came and sowed tares among the wheat, and went his way.

The tares or weeds represent those who appear to be true believers but in actuality are under the authority of Satan. (For a more complete discussion of this subject the read in invited to obtain, free of charge, the book *Wheat and Tares* from Family Radio.)

> *The result of this condition of local churches being filled with unsaved believers created spiritual havoc in the churches.*

The result of this condition of local churches being filled with unsaved believers created spiritual havoc in the churches. Many local churches and denominations became so corrupted that the true Gospel became completely obliterated and they became altogether another gospel, a false gospel. The Bible alone and in its entirety no longer was the divine authority that structured and determined the character of the Gospel they were preaching. The authority for their gospel was the Bible plus church tradition or that which they heard through dreams or visions or tongues. Even though they spoke of Christ as their Savior, Satan had become completely their ruler. This could especially be seen in those churches which began to believe that God is still bringing divine revelation to men and women by means of tongues or dreams or visions or angel visitations. Thus, entire denominations came into existence which were altogether ruled over by Satan even though the rulers of these churches were convinced that they were serving Christ.

In God's plan for the unfolding of the timeline of history, God was fully aware of this terrible falling away from truth. Almost 2000 years ago God wrote in Revelation 2 and Revelation 3 about seven churches that were among the first churches of the church age. As He wrote about them, God was actually writing to all of the churches that would come into existence throughout the church age.

God indicated that even at that very early time in church history already Satan was active in the churches (Revelation 2:9, 13, 24; 3:9). Already one of the churches, the church at Sardis, was effectively a dead church, even though it still had a few members who were true believers (Revelation 3:1-4). Fact is, a few hundred years later all seven of these churches had ceased to exist.

This has been the experience of local congregations throughout the church age. However, in spite of the spiritual weaknesses of these churches God still used them to accomplish His purposes to bring the Gospel message to the world.

> *Nothing man or Satan could do could frustrate*
> *God's plan of salvation.*

In spite of the weaknesses and failures of mankind God could override this and still accomplish His purpose of saving each and every individual He had planned to save. Fact is, nothing was happening outside of God's control. Nothing man or Satan could do could frustrate God's plan of salvation.

Finally, however, the time came when God was finished with the utilization of the institution of local churches to accomplish His plan of salvation. At least three things had developed within the local churches.

First of all, the churches were increasingly departing from truth. Gospels that focused on miracles, visions, voices, and tongues were proliferating. The Bible itself became increasingly less authoritative in the churches. For example, the marriage institution was destroyed as churches began to sanction divorce in opposition to the Biblical law that there was not to be divorce for any reason. Or, for example, churches increasingly taught that one can initiate one's own salvation by doing certain things, such as "accepting Christ" as Savior or becoming baptized in water.

Secondly, the population of the world was exploding so that at this time in history every hour the world population is about 8,300 individuals greater than the hour before. Thus by today the world population is substantially greater than six billion people.

Thirdly, there was an enormous explosion in scientific knowledge. For almost 13,000 years the fastest means of travel was a running horse. The fields were plowed by horses or oxen. There was no electricity, no understanding of atoms, or neutrons or protons. No understanding of DNA. This was not because men of the past were less intelligent or less desirous to learn about these things. It was the simple fact that in the unfolding of God's timeline of history it was not the time for this knowledge to be given to mankind.

In the last 200 years, however, there has been an explosion of knowledge. The time has come when God is allowing mankind to increasingly understand the intricate nature and awesome complexity of God's creation. This should cause mankind to realize that only God could create such a complex and beautiful world. Instead, because of the total perverseness of man's heart, it is causing mankind to believe that they are in charge of this universe and they in turn are increasingly in control of their own destiny.

This same wicked mind of man also becomes the engine that drives the desire to learn more and more about all of these things. Large sums of money can be made and great satisfaction of the lusts of the flesh can be achieved as these secrets of God's creation are unfolded and applied to practical applications.

Significantly, this explosion of scientific knowledge which has resulted in shrinking the world so that there is virtually instant communication to almost every person in the world coincides perfectly with the unfolding of God's salvation plan. Just as pornographic material and secular knowledge can now blanket the world, so, too, the same means can be used to blanket the world with the Gospel.

Moreover, even as secular knowledge becomes more accurate and available to the world so, too, we are at a time in the unfolding of God's salvation plan when we can be much more accurate in the presentation of the Gospel details.

For example, the whole world can be told that the Bible teaches that God alone, in the person of our Lord Jesus Christ, has done all of the work required to save those whom He sovereignly plans to save.

> *God delayed the explosion of secular knowledge*
> *for this time when the spiritual knowledge of the Bible*
> *is to blanket the world.*

Indeed, it becomes quite obvious that God delayed the explosion of secular knowledge for this time when the spiritual knowledge of the Bible is to blanket the world. While secular man seeks to satisfy his own lusts for money and for satisfaction of the lusts of the flesh, the spiritual man, the true believer in Christ, commandeers this exploding scientific knowledge, putting it to work to blanket the world with the true Gospel.

All of the above factors set the stage for the tremendous drama that is presently taking place as Christ is making the final preparations for His return.

When we go back to the Jubilee year of 7 B.C., we witness that God's tremendous plan to publish the good news of salvation to the whole world became a reality. In that Jubilee year of 7 B.C. it was first a band of shepherds that **"made known abroad"** (Luke 2:17), the wonderful news given to them by the angelic host. Luke 2:10-11 records:

And the angel said unto them, Fear not: for, behold, I bring you good tidings of great joy, which shall be to all people. For unto you is born this day in the city of David a Savior, which is Christ the Lord.

The proclamation of this wonderful news of spiritual liberty was further declared to the world as Jesus was announced as the **"lamb of God which taketh away the sin of the world."** That is, through Jesus there existed the means by which anyone who became saved did have his sins paid for. He would be liberated from bondage to sin and to Satan. He was spiritually liberated so that he would be free to serve Christ as his Savior and King for ever.

This announcement was made in A.D. 29. It was the first day of the seventh month. Remember it was at the Feast of the seventh month new moon that there was to be a remembrance of the Jubilee. Thus, effectively, the Jubilee year that began with the birth of Jesus in 7 B.C. was now in full motion because Christ who is the very essence of the Jubilee had now been announced to the world.

Jesus had come to free people from bondage to sin. Jesus Himself expressed this in Luke 4:18-19:

The Spirit of the Lord is upon me, because he hath anointed me to preach the gospel to the poor; he hath sent me to heal the brokenhearted, to preach deliverance to the captives, and recovering of sight to the blind, to set at liberty them that are bruised, To preach the acceptable year of the Lord.

The term "acceptable year" was synonymous with the term "Jubilee Year" because both terms identify with the concept of preaching or publishing deliverance to the captives. The captives include each and every human being who is not saved. To be without salvation is to be still in bondage to sin and to Satan. This is spoken of in connection with the Jubilee year in Leviticus 25:10:

And ye shall hallow the fiftieth year, and proclaim liberty throughout all the land unto all the inhabitants thereof: it shall be a jubile unto you; and ye shall return every man unto his possession, and ye shall return every man unto his family.

This publishing or preaching of the deliverance of people from their sins became officially recognized on Pentecost in A.D.

Later in our study we will discover that the Jubilee year of the preaching of the Gospel would continue for 1955 years until the year 1988 A.D. In that year the "acceptable year," the Jubilee Year, came to an end. In that year the Church Age came to an end. How do we know 1988 was the year that ended the "Church Age" and how does the Bible speak of that awful time of the end of the Church Age? These are questions we will address as we continue this study.

The Great Tribulation*

We are continuing with our task of unfolding the timeline of history, fully recognizing that it is securely tied to God's wonderful salvation plan.

We are learning that for 1955 years the focus of God's salvation plan was the church age. The local churches were the divine institution God had established to be the means by which the whole world was to become acquainted with the Bible. Thus, those who had been chosen by God to become saved might come under the hearing of the Word of God.

The following is a brief summary of some of the Biblical references to this terrible end of the church age, which coincides with the beginning of the Great Tribulation.

1. Revelation 7 indicates it cannot happen until the complete fullness (144,000) of all of those who are to be saved during the church age has been accomplished. (Remember, the number 144,000 is not to be understood literally.)

2. 1 Peter 4:17 teaches that Christ will come to judge the house of God (the local churches).

3. Matthew 24:21, there will be great tribulation such as the world has never known.

4. Revelation 20:1-4, Satan will be loosed so that he can be used by God as a judgment in the local churches.

5. Revelation 9:1-5, Christ as a star looses Satan.

---

* For a more complete discussion of the end of the church age, the reader is invited to obtain, free of charge from Family Radio, a copy of the books *The End of the Church Age and After* and *Wheat and Tares*.

6. Revelation 13:1-2, the beast (Satan) comes out of the sea to make war with the saints and overcome them.

7. Revelation 13:11, the beast (Satan) comes out of the earth appearing as a lamb but speaking like a dragon.

8. Revelation 17:12, Satan rules throughout the Great Tribulation time as a beast with crowns on its ten horns.

9. Revelation 9:15, the four angels are loosed to slay the third part (those unbelievers who externally represent the kingdom of God), of men.

10. Revelation 8:1, the first half hour of the Great Tribulation begins during which heaven is silent (nobody in the whole world will become saved).

11. 2 Thessalonians2:3, the man of sin (Satan) takes his seat (becomes the sole ruler) in the temple (the local congregations).

12. Revelation 11:7, the two witnesses (the true believers) are killed (driven out of the local congregations).

13. Revelation 11:2, the holy city (the true believers in the local congregations) is trodden underfoot.

14. 2 Thessalonians 2:7, He (that is, the Holy Spirit) who restrains is taken out of the midst of each and every local congregation.

These are a sampling of verses found throughout the Bible that instruct us concerning the reality and character of the Great Tribulation we are presently experiencing.

The Bible greatly assures us that just before the end of time there will be this period of Great Tribulation. That this dreadful time comes just before the end of the world is clearly stated in Matthew 24:29:

Immediately after the tribulation of those days shall the sun be darkened, and the moon shall not give her light, and the stars shall fall from heaven, and the powers of the heavens shall be shaken

As we continue this study, we will learn how the Bible speaks of the end of the Church Age. We will also learn from the Bible when it, in all likelihood, came to an end. Further we will learn what follows the end of the Church Age.

Silence In Heaven

In Revelation 8:1 God gives us a very unusual and ominous prophecy. There we read:

And when he had opened the seventh seal, there was silence in heaven about the space of half an hour.

To understand this verse, a couple of Biblical teachings should be kept in mind. Mankind can preach as perfect sermons as possible. However, these messages will not benefit the hearers unless God applies the message to those whom God wishes to bless by that message (Matthew 13:14-17, John 16:13-15).. If heaven is silent it implies that there is no action coming from God to bless that message. Thus, however faithful to the Bible that message may be; it is not being used of God as a means through which God saves any of the hearers.

Moreover we read in Luke 15:7:

I say unto you, that likewise joy shall be in heaven over one sinner that repenteth, more than over ninety and nine just persons, which need no repentance.

Luke 15:10 further adds:

Likewise, I say unto you, there is joy in the presence of the angels of God over one sinner that repenteth.

> *If heaven is silent, we can surely understand that this joyful activity identified with the moment of salvation of any individual is not going on in heaven.*

If heaven is silent, we can surely understand that this joyful activity identified with the moment of salvation of any individual is not going on in heaven. Indeed, the most terrible situation existed in the world during the **"about a half hour of silence."** During this half hour, which we will learn is the first part of the Great Tribulation, no one anywhere in the world could become saved. Later in our study we will indicate when this dreadful half hour occurred. Indeed, all the evidence of the Bible indicates we have already gone through this awful time.

There will be many who will claim they became saved during the time of those years. Or they will testify that during those years their church witnessed the salvation of a great many people.

We must remember, however, that no one can see the heart of men. The churches of our day are filled with men and women who are altogether convinced that they are saved. But by their disobedience to the command of God to come out of their local congregation, because God's judgment has come upon it, they are showing that they may not be a true believer. We must listen to the Bible and not trust at all in what we think. Therefore, during this half hour of silence we can know that those who were convinced they were saved in that time could not have become saved.

God typified the bringing of the Gospel to the world by means of the local churches by describing them as two witnesses. We read in Revelation 11:3-6:

> **And I will give power unto my two witnesses, and they shall prophesy a thousand two hundred and threescore days, clothed in sackcloth. These are the two olive trees, and the two candlesticks standing before the God of the earth. And if any man will hurt them, fire proceedeth out of their mouth, and devoureth their enemies: and if any man will hurt them, he must in this manner be killed. These have power to shut heaven, that it rain not in the days of their prophecy: and have power over waters to turn them to blood, and to smite the earth with all plagues, as often as they will.**

The time these two witnesses are to preach is 1260 days. This equals 42 months of 30 days which equals three and a half years. These three and a half years can be shown to be the last half of the seven years spoken of in Daniel 9:27, where we read:

> **And he shall confirm the covenant with many for one week: and in the midst of the week he shall cause the sacrifice and the oblation to cease, and for the overspreading of abominations he shall make it desolate, even until the consummation, and that determined shall be poured upon the desolate.**

The three and a half years or 1260 days is the period from the middle of the seventieth seven, **"the midst of the week,"** when sacrifice and offering was to cease until the consumation, which comes at the end of the world. This 1260 days is the same period spoken of in Revelation 12:6 which identifies with the body of believers throughout the New Testament era. The fire that proceeds out of the mouths of these two witnesses (Revelation 11:5), refers to the Word of God which they publish. That Word is the fragrance of life unto life and death unto death (2 Corinthians 2:15-16). That is, the Word of God brings eternal life to those who become saved, but it also will condemn the unsaved to hell forever. The language that speaks of these two witnesses having the power to shut up heaven, to turn waters into blood, and smite the earth with all plagues (Revelation 11:6), are a reminder of two Old Testament men. The prophet Elijah prayed and the rain stopped for three and a half years (James 5:17). Moses was used of God to turn the waters of Egypt into blood (Exodus 7:20) and to bring ten terrible plagues upon Egypt.

Moses represents the law and Elijah the prophets. The Bible is called Moses and the prophets (Luke 16:29) or the law and the prophets (Luke 16:16). Therefore, whenever these two witnesses are prophesying it is the Bible that is the power and authority of their witnessing.

The time would come when these two witnesses would become silenced because they are killed. This must coincide with the approximate half hour when heaven is silent. Revelation 11:7-8 explains this:

And when they shall have finished their testimony, the beast that ascendeth out of the bottomless pit shall make war against them, and shall overcome them, and kill them. And their dead bodies shall lie in the street of the great city, which spiritually is called Sodom and Egypt, where also our Lord was crucified.

The two witnesses are killed, that is, the Gospel has been silenced. It does not mean that they are physically dead. In John 16:2 God explains that being killed is equivalent to being put out of the synagogue (also translated "assembly"). There we read:

They shall put you out of the synagogues: yea, the time cometh, that whosoever killeth you will think that he doeth God service.

> *When an individual is driven from the assembly, spiritually they have been killed because their voice can no longer be heard in the assembly.*

When an individual is driven from the assembly, spiritually they have been killed because their voice can no longer be heard in the assembly. They are killed in the sense that they have been driven out by the congregation itself.

Please note the language God uses in Revelation 11:8. There God indicates their dead bodies lie in the streets of the great city called Sodom and Egypt where also our Lord was crucified. Jesus was crucified in Jerusalem. Jerusalem in Jesus' day was the external representation of the Kingdom of God. During the church age the local congregations became the external representation of the Kingdom of God so they are the Jerusalem that is in view in these verses.

But now Jerusalem -- the local churches -- have become Sodom and Egypt. That is, they, like ancient Sodom which was destroyed because of its extreme wickedness, are under the judgment of God. They have become like ancient Egypt of Moses' day which God used to typify being in bondage to sin and being under the rule of Satan (typified by Pharaoh).

That is why Revelation 11:7 speaks of the beast that comes from the bottomless pit making war against these true believers who are the two witnesses. The beast represents Satan. As Revelation 9:1-2 discloses, it is Christ Himself who has loosed Satan from the bottomless pit. The bottomless pit typifies hell. Satan was loosed from the bottomless pit in the sense that he would be allowed to rule in all of the local churches throughout the world as the man of sin. Therefore, Satan (the beast) is now ruling in the local congregations and is able to drive out the true believers (the two witnesses). He is ruling in the local congregations because God Himself has abandoned these churches. God has shifted the responsibility of evangelizing the world away from the institution of the local churches.

You will remember we learned that for the first approximately 9,000 years, God had used single individuals like Enoch and Noah to represent the kingdom of God to the world. Then beginning with Abraham, God raised up the nation of Israel to be the external representation of the kingdom of God.

Then we have seen that after Jesus was crucified, as God continued to unfold His salvation plan to the world, God shifted to the utilization of local churches to provide external representation of the Kingdom of God to the world.

God's utilization of the local churches ended when the half an hour of silence from heaven commenced. The world temporarily was without the Gospel. True, preachers continue to preach and individuals continued to witness. However, remember we learned that there are two very important things that are required before God can save His elect. The elect are those who were chosen by God to become saved. First of all, they must read or hear the Word of God which is the Bible. Secondly, God Himself must apply that Word to the hearts of those whom He plans to save.

These principles were in evidence in a striking way when Jesus preached. He was the perfect preacher since He was God Himself. Yet do you remember that even though He diligently preached for three and a half years virtually no one became saved. Yet when the Holy Spirit was poured out on Pentecost about 3,000 became saved.

Thus, when Revelation 8:1 reports that heaven was silent for about half an hour, it means that for this period of time, no one is being saved throughout the whole world. It was at this time that the churches lost their commission to represent the Gospel to the world.

This dreadful situation is called in the Bible "the Great Tribulation." This is referred to in Matthew 24:21-22:

> **For then shall be great tribulation, such as was not since the beginning of the world to this time, no, nor ever shall be. And except those days should be shortened, there should no flesh be saved: but for the elect's sake those days shall be shortened.**

The entire period of the Great Tribulation is referred to as a period of one hour in several verses (Revelation 17:12, 18:17, 19). Revelation 17:12 is especially significant:

> **And the ten horns which thou sawest are ten kings, which have received no kingdom as yet; but receive power as kings one hour with the beast.**

We must understand that the ten horns represent the rule of Satan within the local churches throughout the entire time of the Great Tribulation.

If no one could become saved, it means there was no hope for the world.

Matthew 24:21 effectively speaks of this time of Great Tribulation as a trauma, a catastrophe, by using the language **"tribulation, such as was not since the beginning of the world."** Nowhere in the Bible do we read of another time when there was silence in heaven for a period of time. If no one could become saved, it means there was no hope for the world. Each and every human being who had not become saved before the Great Tribulation began is guaranteed to end up in hell.

No situation can be imagined that is more terrible, more awful, more traumatic than this. During this half hour of silence in heaven, which identified with the first part of the Great Tribulation, even though many true believers, who are eternally secure as saved people, brought the Gospel outside of the local congregations, no one was becoming saved. Indeed, during the half hour of silence which was the first part of the Great Tribulation the whole world was in the most awful predicament, the greatest spiritual trouble it had ever been.

During the entire period of Great Tribulation, Satan had been given full rule in each and every local congregation throughout the world. We read in 2 Thessalonians 2:3-4:

> **Let no man deceive you by any means: for that day shall not come, except there come a falling away first, and that man of sin be revealed, the son of perdition; Who opposeth and exalteth himself above all that is called God, or that is worshipped; so that he as God sitteth in the temple of God, shewing himself that he is God.**

The man of sin spoken of in this verse can be shown to be Satan. He is called the man of sin because he is typified by the King of Babylon who God used to represent Satan. (Isaiah 14). While Satan is a spirit being and not a human being he is called a man in Isaiah 14:16 because he was typified by the king of Babylon.

The phrase he "sitteth in the temple" means he rules in the temple. The temple signifies the local congregations. In the Old Testament, the temple was the external representation of the kingdom of God. In the church age, the local churches are the external representation of the kingdom of God.

Thus, the phrase "he . . . sitteth in the temple" refers to Satan ruling in the local congregations throughout the world.

This terrible condition in the local congregations will continue to the last day of this world's existence.

This terrible condition in the local congregations will continue to the last day of this world's existence. That is why God commands in Matthew 24:15-16:

> **When ye therefore shall see the abomination of desolation, spoken of by Daniel the prophet, stand in the holy place, (whoso**

readeth, let him understand:) Then let them which be in Judaea flee into the mountains:

The "holy place" in this verse refers to the local congregations which throughout the church age were the caretakers of the Bible. They had been mandated by God to send the Gospel into all the world. But during the Great Tribulation the abomination of desolation is in all of the local congregations. The abomination of desolation is Satan who now rules in the churches. The word "Judea," like the word "temple" in 2 Thessalonians 2:3 was used in the Old Testament as a representation of the external kingdom of God. In the church age it therefore refers to the local churches. The "mountains" are referring to Christ Himself. We read in Psalm 121:1, **"To the hills [or mountains] will I lift up my eyes from whence cometh my help."**

Thus, Matthew 24:15 is teaching that the true believers, if they have not already been driven out, are commanded to flee from the local congregations. This terrible condition of the local churches being ruled by Satan will continue throughout the entire Great Tribulation period.

Outside of the Churches There Is an End to the Silence

However, wonderfully, throughout the world outside of the local congregations, this terrible situation ends at the end of the first part (the time of the half hour of silence), of the Great Tribulation and gives place to a great Gospel salvation program during the second part of the Great Tribulation. During this second part that will continue to the end of time the Jubilee is again being sounded. All through the world there is a great multitude being saved outside of the local congregations. We will examine this wonderful news later in our study.

The logical questions that follow are, "The Great Tribulation" lasted one hour, how long is that? And how long is the period that is spoken of as "about half an hour?" When did the Great Tribulation begin? We will examine these questions as we continue our study.

We do know that the period called "The Great Tribulation" is an event that closes with the return of Jesus Christ at the very end of the world. We read in Matthew 24:29-30:

Immediately after the tribulation of those days shall the sun be darkened, and the moon shall not give her light, and the stars shall fall from heaven, and the powers of the heavens shall be shaken: And then shall appear the sign of the Son of man in heaven: and then shall all the tribes of the earth mourn, and they

**shall see the Son of man coming in the clouds of heaven with
power and great glory.**

Therefore, as we begin to understand the length of time of that dreadful
period we will also be given some understanding of the timing of the end of the
world. But first we must search the Bible to determine when that period began.
We can use the past tense "began" because we can know that we are already
living in the period of time. The beginning of the Great Tribulation identifies with
a great many Biblical expressions spread throughout the Bible.

My People Are Under God's Judgment

God indicated why the local churches are experiencing judgment in our
day by such verses as have been quoted below. Please note the references in
these verses to the phrase "**my people**." The entire nation of Israel was called
"**my people**" by God. Likewise, all of those who became members of local
churches throughout the New Testament era were known to God as "**my
people**," that is, as God's very own people.

---

*Unless someone has become truly saved, he is still headed for
hell, even though he may appear to be a fine church member.*

In both instances, they were God's people in the sense that they were an
external representation of the kingdom of God. However, the fact that these
verses, which we will cite below, show that God's wrath is on "**my people**"
indicates that blood descent from Abraham (national Israel) or church
membership does not in anyway guarantee salvation. Unless someone has
become truly saved, he is still headed for hell, even though he may appear to be
a fine church member.

As indicated above, these verses are representative of a great many
verses sprinkled throughout the Bible that bring these solemn and awful warnings.

Jeremiah 2:12-13:

**Be astonished, O ye heavens, at this, and be horribly afraid, be ye
very desolate, saith the LORD. For <u>my people</u> have committed
two evils; they have forsaken me the fountain of living waters, and
hewed them out cisterns, broken cisterns, that can hold no water.**

Jeremiah 4:22:

For <u>my people</u> is foolish, they have not known me; they are sottish children, and they have none understanding: they are wise to do evil, but to do good they have no knowledge.

Jeremiah 5:30-31:

A wonderful and horrible thing is committed in the land; The prophets prophesy falsely, and the priests bear rule by their means; and <u>my people</u> love to have it so: and what will ye do in the end thereof?

Jeremiah 6:13-15

For from the least of them even unto the greatest of them every one is given to covetousness; and from the <u>prophet</u> even unto the <u>priest</u> every one dealeth falsely. They have healed also the hurt of the daughter of my people slightly, saying, Peace, peace; when there is no peace. Were they ashamed when they had committed abomination? nay, they were not at all ashamed, neither could they blush: therefore they shall fall among them that fall: at the time that I visit them they shall be cast down, saith the LORD.

Jeremiah 7:23-24:

But this thing commanded I them, saying, Obey my voice, and I will be your God, and ye shall be <u>my people</u>: and walk ye in all the ways that I have commanded you, that it may be well unto you. But they hearkened not, nor inclined their ear, but walked in the counsels and in the imagination of their evil heart, and went backward, and not forward.

Isaiah 1:21:

How is the <u>faithful</u> city become an harlot! it was full of judgment; righteousness lodged in it; but now murderers.

Isaiah 3:12:

As for <u>my people</u>, children are their oppressors, and women rule over them. O <u>my people</u>, they which lead thee cause thee to err, and destroy the way of thy paths.

Lamentations 1:8:

Jerusalem hath grievously sinned; therefore she is removed: all that honoured her despise her, because they have seen her nakedness: yea, she sigheth, and turneth backward.

Ezekiel 9:9-10:

Then said he unto me, The iniquity of the house of Israel and Judah is exceeding great, and the land is full of blood, and the city full of perverseness: for they say, The LORD hath forsaken the earth, and the LORD seeth not. And as for me also, mine eye shall not spare, neither will I have pity, but I will recompense their way upon their head.

Ezekiel 34:2-5:

Son of man, prophesy against the shepherds of Israel, prophesy, and say unto them, Thus saith the Lord GOD unto the shepherds; Woe be to the shepherds of Israel that do feed themselves! should not the shepherds feed the flocks? Ye eat the fat, and ye clothe you with the wool, ye kill them that are fed: but ye feed not the flock. The diseased have ye not strengthened, neither have ye healed that which was sick, neither have ye bound up that which was broken, neither have ye brought again that which was driven away, neither have ye sought that which was lost; but with force and with cruelty have ye ruled them. And they were scattered, because there is no shepherd: and they became meat to all the beasts of the field, when they were scattered.

Jeremiah 1:16:

And I will utter my judgments against them touching all their wickedness, who have forsaken me, and have burned incense unto other gods, and worshipped the works of their own hands.

Jeremiah 6:19:

Hear, O earth: behold, I will bring evil upon this people, even the fruit of their thoughts, because they have not hearkened unto my words, nor to my law, but rejected it.

Jeremiah 2:8:

The priests said not, Where is the LORD? and they that handle the law knew me not: the pastors also transgressed against me, and the prophets prophesied by Baal, and walked after things that do not profit.

Jeremiah 9:11:

And I will make Jerusalem heaps, and a den of dragons; and I will make the cities of Judah desolate, without an inhabitant.

Jeremiah 23:1-2:

Woe be unto the pastors that destroy and scatter the sheep of my pasture! saith the LORD. Therefore thus saith the LORD God of Israel against the pastors that feed my people; Ye have scattered my flock, and driven them away, and have not visited them: behold, I will visit upon you the evil of your doings, saith the LORD.

Lamentations 2:5:

The Lord was as an enemy: he hath swallowed up Israel, he hath swallowed up all her palaces: he hath destroyed his strong holds, and hath increased in the daughter of Judah mourning and lamentation.

Isaiah 5:5-7:

And now go to; I will tell you what I will do to my vineyard: I will take away the hedge thereof, and it shall be eaten up; and break down the wall thereof, and it shall be trodden down: And I will lay it waste: it shall not be pruned, nor digged; but there shall come up briers and thorns: I will also command the clouds that they rain no rain upon it. For the vineyard of the LORD of hosts is the house of Israel, and the men of Judah his pleasant plant: and he looked for judgment, but behold oppression; for righteousness, but behold a cry.

Isaiah 5:13:

Therefore <u>my people</u> are gone into captivity, because they have no knowledge: and their honourable men are famished, and their multitude dried up with thirst.

Ezekiel 8:17-18:

Then he said unto me, Hast thou seen this, O son of man? Is it a light thing to the house of Judah that they commit the abominations which they commit here? for they have filled the land with violence, and have returned to provoke me to anger: and, lo, they put the branch to their nose. Therefore will I also deal in fury: mine eye shall not spare, neither will I have pity: and though they cry in mine ears with a loud voice, yet will I not hear them.

I Peter 4:17:

For the time is come that judgment must begin at the house of God: and if it first begin at us, what shall the end be of them that obey not the gospel of God?

As God wrote the Bible using the nations of Israel and Judah as illustrations of the local churches of our day, at times He included verses that distinctly showed that His focus was not on these nations but upon the local congregations of our day, which in I Peter 4:17 is called the "**house of God**." For example, as we have already noted, the Book of Jeremiah was written about God's wrath on Judah at the time they were to be destroyed by Babylon. But God has included verses to clearly show that the prophecies of impending destruction were ultimately focused on God's judgment on the churches of the New Testament church age.

For example, in Jeremiah 10:20-21 we read:

My tabernacle is spoiled, and all my cords are broken: my children are gone forth of me, and they *are* not: *there is* none to stretch forth my tent any more, and to set up my curtains. For the pastors are become brutish, and have not sought the LORD: therefore they shall not prosper, and all their flocks shall be scattered.

The tabernacle mentioned in these verses was the tabernacle that was constructed about 700 years earlier when Israel was at Mount Sinai. Remember, it was taken to Shiloh where it remained for over 300 years.

But the tabernacle at Shiloh ceased to exist about the year 1067 B.C. It was replaced by the temple, the foundation of which was laid in the year 967 B.C. This citation of Jeremiah 10:20 was written after 609 B.C. How can it be speaking of the tabernacle being destroyed at this time that God is writing the Book of Jeremiah?

The answer is that God used the tabernacle at Shiloh as a picture or representation of the church age. We know this to be true because in Isaiah 54:2-3, God wrote through Isaiah (in about 700 B.C.):

Enlarge the place of thy tent, and let them stretch forth the curtains of thine habitations: spare not, lengthen thy cords, and strengthen thy stakes; For thou shalt break forth on the right hand and on the left; and thy seed shall inherit the Gentiles, and make the desolate cities to be inhabited.

In this citation, God is speaking of thy tent (the Hebrew word for tent is also translated tabernacle), being enlarged. That is, not only has it not been destroyed but it is being enlarged and strengthened. How can that be? It had ceased to exist hundreds of years before Isaiah 54 was written.

The answer is that the language of these verses is pointing to another tabernacle that was typified by the tabernacle that had been located in Shiloh. It is a tabernacle that is made up of the nations (Gentiles) that will come to salvation. This was to occur throughout the church age as the Gospel was sent into all the world.

This is the tabernacle that God is speaking of in Jeremiah 10:20-21. God is telling us that that tabernacle has been destroyed because the pastors are at fault.

Through verses of this nature that are sprinkled throughout the books of Isaiah, Jeremiah, Amos, etc., we are assured by God that we are to learn, by carefully studying these Old Testament books as well as the New Testament, all the reasons why the church age finally did come to an end.

Good works are those actions and beliefs which are obedient to all of the commands of the Bible.

Unfortunately, individuals in local congregations are convinced they are saved because they believe that Jesus is their Savior. But they do not realize that **"faith without works is dead"** (James 2:26). To have true faith or true belief in Christ as Savior will result in good works. Good works are those actions and beliefs which are obedient to all of the commands of the Bible. Thus, to hold a false teaching such as a false hermeneutic will not square with truly believing in Jesus. It is this kind of false teaching that has brought the wrath of God upon the local churches.

The method that God is using to bring His divine wrath upon the churches is especially two-pronged. On the one hand, at the start of this period of Great Tribulation, God Himself left the local churches, and secondly, God has permitted Satan as the enemy of the Gospel to occupy the churches. The Bible speaks of God having left the local congregations in various ways. The following are representative verses that speak to this. We read in Jeremiah 5:1:

> **Run ye to and fro through the streets of Jerusalem, and see now, and know, and seek in the broad places thereof, if ye can find a man, if there be any that executeth judgment, that seeketh the truth; and I will pardon it.**

Christ as the Son of God as well as the Son of Man is the only man who can bring about pardon or forgiveness for those in the congregations but now He is absent. Jeremiah 8:19:

> **Behold the voice of the cry of the daughter of my people because of them that dwell in a far country: Is not the LORD in Zion? is not her king in her? Why have they provoked me to anger with their graven images, and with strange vanities?**

Again God poses a rhetorical question that shows that Christ is absent. Ezekiel 22:30-31:

> **And I sought for a man among them, that should make up the hedge, and stand in the gap before me for the land, that I should not destroy it: but I found none. Therefore have I poured out mine indignation upon them; I have consumed them with the fire of my wrath: their own way have I recompensed upon their heads, saith the Lord GOD.**

Only Christ is the man (the son of God, the son of man) who can keep

God from destroying . He does so by taking upon Himself the sins of those who had been under the wrath of God. But now He is gone from the churches.

Each and Every Local Church Is Under God's Wrath

We have learned that it is God's plan that He would entirely reject the local congregations. The Bible teaches us that there is not a single congregation that is not under God's righteous judgment. We learn this from such language as that given in Mark 13:1-4:

> **And as he went out of the temple, one of his disciples saith unto him, Master, see what manner of stones and what buildings are here! And Jesus answering said unto him, Seest thou these great buildings? there shall not be left one stone upon another, that shall not be thrown down. And as he sat upon the mount of Olives over against the temple, Peter and James and John and Andrew asked him privately, Tell us, when shall these things be? and what shall be the sign when all these things shall be fulfilled?**

This same incident is reported in Matthew 24:1-3:

> **And Jesus went out, and departed from the temple: and his disciples came to him for to shew him the buildings of the temple. And Jesus said unto them, See ye not all these things? verily I say unto you, There shall not be left here one stone upon another, that shall not be thrown down. And as he sat upon the mount of Olives, the disciples came unto him privately, saying, Tell us, when shall these things be? and what shall be the sign of thy coming, and of the end of the world?**

These citations are clearly teaching that at the end of the world, the temple buildings will be thrown down so that not one stone will be left upon another. The words "temple" and "building" are used by God in 1 Corinthians 3:9 to describe the body of believers that would develop during the church age. We read there:

> **For we are labourers together with God: ye are God's husbandry, ye are God's building.**

1 Corinthians 3:16 adds:

Know ye not that ye are the temple of God, and that the Spirit of God dwelleth in you?

Two kinds of building blocks are built into this building or temple. We read in 1 Corinthians 3:12:

Now if any man build upon this foundation gold, silver, precious stones, wood, hay, stubble;

Gold, silver, and precious stones refers to those who are true believers like the wheat in the parable of the wheat and tares. Wood, hay and stubble would be like the tares. Throughout the church age every true believer is a living stone in the temple of God which is externally represented by the local congregations. However, in the opening verses of Matthew 24 and of Mark 13 God is indicating that as a sign that Christ is coming not one stone will be left upon another. That is, there will not be one local congregation that still has living stones (true believers) within it. From other Biblical citations we know that they will have been driven out or will be commanded to come out.

The end of the church age which coincides with the beginning of the Great Tribulation which immediately precedes the end of the world is awful, traumatic, disastrous to the divine institution of the local congregations. Furthermore, it is worldwide in its scope.

In Which Century Will The Great Tribulation Begin

The big question that should be asked is: In which century will that be? One of the first Bible clues that help us know the approximate timing of the Great Tribulation which comes just before the end of the world is recorded in Matthew 24:32:

Now learn a parable of the fig tree; When his branch is yet tender, and putteth forth leaves, ye know that summer is nigh:

In this verse, God is speaking of a fig tree coming into leaf. Shortly before this prophetic statement was made we read that Jesus came to a fig tree seeking fruit and there was nothing but leaves. Jesus then cursed the fig tree and declared that it was never to bear fruit (Mark 11:12-14).

> *God's curse came upon Israel so that they were rejected by God.*

From the context we must realize that Jesus was looking at that fig tree as a portrait or representation of national Israel. They, like the fig tree with its leaves, appeared to be a healthy spiritual nation. They had the temple. They kept the spiritual feast days etc. But when Christ looked for spiritual fruit there was none. Fact is, they wanted to kill the source of all spiritual fruit, the Lord Jesus. Therefore, God's curse came upon Israel so that they were rejected by God. They no longer could be the external representation of the Kingdom of God. More than that, in A.D. 70, they were utterly destroyed by the Roman armies, so that for almost 2,000 years they were a scattered people without a land they could call their own.

However, in the parable of Matthew 24:32 Jesus speaks of a time when the fig tree would bear leaves. This appearance of life and vitality would be an indicator that summer was close at hand. This also would be an indicator that all the things spoken of in the context of this verse were in the process of being fulfilled. The entire chapter of Matthew 24 is speaking of the Great Tribulation that immediately precedes the end of the world. Thus, when this sign of the fig tree in leaf can be seen, we will know we are very near the end of the world.

But what about the phrase that says that when the fig tree is in leaf summer is nigh?

In the Bible, harvest time is associated with summer. This is readily understood because winter is never the time of harvest. Therefore, we must understand that this verse is prophesying that there will be a time of spiritual harvest during this time of Great Tribulation. How can that be? The entire chapter of Matthew 24 is speaking about Great Tribulation when Satan is ruling in the local congregations. It is a time of spiritual winter. So how can we understand this prophecy of Matthew 24:32 which ties all of these things to summer; that is, to a time of harvest?

The solution can be known if we realize that outside of the local congregations during the last part of the Great Tribulation there will be a great harvest of believers even as we read in Revelation 7:9-14. There we read that there will be a great multitude of believers which will come out of Great Tribulation. This great multitude of believers will be harvested from nations all over the world. Indeed, it will be a summer time of spiritual harvest.

Indeed, this is the meaning of Matthew 24:22 in which God indicates that for the sake of the elect those days will be shortened. We will learn that during the second part of the Great Tribulation outside of the local churches there will be a great harvest of souls. That is, the Great Tribulation is the time that God no longer uses any local churches anywhere in the world to evangelize the world. Instead in the second part of the Great Tribulation He will save a great multitude by the use of true believers who are under no church authority who bring the Gospel to the world.

With this fact in mind, returning to the prophecy of Matthew 24:32, we learn that God is indicating that when the nation of Israel again becomes a viable nation (a fig tree with leaves) it is a dynamic sign that all of the prophetic statements of Matthew 24 are about to be fulfilled, including the wonderful news that there would still be a great harvest of people becoming saved.

This prophecy of Matthew 24:32 has truly been fulfilled. In the year 1948 A.D. the fig tree, Israel, almost miraculously again began to occupy the land of Israel as a sovereign nation amongst the nations of the world. The prophecy was fulfilled that declared that they were again to be in leaf. It did not predict that there would be any fruit. To be in leaf without fruit means there would be no spiritual fruit. That prophecy also has truly been fulfilled. Except for a tiny trickle of true believers, Israel, as a nation, continues to reject Christ as the Messiah. The prophecy of Matthew 24:32 was indeed fulfilled in the year 1948 A.D.

> *Indeed it will not be long before everything spoken of in Matthew 24 will have taken place.*

This prophecy of Matthew 24:32 declares that all of the events associated with the Great Tribulation and the return of Christ would take place shortly after Israel again became a nation. From our vantage point of living more than fifty years after 1948, we can see that all of these things spoken of in Matthew 24, are taking place. Indeed it will not be long before everything spoken of in Matthew 24 will have taken place.

It is indeed curious that Israel, the fig tree that came into leaf, officially became an independent viable nation on May 16, 1948, A.D. This was almost precisely 40 years before the end of the church age.

As we continue our study, we will learn that the church age, in all likelihood, ended on May 21, 1988, the day before Pentecost of that year. Forty years is certainly a significant period of time given the fact that so many other periods of Gospel history identify with the number 40. (For example, Israel was in the wilderness for forty years.)

Moreover, the period of time from A.D. 1948 to the Jubilee year of A.D. 1994 is 46 years, which breaks down into the significant numbers 2 x 23.

Furthermore, the period of time from A.D. 1948 to A.D. 2011, which we will learn is the likely year that ends the world, is 63 years. The number 63 is made up of the significant numbers 3 x 3 x 7. Is all of this coincidental? Or, does it indicate that God has a carefully designed plan for the unfolding of history?

False Prophets Will Arise

We are learning that the entire Matthew 24 chapter is focused on the Great Tribulation. We have already briefly looked at verse 15 which warns that the abomination of desolation would be standing in the holy place. We have learned that this is speaking of Satan ruling within the local churches after Christ has abandoned these churches. Indeed, remember the true believers were commanded to flee from these churches.

Another striking characteristic of the Great Tribulation is described by the language of Matthew 24:24:

> **For there shall arise false Christs, and false prophets, and shall shew great signs and wonders; insomuch that, if it were possible, they shall deceive the very elect.**

This verse is teaching that during the Great Tribulation there would arise preachers of the Gospel that were under Satan's power but they would preach the Gospel sufficiently faithfully so that even the elect would be deceived by them. The elect are those who are or do become true believers because they had been chosen by God to become saved. These false prophets will be recognizable because they will come with signs and wonders. That is, they will come appearing to be able to do miracles and other supernatural acts.

Significantly about fifty of sixty years ago a gospel came into existence called the charismatic gospel. Sixty years ago when it was still in its infancy it was not called the charismatic gospel but as this gospel has grown into a world-wide phenomena it is generally known as the Charismatic gospel. This gospel is focused on the concept that a true believer filled with the Holy Spirit will receive evidence of this in his life because he will speak in tongues. They believe that to speak in tongues is to speak in a heavenly language words that come from the Holy Spirit. This experience normally occurs during prayer, and the words that are spoken will be interpreted into a known language by a fellow believer who presumably has been given the gift of interpretation. Accompanying this activity will be the possibility of receiving messages from God by means of visions, angel visitation, or hearing a voice. Also accompanying this activity is the possibility of miraculous healing and the supernatural activity of people mysteriously falling backward when they are "slain in the Spirit."

> *...once the Bible was completed such an experience is*
> *impossible because the Bible indicates the Bible*
> *alone and in its entirety gives to us the Word of God.*

All of the above is based on an altogether wrong understanding of a phenomena that was of a short time duration in the church of Corinth as the Bible reports in 1 Corinthians 12-14. The possibility of receiving a verbalized or articulated message directly from God was possible before the Bible was completed. This phenomena was experienced by a few people in the early church of Corinth. However, once the Bible was completed such an experience is impossible because the Bible indicates the Bible alone and in its entirety gives to us the Word of God. We read in Revelation 22:18-19:

For I testify unto every man that heareth the words of the prophecy of this book, If any man shall add unto these things, God shall add unto him the plagues that are written in this book: And if any man shall take away from the words of the book of this prophecy, God shall take away his part out of the book of life, and out of the holy city, and from the things which are written in this book.

This book mentioned in these verses can only be the Bible. The reader of the Bible always knows for certain he is hearing words from the mouth of God because that is precisely what the Bible is. God, therefore will not and cannot satisfy the desires of the charismatic gospel people to hear directly from God apart from the Bible.

But there is a spirit being who can satisfy their desires. He is Satan whom the Bible speaks of as coming as an "angel of light." God warns in 2 Corinthians 11:13-15:

For such are false apostles, deceitful workers, transforming themselves into the apostles of Christ. And no marvel; for Satan himself is transformed into an angel of light. Therefore it is no great thing if his ministers also be transformed as the ministers of righteousness; whose end shall be according to their works.

Satan, almost perfectly counterfeiting Christ, is active in our day completely fulfilling the prophecy of Matthew 24:24 and 2 Corinthians 11:13-15. The Charismatic gospel from its earliest beginnings a few decades ago has spread like wild fire throughout the world. For example, the largest church in the world is a charismatic church located in Korea. This false gospel is successfully active in virtually every city or village in the whole world. All the dear people who are snared by it are convinced they have the true Gospel, when in fact the gospel they are following is totally false. This false gospel is dramatic evidence that the prophecy of Matthew 24:24 had now been fulfilled. (See the pamphlet "Speaking in Tongues," available free of charge from Family Radio.)

Returning to the prophecy of the fig tree remember we read that when the fig tree would be in leaf it would be a sign that summer was near. Remember, too, that summer relates to harvest. Biblically harvest has to do with salvation. Since we are many years past the year 1948 when Israel became a nation in fulfillment of this prophecy should we not be witnessing the summertime harvest.

Indeed there is a harvest going on. The Bible speaks of this in Revelation 7:9, and 13-14:

> **After this I beheld, and, lo, a great multitude, which no man could number, of all nations, and kindreds, and people, and tongues, stood before the throne, and before the Lamb, clothed with white robes, and palms in their hands; . . . And one of the elders answered, saying unto me, What are these which are arrayed in white robes? and whence came they? And I said unto him, Sir, thou knowest. And he said to me, These are they which came out of great tribulation, and have washed their robes, and made them white in the blood of the Lamb.**

These verses are clearly speaking of a great multitude of those who will become saved during the Great Tribulation. We will learn about this a bit later in our study.

The Noachian Flood Offers a Clue

The Bible gives another clue that may help us understand more precisely the timing of the end. This clue is so important we are going to study it in great detail. Earlier in our study we considered the Biblical information concerning the flood of Noah's day. Remember we looked carefully at the language of 2 Peter 3 in which God tied together the flood of Noah's day and the destruction of the universe at the end of the world. We read in 2 Peter 3:3 -8:

**Knowing this first, that there shall come in the last days scoff-
ers, walking after their own lusts, And saying, Where is the promise of his coming? for since the fathers fell asleep, all things
continue as they were from the beginning of the creation. For
this they willingly are ignorant of, that by the word of God the
heavens were of old, and the earth standing out of the water and
in the water: Whereby <u>the world that then was, being overflowed
with water, perished: But the heavens and the earth, which are
now, by the same word are kept in store, reserved unto fire
against the day of judgment and perdition of ungodly men.</u> But,
beloved, be not ignorant of this one thing, that one day is with
the Lord as a thousand years, and a thousand years as one day.**

The final worldwide judgment was typified by the first worldwide
judgment that the world experienced in Noah's day. Both judgments have a
number of things in common, some of which are as follows.

1. They both are a result of man's sin.
2   They both are totally worldwide in scope.
3. They both come when mankind in general do not expect that such
    a calamity could take place.
4. In both cases there is a remnant of people who escape the dire and
    dreadful consequences of this terrible judgment of God.

> *...we can know that without question the first judgment
> by water assures us that the final judgment by fire will take place.*

A most significant fact is that in these verses of 2 Peter 3 God links these
two judgments together. Thus, we can know that without question the first
judgment by water assures us that the final judgment by fire will take place.

God then inserts into this solemn declaration of a fiery end to this world's
existence this very interesting and very significant verse that we should now very
carefully examine. 2 Peter 3:8 declares:

**But, beloved, be not ignorant of this one thing, that one day is
with the Lord as a thousand years, and a thousand years as one
day.**

What can this verse mean? To understand it we should look very carefully at each word and phrase.

The first one we should carefully examine is the phrase "**beloved, be not ignorant**."

Beloved Be Not Ignorant

The word "beloved" assures us that this verse is specifically addressed to the true believers. Only they are the beloved of God. Only they will take seriously and will have understanding of what follows in this verse. Even as verse 3 of 2 Peter 3 speaks of scoffers, we can expect the unsaved will ridicule and disbelieve what God will tell us in this verse.

Secondly, the verse tells the beloved **"be not ignorant."** By this phrase, God is effectively telling the truly saved "I am telling you something that should not be hidden from you. It is my plan that what I tell you in this verse <u>will</u> be understood by you." What can that be that God is insisting should not be hidden from the true believers.

One Thing

Thirdly, the verse teaches that there is "**one thing**" that should not be hidden from the true believers knowledge. The phrase "**one thing**" is a fairly unusual phrase but when it is used it is speaking of something of very great importance. There are at least four other places in which the term "**one thing**" is used. In each passage in which it is used we will learn that it is referring to a fact of very great significance and importance.

John 9 records the healing of the blind man. As the Jewish leaders ridiculed the one who was healed together with the one who healed him, the man with his new eyesight declared in John 9:25:

> **He answered and said, Whether he be a sinner or no, I know not: <u>one thing</u> I know, that, whereas I was blind, now I see.**

Regardless of anything else, the fact could not be denied that a mighty miracle had been performed. A man hopelessly blind could now see, ". . . **one thing I know, that, whereas I was blind, now I see**."

In Luke 10:38-42, we read of Jesus in the home of Mary and Martha. Martha is beside herself trying to be the perfect hostess. Mary sat at Jesus's feet drinking in the words of spiritual life. Finally Martha could stand it no longer that her sister Mary was not assisting her with her hostess duties and voiced her complaint to Jesus. Jesus answer to her is given in Luke 10:41-42:

And Jesus answered and said unto her, Martha, Martha, thou art careful and troubled about many things: But <u>one thing</u> is needful: and Mary hath chosen that good part, which shall not be taken away from her.

Obviously, the phrase "one thing" in this answer is pointing to that which is supremely important as compared with all other things. Spiritual nourishment as Mary is receiving is far more important than the physical nourishment that Martha wishes to provide.

In Luke 18:18-24, the Bible tells us of ruler who asked Jesus what he must do to inherit eternal life. The context assures us that this man lived an exemplary godly life.

But Jesus told him in verse 22:

Now when Jesus heard these things, he said unto him, Yet lackest thou <u>one thing</u>: sell all that thou hast, and distribute unto the poor, and thou shalt have treasure in heaven: and come, follow me.

This verse also emphasizes that the term "one thing" is referring to something of enormous importance. In this case it was to look only to Jesus for salvation and not to any of our good works.

In Philippians 3:13-14 we read:

Brethren, I count not myself to have apprehended: but this <u>one thing</u> I do, forgetting those things which are behind, and reaching forth unto those things which are before, I press toward the mark for the prize of the high calling of God in Christ Jesus.

In these verses the phrase "**one thing**" is also indicating that our trust cannot be in anything we have done. Forget all of that. The one thing that is supremely important is that we look only for the salvation which God has provided in Christ.

In each of these four citations, the term "**one thing**" is pointing to something of supreme importance. Therefore, when we read in 2 Peter 3:8 that true believers are not to have hid from them one thing, we wonder what thing it is that is so tremendously important.

One Day is As A Thousand Years

The Bible then tells us what this all important information is. We read in 2 Peter 3:8:

> **. . . one day *is* with the Lord as a thousand years, and a thousand years as one day.**

What is this language telling us?

To help us understand this, God placed a related verse in Psalm 90:3-7. There we read:

> **Thou turnest man to destruction; and sayest, Return, ye children of men. For a thousand years in thy sight are but as yesterday when it is past, and as a watch in the night. Thou carriest them away as with a flood; they are as a sleep: in the morning they are like grass which groweth up. In the morning it flourisheth, and groweth up; in the evening it is cut down, and withereth. For we are consumed by thine anger, and by thy wrath are we troubled.**

This language is quite parallel to that which we are reading in 2 Peter 3. For example, verse 3 warns mankind of judgment as God declares **"thou turnest man to destruction."** The final Judgment is also emphasized by the phrase **"a watch in the night."** In several citations Christ speaks of His return during a watch in the night. For example, we read in Luke 12:38:

> **And if he shall come in the second watch, or come in the third watch, and find them so, blessed are those servants.**

Verse 5 of Psalm 90 reminds us of the flood of Noah's day as God uses the language, **"thou carriest them away as with a flood."**

This is also emphasized by the language of verse 7, where we read:

> **For we are consumed by thine anger,**

Each and every one of the above phrases given in Psalm 90 are concerned with Christ coming as the Judge of all of the earth. This is directly parallel to the verses we are presently examining which speak about the Judgment at the end of the world.

Verse 4 of Psalm 90 is likewise very parallel to 2 Peter 3:8 as it speaks of a thousand years. The term **"a thousand years"** in this verse offers a bit more information that is not found in 2 Peter 3:8. Psalm 90:4 states **"For a thousand years in thy sight are but as yesterday when it is past."** Literally the phrase **"as yesterday when it is past"** is **"a day of old when it is past."** Therefore, the phrase in Psalm 90:4 can be translated literally **"For a thousand years are but as a day of old when it is past."** Thus God is assuring us that the 1000 years is as a day. However it is not referring to a future 1000 years. Instead it is a past 1000 years. Given these numerous parallels between the account of 2 Peter 3 and that of Psalm 90, we can thus be assured that the reference to a day being 1000 years that is spoken of in 2 Peter 3:8 is a reference to a past period of time.

Furthermore, as we look again at the flood of Noah's day in which God gave a definite time reference of seven days and then the flood would begin (Genesis 7:4), we can't help but wonder. Is God in 2 Peter 3:8 giving a time reference? Are the seven days before the flood to be looked upon as seven days before the end of the world? No, not seven literal days. Seven days each 1000 years in length. God, both in 2 Peter 3 and in Psalm 90, is speaking about both the destruction of the whole world by the flood and also about the destruction of the whole universe by fire on the last day?

When Did The Flood Occur?

One fact is abundantly clear, if we did not know with any precision the year when the flood occurred, then, even if 2 Peter 3:8 were pointing to the end of the world coming 7000 years later, we would still be without any clear idea concerning the possible time of the end.

However, there are two very striking facts of which we should be aware. The first is that we have just learned that whatever the meaning of the phrase **"one day with the Lord is a thousand years"** God is insisting that every true believer (beloved) is to understand that meaning because it is super, super important. I believe that each of us should be thoroughly impressed by the language **"beloved, be not ignorant of this one thing."**

> *God has given us knowledge of the very accurate calendar of time that has been hidden in the pages of the Bible.*

The second fact is that at this time of history when God is opening the believers eyes to a great many Biblical truths that heretofore were not known,

God has given us knowledge of the very accurate calendar of time that has been hidden in the pages of the Bible. And included in that calendar is the precise year when the flood of Noah's day did occur.

Fact is, we know that the year was 4990 B.C. Seven thousand years after 4990 B.C. is A.D. 2011. Remember that when we compute the passage of time between an Old Testament event and a New Testament event we must add the two calendar dates together and subtract one. This is because there is no year zero. Thus, 4990 plus 2011 = 7001. 7001 - 1 = 7000 years.

Is God disclosing to us that A.D. 2011, which is so close at hand, is the last year of this earth's existence? That is a decision each reader of the Bible must make.

Certainly, as each one of us considers this awesome possibility, a few thoughts should be kept in mind.

1. We learned that 120 years before God destroyed the whole world in Noah's day God gave to the preacher Noah the exact year when the flood was to occur. Remember God said in Genesis 6:2:

And the LORD said, My spirit shall not always strive with man, for that he also is flesh: yet his days shall be an hundred and twenty years.

We know that this 120 years is not a statement giving the normal life expectancy of humans. For thousands of years after the flood men lived much longer than 120 years. Therefore, this statement could only relate to the amount of time Noah had been given to construct the ark. Since Noah was a preacher (2 Peter 2:5), as a faithful preacher, he would publish everything that God told him. That would have had to include the fact that at the end of these 120 years, a terrible earth-destroying flood was coming.

2. Seven days before the flood, God gave to Noah the precise day of the flood.

3. Hebrews 13:8 declares, **"Jesus Christ the same yesterday, and today and forever."** We can know by examining how God acted in the past, how He will act in the future. If He gave Noah information concerning God's destruction timetable, we can surely expect that likewise today, He will also give us similar information concerning the end of the world destruction timetable.

4. Earlier in our study we learned that when God was ready to destroy the ancient city of Nineveh in Jonah's day, God gave Nineveh a precise time. In 40 days destruction would come.

It is true the Bible clearly teaches that no one is to know the day or the hour of Christ's return. Therefore, we should understand that quite literally. However, the Bible nowhere says we cannot know the century or the decade or the year of Christ's return.

Having said these things this study is not attempting to make a precise declaration of the day and hour of the end of the world. It is a historical study of the time-line of history. But history is not finished until the end of the world. Therefore, as we continue this study we will note those teachings that relate to the end of the world. Of course, these verses of 2 Peter 3 definitely focus our eyes on the end of the world as they speak of Christ's coming and the total destruction of the universe.

We briefly considered the possibility that the flood occurred 7 days or 7000 years before the end of the world. The number 7 is featured very prominently in the Bible as a number of completeness or perfection. For example, we find:

1. Seven days of creation

2. Seven years of plenty, seven years of famine (Genesis 41)

3. Seven days of the feast of unleavened bread

4. Sprinkle the blood seven times before the Lord (Lev. 4:6, 17)

5. Miriam given leprosy seven days

6. Seven sabbaths between Passover and Pentecost

7. Feast of tabernacles seven days

8. Seven days in a week

9. Final Great Tribulation typified by 70 years

These examples are among the many in which God uses the number seven to illustrate completion or perfection. We know that presently we are in the time of Great Tribulation which immediately precedes the end of this world. We immediately wonder if God is telling us that seven thousand years is the period between the flood on the one hand and the end of the world on the other.

Continuing to look closely at the words God speaks in 2 Peter 3:8 and its companion verse in Psalm 90:4 we might recall that there are many very important concepts we must keep in mind. First of all let us recall that both of the verses indicate a day is as 1000 years. Secondly, both have in view both the flood of Noah's day and the wrath of God at the end of the world. When we further harmonized these two passages we discovered a number of very important principles that are in evidence.

1. Psalm 90:4 emphasizes that it is an olden day that is past that is as 1000 years.

2. 2 Peter 3:8 emphasizes that the message given these verses is particularly for believers.

3. 2 Peter 3:8 indicates the message given in these verses is not to be hid from the believers.

4. 2 Peter 3:8 indicates that the principle that one day is as 1000 years is super important as God speaks of "**one thing**." We understand this as God uses the expression "one thing" in a number of other Biblical passages.

5. 2 Peter 3:8 underscores and emphasizes the super importance of the truth that must not be hidden from the true believers by doubling the statement so that we read:

One day is as a thousand years.
A thousand years is as one day.

6. Completely apart from these verses we know that presently we know from a great amount of Biblical data that we are presently very close to the end of the world.

7. Seven days before God closed the door of the ark on the day that the flood waters began Noah, who was a true believer, was told very precisely which day the flood would begin.

8. Until our present generation no believer had been given exact information as to when the flood of Noah's day began.

9. Presently we know that the Biblical Calendar teaches us that the flood of Noah's day occurred in the year 4990 B.C.

10. The number seven is repeatedly used in the Bible as a completed cycle.

11. If by these verses which we are studying, God has in mind seven days of the past, then it appears the focus of these verses is 7000 years after the long past year of 4990 B.C.

12. Seven thousand years after 4990 B.C. is the year 2011. <u>Is this the year of Christ's return to which God is calling the attention of every true believer?</u>

13. God is the same yesterday, today, and forever. Is there any reason that God cannot or will not give to the true believers of our day the precise year of the end of the world even as He gave the precise year of the flood to Noah? Is this the one thing God wants every true believer to know?

14. Curiously in several situations recorded in the Bible God uses one day for one year (Numbers 14:34, Ezekiel 4:6). Curiously we have begun the serious discussion of 2 Peter 3:8 in the marketplace of the world in the year 2004 -- just seven years before 2011. Are these last seven years also related to the idea that seven days before the flood Noah was given an exact time-table as to when the flood would begin?

Are We Now Near The End of Seven Days

Before we complete our study of 2 Peter 3 and Genesis 7 we should consider one other possibility.

Is it possible that the references recorded in Genesis 7 to seven days have a double meaning? In the historical setting they truly declare that Noah was told that in seven days all of mankind and animals that were to escape the flood were to enter the ark during this seven day period. The ark was the place of safety. It was the only place in which the destruction of the flood could be avoided. In Genesis 7:4 we read:

For yet seven days, and I will cause it to rain upon the earth forty days and forty nights; and every living substance that I have made will I destroy from off the face of the earth.

But the Bible teaches that a day is a thousand years. Could the command to Noah to enter the ark during the time of the next seven days be a command that all who are to escape the final judgment of God are to enter into the safety of the Lord Jesus Christ during the next seven days, that is, the next 7000 years? Jesus is surely typified by the ark. The seven days can surely be understood as 7000 years. Only by entering the ark could the people of Noah's day escape the judgment of the flood. Only by becoming saved by having entered into Christ can we escape the final judgment of the last day.

Genesis 7:16 tells us that when all were in the ark God shut the door. God is the only one who knows when the last of God's elect will have become saved. Only then will He shut the door so that the time of mercy is past. We must take note that it is God who shut the door of the ark even as it si God who determines when the last of the elect have become saved. Luke 17:26 records:

And as it was in the <u>days</u> of Noah, so shall it be also in the <u>days</u> of the Son of man.

In a real sense are not the days of the Son of Man the whole time from the time of the flood all the way to the end of the world?

Could this verse be understood to tie the seven days just before the flood to the seven thousand years just before the end of the world? Genesis 7:1 declares:

And the Lord said unto Noah, Come thou and all thy house into the ark; for thee have I seen righteous before me in this generation.

Are not all true believers spiritually a part of the house of Noah who was a true believer? Certainly every true believer is a direct descendant of Noah. Therefore, is this not the command that is obeyed by all who do become true believers? Is this not the activity that has been going on during the entire period of time following the flood? Surely we can see this added teaching which comes to us from the language of Genesis 7.

Judgment Day Has Already Begun

Now that we have seen this focus on A.D. 2011 are not we in danger of violating other Scriptures? Isn't the Bible emphatic that no one can know the day or hour of Christ's coming. We have already noted that we are not to look for a precise day or hour. We may be surprised but in a real way this truth that we cannot know the day or hour has already been realized. For some time a great many true believers have known that the period of time called the "Great Tribulation" possibly began in the year 1988. We will develop this concept later in our study. What was not known until only very recently was the fact that the beginning of the "Great Tribulation" was the beginning of God's final judgment on the world.

During these past several years the true believers have become increasingly aware of the fact that the world is now experiencing the Great Tribulation. They have also become increasingly aware that the beginning of the Great Tribulation is the beginning of Judgment Day. Therefore, God's final judgment that began with God's judgment on all of the local congregations and transitions to the time when Christ appears in person has already begun. Therefore, we now know that Judgment Day is not a single day of 24 hours. Instead it is a period of time stretching from the beginning of the time of the Great Tribulation to the actual end of this world's existence.

A somewhat parallel situation is found in connection with creation. Creation of the universe encompassed six days of 24 hours. However, in Genesis 2:4 God speaks of a <u>day</u> when everything was created, thus indicating that a day can be longer than 24 hours if the context allows it. However, insofar as we can tell there is not anyone who was living at the time that the Great Tribulation began who was aware that Judgment Day had begun in that year.

Judgment Day coincides with the coming of Christ as Judge. Therefore, since Judgment Day began at the beginning of the Great Tribulation and since we will presently learn that the Great Tribulation in all probability began in the year 1988 Christ must have already come as the Judge and no one knew the day or hour when He did come.

Christ Has Already Come As the Judge

Let us further develop this conclusion. In Revelation 2:5 God warned the church at Ephesus:

Remember therefore from whence thou art fallen, and repent, and do the first works; or else I will come unto thee quickly, and will remove thy candlestick out of his place, except thou repent.

The candlestick signifies the light of the Gospel. A local church without a candlestick is a church that no longer is being used of God in such a way that people are becoming saved. It is a church without the light of the Gospel. Its purpose and work of bringing the Gospel to the world has been finished.

The significant fact is that while in Revelation 2 and Revelation 3 God is speaking of seven churches, including the church at Ephesus, that were in existence even before the Bible was completed, we must recognize that these seven churches represented all of the local churches throughout the church age. We can be assured of this as we note that after speaking of each one of these seven churches the words were added. **"He that hath an ear, let him hear what the Spirit saith unto the <u>churches</u>"** (Revelation 2:6, 11, 17, 29 and Revelation 3:6, 13, 22). In other words, the commendations and the warnings given to anyone of these seven churches apply to each and every local church that has come into existence throughout the church age.

This truth is further emphasized in the statement of Revelation 2:22 in which God warns the church of Thyatira that a false prophetess named Jezebel operating within that church would be cast, together with her followers, into Great Tribulation. We must remember the term "Great Tribulation" is the time when God's judgment has come on the local congregations just before the end of the world. Therefore, as God is speaking to the church of Thyatira He is speaking to all of the local congregations that would come into existence throughout the church age.

This is further emphasized as God warns the church at Sardis, **"If therefore thou shalt not watch, I will come on thee as a thief"** (Revelation 3:3). He also warned the church at Thyatira to **"hold fast till I come"** (Revelation 2:25). The local congregations of Sardis and Thyatira had ceased to exist hundreds of years before the coming of Christ at the end of the world. However, we must remember the warning to them that they were to hold fast until I come etc. in actuality was to all the churches throughout the world throughout time. We will discover that indeed today He has already come as the judge to each and every church.

> *...we should also be aware that the nature of the Great Tribulation was the fact that it brought the local churches' role in sending the Gospel to the world to an end.*

With this in mind we should also be aware that the nature of the Great Tribulation was the fact that it brought the local churches' role in sending the

Gospel to the world to an end. Remember in Matthew 24:21 describes a time when there would be Great Tribulation. There we read:

For then shall be great tribulation, such as was not since the beginning of the world to this time, no, nor ever shall be.

In verses 15 and 16 of Matthew 24 God adds:

When ye therefore shall see the abomination of desolation, spoken of by Daniel the prophet, stand in the holy place, (whoso readeth, let him understand:) Then let them which be in Judaea flee into the mountains.

During the church age the only holy place was the place where the Bible should be found. This would have been the local congregations which had been mandated and assigned the task of sending the Gospel into all of the world. These local congregations are called Jerusalem or Judea because they in an external way represent the Kingdom of God. Prior to the church age the nation of Israel with its capital in Jerusalem, which in turn was located in the land of Judea, which in turn was located in the land of Canaan, was the external representation of the kingdom of God. Abraham and his seed had been given the land of Canaan as an eternal possession (Genesis 17:8).

God spoke of the land of Canaan as an eternal possession not because the physical land was the kingdom of God but because it was a representation of the kingdom of God. Thus, throughout the Bible words like Jerusalem, Zion, Judea, Israel, which identify with the land of Canaan or with the nation of Israel are used to point to the eternal kingdom of God. Therefore, when the church age began in A.D. 33, because it was the external representative of the kingdom of God, the Bible frequently speaks of the local churches which are the focus of the church age as Jerusalem, Zion, Israel, Judea, the temple, etc.

> *...when a person becomes saved, he has eternally entered the actual kingdom of God.*

Incidentally, we must remember in this connection that when a person becomes saved, he has eternally entered the actual kingdom of God. Therefore, the true believers are also frequently called Jerusalem, Zion, Israel, the temple, etc. The reader of the Bible must look carefully at the context where these words are used to determine whether God is speaking of the external representation of the kingdom of God or of the true believers who are the only eternal citizens of the kingdom of God.

Returning to Matthew 24:15-16, we read the words "Judea" and "holy place." In this instance, the words "holy place" and "Judea" are referring to the local congregations which throughout the church age externally represented the kingdom of God. Throughout the time of the church age God the Holy Spirit was present in each and every local congregation which was reasonably true to the word of God. The Holy Spirit was present in these congregations to apply the Gospel to the lives of those whom God wished to save. Christ was present within that congregation as King of the church.

Unfortunately, there were some individuals, and frequently very many individuals, who were preachers or elders or members of that local congregation who were not saved. In the parable of the wheat and tares recorded in Matthew 13 these are called the "tares" or "weeds." They are virtually indistinguishable from the true believers. Because they are not saved, they are still under the authority of Satan. Thus, throughout the church age, Satan, through these individuals, to some degree, ruled in the congregation, even though Christ was the King of that local congregation.

However, at the beginning of the Great Tribulation, Christ and the Holy Spirit left the local churches, abandoning them completely to Satan. The true believers were driven out or were commanded by God to come out. Thus, the situation described in Matthew 24:15-16 took place. The abomination of desolation (Satan) now had become the only spiritual ruler in every local congregation throughout the world. That is why the true believers were commanded to flee from Judea. Remember Judea in this context is the local congregation which during the church age had been an external representation of the kingdom of God. The local churches were now ruled by the man of Sin (Satan) who had taken his seat (he became the ruler) in the temple (the local congregation which previously had been an external representation of the kingdom of God). In 2 Thessalonians 2:3-4 we can read about this:

Let no man deceive you by any means: for *that day shall not come*, except there come a falling away first, and <u>that man of sin be revealed</u>, the son of perdition; Who opposeth and exalteth himself above all that is called God, or that is worshipped; so that he as God sitteth in the temple of God, shewing himself that he is God.

Who Is The Antichrist

This verse teaches that the man of sin will be revealed. The man of sin is the anti Christ who will be very prominent near the end of the world. Who is he?

Throughout the church era theologians have believed that Satan would finally rule in the world by means of indwelling a very prominent political-religious man. This man, because Satan indwells him, would have enormous evil power throughout the world. In the past such notorious rulers as Kaiser Wilhelm, Adolf Hitler, Mussolini, or some supreme ruler of the Catholic church have in their time of power been looked at as possible candidates for the antichrist. However, each of these individuals have died and the world has continued, thus indicating the speculation concerning them was altogether incorrect.

However, in our day we know for certain who this man of sin, this antichrist, is. The Bible verse that exposes him is 1 John 4:3:

And every spirit that confesseth not that Jesus Christ is come in the flesh is not of God: and this is that of antichrist, whereof ye have heard that it [he] should come; and even now already is it [he] in the world.

The fact that the antichrist was already in the world when God was writing this verse, about two thousand years ago, and would also come at the time of the closing events of the history of the world, proves that he cannot be a human being. Each and every human lives out his life and then dies, never to reappear until the end of time when the resurrection of all of the dead will occur.

However, the description of the antichrist in this verse fits perfectly with Satan. He was in existence 2000 years ago and is still very much in existence today. He is the pseudo-Christ, the false Christ, the antichrist, who heads up the kingdom of Satan, which includes all of the unsaved throughout the world. He is a counterfeit Christ constantly endeavoring to destroy Christ. He is described together with those who blindly assist him in 2 Corinthians 11:13-15:

For such are false apostles, deceitful workers, transforming themselves into the apostles of Christ. And no marvel; for Satan himself is transformed into an angel of light. Therefore it is no great thing if his ministers also be transformed as the ministers of righteousness; whose end shall be according to their works.

Satan indeed fits all the Biblical statements that speak of "the man of sin" or the "antichrist." He is called a man because he was typified by the King of

Babylon in Isaiah 14:4-20. In verse 16 of Isaiah 14 God is speaking of Satan in this context by the language, "**Is this the man that made the earth to tremble, that did shake Kingdoms; that made the world as a wilderness . . . .**"

Satan indeed fits all the Biblical statements that speak of "the man of sin" or the "antichrist."

Indeed the "**man of sin**" has been revealed. He is Satan who now rules in all of the local churches throughout the world. He is given this rulership over the churches because the Holy Spirit, who had previously always been present within these churches to apply the Words of the Bible to the hearts of those whom Christ intends to save, is no longer present in the congregations. God has abandoned the congregations and is no longer doing the work of saving within them. Instead, as we are presently learning, He is now in the congregation as the Judge to prepare those remaining within the congregations for their commitment to hell.

Because Christ and the Holy Spirit have abandoned the local congregations, these churches now no longer can serve as the light of the world. Effectively, their candlestick had been removed.

This is the awful calamity about which God warned in Revelation 2:5. Remember we read there that if the church did not repent, Christ would come quickly and remove their candlestick. Remember, we have learned that this warning to the church at Ephesus, a local church existing at the time the Book of Revelation was being written, in actuality was addressed to every local congregation that throughout time would come into existence. The local church of Ephesus was an example God used to illustrate a principle that applies to each and every one of the churches of the world. We know that this is true as Jesus warned in Revelation 2:5, **"I will come quickly."** This most significant phrase can only apply to the time when Christ has come as Judge of all the earth. This phrase, therefore, greatly helps us to understand that the second coming of Christ includes and extends over a period of time rather than being focused on a single day.

I Will Come Quickly

We should look more carefully at the Biblical language that speaks of Christ's second coming to make certain that we are correctly understanding that Christ at this time in history has already come as Judge of all the earth.

Over sixty times the Bible makes references to the coming of Christ at the time He brings this world to its end. Several verses teach that when He comes everyone will see Him (Matthew 16:28, 24:30, etc.). Numerous verses teach that we will not know when He comes (Matthew 24:42, 25:13, etc.). In John 14:3, Jesus promised that when He comes He will receive the true believers.

Several verses teach that the wrath of God is coming (Ephesians 5:6, Colossians 3:6, etc.). The Bible speaks of the hour of judgment (Revelation 14:7) and the day of His wrath (Revelation 6:17).

Six times Christ declares, **"I will come quickly."** This is the phrase that is most significant in helping us understand that Christ has already come.

> *...because of the great amount of evidence that the church age has ended and their candlesticks have been removed, Christ must have already come.*

First, we will learn that it is a phrase that definitely identifies with Christ's second coming to bring this world to its end. Then we will learn that because of the great amount of evidence that the church age has ended and their candlesticks have been removed, Christ must have already come.

In Revelation 2:16 God warns the church of Pergamos:

Repent; or else I will come unto thee quickly, and will fight against them with the sword of my mouth.

This verse may be understood when we read in Revelation 19 wherein God describes Christ coming to bring judgment upon the world. He is pictured riding on a white horse and having a sword protrude from His mouth.

We read in Revelation 19:15:

And out of his mouth goeth a sharp sword, that with it he should smite the nations: and he shall rule them with a rod of iron: and he treadeth the winepress of the fierceness and wrath of Almighty God.

That sword can only by the Word of God (Ephesians 6:17) that will bring judgment upon the unsaved as they stand before the Judgment Throne of Christ. Therefore, God is telling the churches in Revelation 2:16 that Christ will come quickly at the time He comes as Judge of all the earth. Thus, the phrase, **"I will come quickly"** identifies with Christ coming as the Judge.

Likewise we read in Revelation 22:12:

And, behold, I come quickly; and my reward is with me, to give every man according as his work shall be.

> *The reward for the true believers will be the completion of their salvation as they are given their eternal resurrected bodies.*

It is at the end of time that Christ comes with rewards. The reward for the true believers will be the completion of their salvation as they are given their eternal resurrected bodies. The rewards for the unsaved will be that which they have earned - the wages of sin is death (Rom 6:23). The wages will be the terrible fact that they are judged, found guilty, and sentenced to eternal damnation.

From the above we can know that there is ample Biblical evidence that the phrase, **"I will come quickly"** can only identify with Christ's second coming to judge the world.

The second principle we must keep in mind is that we are now in the time of Great Tribulation, a time in which God has abandoned the churches. They no longer are the light of the Gospel because God is not any longer applying the Word of God that may be preached by them, to the lives of the unsaved. Therefore the candlestick has been removed from them.

Thus, if the candlestick has been removed from all of the churches it means that based on the truth we learned from our study of Revelation 2:5 we can be sure that Christ has already come quickly. He already has come as Judge of all the earth. This agrees with all of the other references such as 1 Peter 4:17 which teaches that judgment will begin with the house of God. Remember that in 1 Peter 4:17 the house of God is the external physical representation of the kingdom of God which are the local churches.

Therefore, since Christ has already come quickly to remove the candlesticks from each and every local congregation and, therefore, since Judgment Day is already in process, we need not worry that we might be guilty of violating the Scriptures that declare that no one can know the day or the hour when we ask the question, "Could the year 2011 be the year of the actual end of the world?"

No One Knows the Day or Hour of Christ's Return

We have learned that Jesus has already come to begin the judging process in the world. Judgment has begun in all of the local congregations throughout the world. And no one knew the day or hour when He came.

> *His coming in a visible way so that everyone will see Him with their physical eyes will not occur until the very end of the world, which the Bible speaks of as the last day.*

Remember, Christ has not already come in a visible form in which we can see Him with our physical eyes. Later in our study we will learn that He has come as the Holy Spirit to begin the judgment process in the local churches. From everything we read in the Bible, His coming in a visible way so that everyone will see Him with their physical eyes, will not occur until the very end of the world, which the Bible speaks of as the last day. That is the day when every eye shall see Him.

The Feast of Tabernacles

We believe this last day must identify with the timing of the Feast of Tabernacles, which was to be observed by Old Testament Israel during the fifteenth to the twenty-second day of the Biblical seventh month. We believe this for a number of reasons.

It is the only Biblical feast day wherein there has not yet been literal fulfillment. Remember, the Passover focused on the crucifixion of Christ and Christ as the Passover Lamb was actually crucified in the A.D. 33 on the fourteenth day of the first month, which was stipulated to be the Passover day.

Remember, the Feast of Weeks (also called Pentecost), was to be observed seven weeks after the first Sabbath after the Passover Feast. It was literally fulfilled in A.D. 33 when the Holy Spirit was poured out and about 3,000 were saved (Acts 2).

The feast of the first day of the seventh month, which was to be a reminder of the Jubilee, was literally fulfilled in A.D. 29 on the first day of the seventh month when Jesus was announced as the Lamb of God. Remember, at the same time, heaven announced, **"This is my beloved Son, in whom I am well pleased"** (Matthew 3:17).

> *The Jubilee in which liberty was to be proclaimed throughout the world was literally fulfilled on two occasions.*

The Jubilee in which liberty was to be proclaimed throughout the world was literally fulfilled on two occasions. Remember, we learned there were to be two Jubilees. The first was the year 7 B.C., a Jubilee year in which Jesus was born. At that time, the shepherds and the angelic host published to the world that Christ the Savior had come.

The second Jubilee year was A.D. 1994 at which time the half hour of silence ended in heaven, and once again the Gospel is being published throughout the world so that **"a great multitude, which no man could number"** is being saved (Revelation 7:9).

The day of atonement was to be observed on the tenth day of the seventh month. It identified with the Jubilee as Israel afflicted themselves (fasted), and we learned that fasting identifies with sending the Gospel into the world (Isaiah 58:3-7). We learned that in all likelihood it was literally on the day of atonement in the Jubilee year 7 B.C. that Jesus was born.

Thus, we have learned of the intimate relationship that exists between the Old Testament ceremonial feasts and the actual literal fulfillment of these feast days.

> *...there was one additional very prominent feast that was called for by the Old Testament ceremonial laws.*

However, there was one additional very prominent feast that was called for by the Old Testament ceremonial laws. It was the Feast of Tabernacles or the Feast of Ingathering (Leviticus 23:34-36, 23:39-43). It was to be observed during the seven-day period that began on the fifteenth day of the seventh month and ended on the twenty-second day of the seventh month. It was a feast that pointed to the ingathering of the year's final harvest. It was linked to the end of the world because it identified with the sending of the Gospel into the world during the time of the latter rain, which is also the time of the second Jubilee. It is during this time that we are presently living and a great multitude is being saved.

The Feast of Tabernacles was definitely linked to the end of the world by the phrase **"last day."** Surprisingly, this phrase is found only once in the Old Testament and seven times in the New Testament. In the New Testament, four of the citations that speak of the **"last day"** are virtually identical and all are found in John 6. The four verses are verses 39, 40, 44, and 54. Each verse is speaking of true believers who will be resurrected on the **"last day."** Verse 40 is typical, and we read there:

> **And this is the will of him that sent me, that every one which seeth the Son, and believeth on him, may have everlasting life: and I will raise him up at the last day.**

The Bible also speaks of the resurrection of the last day in John 11:24:

Martha saith unto him, I know that he shall rise again in the resurrection at the last day.

The sixth place the phrase "**last day**" is found is in John 12:48, where God speaks of the unbelievers being judged on the last day. We read there:

He that rejecteth me, and receiveth not my words, hath one that judgeth him: the word that I have spoken, the same shall judge him in the last day.

> *Significantly, the remaining two Biblical citations in which God includes the phrase "**last day**" are speaking of the last day of the Feast of Tabernacles.*

Significantly, the remaining two Biblical citations in which God includes the phrase "**last day**" are speaking of the last day of the Feast of Tabernacles. They are given in John 7:37 and in Nehemiah 8:18. We read in John 7:37:

In the last day, that great *day* of the feast, Jesus stood and cried, saying, If any man thirst, let him come unto me, and drink.

And we read in Nehemiah 8:18:

Also day by day, from the first day unto the last day, he read in the book of the law of God. And they kept the feast seven days; and on the eighth day *was* a solemn assembly, according unto the manner.

These last two citations definitely link the last day of the Feast of Tabernacles to the return of Christ at the end of the world.

Given all of the foregoing information, we wonder, if all the Biblical evidence points to the year 2011 as the most likely year for the end of the world, then by determining the date of the twenty-second day of the seventh month of the Jewish calendar in the year 2011 we would also know the likely day that ends the world.

However, it is very curious that in the year 2011, the twenty-second day of the seventh month could come in the month of September or it might come in October. This problem exists because the Jewish Biblical calendar is determined by the moon cycles and those cycles do not neatly fit into the yearly cycle. Let me explain.

Each year consist of 365.242 days. Each moon cycle (one new moon to the next new moon), averages 29.53059 days. The Biblical or Jewish calendar therefore consists of 29 day or 30 day months. Twelve months averaging 29½ days equals 354 days, but 354 days is about 11 days short of a year of 365 days. Therefore, every two or three years in the Jewish calendar an extra month must be added so that, for example, the first month will always be as close as possible to the same location in the year.

> *The vernal equinox is the day when all over the world,*
> *the daytime hours are exactly equal to the   nighttime hours.*

When the Jewish calendar was instituted by God as reported in Exodus 12, we can calculate that the first Passover was on March 21, 1447 B.C. Significantly, March 20 or 21 is always the date of the vernal equinox. The vernal equinox is the day when all over the world, the daytime hours are exactly equal to the nighttime hours. Therefore, it would appear that the extra month should be added whenever it was necessary in any year to keep the Passover as close as possible to March 20 or 21, the date of the vernal equinox.

The Bible, however, has given no rules concerning this. Therefore, in Jewish tradition, rules to govern the time when the extra month was to be inserted in the Jewish calendar are obviously man-made because the Bible does not give any rules concerning this. Therefore, it is possible to argue for the inclusion of the extra month in either of two years close to 2011 so that the twenty-second day of the second month comes either in September or October. The Jewish calendar according to its rules places the twenty-second day in October, but it is possible that it should be in September.

Additionally, the Bible speaks of the Feast of Tabernacles as having seven day. But it also associates the eighth day as a day of solemn assembly that intimately identified with the Feast of Tabernacles. Was it the seventh day or the eighth day that was the great day, the last day, of the Feast of Tabernacles spoken of in John 7:37?

For all of these reasons, it does not appear that we can know with any certainty the calendar date that will be the last day of the history of the world. We probably are far wiser in simply indicating that it will in all likelihood occur in the fall of the year 2011.

> *...it does not appear that we can know with any certainty the calendar date that will be the last day of the history of the world*

The Unsaved Do Not Hear Because They Do Not Believe

> *Unsaved people can hear the truths of the Bible concerning the coming end of the world and Judgment Day but spiritually they remain in ignorance as if they never heard these truths even with their physical ears.*

One other fact must be kept in mind. Except for true believers who implicitly trust the Bible, no one truly believes what the Bible declares. Unsaved people can hear the truths of the Bible concerning the coming end of the world and Judgment Day but spiritually they remain in ignorance as if they never heard these truths even with their physical ears. That is why God says in Matthew 24:36-39:

> **But of that day and hour knoweth no man, no, not the angels of heaven, but my Father only. But as the days of Noe were, so shall also the coming of the Son of man be. For as in the days that were before the flood they were eating and drinking, marrying and giving in marriage, until the day that Noe entered into the ark, And knew not until the flood came, and took them all away; so shall also the coming of the Son of man be.**

The people of the world in Noah's day heard him preach that at the end of 120 years the Flood would come. They witnessed the gigantic construction project as Noah and his sons constructed the huge ark on dry ground. It was a tremendous testimony to the fact that Noah absolutely believed the truths that he was preaching, but none of these truths registered in their sinful minds. They continued to live as if they had never hear nor seen Noah. Then right near the end, they heard the truth that in seven days the Flood would begin, but neither did these truths register with them. They continued to live as if they had never been told. The Flood came upon them as a thief in the night.

This matches the language we read in 1 Thessalonians 5:2:

For yourselves know perfectly that the day of the Lord so cometh as a thief in the night.

We thus learn that the Biblical emphasis that indicates that no one can know the day of hour of Christ's return is literally true for the many reasons we have just related.

We must recognize, however, that 1 Thessalonians 5:4-5 goes on to declare:

But ye, brethren, are not in darkness, that that day should over-take you as a thief. Ye are all the children of light, and the chil-dren of the day: we are not of the night, nor of darkness.

...it is the unsaved who are especially in view when God speaks of people not knowing the day or the hour

---

The language of this verse surely tells us that in the lives of the true believers the knowledge of the timing of Christ's return will be entirely different from that of the unsaved. The additional information of verse 3 particularly emphasizes that it is the unsaved who are especially in view when God speaks of people not knowing the day or the hour.

The people living in Noah's day heard with their physical hearing the timing of the flood. But they continued their earthly lifestyle of living in complete denial that destruction was imminent. They did not hear the warning with their spiritual ears. Therefore, for them Christ came as a thief in the night. So, too, it will be with most of the unsaved of the world of our day, Christ will come as a thief in the night.

True Believers Must Warn The World

Let us now return to 2 Peter 3 and the one thing every true believer must know. "**But, beloved, be not ignorant of this one thing, that one day *is* with the Lord as a thousand years, and a thousand years as one day**." Again the question hammers on the true believer. Is the year 2011, which we know is exactly 7000 years after the beginning of the flood of Noah's day, the final year of this world's existence?

True, the unbelievers will scoff. They have to ridicule. The last thing they want to think seriously about is that the end of the world is almost here. On the other hand, the true believers are faced with an enormous responsibility. Repeatedly God warns them that they are watchmen who must sound the warning the enemy is coming.

The true believers have been commanded to declare the Gospel to the whole world. The Gospel begins with the warning of the fact that this world is heading for Judgment Day. It also includes the wonderful news that there is salvation through the Lord Jesus Christ.

This is the reason God declares in Ezekiel 3:17-19:

Son of man, I have made thee a watchman unto the house of Israel: therefore hear the word at my mouth, and give them warning from me. When I say unto the wicked, Thou shalt surely die; and thou givest him not warning, nor speakest to warn the wicked from his wicked way, to save his life; the same wicked man shall die in his iniquity; but his blood will I require at thine hand. Yet if thou warn the wicked, and he turn not from his wickedness, nor from his wicked way, he shall die in his iniquity; but thou hast delivered thy soul.

God gives the true believer no option.
He must warn the world
that Christ is coming as Judge of all the earth.

God gives the true believer no option. He must warn the world that Christ is coming as Judge of all the earth. He must send forth the news that only in Christ as Savior is there any hope.

Is this perhaps the reason that God insists in 2 Peter 3:8 that He wants every true believer to know this super important fact that one day is as 1000 years? For is it possible that this shows us that the year 2011 must be published to the world as the end of the world? Every true believer must think carefully about these matters.

There still remains a question that must be answered. Haven't we learned long ago that when Jesus comes again every eye will see Him (Matthew

24:30). Didn't He promise in Acts 1:11 that He would **"come in like manner as ye have seen Him go into heaven."** How then do we dare to say that at this moment He has already come? This is a fair question that we must honestly face.

Christ Has Already Come As The Judge

When we search the Bible we learn that Christ can come as a spirit or He can come so that every person on earth can see Him with their physical eyes. First let us hear God's Word concerning Him coming as a Spirit.

In John 14:23 Jesus declared:

Jesus answered and said unto him, If a man love me, he will keep my words: and my Father will love him, and we will come unto him, and make our abode with him.

This is a faithful promise. Those who have become saved are indwelt by Jesus and their heavenly Father. That is God has come to dwell within the life of the true believer.

This is emphasized in 1 John 4:12-16:

No man hath seen God at any time. If we love one another, God dwelleth in us, and his love is perfected in us. Hereby know we that we dwell in him, and he in us, because he hath given us of his Spirit. And we have seen and do testify that the Father sent the Son to be the Saviour of the world. Whosoever shall confess that Jesus is the Son of God, God dwelleth in him, and he in God. And we have known and believed the love that God hath to us. God is love; and he that dwelleth in love dwelleth in God, and God in him.

This is why we read in Galatians 2:20:

I am crucified with Christ: nevertheless I live; yet not I, but Christ liveth in me: and the life which I now live in the flesh I live by the faith of the Son of God, who loved me, and gave himself for me.

These citations assure us that Christ can come to us without our seeing Him with our physical eyes.

If Christ can come into our lives as the Savior without our seeing Him with physical eyes, then He certainly can come into this world as the Judge of all the world without anyone seeing Him with their physical eyes.

This is precisely the situation today. Christ as the Judge of all the earth has already come even as later He will come so that every eye shall see Him.

Thus, in Biblical passages such as Matthew 24:42-46 or Luke 12:36-45 which indicate that we cannot know the day or the hour when He shall come, in all likelihood have already been fulfilled. He has come to bring the local churches under His judgment even as prophesied in 1 Peter 4:7, **"judgment begins at the house of God."**

This also means that such a passage as Revelation 2:5, **"I will come unto thee quickly"** and remove your candlestick has already been fulfilled.

> *That will be the awful moment*
> *when there is no more mercy,*
> *no more the possibility of salvation.*

On the other hand, the Bible speaks of His coming in a way that every person can see Him with their physical eyes. This will be fulfilled at the end of the "last day." That will be the time when all of the true believers will be raptured and all the unbelievers who had died will be resurrected to stand for judgment. That will be the awful moment when there is no more mercy, no more the possibility of salvation. That will be the **"last day"** spoken of in connection with the resurrection of the bodies of the believers (John 6:39, 40, 44, 54).

The Bible speaks in many ways about the second coming of Christ. For example, the Bible uses phrases such as **"the great and notable day"** (Acts 2:20), **"the great day of His wrath"** (Revelation 6:17), **"the hour of His judgment"**(Revelation 14:7), etc. All of these references are speaking of the time of the second coming of our Lord.

Because we are living at that time that the day of God's wrath is already taking place, we can now begin to better understand all of these phrases that identify with Judgment Day and the end of the world. We may conclude that the hour or day of judgment, the day of God's wrath, the fact of Christ's coming etc. are all speaking of the time in history that began with the beginning of the Great Tribulation (Matthew 24:21) and ends with the entire universe being dissolved (2 Peter 3:10).

What Is the Judging Process

However, now a question arise. How is it possible that Christ has already come as the Judge. Where is His Judgment Throne where He is busy judging?

To answer this question we must understand what the Bible means when it speaks of Judgment. The word "judgment" or "judgments" is used very frequently in the Bible as a synonym for "law" or "precept" or "commandment." In Psalm 119 for example God repeatedly uses the word "judgments" as a synonym for "laws." Thus we know that the laws of God are the judgments of God. Thus, since sin is transgression of the law of God, it is therefore a transgression of the judgment of God. We must, therefore, examine carefully the meaning of the word "judgment."

The law or judgment of God stipulates how mankind is to live. For example, it declares **"Thou shalt not commit adultery?"** Thus if an individual does commit adultery he has broken the law or judgment of God. However, now that he has committed adultery and thus has broken the judgment of God that is not the end of the matter. The law or judgment of God also stipulates that **"the wages of sin is death."** That is, the law decrees that a penalty must be imposed upon the person who has broken the judgment of God by committing adultery.

But this person who has committed adultery lives his whole life without consciously experiencing any penalty for his sin of adultery. Yet the law or judgment of God demands that the penalty must be paid. Therefore, the law or judgment of God stipulates that the hour will come that every person who has previously lived on the earth and subsequently died (remember physical death is not payment for sin) will be resurrected and will stand before the throne of God to answer for his sins. The resurrection of this person is decreed by the law of God even as the appearance before the judgment throne of God and the subsequent sentencing and removal into eternal damnation are an integral part of the law or judgment of God.

Thus, we can know that when a person is brought to judgment it means that all of the laws that deal with the procedures that must be carried out in bringing that person to justice have been fully carried out.

We see this in our modern legal system. A person has committed murder. Therefore, he has broken the law. But then a whole series of procedures governed by the law must be carried out in order for judgment or justice to be carried out. This includes such things as allowing adequate representation by a defense attorney, pre-trial hearings, proper submission of evidence, proper courtroom procedures, etc. Sometimes the period of time required to properly bring judgment against an individual may require months of time. Closure on the case will occur only when the suspect has been actually tried and has either been exonerated and set free, or when he has been found guilty and has been executed or has experienced whatever punishment the judge has decreed is a lawful penalty for his crime.

Returning to the laws or judgments of the Bible, we likewise discover that God had established many judgments or laws concerning the conduct of the local congregations. They were to follow strict rules in the appointment of elders and deacons (1 Timothy 3). They faithfully were to be representatives of the kingdom of God on this earth. They were to faithfully send the whole Gospel into the world. They were to be a divine institution wherein only God is worshiped. Any violation of the Biblical laws or judgments by these churches calls for certain Biblical legal action to be taken against them. This includes the fact that the time would come that the Holy Spirit would forsake these churches. It includes the fact that finally Satan as the man of sin would be allowed to rule in them. It includes the fact that the true believers would be driven out of them or would be commanded to come out. It includes the fact that God would send a strong delusion upon those who remain within those churches. It includes the fact that finally those who remain in these churches must individually appear before the Judgment Throne of God to answer for their individual sins.

All of the forgoing actions which are an integral part of the law of God are an integral part of God's judgment coming upon the local congregations. All of these actions are included in the warning of 1 Peter 4:17:

For the time is come that judgment must begin at the house of God: and if it first begin at us, what shall the end be of them that obey not the gospel of God?

We can know that Christ has already come as the Judge.

Christ is the Judge of all the earth. Thus, many of the above actions are already taking place in the local congregations. We can know that Christ has already come as the Judge. Fact is, we know, from the extensive Bible information that speaks to this subject, that the beginning of the Great Tribulation signaled the beginning of the final judgment. The hour of judgment has begun.

Therefore, we need not be concerned with wondering about the day or hour when Christ will come as the Judge. He already has come as the Judge and the various actions required by the final judging process to be carried out are now in full swing. Each day brings us closer to that aspect of the Judging process when Christ will appear and each and every person will see Him with their physical eyes. It is then that each and every unsaved person will stand individually before the Judgment Throne of Christ to receive sentencing and from there will be removed into eternal Hell to pay for their sins. It is at that time that time will be no more and the true believers will be evermore with Christ in the New Heavens and New Earth.

No One Can Become Saved

We should now begin to analyze in more detail the Great Tribulation period that is spoken
of as occurring immediately preceding the end of the world. Remember Matthew 24:21 speaks of it. We read there:

> **For then shall be great tribulation, such as was not since the beginning of the world to this time, no, nor ever shall be.**

Remember, too, we learned that the chief character of the Great Tribulation was the fact that no one could become saved anywhere in the world. Matthew 24:22 declared that:

> **And except those days should be shortened, there should no flesh be saved: but for the elect's sake those days shall be shortened.**

But we must also recall that this verse also teaches that for the sake of the elect the days of the Great Tribulation were shortened. This is in agreement with the teaching of Revelation 17 which speaks of Satan ruling, under the figure of a beast with ten crowned horns, for a period of one hour. However, remember Revelation 8:1 speaks of about a half hour of silence. We are learning that the Great Tribulation, therefore, is the entire period when Satan is ruling so that no one is becoming saved in any local church. This is so because Christ has abandoned each and every local church to the rule of Satan. However, for the sake of the elect, while Satan's rule in the churches continues for the entire one hour (entire Great Tribulation), outside of the churches at the end of about half and hour of silence, God again begins to save. This He does for the sake of the elect whom God had named to be saved and who had not yet become saved when the Great Tribulation began.

> *Thus, the Great Tribulation is divided into two distinct parts.*

Thus, the Great Tribulation is divided into two distinct parts. During the first part no one could become saved anywhere in the world. During the second part no one can become saved in any of the local churches. But outside of the local churches there is a great harvest of people becoming saved as the Gospel goes into all the world outside of the local congregations.

We have learned that the end of time appears to focus on A.D. 2011. Thus, A.D. 2011 must in all likelihood be the year that coincides with the end of the Great Tribulation. We should now begin to learn what we can about the duration of the Great Tribulation and the length of each of the two parts of the Great Tribulation.

First, we should try to determine the precise length of time of the first part of the Great Tribulation. Remember, it identifies with the about half an hour of silence recorded in Revelation 8:1.

2300 Days

The Biblical statement most likely to give us the duration of the half hour of silence is found in Daniel 8. In that chapter, God describes the period of the Great Tribulation by the citation of Daniel 8:10-12:

> **And it waxed great, even to the host of heaven; and it cast down some of the host and of the stars to the ground, and stamped upon them. Yea, he magnified himself even to the prince of the host, and by him the daily sacrifice was taken away, and the place of his sanctuary was cast down. And an host was given him against the daily sacrifice by reason of transgression, and it cast down the truth to the ground; and it practised, and prospered.**

The question was then asked in Daniel 8:13:

> **Then I heard one saint speaking, and another saint said unto that certain saint which spake, How long shall be the vision concerning the daily sacrifice, and the transgression of desolation, to give both the sanctuary and the host to be trodden under foot?**

The answer was given in Daniel 8:14:

> **And he said unto me, Unto two thousand and three hundred days; then shall the sanctuary be cleansed.**

The Hebrew words translated as "days" in this verse actual should be translated "evening mornings." It is unique language that is very similar to that employed by God when God describes the six days of creation. After each day's creation activities, God declared, **"And the evening and the morning were the first day,"** etc. We can be certain that these days of creation which were spoken of as evening and morning were literal days of 24 hours. Therefore, we strongly suspect we are to understand the evening mornings of Daniel 8:14 to be literal 24 hour days.

Secondly, at the end of 2300 evening mornings the sanctuary was cleansed (literally made righteous) . The only sanctuary or holy place that could have become righteous during the Great Tribulation period are the true believers who are sending the true Gospel into the world completely outside the local church.

Remember we learned that the entire one hour of the Great Tribulation, the rule of Satan, continues in the local churches until the end of the world. Therefore, it can only be outside of the church where righteousness can be found.

The twenty-three hundred evening mornings of Daniel 8:13-14 ties us to the language of Revelation 11:2 which speaks of the 42 months.

Daniel 8:13: **"How long the vision of the daily and the transgression of desolation to give both the <u>sanctuary</u> and the host <u>to be trodden under foot."</u>**

Revelation 11:2: **"and the holy city shall they tread under foot forty and two months."**

The sanctuary and host of Daniel 8:13 is the representation of the kingdom of God which are the true believers, even as the holy city of Revelation 11:2 are the true believers who are the kingdom of God. Both citations therefore speak of believers being trodden under foot.

This language in turn identifies with the believers being killed. Revelation 11:7-9:

And when they shall have finished their testimony, the beast that ascendeth out of the bottomless pit shall make war against them, and shall overcome them, and kill them.. And their dead bodies shall lie in the street of the great city, which spiritually is called Sodom and Egypt, where also our Lord was crucified. And they of the people and kindreds and tongues and nations shall see their dead bodies three days and an half, and shall not suffer their dead bodies to be put in graves.

It identifies with Revelation 13:7:

And it was given unto him to make war with the saints, and to overcome them: and power was given him over all kindreds, and tongues, and nations.

It identifies with Daniel 8:23-24:

And in the latter time of their kingdom, when the transgressors are come to the full, a king of fierce countenance, and understanding dark sentences, shall stand up. And his power shall be mighty, but not by his own power: and he shall destroy wonderfully, and shall prosper, and practise, and shall destroy the mighty and the holy people.

It identifies with Revelation 8:1:

And when he had opened the seventh seal, there was silence in heaven about the space of half an hour.

During this literal period of 2300 days which we are presently considering, no one anywhere in the world could become saved. It is the same period of time God speaks of as 42 months in Revelation 11:2:

But the court which is without the temple leave out, and measure it not; for it is given unto the Gentiles: and the holy city shall they tread under foot forty *and* two months.

It is the same period of time God speaks of as 3½ days in Revelation 11:8-9:

And their dead bodies *shall lie* in the street of the great city, which spiritually is called Sodom and Egypt, where also our Lord was crucified. And they of the people and kindreds and tongues and nations shall see their dead bodies three days and an half, and shall not suffer their dead bodies to be put in graves.

It is the same period of time God speaks of as "**time and times and the dividing of time**" in Daniel 7:25:

> **And he shall speak *great* words against the most High, and shall
> wear out the saints of the most High, and think to change times
> and laws: and they shall be given into his hand until a time and
> times and the dividing of time.**

The closest approximation to this terrible period of 2300 days is the 3½
years during which Jesus preached. Jesus the perfect preacher preached 3½
years. During this time virtually no one was saved. When Jesus was preaching,
Satan had not yet been bound and the Holy Spirit had not yet been poured out.
Thus, Satan was able to snatch away the perfect words of Jesus, even as Christ
indicated in the parable of the sower in Luke 8:12:

> **Those by the way side are they that hear; then cometh the devil,
> and taketh away the word out of their hearts, lest they should
> believe and be saved.**

Moreover, it was a time when the Holy Spirit had not yet been poured
out. Therefore, God at that time was rarely applying the perfect Words of God
spoken by Jesus to the hearts of the hearers so that they might become saved.

But on Pentecost day in A.D. 33, a great number of about 3000
individuals did become saved. Satan had been bound in the sense that he could
not snatch away the Word of God; and the Holy Spirit was now applying the Word
of God to the hearts of the elect so that they did become saved.

---

*...when the first part of the Great Tribulation began all
over the world within the churches and outside of
the churches Satan had become loosed.*

Thus, when the first part of the Great Tribulation began all over the world
within the churches and outside of the churches Satan had become loosed so that
he could again snatch away the Word from the hearers. During this same period
of time, the Holy Spirit was not applying the Word of God to the hearts of any who
were chosen to salvation but who had not yet become saved.

It was during this first part of the Great Tribulation that Satan took his
seat, that is, he began to rule in all of the local congregations (2 Thessalonians 2:3).
Throughout the church age, which we are learning was in place from A.D. 33 to
A.D. 1988, Satan had been planting within the local congregations tares or weeds.
These tares were individuals who were not saved but who gave every outward
appearance of having become saved. They were virtually indistinguishable from

the true believers. They were individuals who were faithful to all of the doctrines and practices of the church wherein they had become a member. They were altogether convinced they were serving Christ as their Savior and King.

But they had not become saved and, therefore, they were still under the authority of Satan. They frequently included the vast majority of people within the local congregations. This is abundantly evident today as we witness how few people there are in the local congregations who are obeying God's command to leave the local congregation, now that we are in this time of Great Tribulation. Those who are unsaved , that is, those who are under the authority of Satan, will not want to obey God's command to come out of the churches.

> *When the Great Tribulation began, the impact of God withdrawing from the local churches throughout the world was hardly noticed in these churches.*

When the Great Tribulation began, the impact of God withdrawing from the local churches throughout the world was hardly noticed in these churches. In many instances most of the true believers which had been members in these churches had already been driven out. Frequently this was a result of their criticism of some of the doctrines or practices observed by this congregation which were not faithful to the Bible.

Thus, when the Holy Spirit abandoned these churches it made hardly a ripple. Only because of what we read in the Bible can we know what has been truly happening in the churches.

During this 2300 day first part of the Great Tribulation, not only was Satan the Prince of the secular world but he also had become the ruler in all of the local congregations. Moreover, throughout the world no one was being saved regardless of how they heard the Gospel. Indeed the world had come into Great Tribulation. This is why that during this 42 months (Revelation 13:5), the first part of the Great Tribulation, the Bible declares in Revelation 13:7-8:

> **And it was given unto him to make war with the saints, and to overcome them: and power was given him over all kindreds, and tongues, and nations. And all that dwell upon the earth shall worship him, whose names are not written in the book of life of the Lamb slain from the foundation of the world.**

The Holy Place is Made Righteous

But after this 2300 days there is a change in the world. We read in Daniel 8:14:

And he said unto me, Unto two thousand and three hundred days; then shall the sanctuary be cleansed.

Literally this is teaching that after 2300 days the holy place will be made righteous. What can this mean?

The holy place is where the true believers are. Throughout the church age the true believers had been found mainly in the local congregations. But now they have been driven out into the world. While these true believers continue to be in-filled by the Holy Spirit, and have been continuing to bring the Gospel throughout the world throughout the first part of the Great Tribulation, no one is becoming saved.

> *The Holy Spirit is again saving people.*
> *Christ, the Jubilee is again being proclaimed*
> *throughout the world.*

But at the end of 2300 days, the holy place is cleansed. That is, the true believers, typified by the two witnesses of Revelation 11, are now standing on their feet with the Spirit of life from God having entered into them. They are bringing the true Gospel to the world. That is, heaven is no longer silent. The about "half an hour" has ended. The Holy Spirit is again saving people. Christ, the Jubilee is again being proclaimed throughout the world. A great multitude which no man can number is becoming saved.

This is the time of the latter rain. (See *The End of Church Age and After*, available free of charge from Family Radio.) This is the time of the final summer of harvest. This is the time of the final ingathering. This is the time of the second Jubilee. Indeed, Christ has come again as the Savior. We will find that this time of the end of the first part of the Great Tribulation, the end of the 2300 days, the beginning of the latter rain, the beginning of the final ingathering of the elect from all over the world coincides with the year 1994. Remember, 1994 is a Jubilee year. It, like the Jubilee year of 7.B.C., coincides with the coming of Christ as Savior. Remember, Jubilee identifies with the proclamation of the Gospel throughout the world.

True, during this last half of the Great Tribulation Satan continues to rule in the local churches. Within the churches located all over the world Christ continues to bring judgment upon them as He prepares the members of these churches for their appearance before the Judgment Throne of God. He continues to send these people, which corporately or externally had been His people, a strong delusion that they should believe a lie (2 Thessalonians 2:11).

In the secular world outside of these churches God is also preparing the unsaved who are not chosen for salvation for their appearance at the Judgment Throne of God. He has given them up (Romans 1:24, 26). He has given them over (Romans 1:28) to vile affections and reprobate mind.

> *The two witnesses again are standing on their feet,*
> *filled with the Spirit, declaring the Gospel*
> *throughout the world.*

Indeed, throughout the one hour which is the entire time of the Great Tribulation Satan is ruling both in the local churches and in the secular world as sin multiplies in both the churches and throughout the world. But there is a major difference throughout the world during the second part of the Great Tribulation as compared with the first part of the Great Tribulation. During the second part it is again the time of Jubilee. The two witnesses again are standing on their feet, filled with the Spirit, declaring the Gospel throughout the world. We read in Revelation 11:11:

And after three days and an half the Spirit of life from God entered into them, and they stood upon their feet; and great fear fell upon them which saw them.

The three and a half days corresponds to the 2300 days. It is called three and a half days because it is one half of seven. Later we will learn how the number seven identifies with the entire time of the Great Tribulation.

The language in the above verse that speaks of the Spirit coming upon the witnesses and they stand on their feet means they are to again bring the Gospel to the world. Similar language is used in Ezekiel 2:1-2, 4 to describe the declaration of the Gospel to the world. There we read:

> **And he said unto me, Son of man, stand <u>upon thy feet</u>, and I will speak unto thee. And the <u>spirit entered into me</u> when he spake unto me, and set me upon my feet, that I heard him that spake unto me.**
>
> **For they are impudent children and stiffhearted. <u>I do send thee unto them; and thou shalt say unto them, Thus saith the Lord GOD.</u>**

This passage assures us that standing on one's feet endowed with the Holy Spirit signifies the sending forth of the Gospel.

> *It is a time when each saved person has placed his trust entirely in the Bible alone.*

This is the time that a great multitude which no man can number is coming out of Great Tribulation. We read in Revelation 11:11 that when the two witnesses stood on their feet **"great fear fell upon them that saw them."** This is the fear of God that every true believer receives when he has become a true believer. This is the time in which those who do become saved are not certified by spiritual rulers who have been appointed to rule over a divine institution called the nation of Israel or which is a local New Testament church. It is a time when each saved person has placed his trust entirely in the Bible alone. He knows that God will work in him to will and to do of His good pleasure (Philippians 2:13).

The Gospel Goes Into All of the World

This is the time that the world which has exploded to more than six billion people is being blanketed with the true Gospel. It is a Gospel that attempts to be as faithful as possible to the Bible. It is a Gospel that entirely rejects any doctrine that suggest that man's work of being baptized in water, or accepting Christ or believing in Christ or any thing else has a part together with the grace of God in providing for our salvation.

We must realize, of course, that false gospels that teach many doctrines contrary to the Bible will continue to bombard the world by such means as radio, television, and Internet. These, however, will make no impact on bringing the true message of salvation to the world. The two witnesses who stand upon their feet include only those who faithfully bring the true Gospel.

By means of this faithful proclamation of the true Gospel the language of 2 Chronicles 36:21, **"the land is enjoying her sabbaths,"** will occur. Remember the "land" represents the kingdom of God which consists of all true believers. The sabbath is the seventh-day sabbath that points to the fact that we are not to trust in any work of any kind that we do as an assist in our becoming saved. Thus, during this time of the second part of the Great Tribulation, the land (the kingdom of God, which consists of the true believers scattered throughout the world), is enjoying the sending forth of the true Gospel which insists that <u>all</u> of the work of saving was done by Christ.

It is the time the "holy place" (Daniel 8:14) has been cleansed. No longer are denominational doctrines or practices the kind of Gospel being sent into all the world. Now it is the Bible alone and in its entirety that is the ultimate and only spiritual authority.

> *We will learn that the duration of time encompassed by the entire Great Tribulation appears to be 23 years.*

We will learn that the duration of time encompassed by the entire Great Tribulation appears to be 23 years. The first part of that period is 2300 days which is a few months longer than six years. Thus, the last part of the Great Tribulation appears to be 23, 6, or 17 years.

We have learned that the number 23 is intimately associated with judgment and the wrath of God. We can also know that the number 17 is intimately associated with heaven. Given this much information we now can suggest a timeline for the time of the Great Tribulation and the end of the world.

If we begin with the Jubilee year of 1994 as the end of the "about half hour of silence" then 2300 days earlier would be sometime in the year 1988. Thus, 1988 would have been the year in which the church age came to an end and the Great Tribulation of Matthew 24:21 began. Then the period from 1994 to 2011, a period of seventeen years, would have been the second part of the Great Tribulation. Thus, the entire length of the Great Tribulation would have been a total of 23 years.

The Great Tribulation: 23 Years

Immediately we can see that 23 years is quite in agreement with the manner in which God uses numbers. Throughout the Bible God uses numbers to illustrate or symbolize the spiritual truth. The number 23 consistently identifies with God's judgment which is the essential character of the Great Tribulation period.

We have already seen the number 23 used in connection with the 2300 days of Daniel 8:14. Another example is 1 Corinthians 10:8. God is describing a plague which was recorded in Numbers 25:9. Actually 24,000 were killed in the plague (Numbers 25:9) but in 1 Corinthians 10:8 the Bible declares that 23,000 fell in one day. This obviously means that 1000 must have fallen the second day to make a total of 24,000. But God is certainly identifying the number 23 with judgment.

> *The 276 survivors represent the true believers who are driven out or commanded to come out of the churches beginning with the time of the Great Tribulation.*

Earlier we also saw this, for example, in Acts 27:37. There God made certain that when the ship on which Paul was a prisoner was destroyed, there were 276 individuals aboard that ship which were saved. Although we will not develop this in this study, it can be shown that the destroyed ship is typifying or representing the local churches that come under the wrath of God at the end of the church age. The 276 survivors represent the true believers who are driven out or commanded to come out of the churches beginning with the time of the Great Tribulation. Significantly, the number 276 can be broken down into two or three important numbers, as follows.

12 x 23 = 276

3 x 4 x 23 = 276

Twelve signifies fullness

Three signifies God's purpose

Four signifies universality or the end

Twenty-three signifies judgment

Thus, the number 276 spiritually is teaching that the fullness (12) of all true believers will escape the judgment (23) of God. Or we could understand the number 276 to signify that it is God's purpose (3) that the believers all over the world at the end of the church age (4) will escape God's judgment (23).

We might note again another interesting and perhaps significant fact in connection with the number 23. The flood of Noah's day occurred in the year 4990 B.C. Creation occurred in the year 11,013 B.C. Thus, there were exactly 6000 plus 23 years from creation to the flood.

> *The year 1988 coincides with the 13,000th anniversary of the history of the world.*

The next great judgment that took place was the judgment which our Lord Jesus endured when He paid for our sins. That judgment occurred in A.D. 33. It is very curious that the time from the judgment in Noah's day -- 4990 B.C. -- to that experienced by Jesus in A.D. was precisely 5000 plus 23 calendar or inclusive years. Likewise, the year 2011 is exactly 13,000 plus 23 years from creation. Is all of this coincidental. Or does it show the majestic consistently of the unfolding of God's salvation plan. We might also note another interesting fact. The year 1988 coincides with the 13,000th anniversary of the history of the world. Is this a significant fact or is it merely a curiosity?

The Church Age : Pentecostal First Fruits

The church age, in the unfolding of God's salvation plan, was the harvest of the Pentecostal firstfruits. Remember that at the feast of weeks which in the New Testament is called Pentecost, the first fruits were brought in.

In this connection we know that God officially began that harvest very literally on Pentecost day in A.D. 33. That day about 3,000 were saved (Acts 2:41). The occurrence of each following Pentecost day in a real sense signified the continuing of the harvest of the firstfruits (the salvation of additional people). Therefore, we can call those who became saved at any time during the church age, Pentecostal firstfruits.

If the church age, the age of gathering in the firstfruits of the harvest, ended in 1988, we would suspect that it would have ended the day before the 1988 Pentecost day. We can calculate very accurately the date of the Pentecost of A.D. 33. It was May 21. We also know that in A.D. 1988 Pentecost occurred on May 22. This in itself is striking because the date of Pentecost is controlled by its relationship to the Passover day. And the Passover day is always the 14th day of a lunar month. Thus, the Passover and likewise Pentecost could be any one of about 29 different calendar days. Yet in God's timeline of history, the day of Pentecost in A.D. 1988 came on a day so that the church age continued exactly

1955 complete years to the very day. It is indeed curious that similarly, Israel was in Egypt exactly 430 years to the very day (Exodus 12:40-41).

The Church Age: Exactly 1955 Years

> *We would suspect that the official end of the church   age would have occurred the day before the day of Pentecost.*

Since we are presently learning that the church age ended in 1988 and since the church age was entirely related to Pentecost, we would suspect that the church age would not include Pentecost of 1988. We would suspect that the official end of the church age would have occurred the day before the day of Pentecost. That would have been May 21, in 1988. This means that the duration of the church age in all likelihood was 1955 years (1988 - 33 = 1955) exactly to the very day. Its duration would have been May 21, A.D. 33 to May 21, A.D. 1988.

Moreover, it is indeed interesting that when we add 2300 days, the duration of the first part of the Great Tribulatiom, to May 21, 1988, the end of the church age, we come to September 6, 1994. September 6 was a very special day in the year 1994. It is the first day of the seventh month. Remember we learned that this feast day identified with the Jubilee. Thus, we learn that the end of the "about half hour of silence" of Revelation 8:1 which ended with the Jubilee again being sounded throughout the world identifies perfectly with September 6, 1994. Both the day of September 6 and the year 1994 are identified with the Jubilee.

> *We thus learn that in all likelihood the church age encompassed exactly 1955 full years to the very day.*

We thus learn that in all likelihood the church age encompassed exactly 1955 full years to the very day. We also have learned that in all likelihood the end of the half hour of silence, the first part of the Great Tribulation, coincided with the Jubilee day of September 6 in the Jubilee year of 1994. We surely can see how carefully God all the way to the end of time has preplanned the unfolding of the timeline of history -- the Gospel.

A Brief Summary

Thus far we have discovered considerable Biblical evidence that appears to give us a good understanding of the major events and the timing of those events that bring us to the very end of the world.

In summary, those events are as follows.

1. The church age which began on the Day of Pentecost May 21, A.D. 33 probably continued for precisely 1955 years until the day before Pentecost. May 21, in A.D. 1988.

2. This tremendous period during which the Gospel reached into all the world and during which local congregations were established in virtually every city and village of the world coincided with the first great Jubilee period. During this great period that in principle began with the birth of Christ in the Jubilee year 7 B.C. the Gospel went forth as a two-edged sword. It was a sweet fragrance to Christ to those who became saved. But it was the stench of death unto death to those who did not become saved. As we learned it was typified by the conquest of the land of Canaan that began in the year 1407 B.C. Those individuals like Rahab the harlot or like the inhabitants of the city of Gibeon who wanted peace with Israel (Joshua 9) were spared. Those like other cities of the land of Canaan who resisted Israel were destroyed.

> *This worldwide activity of the church age probably came to an abrupt end in the year 1988. In that year the judgment preparations for the end of the world began.*

3. This worldwide activity of the church age probably came to an abrupt end in the year 1988. In that year the judgment preparations for the end of the world began. It was in this year that the brief period of time the Bible calls the Great Tribulation began. We learned that it probably began in the year 1988 and will probably end in the year 2011 which according to our present understanding will be the last year of this present word's existence.

4. The Great Tribulation began at the moment this first great Jubilee period came to an end probably on May 21, 1988, which was the day just before Pentecost in that year. As we learned from Rev-

elation 8:1, for a brief period of time heaven became silent, so that for this period of time no one in the whole world could become saved. Christ had come to bring judgment upon every local congregation in the entire world. On the one hand, God was finished using these churches as the external representation of the kingdom of God on this earth. All of those elect of God who were to become saved by God's utilization of the local congregations had become saved.

On the other hand, the local congregations were increasingly unfaithful in presenting to the world the teaching of the Bible. The doctrines of the church Confessions and the man made hermeneutic (the method of Bible interpretation) that were uniquely those of their denomination had become the ultimate authority rather than the Bible. Thus, the local churches had come under the wrath of God. Therefore, Christ had come in judgment, beginning in the A.D. 1988, to prepare those churches for the great Judgment Throne when Christ will judge all of the unsaved of the world.

Satan Appears To Be The Winner

This awesome event that appears to have occurred in the year 1988 that marked the end of the time period of the first Jubilee period and which in turn coincided with the end of the church age, marked the beginning of what appears to be a time of great success for Satan. Throughout the church age he had been unable to frustrate the purpose of the Gospel to save those whom God had elected to salvation. True, he had been able to seed, to plant, within the local churches individuals who were not saved, but who gave the appearance of having become saved. The Bible speaks of these individuals as tares or weeds. Thus, even though Christ was the King of the local churches, Satan as an angel of light had much authority in the local churches through his subjects (the tares) who the Bible calls "ministers of righteousness" (2 Corinthians 11:15).

> *Christ, who had ruled as King in the local churches, abandoned them to the full control of Satan.*

However, at the end of the church age, as a first act of preparing the individuals who were members of the churches for judgment, Christ, who had ruled as King in the local churches, abandoned them to the full control of Satan. The true believers within the churches were driven out or were commanded to come out. Those tares who remained within the local churches were blinded by God so that they were convinced that they were saved Christians and that their local congregation would remain faithful until the very end of the world.*

> *God has taken His hand of restraint from off the unsaved of the world who by nature were in complete rebellion against the laws of God but who throughout the church ag e had been restrained by God from unbridled wickedness.*

At the same time that this terrible situation descended on all of the local congregations throughout the world, God also gave Satan unparalleled rule over the kingdoms of the world. God has taken His hand of restraint from off the unsaved of the world who by nature were in complete rebellion against the laws of God but who throughout the church age had been restrained by God from unbridled wickedness. Therefore, especially beginning with the year 1988 which marked the end of the church age, God also has allowed sin to greatly increase throughout the world. Thus, we have entered a period typified by such things as the enormous growth in sexual perversion and homosexuality.

> *During this first part of 2300 days no one anywhere in the world could have become saved.*

We have learned that this terrible period of Great Tribulation will probably be continuing for a period of twenty-three years ending with the return of Christ at the end of time in A.D. 2011. We have learned that this twenty-three year period appears to be divided into two parts. The first part is exactly 2300 days in length ending in all likelihood on September 6, in the year 1994. The second part began on September 6, 1994 and continues for seventeen years to the fall of A.D. 2011. During this first part of 2300 days no one anywhere in the world could have become saved. There was no longer in existence a Jubilee. The local churches and the whole world were experiencing a tribulation of monumental consequence.

---

* Again, the reader is invited to obtain free of charge from Family Radio the books *The End of the Church Age and After* and *Wheat and Tares.*

Those who were true believers who lived during this period did not lose their salvation. Most of them were not even aware that such a dreadful situation prevailed throughout the world. They may have been concerned about the doctrines and practices that were increasingly Biblically questionable. They may have wondered about the spectacular success of such gospels as the charismatic gospels (those that featured tongues and signs and wonders). But they had no knowledge that Jesus had come to begin the judgment process that would begin with the judgment on the house of God (the local churches) and will transition to the return of Christ at the end of the world. It is at the end of the world that the dreadful time will have come when each and every unsaved individual must personally stand before the Christ as the Judge. They will be found guilty, and they will hear the awful truth that they had been sentenced to an eternity under God's eternal damnation.

As we have learned, this terrible first part of the Great Tribulation ended in all likelihood on September 6, 1994. We learned that September 6 was the first day of the seventh month of the Jewish Calendar. The year 1994 was a Jubilee year and September 6 of that year was the first day of the seventh month. It was a special ceremonial feast day identifying with the Jubilee year. Thus the end of this first part of the Great Tribulation coincided with the beginning of the second Jubilee period which would continue for seventeen years ending in the year 2011.

> *...salvation is again taking place all over the world.*

During the seventeen years of the second part of the Great Tribulation, the period of time in which we are now living, the spiritual conditions in the local churches will continue unchanged. Satan continues to rule precisely as he ruled in the churches during the first part of the time of the Great Tribulation. But in the world outside of the local churches a great change occurred at the beginning of the second part. As we have just noted the Jubilee is again being sounded throughout the world. That is, salvation is again taking place all over the world. It is not taking place by utilizing the local churches as the means to send forth the Gospel. It is taking place utilizing individuals, who have no relationship with local congregations, who faithfully continue to send forth the Gospel throughout the world. It is a time when a great multitude which no man can number are being saved.

During this time Satan continues to rule as "prince of this world." Throughout the time of this last seventeen years God continues to give people up to great wickedness. That is, all kinds of rebellion against God continues to get stronger. The Bible appears to have virtually no authority in the world. But for the sake of the elect who are sprinkled throughout the huge population of the world, the Bible continues to be used of God as the means through which God is doing His work of saving people. Immediately following this twenty-three period of Great Tribulation will come the end of time and the history of planet earth.

Later in our study we will indicate what we can know at this time concerning our understanding of eternity future. But before we examine some of the Biblical citations that speak of the end of time when Christ appears so that every eye shall see Him we should raise a very serious question.

Is There More Biblical Information

It is true that the Bible declares in Matthew 24:21, **"There will be Great Tribulation such as this world has never known nor ever shall know."** It is also true that this period Great Tribulation is immediately followed by the return of Christ and the end of the world. This is clearly indicated by the citation of Matthew 24:29:

Immediately after the tribulation of those days shall the sun be darkened, and the moon shall not give her light, and the stars shall fall from heaven, and the powers of the heavens shall be shaken:

> *The Biblical rule is that we are to compare*
> *Scripture with Scripture until we obtain conclusions*
> *that are in harmony with any and every citation*
> *of the Bible that might relate to the conclusion*
> *that was obtained.*

However, in arriving at the details of this period of Great Tribulation we have had to piece together bits of information from various parts of the Bible. True, because of the awesome nature of this Great Tribulation the Bible presents extensive information about it. It is also true that this is the way all doctrines of the Bible are developed. The Biblical rule is that we are to compare Scripture with Scripture until we obtain conclusions that are in harmony with any and every citation of the Bible that might relate to the conclusion that was obtained.

However, given the enormous nature of the subject we are considering -- the timing and details of the end of the world -- is there anything more in the Bible that would further strengthen and corroborate the conclusions to which we have arrived. Indeed, there is still more that can be learned from the Bible that greatly strengthens our belief that we have properly understood the Biblical information concerning the timing of the end.

What Do We Thus Far Know

1. The fig tree in leaf assures us that the end has to be after the year 1948.

2. The phrase "Summer is nigh" emphasizes that shortly after 1948 there must be a harvest of souls.

3. A harvest of souls means there must a Jubilee.

4. 1994 is the next Jubilee year after the year 1948 when Israel again became a nation.

5. If summer harvest begins in the Jubilee year 1994 it means something must have ended the first Jubilee that identified with the church age.

6. We are very comfortable with two Jubilees because of what we learned when we studied the destruction of Jericho.

7. The ending of the first Jubilee coincided with the beginning of the Great Tribulation.

8. The Great Tribulation is spoken of as one hour in Revelation Chapter 17.

9. Revelation 8:1 speaks of a half hour of silence. This verse assures us that there will be an end to the first Jubilee.

10. Matthew 24:21 speaks of the beginning of the Great Tribulation.

11. But Matthew 24:22 implies there will be some kind of a relenting or change before the full end of the Great Tribulation. "For the

sake of the elect those days will be shortened."

12. This identifies with Rev 8:1 which indicates that the silence in heaven is <u>half</u> an hour. That is, there is a great change somewhere in the middle of the Great Tribulation.

13. Since 1994 must be the beginning of the second Jubilee, it must coincide with the end of the half hour of silence and the beginning of the second period when for the sake of the elect the Gospel is again going forth.

14. The duration of the first part of the Great Tribulation appears to be best described by Daniel 8 where we read of a period of 2,300 days.

15. Since the church age identifies with Pentecost at which time the first fruits were brought in we could expect the end of the church age to be the day before Pentecost in 1988. A date in the year 1988 is 2,300 days earlier than 1994.

16. This makes the church age equal to 1,955 years to the very day. 1955 years breaks down into the significant numbers 5 x 17 x 23.

17. 2,300 days after the day before Pentecost in 1988 comes to the first day of the seventh month in 1994 according to the Jewish calendar. In the Old Testament ceremonial law this day was the feast day for remembering the Jubilee.

18. When we try to place the end of the second part of the Great Tribulation which coincides with the duration of the second Jubilee we find that a time duration of seventeen years is most probable.

19. Seventeen years goes to the year 2011. Thus the entire duration of the Great Tribulation would then be twenty-three years.

20. A time duration of 23 years for the entire Great Tribulation fits with the fact these 23 years are a time of Judgment on the local congregations.

21. 23 years fits with two prior 23 year periods that end with judgment.

    $11,013 - 4,990 = 6000$ plus 23

    $4,990 + 33 = 5,000$ plus 23 yrs. inclusive to judgment on Christ

    $11,013 + 2,011 = 13,000$ plus 23 yrs to judgment by Christ

22. A period of 17 years for the duration of the second part of the Great Tribulation which is the period of the second Jubilee (also called the latter rain or final harvest) fits well with the harvest of souls since the number 17 signifies heaven.

23. The 17 years fits well with the 153 fish caught (See John 21:11) which fish represent all of those saved during the latter rain which we can call the second Jubilee. $153 = 3$ x 3 x 17.

24. The 17 years in a veiled way identify with the 17 years that Jacob lived after he came under the care of Joseph in the year 1877.

25. The 17 years in a veiled way identifies with the 17 shekels Jeremiah paid for the deed to the land which was a proof Israel would again return to the promised land.

26. The year 2011 fits perfectly with statement of 2 Peter 3:8 which speaks of a day being equal to 1,000 years. Precisely 7,000 years after the Noachian Flood of 4990 B.C. is the year 2011 (A.D.).

27. The year 2011, which is the final judgment day for the local church, as well as whole world is 1,978 years after 33 A.D., which breaks down into the significant numbers 2 x 23 x 43.

28. $2,011 - 391 = 2.401$, or 7 x 7 x 7 x 7. In the perfectly complete end of time, Christ will finish speaking to this present world.

29. Nineveh. God gave precise time information as to when His judgment would fall on the Ninevites.

Thus, we have learned that a great many facts harmonize with the conclusion that the Great Tribulation began in 1988, and ended at the end of the world in 2011. Further that it was divided into two parts the first part being 2,300 days and the second part being 17 years also appears to harmonize with any and all Biblical data that relates to this subject.

Before we can feel secure with these conclusions, however, there is one more big test that can be applied to these conclusions.

Chapter 11
Patterns

God uses a very interesting device in conveying truth. That device is the giving of a pattern by which the object to be built or formed will be correctly finished. This is a method or procedure we can readily understand. For example, if an individual is going to make a garment that will fit properly, it is extremely helpful if a pattern can be obtained that will show how each piece of material from which the garment is to be made is to be cut. This insures that the garment will fit well and in the making of it no material is wasted.

Likewise, before the temple was built by Solomon, we read in 1 Chronicles 28:11-12:

> **Then David gave to Solomon his son the <u>pattern</u> of the porch, and of the houses thereof, and of the treasuries thereof, and of the upper chambers thereof, and of the inner parlours thereof, and of the place of the mercy seat, and the <u>pattern </u>of all that he had by the spirit, of the courts of the house of the LORD, and of all the chambers round about, of the treasuries of the house of God, and of the treasuries of the dedicated things.**

This same concept is conveyed in 1 Timothy 1:16:

> **Howbeit for this cause I obtained mercy, that in me first Jesus Christ might shew forth all longsuffering, for a <u>pattern to them</u> which should hereafter believe on him to life everlasting.**

In this citation, the life and conduct of the Apostle Paul is a pattern to follow for those who would live in a God-glorifying way. Likewise, God gave Moses the pattern for the objects that were to be placed in the tabernacle. For example, we read in Numbers 8:4:

> **And this work of the candlestick was of beaten gold, unto the shaft thereof, unto the flowers thereof, was beaten work: according unto the <u>pattern</u> which the LORD had shewed Moses, so he made the candlestick.**

Significantly, this is the method God used when He gave much information concerning His Gospel plan. We read in Hebrews 8:3-6:

For every high priest is ordained to offer gifts and sacrifices: wherefore it is of necessity that this man have somewhat also to offer. For if he were on earth, he should not be a priest, seeing that there are priests that offer gifts according to the law: who serve unto the <u>example and shadow of heavenly things</u>, as Moses was admonished of God when he was about to make the tabernacle: for, See, saith he, that thou make all things according to the pattern shewed to thee in the mount. But now hath he obtained a more excellent ministry, by how much also he is the mediator of a better covenant, which was established upon better promises.

This citation is teaching us that the pattern that typified or showed God's Gospel program were the various laws that governed the activities of the priests as they performed their priestly duties in the temple.

Biblical Patterns of the Great Tribulation

In this study as we have traveled down the highway of time, from time to time we have made reference to three dramatic events that appear to be related. They are as follows:

1.   The experience of Jacob when he was commanded to come out of the promised land of Canaan and go to live with his entire family in the heathen land of Egypt. The year was 1877 B.C.

2.   The experience of the nation of Judah when the armies of Babylon destroyed Jerusalem in the year 587 B.C.

3.   The traumatic experience of true believers of our day as in this time of Great Tribulation they are commanded to leave their local church.

It might be noted that superficially there is no resemblance that can readily be seen between the great tribulation Jacob experienced in 1877 B.C. and that which was experienced by the nation of Israel in 587 B.C. Furthermore, superficially there does not appear to be any resemblance between either of these two tribulations and the Great Tribulation of our day.

> *God provided two distinct patterns that clearly outlined and gave very much detail concerning the Great Tribulation of our day.*

However, God has provided two distinct patterns in the experiences of Jacob and the nation of Judah which clearly sharpen the focus of events relating to the Great Tribulation of our day. Remember, it is during the period of the Great Tribulation that the final activity is taking place as God is completing the unfolding of the calendar of history.

When we discover the precise fit of these two patterns as they are compared with the details of the Great Tribulation that has come just prior to the end of the world we will be greatly encouraged that we have properly understood the Biblical information concerning the end of the world.

> *...as God gives understanding of the metaphors and parables of the Bible, our understanding of the teachings of the Bible is greatly increased.*

Only when we thoroughly understand that Christ spoke in parables so that we clearly see the spiritual meaning of these events can we see the precise relationships that exist between them. This is an excellent illustration of the Lord's assertion in Mark 4:11-12 that He spoke in parables so that those who were not true believers would not understand. For the true believers the fact is that as they understand the metaphors and parables of the Bible, their understanding of the teachings of the Bible is greatly increased.

First, let us briefly outline the two Great Tribulation patterns recorded in the Bible.

Pattern 1. The first pattern is that of Jacob having to leave the promised land, Canaan, to come to Egypt to escape the grievous famine that was occurring (Genesis 46:2-3). The total time duration was seven years. It was divided into two parts in that it was after the first two years of the famine that Jacob and his family left Canaan. The year he left Canaan was 1877 B.C.

The second pattern is that of Judah during the seventy- year period from 609 B.C. to 539 B.C. It, too, was a time of great affliction that was divided into two parts. The first part ended when Jerusalem and the temple were completely destroyed by the armies of the Babylonians.

We will find that the tribulation experience of Jacob and also the tribulation experience of Judah are patterns that identify very closely with the conclusions to which we have already come in this study. Furthermore because our conclusions concerning the present "Great Tribulation" fit these patterns so closely we will be greatly encouraged that we are correctly understanding God's closing program for the churches and for the world which ends with the end of the world.

We will discover at least fourteen distinct parallels or similarities between the two patterns themselves as well as between them and the present Great Tribulation which will end with Christ's return at the end of the world. To facilitate the setting forth of these parallels we will use the word "JACOB" when speaking of the great tribulation Jacob experienced in 1877 B.C. We will use the word "JUDAH" when speaking of the terrible tribulation Judah experienced in 587 B.C. We will use the phrase "PRESENT GREAT TRIBULATION" when speaking of the present time of Great Tribulation.

We must remember the tribulations of "JACOB" and "JUDAH" are facts of past history. They are the patterns that God has given us. The tribulation we call "PRESENT GREAT TRIBULATION" is the Great Tribulation we are presently experiencing. We will find that it is precisely patterned after the "JACOB" and "JUDAH" tribulations.

Parallel No. 1: EACH TRIBULATION WAS A TIME OF GREAT TRIBULATION.

JACOB: Acts 7:11 speaks of this time as a time of "great affliction." The Greek word which is translated "affliction" is the identical word translated as tribulation in Matthew 24:21. Therefore, God speaks of Jacob's experience as "great tribulation."

JUDAH: The Great Tribulation spoken of in Matthew 24:21 was typified by the destruction of Judah in 587 B.C. Therefore, it is very extensively written about in such Old Testament books as Isaiah, Jeremiah, Lamentations, Ezekiel, Zephaniah, etc. In each book the destruction of Judah is used as the example of the end of the church age at which time all of the local churches throughout the world would come into judgment. In the Old Testament God wrote in the Hebrew language rather than in the Greek language which was the language of the New Testament. Therefore, we do not find the exact words, "Great Tribulation." However, the idea of Great Tribulation was expressed in many ways in these books. For example, Lamentations 2:2-7 clearly describes the enormous tribulation the nation of Judah experienced at that time in history. We read in these verses:

The Lord hath swallowed up all the habitations of Jacob, and hath not pitied: he hath thrown down in his wrath the strong holds of the daughter of Judah; he hath brought them down to the ground: he hath polluted the kingdom and the princes thereof. He hath cut off in his fierce anger all the horn of Israel: he hath drawn back his right hand from before the enemy, and he burned against Jacob like a flaming fire, which devoureth round about. He hath bent his bow like an enemy: he stood with his right hand as an adversary, and slew all that were pleasant to the eye in the tabernacle of the daughter of Zion: he poured out his fury like fire. The Lord was as an enemy: he hath swallowed up Israel, he hath swallowed up all her palaces: he hath destroyed his strong holds, and hath increased in the daughter of Judah mourning and lamentation. And he hath violently taken away his tabernacle, as if it were of a garden: he hath destroyed his places of the assembly: the LORD hath caused the solemn feasts and sabbaths to be forgotten in Zion, and hath despised in the indignation of his anger the king and the priest. The Lord hath cast off his altar, he hath abhorred his sanctuary, he hath given up into the hand of the enemy the walls of her palaces; they have made a noise in the house of the LORD, as in the day of a solemn feast.

"PRESENT GREAT TRIBULATION." God declares in Matthew 24:21:

For then shall be <u>great tribulation</u>, such as was not since the beginning of the world to this time, no, nor ever shall be.

2. THE PHYSICAL LOCATION OF EACH PERIOD WAS AN EXTERNAL REPRESENTATION OF THE KINGDOM OF GOD.

JACOB: The land of Canaan from which the family of Jacob must leave was an external representation of the kingdom of God. Abram the grandfather of Jacob had been told in Genesis 17:8:

And I will give unto thee, and to thy seed after thee, the land wherein thou art a stranger, all the land of Canaan, for an everlasting possession; and I will be their God.

JUDAH: The land of Judah from which all of Israel was commanded to leave was also an external representation of the Kingdom of God. This was so because the land of Judah and Jerusalem were an integral part of the land of Canaan.

PRESENT GREAT TRIBULATION: The local churches physically in evidence throughout the world were a divine institution designed by God to be the place identified with true believers. Thus, it, too, was an external representation of the kingdom of God. That is why God frequently speaks of them as Jerusalem, Judaea, Zion, the temple, etc.

3. THE PEOPLE OCCUPYING THAT LOCATION WERE ALSO A REPRESENTATION OF THE KINGDOM OF GOD.

JACOB: The entire family of Jacob was also given the name Israel. Israel which means Prince of God is a name that is repeatedly used to signify the kingdom of God.

JUDAH: All of the nation of Judah which after the year 709 B.C. included anyone who was a blood descendant of Abraham was looked upon by God as the external representation of the kingdom of God.

PRESENT GREAT TRIBULATION: All of the members of the local congregations which are located throughout the world are an external representation of the kingdom of God. They are spoken of as the seed of Abraham (Galatians 3:21).

4. EACH LOCATION HAS A LONG HISTORY OF OCCUPA-TION. THE NUMBERS OF YEARS HAVE WITHIN THEM NUMBERS SIGNIFYING JUDGMENT.

JACOB: Abraham had come to the land of Canaan in the year 2092 B.C. Jacob and his family were commanded to leave Canaan and go to Egypt 215 years later in the year 1877 B.C. The number 215 breaks down into 5 x 43.

5 signifies salvation or judgment
43 signifiessalvation or judgment

JUDAH: Israel became a kingdom with Saul as their first king in the year 1047 B.C. The kingdom of Israel ended in the year 587 B.C. when it was destroyed by Nebuchadnezzar the King of Babylon. 1,047 - 587 = 460 years. The number 460 breaks down into 2 x 10 x 23.

2 = number signifying the witnesses of the Gospel
10 = number signifying completeness
23 = number signifying judgment.

PRESENT GREAT TRIBULATION: The church age began a few weeks after Jesus returned to heaven in A.D. 33. Satan took his seat, that is, he began to rule in the churches most likely in the year 1988 A.D.

1,988 - 33 = 1955 years. The number 1,955 breaks down into 5 x 17 x 23.
5 signifies salvation or judgment
17 signifies heaven
23 signifies judgment.

5. GREAT TRIBULATION BEGAN WITH FAMINE.

JACOB: Genesis 41:54-56 declares:

And the seven years of dearth began to come, according as Joseph had said: and the dearth was in all lands; but in all the land of Egypt there was bread. And when all the land of Egypt was famished, the people cried to Pharaoh for bread: and Pharaoh said unto all the Egyptians, Go unto Joseph; what he saith to you, do. And the famine was over all the face of the earth: And Joseph opened all the storehouses, and sold unto the Egyptians; and the famine waxed sore in the land of Egypt.

The dearth (famine) was in the land of Canaan as well as in Egypt.

JUDAH: Jeremiah 21:6-7 declares:

And I will smite the inhabitants of this city, both man and beast: they shall die of a great pestilence. And afterward, saith the LORD, I will deliver Zedekiah king of Judah, and his servants, and the people, and such as are left in this city from the pestilence, from the sword, and from the famine, into the hand of Nebuchadrezzar king of Babylon, and into the hand of their enemies, and into the hand of those that seek their life: and he shall smite them with the edge of the sword; he shall not spare them, neither have pity, nor have mercy.

Jeremiah 14:1-4 declares:

The word of the LORD that came to Jeremiah concerning the dearth. Judah mourneth, and the gates thereof languish; they are black unto the ground; and the cry of Jerusalem is gone up. And their nobles have sent their little ones to the waters: they came to the pits, and found no water; they returned with their vessels empty; they were ashamed and confounded, and covered their heads. Because the ground is chapt, for there was no rain in the earth, the plowmen were ashamed, they covered their heads.

PRESENT GREAT TRIBULATION.

Amos 8:11 declares:

Behold, the days come, saith the Lord GOD, that I will send a <u>famine</u> in the land, not a famine of bread, nor a thirst for water, but of hearing the words of the LORD:

A famine of hearing the word of God means that God is no longer giving people ears to hear; that is, they hear the Word of God with their physical ears but that Word is not spiritually applied to their hearts because God the Holy Spirit has left the churches.

In Revelation 11:7-8 we read of the killing of the two witnesses (the true believers) by the local congregations. They are not physically killed but they are killed in the sense that their voice is no longer heard in the congregation. They have been driven out of the congregation. This sad fact is recorded in Jeremiah 14:16:

And the people to whom they prophesy shall be cast out in the streets of Jerusalem because of the famine and the sword; and they shall have none to bury them, them, their wives, nor their sons, nor their daughters: for I will pour their wickedness upon them.

I will pour <u>their</u> wickedness upon them is not referring to the wickedness of those who were killed. It is the wickedness of the killers. This idea is further expressed in Psalm 79:1-3:

O God, the heathen are come into thine inheritance; thy holy temple have they defiled; they have laid Jerusalem on heaps. The

dead bodies of thy servants have they given to be meat unto the fowls of the heaven, the flesh of thy saints unto the beasts of the earth. Their blood have they shed like water round about Jerusalem; and there was none to bury them.

Because God has left the local congregations and because the true witnesses have been driven out, God is no longer applying the Word of God that is preached in these congregations to the lives of those people in the congregations. Therefore, it is like there is no Word of God being preached. Thus, the churches are experiencing intense spiritual famine.

6. GREAT TRIBULATION: A TWO-PART PROGRAM.

JACOB: The seven years of famine which endured in the days of Joseph was divided into two significant parts. The first part was two years in length. During these two years Jacob and his family remained in the land of Canaan even though there was great famine within the land of Canaan.

The last five years Jacob and all of his family came into Egypt and remained there for the duration of the famine and even for a long time afterwards. Thus, the seven years was divided into a two year part and a five year part.

JUDAH: The Great Tribulation period which fell on Judah officially began in the year when that last God-fearing king who reigned over Judah was killed. That king was Josiah who was killed in battle in the year 609 B.C. This was the year that the seventy-year tribulation began for Israel. First they were subjugated to Egypt and then they came under the authority of Babylon. In the year 587 B.C. Jerusalem and the ten tribes were totally destroyed by the armies of Babylon. This was 23 years inclusive after King Josiah was killed in battle. During the remainder of the seventy years Israel did not exist as a nation in the land of Canaan.

PRESENT GREAT TRIBULATION: The Great Tribulation spoken of in Matthew 24:21 also was divided into two periods. Revelation 18:8 speaks of this period as "one day" and Revelation 18:10, 17 and 19 as "one hour." Likewise Revelation 17:12 speaks of this time as "one hour." In Revelation 14:7 this time is spoken of as the hour of his (God's) judgment.

The context in which the above one day or one hour citations are to be found show that these phrases refer to the entire Great Tribulation period.

However, in Revelation 8:1, we read:

And when he had opened the seventh seal, there was silence in heaven about the space of half an hour.

This half hour can be shown to be the first part of the Great Tribulation period. This first period is followed by the remainder of the Great Tribulation period during which time, for the sake of the elect, that is, for the sake of those who had been elected by God to become saved and had not yet become saved, the Gospel continues to go into the world. However, it is a Gospel for which the local churches anywhere in the world have no mandate, or authority to bring to the world. This latter period is spoken of in the Bible as the latter rain or as the time of the end of the year harvest.

7. THE FIRST PART OF THE GREAT TRIBULATION PERIOD FEATURES THE NO. 23.

JACOB: As we have learned the great tribulation of Joseph's Day was divided into two parts. The first part was two years in length. Jacob and his family who included all of Israel that lived in the land of Canaan at that time left Canaan and came under the protection of Joseph during the remaining five years of famine. Genesis 45:6 declares:

For these two years hath the famine been in the land: and yet there are five years, in the which there shall neither be earing nor harvest.

A full two years equals 24 months. However, no where does the Bible say two full years in connection with this famine Jacob and the world were experiencing. Therefore, if 23 months had passed at which time Jacob came into Egypt it would still be permissible language to state two years had passed.

There is precedence in the Bible to think of the number 24 as the number 23. In 1 Corinthians 10:8 we read:

Neither let us commit fornication, as some of them committed, and fell in one day three and twenty thousand.

This citation is speaking of a plague that came upon Israel just before they were to cross over the Jordan river into Canaan, the promised land. We read in Numbers 25:9:

And those that died in the plague were twenty and four thousand.

This is truly a curious situation. Why does God give the number 24,000 in Numbers 25 and the number 23,000 in 1 Corinthians 10? We know there is no contradiction. The 23000 is the number of those who were killed in one day. Thus 1,000 of those who were killed in the plague were killed the day earlier or the day following the day when the 23000 were killed.

But this is a significant reference because as we learned earlier God speaks of the Great Tribulation as "one day" (Revelation 18:8). Thus we see by the usage of the phrase "one day" that there exists an identification of the number 23 with the Great Tribulation. Therefore, since the two years of the famine are not specifically spoken of as two full years and because they do identify with the Great Tribulation of Jacob's day, could not the two years be looked upon as 23 months instead of 24 months, even as the plague featured in Numbers 25 in which 24,000 died is identified with 23,000 in 1 Corinthians 10?

JUDAH: As we have learned there was a distinct break in the 70 years of tribulation experienced by Israel. It was in the year 587 B.C. when Jerusalem was destroyed. This terrible tribulation began in the year 609 and was continuing to be experienced in the year 587 B.C. when Jerusalem was destroyed.

Therefore, 609 - 587 inclusive equals 23 years. The tribulation began in the year 609 B.C. and it was during the year 587 B.C. that Jerusalem was destroyed indicating that both of these years can be included as the first part of this 70 year tribulation period. We thus see that these 23 years inclusive identify with the probable 23 months of the tribulation experienced by Jacob.

PRESENT GREAT TRIBULATION: In the Book of Daniel God prophecies concerning the coming of the Great Tribulation at the end of the world. During that time Satan will be the apparent winner in the local churches. Daniel 8:11-12 describes his actions:

> **Yea, he magnified himself even to the prince of the host, and by him the daily sacrifice was taken away, and the place of his sanctuary was cast down. And an host was given him against the daily sacrifice by reason of transgression, and it cast down the truth to the ground; and it practised, and prospered.**

A commentary on these verses is recorded in Daniel 8:23-24 where we read:

> **And in the latter time of their kingdom, when the transgressors are come to the full, a king of fierce countenance, and**

understanding dark sentences, shall stand up. And his power shall be mighty, but not by his own power: and he shall destroy wonderfully, and shall prosper, and practise, and shall destroy the mighty and the holy people.

These are statements that have been fulfilled when the present Great Tribulation began. In this connection the question is raised in Daniel 8:13:

Then I heard one saint speaking, and another saint said unto that certain saint which spake, How long shall be the vision concerning the daily sacrifice, and the transgression of desolation, to give both the sanctuary and the host to be trodden under foot?

The question is, "How long will Satan be able to prevail so that Christ and the Gospel are vanquished?" Remember we read earlier in Revelation 8:1 there was silence for about one half hour. That half hour which was the first part of the Great Tribulation identifies with these verses we are reading in Daniel 8.

In answer to the question of how long this situation would continue the answer is given in Daniel 8:14:

And he said unto me, Unto two thousand and three hundred days; then shall the sanctuary be cleansed.

The word "days" in this verse literally in the original Hebrew reads "evening mornings." This is like the language of Genesis 1 where an evening morning was a day of 24 hours. Therefore we would suspect that Daniel 8:14 is describing 2,300 24-hour days. At the end of these 2,300 days the sanctuary (the holy place) would be cleansed (literally be made righteous). This citation thus appears to be speaking either of the entire tribulation period or it can be speaking of the first part of the Great Tribulation period.

The key to this question must relate to the phrase "the holy place be made righteous." Before the beginning of the Great Tribulation the local churches were the "holy place." This is so because the Bible was present there and these churches had been given the task of evangelizing the world. But then there was silence in heaven for half an hour. Effectively during this half hour period there was no salvation going on. There was no holy place that was the custodian of the Bible and had been mandated to send the Gospel into all of the world. However, immediately following this half hour of silence came the latter rain. During the latter rain, the final harvest of true believers takes place. However the "holy" place has shifted to the sending forth of the Gospel by individuals outside of the local congregations. Therefore, in that sense the holy place has been cleansed or made righteous.

Thus, it would appear that the 2,300 days (evening mornings) of Daniel 8:14 is the literal duration of time of the first part of the tribulation period. Thus in the great tribulation of Jacob's day the first part of this period was in all likelihood to be considered as 23 months. Likewise the first part of the 70 year tribulation period of 23 years inclusively. And the first part of the Great Tribulation of our day when Christ is judging the local congregations is 2300 literal days.

8. THE ENTIRE GREAT TRIBULATION PERIOD RELATES TO THE NUMBER 84.

JACOB: God frequently uses numbers to assist with spiritual truth. The tribulation period experienced by Jacob encompassed seven years or 84 months.

JUDAH: The tribulation period experienced by Israel endured for seventy years which is 840 months. Again the number 84 is in view.

PRESENT GREAT TRIBULATION: Earlier in our study we learned from 2 Peter 3:8 that a day is 1000 years in God's sight and a thousand years is a day. We also learned that this statement was made in the context of reminding us of the Flood of Noah's day and of the coming end of the world at which time the entire universe will be destroyed by fire. We learned that the year 2011 A.D. is precisely 7,000 years after the Noachian Flood. Therefore, there is a distinct possibility that the year 2011 A.D. could be the year when the world is brought to an end.

We will also learn as we have already noted that the year 1988 A.D. is the probable year when the Great Tribulation of our day began. Thus the period of 1988 A.D. to 2011 A.D. is a period of 23 years. Given the fact that the number 23 as used in the Bible to signify judgment we can see the likelihood that the entire period of the Great Tribulation could be 23 years. What is remarkable is the fact that each year has 365.2422 days within it. Thus, our calendar shows each year as 365 days with each fourth year as a leap year with 366 days. In a period of 23 years, there are five leap years. Thus, 18 years of 365 days plus 5 years of 366 days equals a total of exactly 8,400 days. Thus, we see that the number 84 is also prominently in evidence in the Present Great Tribulation period just as it was in the tribulation periods experienced by Jacob and later by Judah.

9. BELIEVERS ARE COMMANDED TO LEAVE THEIR
HOMELAND.

JACOB: As we learned earlier because of the famine in Canaan, the land
which externally typified the Kingdom of God, Jacob and his entire family were
commanded to leave Canaan and go to Egypt. We read in Genesis 45:9-10:

> **Haste ye, and go up to my father, and say unto him, Thus saith thy
> son Joseph, God hath made me lord of all Egypt: come down unto
> me, tarry not: and thou shalt dwell in the land of Goshen, and thou
> shalt be near unto me, thou, and thy children, and thy children's
> children, and thy flocks, and thy herds, and all that thou hast.**

That this was God's plan for Jacob is emphasized by the language of
Genesis 46:2-3:

> **And God spake unto Israel in the visions of the night, and said,
> Jacob, Jacob. And he said, Here am I. And he said, I am God, the
> God of thy father: fear not to go down into Egypt; for I will there
> make of thee a great nation.**

Therefore, we read in Genesis 46:5-7:

> **And Jacob rose up from Beersheba: and the sons of Israel carried
> Jacob their father, and their little ones, and their wives, in the
> wagons which Pharaoh had sent to carry him. And they took their
> cattle, and their goods, which they had gotten in the land of
> Canaan, and came into Egypt, Jacob, and all his seed with him: his
> sons, and his sons' sons with him, his daughters, and his sons'
> daughters, and all his seed brought he with him into Egypt.**

This meant that God had abandoned the land of Canaan leaving it to be
possessed only by unbelievers.

JUDAH: In similar manner at the time great tribulation had come upon
Judah and Jerusalem, God commanded in Jeremiah 21:8-10:

> **And unto this people thou shalt say, Thus saith the LORD;
> Behold, I set before you the way of life, and the way of death. He
> that abideth in this city shall die by the sword, and by the famine,
> and by the pestilence: but he that goeth out, and falleth to the**

Chaldeans that besiege you, he shall live, and his life shall be unto him for a prey. For I have set my face against this city for evil, and not for good, saith the LORD: it shall be given into the hand of the king of Babylon, and he shall burn it with fire.

In similar fashion God declared in Jeremiah 38:2-3:

Thus saith the LORD, He that remaineth in this city shall die by the sword, by the famine, and by the pestilence: but he that goeth forth to the Chaldeans shall live; for he shall have his life for a prey, and shall live. Thus saith the LORD, This city shall surely be given into the hand of the king of Babylon's army, which shall take it.

This meant that God had abandoned Jerusalem and Judea so that they would be possessed only by unbelievers.

PRESENT GREAT TRIBULATION: As we learned earlier the 24th chapter of Matthew teaches very plainly about this time of Great Tribulation that has come just prior to the end of the world. In Matthew 24:15-16, God commands:

When ye therefore shall see the abomination of desolation, spoken of by Daniel the prophet, stand in the holy place, (whoso readeth, let him understand:) then let them which be in Judaea flee into the mountains.

The holy place and Judaea are signifying the local churches located all over the world. They are the holy place because they throughout the church age had been entrusted with the Bible by which they had been commanded to send the Gospel into all of the world. But now Satan as the man of sin, who is called in this verse the "abomination of desolation," is ruling in all of the local congregations and the true believers are commanded to flee to the mountains. The mountains are a figure pointing to God, Himself. We read this in Psalm 121:1:

I will lift up mine eyes unto the hills, from whence cometh my help.

In this verse, the word "hills" can also be translated "mountains." The local churches have become Babylon because Christ has abandoned them and given them to Satan, who is typified by the king of Babylon, to rule over. This is stated, for example, in 2 Thessalonians 2:3-4:

Let no man deceive you by any means: for that day shall not come, except there come a falling away first, and that man of sin be revealed, the son of perdition; who opposeth and exalteth himself above all that is called God, or that is worshiped; so that he as God sitteth in the temple of God, shewing himself that he is God.

Satan is called a man because in Isaiah 14 he is typified by the man Nebuchadnezzar who was king over Babylon. To take one's seat is a figure expressing rulership. Thus, Revelation 18:4 commands the true believers:

And I heard another voice from heaven, saying, Come out of her, my people, that ye be not partakers of her sins, and that ye receive not of her plagues.

Thus, we must understand God has abandoned the local congregations leaving them entirely to unbelievers.

10. BELIEVERS WHO HAVE BEEN COMMANDED TO COME OUT ARE UNDER GOD'S PROTECTION.

JACOB: Jacob and all of his family came to Egypt and settled in the land of Goshen. They were under the care and protection of Joseph who as Prime Minister of Egypt was a type of the Lord Jesus Christ.

JUDAH: Judah was told in Jeremiah 29:4-7:

Thus saith the LORD of hosts, the God of Israel, unto all that are carried away captives, whom I have caused to be carried away from Jerusalem unto Babylon; Build ye houses, and dwell in them; and plant gardens, and eat the fruit of them; take ye wives, and beget sons and daughters; and take wives for your sons, and give your daughters to husbands, that they may bear sons and daughters; that ye may be increased there, and not diminished. And seek the peace of the city whither I have caused you to be carried away captives, and pray unto the LORD for it: for in the peace thereof shall ye have peace.

PRESENT GREAT TRIBULATION: Those who have been driven out of the local congregation or in obedience to God's command have come out of the local congregation continue under the protection of Christ who has promised the true believer **"I will never leave thee nor forsake thee"** (Hebrews 13:56).

11. THE LAND OR LOCATION FROM WHICH THE BELIEVERS HAVE COME OUT WILL CONTINUE TO BE WITHOUT THE PRESENCE OF TRUE BELIEVERS TO THE END OF THE GREAT TRIBULATION.

JACOB: The Great Tribulation is identified with a seven-year famine. When Jacob and his family left Canaan to go into Egypt the land of Canaan was left to those who follow Satan (unbelievers) and the famine continued until the end of the seven-year tribulation period.

JUDAH: When Judah and Jerusalem enter into this seventy-year tribulation period those who remained under the blessing to God lived in Babylon. For the entire time of this tribulation, after Babylon destroyed Jerusalem, the land of Israel remained as a hostage of Babylon, and Israel could not return. It was only at the end of this seventy-year period that Israel could return to Jerusalem.

PRESENT GREAT TRIBULATION: This tribulation will continue until the end of the world when Christ appears as the Judge of all the earth. The local churches will be experiencing the action of God in preparing them for the last day. This action of God's wrath upon them will continue all the way to the end of the world. Those that remain in them will be sent a strong delusion (2 Thessalonians 2:11).

To use the language of the parable of the wheat and tares (Matthew 13:30) they are the tares that are bound in bundles to be burned.

12. EACH TRIBULATION PERIOD IDENTIFIES WITH THE NUMBER 43, MAKING THE NUMBER 43 IDENTIFY WITH GREAT TRIBULATION.

JACOB: The number 43 is prominent in two ways. First of all it was after 215 years of occupancy in the land of Canaan that Jacob came into Egypt. The number 215 is the product of 5 x 43. Secondly, in one sense the great tribulation experienced by Jacob and his family continued for 5 years until the end of the seven year famine. However, it continued in another sense for 430 years because that was the period of time that Israel was in Egypt as they grew into a nation.

JUDAH: In the year 1877 B.C. Jacob and his family left the promised land, Canaan and came into Egypt. This year began the second part of the seven year tribulation. Exactly 3 x 430 years later in the year 587 Jerusalem was destroyed by the king of Babylon. This began the second part of the seventy-year tribulation endured by Israel. This 3 x 430 year period between the tribulation periods of Jacob and Judah was prophesied in Daniel 12:11:

> **And from the time that the daily sacrifice shall be taken away, and the abomination that maketh desolate set up, there shall be a thousand two hundred and ninety days.**

This citation speaks of 1,290 days which equals 3 x 430. However, as we have shown elsewhere in this study, we believe we can look upon one day equaling one year.

PRESENT GREAT TRIBULATION: The time duration between the beginning year of the second part of Jacob's tribulation and the second part of the Present Great Tribulation appears to be exactly 3 x 3 x 430 years. 1,877 + 1,994 - 1 = 3,870 = 3 x 3 x 430. Once again the number 43 identifies with tribulation.

13. THE TRUE BELIEVERS ARE TO BE REPRESENTATIVES OF THE KINGDOM OF GOD WHEN THEY HAVE COME OUT OF THEIR HOMELAND AND LIVE IN THE WORLD.

JACOB: The family of Jacob were shepherds. When they came into Egypt they were to serve as shepherds to the Egyptians. We read in Genesis 46:34 **"every shepherd is an abomination unto the Egyptians."** In Genesis 47:6 Pharaoh declared to Jacob:

> **The land of Egypt is before thee; in the best of the land make thy father and brethren to dwell; in the land of Goshen let them dwell: and if thou knowest any men of activity among them, then make them rulers over my cattle.**

JUDAH: In Jeremiah 29:4-7 we read:

> **Thus saith the LORD of hosts, the God of Israel, unto all that are carried away captives, whom I have caused to be carried away from Jerusalem unto Babylon; Build ye houses, and dwell in**

them; and plant gardens, and eat the fruit of them; take ye wives, and beget sons and daughters; and take wives for your sons, and give your daughters to husbands, that they may bear sons and daughters; that ye may be increased there, and not diminished. And seek the peace of the city whither I have caused you to be carried away captives, and pray unto the LORD for it: for in the peace thereof shall ye have peace.

PRESENT GREAT TRIBULATION: The true believers live in the world but are living there as representatives or ambassadors of the Gospel. They are the two witnesses of Revelation 11:11 who during the second part of the great tribulation stand on their feet and the Spirit of God entered into them and great fear came upon them who saw them. The fear of God comes upon those whom the Holy Spirit is saving as they hear the true Gospel that is sent into all the world during the second part of the Great Tribulation.

14. THE DIVISION OF EACH TRIBULATION PERIOD INTO PARTS IS VERY SIMILAR.

JACOB: First part is 23 or 24 months.

The entire period is seven years or 84 months.

Therefore, if the first part was 24 months the relationship of the first part to the whole period would be as follows:

First part	Entire Tribulation
24 months	Seven years of 84 months

If the first part is 23 months then:

First part	Entire Tribulation
23 months	Seven years or 84 months.

JUDAH:

First part	Entire Tribulation
23 years inclusive	70 years = 840 months.

PRESENT GREAT TRIBULATION:

First Part	Entire Tribulation
2,300 days	8,400 days

We should be greatly impressed by these fourteen parallels that exist between the patterns themselves. We should be even more impressed by these fourteen parallels that exist between the two patterns on the one hand and the present Great Tribulation on the other. These many parallels can only be true if we have correctly understood God's timetable for the final end of history that encompasses this present Great Tribulation period. We are given great assurance that our present understanding of the timetable of the unfolding of God's salvation plan during this present Great Tribulation is accurate. We must remember that all of this material is derived solely from the Bible. Because it is new to our ears does not in anyway diminish its value and authority as truth.

Again it should be emphasized. We should be greatly impressed that God in His divine mercy has hidden within the Bible these two patterns of the Great Tribulation of our present time. Thus we can receive great assurance that our understanding of the bits and pieces of information that were scattered throughout the Bible have been correctly assembled and understood.

Chapter 12
After the Great Tribulation

In our study of the timeline of the unfolding of God's salvation program we have come all the way to the likely year of the end of the world -- the year 2011 A.D. We have purposely avoided discussing the month or day of Christ's return on the clouds of glory.

We do know that the Feast of Ingathering which is also called the Feast of Tabernacles in the Bible is scheduled each year from the fifteenth to the twenty second of the seventh month of the Jewish calendar. This will come in the fall of the year. It could well be that these physical, literal times of these feasts could identify with Christ's return. I believe, however, at this time in our knowledge of Bible truth is it not wise to go past the language that speaks of Great Tribulation. In Matthew 24:29 we read:

> **Immediately after the tribulation of those days shall the sun be darkened, and the moon shall not give her light, and the stars shall fall from heaven, and the powers of the heavens shall be shaken.**

Insofar as my present understanding of the Bible is concerned I do not believe I can adequately understand this verse. That is, it surely is speaking about the visible return of Christ together with the events that will take place at that time. This will include the rapture of the believers, the judging of the unsaved, the physical destruction of the universe and the creation of the New Heaven and New Earth. This is a time when time is about to end and eternity future will have arrived. Will these closing events that occur after the end of the Great Tribulation be in the context of time so that there still will be a few days before eternity future begins? It is beyond my poor ability to know. As a minimum I believe God has spoken about these things to give closure to the Gospel message.

Moreover, when these things which are spoken of in Matthew 24:29 are happening spiritually it will be night time. There will no longer be the possibility of salvation. It will be the time when mankind reacts as we read in Revelation 6:15-16:

> **And the kings of the earth, and the great men, and the rich men, and the chief captains, and the mighty men, and every bondman, and every free man, hid themselves in the dens and in the rocks of the mountains; And said to the mountains and rocks, Fall on us,**

and hide us from the face of him that sitteth on the throne, and from the wrath of the Lamb.

We can, however, summarize what we can know from the Bible concerning the visible return of Christ and the eternity which immediately follows.

We do know that at the time of the end there will be the visible return of Christ as the judge of all the earth. We read in Matthew 24:30:

And then shall appear the sign of the Son of man in heaven: and then shall all the tribes of the earth mourn, and they shall see the Son of man coming in the clouds of heaven with power and great glory.

When Christ ascended into heaven after the atonement, the disciples were told in Acts 1:11:

. . . also said, Ye men of Galilee, why stand ye gazing up into heaven? this same Jesus, which is taken up from you into heaven, shall so come in like manner as ye have seen him go into heaven.

Matthew 24:27 further describes His coming:

For as the lightning cometh out of the east, and shineth even unto the west; so shall also the coming of the Son of man be.

The immediate impact on mankind resulting from His visible return is described in Matthew 24:30 and in Revelation 6:15-17.

And then shall appear the sign of the Son of man in heaven: and then shall all the tribes of the earth mourn, and they shall see the Son of man coming in the clouds of heaven with power and great glory.

And the kings of the earth, and the great men, and the rich men, and the chief captains, and the mighty men, and every bondman, and every free man, hid themselves in the dens and in the rocks of the mountains; And said to the mountains and rocks, Fall on us, and hide us from the face of him that sitteth on the throne, and from the wrath of the Lamb: For the great day of his wrath is come; and who shall be able to stand?

When Christ comes in His visible return He will come as the Judge of all the earth. We read in Revelation 20:12-13:

And I saw the dead, small and great, stand before God; and the books were opened: and another book was opened, which is the book of life: and the dead were judged out of those things which were written in the books, according to their works. And the sea gave up the dead which were in it; and death and hell delivered up the dead which were in them: and they were judged every man according to their works.

At that awesome time every unsaved person who has ever lived on the earth together with every unsaved person who is still physically alive at that time will be individually brought to trial before the Judgment Throne of Christ. John 5:28-29 discloses:

Marvel not at this: for the hour is coming, in the which all that are in the graves shall hear his voice, And shall come forth; they that have done good, unto the resurrection of life; and they that have done evil, unto the resurrection of damnation.

> *...when Christ visibly appears and every person who has ever lived on the earth sees Him in His glory, they no longer can pretend or deceive themselves that there is no God to whom they must answer.*

Mankind was created in the image of God. Intuitively, every human being knows there is a God he must answer to. He also knows he has violated God's laws. He, therefore, knows he is guilty. But when Christ visibly appears and every person who has ever lived on the earth sees Him in His glory, they no longer can pretend or deceive themselves that there is no God to whom they must answer. They no longer can be in denial of this awesome truth. They will know that they must answer to Him.

Wonderfully, at the same time that Christ appears as the Judge of all the earth He also comes to complete the salvation of those who have throughout time become saved. At anytime in the history of the world when an individual became saved, from a legal stand point, he is no longer in any way condemned by the Law of God. This is because the Lord Jesus on behalf of that person has personally paid the penalty, demanded by the Law of God, for that sin.

On the other hand, those who died as unsaved individuals and those unsaved who are still alive on earth when Christ visibly appears must be brought to trial to be examined. Then will be brought to fulfillment the prophecy of 2 Corinthians 5:10:

> **For we must all appear before the judgment seat of Christ; that every one may receive the things done in his body, according to that he hath done, whether it be good or bad.**

Not a single unsaved person will escape this awful judgment.

Not a single unsaved person will escape this awful judgment. Because God knows every thing about every thing, no sin, however slight or seemingly unimportant, will escape the scrutiny of God. We read in Hebrews 4:12-13:

> **For the word of God is quick, and powerful, and sharper than any twoedged sword, piercing even to the dividing asunder of soul and spirit, and of the joints and marrow, and is a discerner of the thoughts and intents of the heart. Neither is there any creature that is not manifest in his sight: but all things are naked and opened unto the eyes of him with whom we have to do.**

In this verse, the phrase **"the word of God"** is pointing to the Lord Jesus Christ. In John 1:1 and 14 we read:

> **In the beginning was the Word, and the Word was with God, and the Word was God. And the Word was made flesh, and dwelt among us, (and we beheld his glory, the glory as of the only begotten of the Father,) full of grace and truth.**

Thus, we can know that as the unsaved stand for judgment at the time of the visible appearing of Christ as the Judge, no sin of that individual can be hidden from God. True the sinner standing before this mighty infinite Judge can argue in accordance with the language of Matthew 7:22-23:

Many will say to me in that day, Lord, Lord, have we not prophesied in thy name? and in thy name have cast out devils? and in thy name done many wonderful works? And then will I profess unto them, I never knew you: depart from me, ye that work iniquity.

Sentence will be pronounced. Hell, the lake of fire, eternal damnation is the penalty that must be paid. How horrible! And there will be no plea bargaining, no parole, no possibility of escaping this terrible experience. Only those who had become true believers in the times when God was saving will escape this awful end. Their escape was made possible because Christ had taken upon Himself each and every one of their miserable, dirty, rotten sins and as their Substitute had paid for their sins.

What a terrible future awaits the billions of people who have never become saved. What an awful, terrible moment that will be when Christ visibly returns as the Judge of all the earth.

New Resurrected Bodies

Wonderfully, at that dramatic moment when times comes to an end another scenario also takes place. It will be the moment of ultimate joy for every true believer in Christ. Remember, we learned that at the moment of salvation, God gave that person a brand new eternal resurrected soul. This saved individual is, therefore, from the moment of his salvation, eternally alive.

But that person also was created with a physical body. When he became saved God did not make a change in his body. Yet his body is an integral part of his personality. Therefore, at some moment his body, too, must be changed into a perfect resurrected body. That moment occurs at the time of the literal, visible return of Christ.

If that saved individual had physically died before the return of Christ there would have been a separation between his soul or spirit essence and his body at that moment of physical death. Because he had received an eternal resurrected soul at the moment of salvation, at the moment of his physical death in his new resurrected soul he would have left his body and instantly have been taken into heaven to live with Christ as a spirit personality without a body. His physical body would have been buried or cremated or disposed of in some other way. But at the end of the world in his soul existence he will return with Christ. At that time his body will be resurrected a perfect spiritual body and rejoined with his soul. Thus his salvation will be complete in every way.

This resurrection of his body is a simultaneous event occurring at the same moment the unsaved are resurrected to stand for judgment. Remember John 5:28-29:

> **Marvel not at this: for the hour is coming, in the which all that are in the graves shall hear his voice, And shall come forth; they that have done good, unto the resurrection of life; and they that have done evil, unto the resurrection of damnation.**

At precisely the same time this resurrection of the unsaved is taking place a similar event is being experienced by all the true believers who are living at the time Christ returns. They instantly will be changed into their eternal resurrected spiritual bodies. We read in 1 Corinthians 15:51-53:

> **Behold, I shew you a mystery; We shall not all sleep, but we shall all be changed, In a moment, in the twinkling of an eye, at the last trump: for the trumpet shall sound, and the dead shall be raised incorruptible, and we shall be changed. For this corruptible must put on incorruption, and this mortal must put on immortality.**

This simultaneous completion of the salvation of both those who had physically died as well as those who are physically living when Christ visibly appears is spoken of in 1 Thessalonians 4:16-17:

> **For the Lord himself shall descend from heaven with a shout, with the voice of the archangel, and with the trump of God: and the dead in Christ shall rise first: Then we which are alive and remain shall be caught up together with them in the clouds, to meet the Lord in the air: and so shall we ever be with the Lord.**

This will be the most notable, most happy, most exciting, most wonderful moment these true believers will have ever experienced. It is far above and beyond our human minds to grasp the import or significance of this. But it will come to pass. As we have followed the timeline of the history of the world beginning at the first day of creation we have learned much about God who is completely in control of every event that has occurred throughout the duration of this universe. We have learned that every prophetic declaration of God does come true in accord with the precise timetable God has established.

God's Overall Plan for this Universe

We have come almost to the end of our study. The last event in the history of the universe will be its complete destruction and its re-creation as the New Heaven and New Earth. To receive a bit of insight into this we should take a moment to review God's commitments to this present universe.

We have learned that the timeline of history is the unfolding of God's salvation plan. We must keep in mind, however, that this salvation program is within the context of this universe which God brought into existence slightly more than thirteen thousand years ago. Therefore, this universe is intimately associated with the development of God's salvation plan.

Before we complete this study we thus should briefly look at a number of Biblical citations which indicates this relationship between mankind and this universe.

The first principle we should note is that this earth was given to mankind. We read in Psalm 115:16:

The heaven, even the heavens, are the LORD'S: but the earth hath he given to the children of men.

Since the earth was given by God to man, we, therefore, are not surprised to read that mankind was to rule over this earth. We read this in Genesis 1:26:

And God said, Let us make man in our image, after our likeness: and let them have dominion over the fish of the sea, and over the fowl of the air, and over the cattle, and over all the earth, and over every creeping thing that creepeth upon the earth.

But then, as we have learned disaster came. Our first parents, Adam and Eve, who represented the entire human race that was to occupy this earth surrendered their will to the fallen angel, Satan. Thus, Satan became the ruler of this universe.

We read in John 12:31:

Now is the judgment of this world: now shall the prince of this world be cast out.

The prince of this world is Satan who heads up the kingdom of Satan to which all of the unsaved of the world belong.

But God's plan is that those who become saved, who in the Bible are called the righteous, are to inherit this earth. We read in Psalm 37:9 and 11:

For evildoers shall be cut off: but those that wait upon the LORD, they shall inherit the earth. But the meek shall inherit the earth; and shall delight themselves in the abundance of peace.

On the other hand, the wicked who have remained under the rule of Satan are to be cut off from this earth as we just read in Psalm 37:9. In Psalm 37:20 God declares:

But the wicked shall perish, and the enemies of the LORD shall be as the fat of lambs: they shall consume; into smoke shall they consume away.

This verse is effectively indicating that when God comes as the Judge of all the earth all of the wicked will be cast into Hell which is also called a lake of fire (Revelation 20:15). This verse anticipates what is required in order that this world be rescued from the possession and tyranny of Satan and restored to the possession and rule of mankind who are to inherit this earth.

This rescue operation was accomplished by Jesus, who is eternal God, Himself, taking on a human nature so that He could rightfully pay for the sins of those individuals He came to save. In the process of paying for their sins He also guaranteed that Satan and all the other fallen angels who rule over the unsaved (the wicked) of this world were also judged. This means that when the end of this world comes Satan will no longer be the ruler of this world but will be cast into Hell which is eternal damnation.

It is true that when mankind sinned so that they effectively surrendered the rule of this earth to Satan, God cursed the earth which He had created as a perfect earth. Therefore the whole creation which consists of this entire universe has been subject to decay and corruption throughout the 13,000 years of its history. That is why man and animals die, why there are thorns and thistles, poisonous bacteria, volcanoes, earthquakes etc. This curse will be removed when the end of time comes and God will destroy this entire universe so that it can be re-created a perfect universe wherein the results of God's curse will have been completely removed. This is why we read in Romans 8:19-21:

For the earnest expectation of the creature waiteth for the manifestation of the sons of God. For the creature was made subject to vanity, not willingly, but by reason of him who hath

subjected the same in hope, Because the creature itself also shall be delivered from the bondage of corruption into the glorious liberty of the children of God.

The Bible speaks of the end of this existing corrupted earth by the language of 2 Peter 3:10-12:

But the day of the Lord will come as a thief in the night; in the which the heavens shall pass away with a great noise, and the elements shall melt with fervent heat, the earth also and the works that are therein shall be burned up. Seeing then that all these things shall be dissolved, what manner of persons ought ye to be in all holy conversation and godliness, Looking for and hasting unto the coming of the day of God, wherein the heavens being on fire shall be dissolved, and the elements shall melt with fervent heat?

The final destruction of the present universe will be followed by the creation of a new heaven and earth as we read in 2 Peter 3:13:

Nevertheless we, according to his promise, look for new heavens and a new earth, wherein dwelleth righteousness.

We thus must understand that the unfolding of the timeline of history is particularly focused on God's salvation plan for mankind. However, this salvation plan is altogether identified with the whole universe in which mankind lives.

Eternity Future

As we have just noted the last event in the history of the universe will be its complete destruction. In the first chapter of Genesis, God gives us the details of the creation of this universe about 13,000 years ago. In 2 Peter 3, verses 10 to 13, which are quoted above, God gives us the information concerning the end of this universe. Remember, when God created the universe in six days He gave it the appearance of age. The moment Adam was created he looked like he was a man several decades old. The moment the distant stars were created God created the light of these stars to earth so they appear to have been created billions of years ago. Likewise, at the end of time the entire universe simultaneously will burn with fire. Distant stars will disappear together with the light from them that presently can be seen.

It is at this moment according to what we read in the Bible along with many other events that two major events should be noted. One is the development of the locale of all those who became saved during the history of the world. The other is the locale of hell which is also called the lake of fire.

The Bible speaks of the New Heavens and the New Earth. We can only speculate what God means by this. We do know certain facts that can provide some help in understanding this language. We do know the following.

1. This present earth is separated from heaven where God dwells. For example Elijah went into heaven in a whirlwind and in a chariot of fire (2 Kings 2:11). Jesus, forty days after rising from the dead, ascended into heaven (Acts 1:3, 11).

2. This present earth is under the curse of God because of man's sin (Romans 8:19-22).

3. This present universe will be completely destroyed by fire (2 Peter 3:10-12).

4. True believers who die are presently living in their soul existence or spirit essence in heaven (2 Corinthians 5:8, 1 Thessalonians 4:15).

5. In eternity future the true believers will be literally with Christ. In 1 John 3:2 we read:

    Beloved, now are we the sons of God, and it doth not yet appear what we shall be: but we know that, when he shall appear, we shall be like him; for we shall see him as he is.

Based on the above information it appears that in eternity future there will not exist a heaven up there and an earth down here. It appears that heaven and earth will be a single entity.

We also know the following.

1. Since the true believers were given eternal life it definitely means they will never again fall into sin. This means that they never come under the wrath of God.

2. There will be no sorrow or suffering (Revelation 21:2-4).

3. There will be no day or night (Revelation 22:5).

4. There will be no sun. Christ will be the light (Revelation 22:5).

5. This earth and its sorrows will not be remembered. Isaiah 65:17 declares:

   For, behold, I create new heavens and a new earth: and the former shall not be remembered, nor come into mind.

Unfortunately, during eternity there will somewhere exist a place of eternal torment. It will be inhabited by Satan and all of the fallen angels who are called devils or evil spirits. It will also be eternally inhabited by the billions of human beings who did not become saved.

It will be a place:

1. where there is weeping and gnashing of teeth (Matthew 13:41-42),

2. where the smoke of their torment ascendeth for ever and ever (Revelation 14:10-11),

3. where those present there will be under eternal damnation (2 Thessalonians 1:8-9, Matthew 25:46),

4. which is called a lake of fire (Revelation 20:15),

5. that is altogether outside of the new heavens and the new earth where the true believers live in the highest happiness with Christ forevermore (Revelation 21:8).

MAY GOD HAVE MERCY ON EACH ONE OF US.

Because He is God who spoke and brought this complex universe into existence, He is also fully qualified to bring to completion all that He has prophesied concerning His visible return and the end of the world. Thus, when we realize that as we have understood God's plan for the remaining few years of the existence of this earth we should tremble with fear. AM I READY TO MEET GOD? Remember this study of the Biblical history of the world was not made in any sense as a speculation, as a novel, as something imaginative, or something based on intuition, a dream, or on a vision. It is based on a careful analysis of the truths of the Bible.

We are almost to the end of time. Whether we like it or not makes no difference whatsoever. The end of time that is coming with all the horror of Christ's judgment throne is almost here. True, the Bible reveals that most people will scoff at the concepts set forth in this study. As we noted earlier they have to be in denial; they have to believe it cannot happen. The idea that in a few short years they will be sent to Hell forever is completely unacceptable.

Unfortunately, it will happen. The world of Noah's day were amply warned that a flood was coming that would completely destroy every living person or animal that was not in the safety of the ark. The Bible tells us that they continued to live with complete disregard of the warning. The Bible declares in Matthew 24:37-39:

> **But as the days of Noe were, so shall also the coming of the Son of man be. For as in the days that were before the flood they were eating and drinking, marrying and giving in marriage, until the day that Noe entered into the ark, And knew not until the flood came, and took them all away; so shall also the coming of the Son of man be.**

People living today are no different than those living in Noah's day who perished in the flood. The great comfort we receive is that it is still the day of Salvation. God presently is saving a great multitude which no man can number (Revelation 7:9). That is why this History book is written. That is why an organization like Family Radio, which is completely unrelated to any local church or denomination is so extensively and intensively sending the Gospel into the world. That Gospel seeks to be as faithful as possible to the authority of the Bible.

In the next chapter, we will seek to answer the big question, "What Must I Do To Be Saved?"

Chapter 13
What Must I Do To Become Saved?

Anyone who hears the Gospel message that Jesus Christ is the Savior of sinners and then seriously considers that message, eventually will begin to ask the question, "What must I do to become saved?" An additional question will follow, that is, "How can I know for certain that I have become saved?" These are the two most important questions that any human being can and should ask.

The correct answer to these questions requires an understanding of why we must be saved and also an understanding of what was required to make salvation possible. We will discover these truths as we learn, from the Bible, the actions that God must perform to save any individual at any time in history.

We will address the second question first.

Certainty of Salvation

How can I know for sure that I have become saved?

How can I know for sure that I have become saved? This has to be the most important question anyone on earth will ever face. To answer this question, we must first discover precisely what happens in a person's life at the moment he becomes born again.

There are three exceedingly important actions taken by God Himself that are absolutely required before anyone can experience salvation in his life. These three actions are required for every person who becomes saved. There are no exceptions.

Chosen of God

The first action performed by God on behalf of the individuals He plans to save was that, before the creation of the world, God chose every person that He would save.

We read in Ephesians 1:3-5:

Blessed be the God and Father of our Lord Jesus Christ, who hath blessed us with all spiritual blessings in heavenly places in Christ: according as he hath chosen us in him before the

foundation of the world, that we should be holy and without blame before him in love: having predestinated us unto the adoption of children by Jesus Christ to himself, according to the good pleasure of his will.

As God prepared to create this world and its billions of human inhabitants, He looked down the corridors of time and saw a miserable mass of humanity that was altogether in rebellion against Him. Even though God created mankind as perfect beings, in the image and likeness of God, the Bible is clear that no one is righteous before God and no one of himself will seek after God. God knew that mankind would rebel against Him. He also knew that no one would seek a right relationship with God.

We read in Romans 3:10-12:

As it is written, There is none righteous, no, not one: there is none that understandeth, there is none that seeketh after God. They are all gone out of the way, they are together become unprofitable; there is none that doeth good, no, not one.

> *in spite of the total disaster of mankind's rebellion*
> *against God, God made a decision to redeem*
> *some of the rebellious humans*

Yet, in spite of the total disaster of mankind's rebellion against God, God made a decision to redeem some of the rebellious humans so that they would not have to pay the consequences of their rebellion. The consequences are horrendously awful because the sin of the human race is horrendously awful.

And so, from before the foundation of the world, God chose those whom He wished to sanctify for Himself. His choice had nothing at all to do with any action or desire of mankind.

God declares in Romans 9:15:

. . . I will have mercy on whom I will have mercy, and I will have compassion on whom I will have compassion.

Through the emphasis of this all-important first action of God, God provides an enormous hope to every unsaved person. God insists that He is not a respecter of persons (Romans 2:11, Ephesians 6:9, Colossians 3:25). No nationality or class of people is likely to include more of God's elect than any other group. No class of sinners is farther outside the possibility of containing elect people than any other.

The Bible records the salvation of the adulterous woman in John Chapter 8, and it records the salvation of the criminal who was crucified alongside Jesus. Therefore, regardless of how great our sins may be, if we have a deep desire for salvation on God's terms, there is a definite possibility that we could be among God's elect. Given the fact that today, God is saving a great multitude (Revelation 7:9), we can know that, "It is possible that I, too, can be one of that great multitude who is saved."

The Chosen Ones Were Given to Christ

Those whom God chose to be redeemed or saved were given to the Lord Jesus Christ, as we read in John 6:37:

All that the Father giveth me shall come to me; and him that cometh to me I will in no wise cast out.

However, if Jesus is to have these chosen ones as His eternal possession, something had to be done about their sins. The perfect Law of God decreed that because mankind was created in the image of God, every individual must pay the penalty, demanded by God's Law, for their sin. Therefore, even though they were elected by God and given to Christ to become His eternal possession, Christ could not have them unless the payment for their sins was paid. God's Law decrees that the penalty for sin is eternal damnation, so effectively, those who were chosen and given to Christ would never be able to come into Christ's possession because they would be forevermore in hell paying for their sins.

That brings us to the second dramatic action that God took on behalf of those who become saved.

The Sin Bearer

When God viewed the universe, which He created at the beginning of time, He saw that there was no one He could utilize to bear the wrath of God on behalf of the elect or chosen by God who were given to Christ as His eternal possession. This is taught in Isaiah 63:5 and Ezekiel 22:30. However, God's perfect Law decreed that the penalty of eternal damnation must be paid before any individual could be allowed to enter into God's holy heaven. Every aspect of God's perfect Law had to be satisfied perfectly.

> *in an act of mercy and love that is unparalleled,*
> *Christ Himself became the sin bearer on behalf of those*
> *individuals who had been given to Him*

Therefore, in an act of mercy and love that is unparalleled, Christ Himself became the sin bearer on behalf of those individuals who had been given to Him. We read in Isaiah 53:6:

All we like sheep have gone astray; we have turned every one to his own way; and the LORD hath laid on him the iniquity of us all.

This is why Jesus had to take on a human nature. He was paying for man's sins, and therefore, Christ had to become the Son of man. He had to become a human being so that He would legally qualify to be a substitute or stand-in for the human beings He had come to save. He had to be the substitute who could bear the curse of God on behalf of those cursed individuals He had come to save. This is why He had to go to the cross. The fact that He was hanging on the cross declared and demonstrated to the world that He had become a curse. We read in Galatians 3:13:

Christ hath redeemed us from the curse of the law, being made a curse for us: for it is written, Cursed is every one that hangeth on a tree.

This is why He was forsaken by God. To be forever forsaken by God is one description of the awfulness of hell. We see this truth in the cry of Jesus when He was hanging on the cross. We read in Matthew 27:46:

. . . My God, my God, why hast thou forsaken me?

Only because Jesus was God and He never ceased to be infinite God could the hours of the cross experience be sufficient time to pay for each and every sin of each and every one chosen to be given to Christ. No sin of these elect persons could be left unpaid.

So now, there are many individuals in this world who, from before creation, were chosen to salvation and who have been given to Christ as His eternal possession, and whose sins have been totally and eternally covered because Jesus became their Savior by paying for their sins.

But one more great act of God is required. These individuals, who were chosen to salvation, are sinful humans. They do not know anything about God's plans for them. Like the rest of the human race that will never become saved, they are essentially a body and a soul. Their body is that part of their personality that is buried at the time they die. Their soul is their spirit essence that is just as real a part of their personality as their body. We know that the soul is completely substantive because in the case of a saved person, at the moment of his physical death, his soul leaves his body and is taken into heaven where he lives and reigns with Christ. Then at the end of the world, when Christ returns, God will resurrect his body (2 Corinthians 5:8, 1 Thessalonians 4:14-17).

However, the chosen individual now lives in this world like any individual who is not chosen to salvation. We read of him in Ephesians 2:1-3:

> **And you hath he quickened, who were dead in trespasses and sins; wherein in time past ye walked according to the course of this world, according to the prince of the power of the air, the spirit that now worketh in the children of disobedience: among whom also we all had our conversation in times past in the lusts of our flesh, fulfilling the desires of the flesh and of the mind; and were by nature the children of wrath, even as others.**

In his body, he lusts after sin, and in his soul, he lusts after sin. Before he becomes saved, he is as spiritually dead as any individual who will end up in hell eternally paying for his sins.

That brings us to the third giant act of God which He does on behalf of those whom Christ came to save.

The Miracle of the New Birth

> *God performs the miracle of giving the elect person a brand new resurrected soul.*

The third act performed by God on behalf of those who were given to Christ as His eternal possession is that God performs the miracle of giving the elect person a brand new resurrected soul. Jesus spoke to Nicodemus about this in John 3:5, where we read:

> **. . . Verily, verily, I say unto thee, Except a man be born of water and of the Spirit, he cannot enter into the kingdom of God.**

Ahead of that He said in John 3, verse 3:

. . . Verily, verily, I say unto thee, Except a man be born again, he cannot see the kingdom of God.

To be born of water and of the spirit means to be born of the Gospel (water), by the action of God the Holy Spirit (John 4:10-15; 7:38). God speaks of this action in Romans 10:17:

So then faith cometh by hearing, and hearing by the word of God.

In God's divine arrangement, He established the environment in which He saves people. That environment is the Bible, which is the only Word of God. Therefore, it is impossible for anyone in the world to become saved unless they hear words from God, and the only Word is the Bible. That is why, throughout the church age, God commanded the local congregations to send the Gospel into all the world. That is why, in our day, true Christians are to continue zealously to send the Gospel into the world but now, as individuals, the true believers serve as Christ's ambassadors.

> *...a baby can be saved as readily as a mature adult.*
> *A person with the mind of a two-year-old can be*
> *saved as readily as a college professor.*

God does the entire work of saving, and therefore, He can save an elect individual at any time during that person's life. The only requirement is that the individual be under the hearing of the Bible. At the moment of salvation, God gives that individual spiritual ears and a new eternal soul. Thus, a baby can be saved as readily as a mature adult. A person with the mind of a two-year-old can be saved as readily as a college professor.

At the cross, Christ paid for all the sins of the elect person. So, what remains to be done is that at an appropriate time known only to God, God will cause this person to actually experience the wonderful fact of salvation.

A Mighty Transformation

Now the question must be asked: How does salvation affect this person? What does it mean in his life that he is born again? Remember, before he was saved, in his whole personality, he was exactly like all the non-elect people who will never become saved. In body and in soul, he lusted after sin and was in rebellion against God.

But now, he has been given a new resurrected soul. In that part of his personality, he is a new creature in Christ. When he was born physically, he was a baby with a personality that consists of a body and a soul. At the moment of salvation, he is born again. He is given a new soul. It is a miracle our human minds cannot understand. There is no physical evidence of this transformation. However, the result of the miraculous transformation of his soul can be seen, that is, a brand new soul in a person's unchanged body will seriously impact and change his behavior. This is proven by God's declaration in 1 John 3:9:

Whosoever is born of God doth not commit sin; for his seed remaineth in him: and he cannot sin, because he is born of God.

In this verse, God teaches us that beginning at the moment of salvation, an enormous change occurs in the individual's personality. In his new resurrected soul, he cannot sin. Since sin is transgression of God's Law, it means that in the soul part of his personality, he cannot initiate sin. It means that in the soul part of his personality, he loves God and God's laws. It means that he always has a great desire to be obedient to all of the commandments of the Bible.

> *a true believer can never lose his salvation*

Since God has done everything to accomplish these three things that are necessary for the salvation of the elect individual, that person can be certain that he can never lose his salvation. Once he becomes saved, he has eternal security. God has already accomplished everything necessary to give him eternal life. Therefore, a true believer can never lose his salvation. The Bible says there is no sin nor anything else that can separate a true believer from the love of God (Romans 8:35-39).

But in his new soul, he still must live in his old body that was not at all changed at the moment of his salvation. Therefore, he has become a personality with two mutually exclusive desires. On the one hand, he always wants to be obedient to God's laws, and on the other hand, he still lusts after sin. This awkward situation is described by God as the Apostle Paul, under the inspiration of the Holy Spirit, declares in Romans 7:21-24:

I find then a law, that, when I would do good, evil is present with me. For I delight in the law of God after the inward man: but I see another law in my members, warring against the law of my mind, and bringing me into captivity to the law of sin which is in my members. O wretched man that I am! who shall deliver me from the body of this death?

To be free of our sinful body is the continuing desire of every true believer.

However, the tug of war that goes on in the saved personality is not static. There will be progress toward increasing victory for the new resurrected soul. This will be true because one other wonderful event occurred in that individual's personality at the moment of salvation. That event is that God the Holy Spirit has begun to indwell the life of that person. We read in Romans 8:9 that if we do not have the spirit of God, we are **"none of his."**

> *The indwelling presence of God Himself in the life and personality of the saved person further stimulates him to obey God and desire only that which is pleasing to God.*

We do not at all understand how Almighty God can dwell in a saved person's life. We must admit it is a complete mystery to us. But because the true people of God absolutely trust the Bible, they know that this mysterious fact is true. The indwelling presence of God Himself in the life and personality of the saved person further stimulates him to obey God and desire only that which is pleasing to God.

Moreover, the saved person has been taken out of Satan's dominion and has become an eternal citizen of Christ's kingdom. God tells us about this in Colossians 1:13, where He says:

Who hath delivered us from the power of darkness, and hath translated us into the kingdom of his dear Son.

In Philippians 3:20, we read that our "conversation" (better translated "commonwealth"), that is, our citizenship, is in heaven. This is true for every individual who becomes saved.

Thus, at the moment of salvation, many factors are at work in the life of the newly-saved individual that cause a very decided and important change in his conduct and desires. He will understand and identify with statements such as those found in Psalm 119 and elsewhere in the Bible.

A few samples of the beautiful language found in Psalm 119 that demonstrate the true believer's love and respect of the Bible follow.

Verse 10: **"With my whole heart have I sought thee: O let me not wander from thy commandments."**

Verse 11: **"Thy word have I hid in mine heart, that I might not sin against thee."**

Verse 16: **"I will delight myself in thy statutes: I will not forget thy word."**

Verse 24: **"Thy testimonies also are my delight and my counsellors."**

Verse 47: **"And I will delight myself in thy commandments, which I have loved."**

Verse 77: **"Let thy tender mercies come unto me, that I may live: for thy law is my delight."**

Verse 97: **"O how love I thy law! It is my meditation all the day."**

> *Anyone who has truly become saved will increasingly experience these desires and motivations in his life.*

These kinds of statements can be found all through the Bible. Anyone who has truly become saved will increasingly experience these desires and motivations in his life. Thus, he recognizes and identifies with the truth expressed in 1 John 2:3-5, where we read:

And hereby we do know that we know him, if we keep his commandments. He that saith, I know him, and keepeth not his

commandments, is a liar, and the truth is not in him. But whoso keepeth his word, in him verily is the love of God perfected: hereby know we that we are in him.

The true believer knows that the commandments of God include the whole Bible. He also knows that awful feeling he has when he allows the lustful desires of his body to cause him to sin. He empathizes with a true man of God, David, who fell into grievous sin. And then David, under the inspiration of the Holy Spirit, recorded his heartfelt remorse, which we read about in Psalm 51.

So, God has to do these three things, and this is why no one can get himself saved. Every human being knows that he must answer to God. But until he becomes saved, he wants to get right with God on his own terms and with his own salvation plan. Therefore, he will not call upon God in a God-pleasing way until God has saved him (John 6:44, Romans 3:10-12, Ephesians 2:2-5).

Fear and Trembling

One aspect of the truly saved person's character is his recognition of the holiness and righteousness of God and the fact that God is the righteous Judge of all the earth. In Philippians 2:12, God declares:

. . . work out your own salvation with fear and trembling.

The salvation the genuine believer is to "work out" in his life is the salvation that God has given him. But as he grows in grace (2 Peter 3:18), that is, as he increasingly lives to God's glory and away from following the sinful desires of his unsaved body, he does so with fear and trembling.

This is a surprising statement because we might expect that as a result of salvation, all fear of God would be removed. To still tremble and fear before God would appear to be altogether alien to the wonderful security the saved person has been given, for example, he knows that Christ has paid for all his sins, and he knows he will never be threatened by the possibility of hell.

The true believer is aware that he himself still has sins even though he is dramatically more obedient to God's laws than he was before he was saved.

We must remember, however, the saved person is indwelt by the Holy Spirit. The saved person also has begun to increasingly love and respect everything the Bible teaches. Therefore, he learns and becomes increasingly aware of the greatness of God. He knows that God is the Almighty God who spoke and brought this tremendous universe into existence. He knows that God is the Almighty Judge who is completely aware of even the smallest sin in every human being. He knows that God is so righteous that even the smallest sin is sufficient to cause a person to be eternally damned. The true believer is aware that he himself still has sins even though he is dramatically more obedient to God's laws than he was before he was saved. He is thoroughly aware of the fact that except for the mercy and grace of God, he deserves eternal damnation.

A poor illustration of this might be offered. Suppose that by his own stupid and uncalled for action, a person placed himself in an exceedingly dangerous situation. For example, we might think of a child playing with matches. The impact of this action is that he causes the house in which he lives to burn to the ground. By some miracle, at great cost to his rescuer, he is brought to safety. And for days afterward, this child has nightmares as he contemplates his narrow escape. Furthermore, for the rest of his life, he may have a phobia, that is, an enormous fear of fire, even though he is never again threatened by fire. This, of course, is a poor illustration of the life of someone who has become saved, but it may help us to see what God means when He uses the phrase "fear and trembling."

On the one hand, because of his intense love and trust in the Bible, the believer increasing knows he is eternally secure in Christ, and he knows that he can never be threatened by hell. He knows that all of his sins have been covered by Christ. On the other hand, the more he becomes acquainted with the teachings of the Bible, the more he recognizes that he rightly deserves the awful wrath of God as payment for his sins. He is aware that it was only God's mercy and grace that caused his salvation. He therefore trembles in fear and awe before God. He recognizes that his salvation was entirely undeserved.

But Perfect Love Casts Out Fear

It is true that the Bible teaches that perfect love casts out fear. We read in 1 John 4:18:

There is no fear in love; but perfect love casteth out fear: because fear hath torment. He that feareth is not made perfect in love.

We might conclude that because the true believer has experienced the perfect love of Christ, he should no longer fear. But that conclusion is contrary to all the verses that teach that a characteristic of the believer is that he fears God (Acts 9:31,10:35; Philippians 2:12; I Peter 2:17; Proverbs 1:7; Ecclesiastes 8:12-13). How then are we to understand 1 John 4:18, which teaches that perfect love casts out fear? The solution comes when we learn the Biblical definition of love. In John 14:21, we read:

He that hath my commandments, and keepeth them, he it is that loveth me . . .

In John 14, verse 23, this law of God is reiterated:

Jesus answered and said unto him, If a man love me, he will keep my words . . .

In other words, love is altogether identified with obedience to God's Commandments, the Bible. Regardless of how convincingly an individual tries to proclaim his love for Christ, the litmus test of his love is his fidelity, his obedience to God's Law Book, the Bible.

But that means that perfect love would require perfect obedience. Perfect obedience, however, is impossible until God's elect receive their new resurrected bodies, and those will not be given until the last day when Christ returns. In the meanwhile, in new resurrected souls, which true believers received at the moment of their salvation, they continue to live in a body that still lusts after sin. Therefore, at the present time, they do not have perfect love, and therefore, they cannot live without fear.

Earlier in our study, we learned one reason why true believers fear and tremble before God. But more should be said about that. When David, a man after God's own heart, a man greatly loved by God, committed sin, God tells us the reaction of this man's heart in Psalm 51. The entire psalm records David's reaction, but we will quote only one verse.

Psalm 51:11:

Cast me not away from thy presence; and take not thy holy spirit from me.

David had received eternal life. He was eternally secure in the kingdom of God. How could he say the words of this psalm, which God the Holy Spirit gave him to say. The answer comes when we realize the enormous consequences of sin. Every sin requires the penalty of eternal damnation. Therefore, when the true believer sins, two truths should permeate his whole personality.

> *...the true believer fears and trembles as he realizes that*
> *each time he sins, this sin, too, had to be laid*
> *upon our blessed Savior.*

The first truth is that the sins he commits after he has become saved had to be paid for by the Lord Jesus Christ. It is true, of course, that God knew from the beginning that these sins in the life of the true believer would occur, and therefore, He has already laid them on Jesus. But that does not change the fact that these sins are being committed by a person who has learned how dreadful sin is and the enormous payment for sin that is required by God's perfect justice. Thus, the true believer fears and trembles as he realizes that each time he sins, this sin, too, had to be laid upon our blessed Savior.

The second truth is that the true believer becomes increasingly acquainted with the seriousness of sin and the awful penalty that God's perfect justice demands as payment for sin. He also recognizes that each time he sins, he is engaging in an act of rebellion against his beloved Savior. On the one hand, he knows that his sin is covered by Jesus' shed blood and will never be counted against him. On the other hand, he recognizes that forgiveness of his sin is only because of the completely undeserved mercy and grace of God. Therefore, the fact that he dared to sin again causes him to live his life in fear and trembling before God and that stimulates his desire that he not sin, that, indeed, he might live more and more obediently to all of God's laws.

Thus, we understand that the saved person will have an entirely different lifestyle and an entirely different attitude toward sin, and God, and the Bible, from that which is found in the life of the unsaved.

What Must I Do To Become Saved?

The logical question then is: What can I do to become saved? With all of the information I have learned concerning salvation, I know that the answer must be: <u>I cannot do anything.</u> Salvation is entirely the work of God. I am entirely dependent upon God's sovereign mercy to choose me and pay for my sins and make me a new creature in Christ. I must patiently wait upon the mercy of God.

Is there no hope for me? Well, in fact, there is great hope. <u>It is entirely possible that I, too, despite the enormous sins I have committed, could be one of those who are chosen by God to become saved.</u> And because I have learned that the environment that God has established for saving His elect is the hearing of the

Word of God, I want to read and listen to the Bible as much as possible.
Remember what the Bible says in Romans 10:17:

So then faith cometh by hearing, and hearing by the word of God.

The fact that I carefully read the Bible will not guarantee my salvation
but it will provide several great blessings to me, including the following.

1. It will place me in an environment in which God can save me if He
so desires.

2. It will make me more acquainted with God in all of His majesty and
glory.

3. It will make me more aware of my sins and my need of salvation.

4. I will realize more fully that God is merciful.

5. I will learn that if it is God's plan to save me, He will do so in His
own time. Therefore, I am to patiently wait on Him.

As I carefully read and listen to the Bible and become increasingly aware
of my sins, I can pray and I can plead with God. I can beg God for His mercy and
for some understanding of what I am reading, and I can pray for Him to make
me more obedient to His Law Book, the Bible. I will become increasingly aware
that the words of the Bible are God's voice speaking directly to me.

The Bible gives us a beautiful statement that tells us to wait upon God in
Lamentations 3:26, where we read:

**It is good that a man should both hope and quietly wait for the
salvation of the LORD.**

We must wait upon God for salvation because, as we learned earlier in
this study, God must do all the work that is required to bring about salvation.

God Tests Us

We have learned that God must do all the work to accomplish salvation.
But why then did God the Holy Spirit, speaking through the Apostle Paul,
command the jailor of Philippi to believe on the Lord Jesus Christ?

Remember the jailor's question to Paul and Silas in Acts 16:30 and 31, where we read:

> **. . . Sirs, what must I do to be saved? And they said, Believe on the Lord Jesus Christ, and thou shalt be saved, and thy house.**

On Pentecost day, the people asked, "what shall we do?" Why did God, through the Apostle Peter, answer by saying in Acts 2:38:

> **. . . Repent, and be baptized every one of you in the name of Jesus Christ for the remission of sins, and ye shall receive the gift of the Holy Ghost.**

Why does God say in Romans 10:9:

> **That if thou shalt confess with thy mouth the Lord Jesus, and shalt believe in thine heart that God hath raised him from the dead, thou shalt be saved.**

Why does God tell us in Romans 10:13:

> **For whosoever shall call upon the name of the Lord shall be saved.**

Why does God say in Revelation 3:20:

> **Behold, I stand at the door, and knock: if any man hear my voice, and open the door, I will come in to him, and will sup with him, and he with me.**

> *...the correct understanding of any Bible verse*
> *can come only as that verse is carefully examined in the light*
> *of everything the Bible teaches that may*
> *relate to that verse*

Unfortunately, when theologians and Bible teachers have examined these verses, they seem to have forgotten that the correct understanding of any Bible verse can come only as that verse is carefully examined in the light of everything the Bible teaches that may relate to that verse. These verses apparently teach that before God saves someone, that person is required to believe, repent, and obey. However, when we examine the whole Bible, we discover the sad news that when God is speaking to unsaved people, He is speaking to spiritual corpses. Before we are saved, we are absolutely and totally unable to obey any of the above commands. As we learned earlier in this study, God must do all the work to save us.

But why then did God give these commands to believe and to repent when mankind is totally incapable of obeying these commands? In our consideration of that question, at least two very important truths must be kept in mind.

The first truth is that God created mankind in His image and in His likeness. Therefore, God holds mankind completely accountable for his actions. Even though mankind will not and cannot obey these commands, God addresses all of us as those who were created by God to obey these commands. Therefore, God can rightfully expect mankind to obey His commands. However, because of mankind's rebellion against God, we are so infected by sin that we can never obey God as we should. It is only after a person becomes saved that that individual can begin to obey God in a God-glorifying way.

A second major reason why God gives these imperative commands to believe, to repent, etc., is to test man. By means of these commands, God puts man on trial. The issue is does he trust in God alone for salvation or does he trust in his own ability or something or someone other than God? Remember, God gives the command to believe, etc., to all of mankind. However, in the same Law Book, the Bible, God informs us that we are spiritually dead and we are slaves of sin and of Satan. Therefore, we are totally incapable of obeying these commands. Anyone who relies upon obeying these commands somehow by his own effort or will or ability will not have true salvation because his reliance is not sourced and founded in God. In fact, this person, in effect, has come up with a "do-it-yourself" salvation.

Therefore, when God commands us to believe, etc., as He does very plainly in so many verses of the Bible, we should understand that we cannot obey these commands. We should realize the truth of John 6:44, where God says:

No man can come to me, except the Father which hath sent me draw him: and I will raise him up at the last day.

...only God can save us and that He must do all of the work required to save us.

We should, therefore, realize that only God can save us and that He must do all of the work required to save us.

Unfortunately, in our human depravity, we hear and read these commands to believe, to repent, etc., and we believe that somehow we can begin to obey them. At the moment we believe we can obey these commands, we are guilty to some degree of putting our trust in our ability to assist with our salvation. In this study, we learned that the idea that we can assist in any way is impossible. Not only is it not possible but it means we have a "do-it-yourself" salvation plan. Unfortunately, any "do-it-yourself" plan guarantees that those who follow it will end up under eternal damnation. Those who conclude that they can sufficiently obey God's commands so that through their obedience they can be right with God are rejecting the Law of God that declares there must be payment for our sins, and only God in the person of the Lord Jesus Christ can make that payment and save us.

Lazarus is Resurrected to Show Us How God Saves

In His patient mercy God gives us a vivid illustration of what is required to become saved when He brings a dead man named Lazarus to life. We read about this true historical event in John Chapter 11. Lazarus had been dead for four days. The Bible records that he stank (John 11:39). So it was abundantly obvious that he was a stinking corpse and there was no vestige of life remaining in that corpse. But Christ stood outside of that tomb and commanded, **"Lazarus, come forth"** (John 11:43).

Jesus was about to demonstrate how He brings spiritually dead people to spiritual life. When He stood outside the tomb of Lazarus, He declared in John 11:25-26:

> **. . . I am the resurrection, and the life: he that believeth in me, though he were dead, yet shall he live: and whosoever liveth and believeth in me shall never die. Believest thou this?**

Clearly, it was Christ's intention to bring the physically dead Lazarus to life as a dynamic illustration of how Christ can and does bring spiritual life to those whom He came to save.

Before a person is saved, he is a spiritual corpse. He is as spiritually dead as Lazarus was physically dead. In the historical event of Lazarus being brought to life, Jesus demonstrates how He does all of the work that is required to bring an individual to salvation.

Jesus commanded that stinking corpse of Lazarus to come out of the tomb. Because Jesus was speaking the Word of God, that stinking corpse was now in an environment in which he was under the hearing of the Word of God. This is precisely parallel to the requirement that those whom God plans to save must be under the hearing of the Word of God.

Jesus' command to the dead Lazarus is parallel to the commands God gives to spiritually dead people, that is, they are to call upon Him, they are to believe, etc. These are the commands they hear when they listen to or read the Bible. This meets the requirement of God's Law expressed in Romans 10:17, where we read:

. . . faith cometh by hearing, and hearing by the word of God.

Returning to John Chapter 11 and the dead Lazarus, could that stinking corpse in the tomb hear the voice of Jesus? Was there some way that the dead Lazarus could obey that command? It is obvious that such a response to Jesus' command was impossible. There was no possible way that Lazarus could obey that command.

> *...when God commands unsaved mankind to believe and to repent, there is no way possible for the unsaved (that is, the spiritually dead) to obey these commands.*

Likewise, when God commands unsaved mankind to believe and to repent, there is no way possible for the unsaved (that is, the spiritually dead) to obey these commands.

However, that stinking corpse in the tomb did obey the command of Jesus. John 11, verse 44, declares:

And he that was dead came forth, bound hand and foot with graveclothes: and his face was bound about with a napkin. Jesus saith unto them, Loose him, and let him go.

How could that be? Remember, Jesus had said, **"I am the resurrection, and the life."** When Jesus commanded the dead Lazarus to come out of the tomb, Jesus as eternal God, who is the creator of life, had to give physical life to that stinking corpse. Jesus had to give the physically dead Lazarus ears to hear and strength and a will to respond to Christ's command to him to come forth.

Likewise, God commands the spiritually dead of the world to believe, to repent, to become saved. But with that command, God creates eternal life in the souls of those He has chosen to salvation.

The Bible declares, **"many are called, but few are chosen"** (Matthew 22:14). That is, every individual who reads or hears the Gospel is being commanded to believe in Jesus as their Savior. But no one can or wants to believe. Spiritually, everyone is a stinking corpse.

Yet, within the spiritual graveyard of the world, there is one here, one there, one in another place who begins to believe and who finds in their life a strong desire to obey the Bible. What has happened to those few? Their spiritual experience was precisely like the physical experience of the dead Lazarus. Jesus, through His Word the Bible, commanded them to believe, and Jesus applied His Word to their life and created within them a new soul in which they were given eternal life. This could only happen because they had been chosen by God from before the beginning of creation.

Now we can understand the illustration of Revelation 3:20, where we read:

> **Behold, I stand at the door, and knock: if any man hear my voice, and open the door, I will come in to him, and will sup with him, and he with me.**

> *...when Jesus knocks on the door of the sinner's heart,*
> *giving the command to believe, at the same time, He*
> *creates eternal life in the corpse that lies behind that door*
> *if that individual is one of God's chosen people.*

The individual behind that door is spiritually a stinking corpse. He could never hear that knock on the door. But when Jesus knocks on the door of the sinner's heart, giving the command to believe, at the same time, He creates eternal life in the corpse that lies behind that door if that individual is one of God's chosen people. At the moment that person is given eternal life, he also receives spiritual ears to hear and understand the Bible, and he is given the desire to obey God's commands, and he does obey God's commands.

Truly, we should be learning that God alone can save us. We are totally dependent on Him to do all the work.

Is There Hope for Me?

Does that mean that the possibility of becoming saved is hopeless? Yes, it is indeed hopeless if we are depending in any way upon our efforts, our faith, our desires, our obedience, to provide even the smallest contribution to our salvation. Such thinking is evidence of an arrogant disregard concerning all that the Bible teaches about the
astounding, sublime provision of God. It means we are trusting in a salvation plan that can never save and actually makes a mockery of God's perfect salvation plan.

But when we understand God's salvation plan, that He is the only one who can do all the work required for salvation, we can have hope, abundant hope. We are living in a day when God is saving a great multitude which no man can number (Revelation 7:9). Moreover, the Bible's declaration that God has elected certain individuals and given them to Christ, and that Christ has paid for all of their sins, provides enormous hope to unsaved individuals.

> *Any unsaved person who has an intense desire to become saved and recognizes that he can become saved only on God's terms, possibly could be one of God's elect or chosen ones.*

Any unsaved person who has an intense desire to become saved and recognizes that he can become saved only on God's terms, possibly could be one of God's elect or chosen ones. Since God's election plan has nothing to do with our personal worthiness (we have none), and regardless of how great and terrible an individual's sins have been, he or she could just as readily be one of God's elect as any saved individual. Indeed, God's elective plan gives great encouragement to the unsaved person who begins to earnestly desire that he, too, might become saved.

There are at least seven additional truths revealed in the Bible that should be of great encouragement to the individual who truly wishes that his sins, also, were covered by the blood of Jesus. We have already made reference to some of these truths. However, they are so important that we will briefly outline them again.

1. Presently, it is the day of salvation. We have correctly learned that God is no longer saving people by utilizing the efforts of the local congregations, its leaders, or its people. (For more information, contact Family Radio and request the free book, *The End of the Church Age . . . and After.*) However, outside of the local congregations, a great number of individuals are faithfully bringing the true Gospel to the world. They are witnessing individually and banding together collectively to send the Gospel into the world by radio and other methods of mass communication, and **"a great multitude which no man can number"** (Revelation 7:9) is being saved. Any unsaved person potentially could be one of that great multitude. What a blessing to know that we are living at a time when all over the world, many individuals are becoming saved.

2. The setting or the environment in which God saves is the hearing of the Word of God, the Bible. The Bible declares in Romans 10:17:

So then faith cometh by hearing, and hearing by the word of God.

> *we parents want our babies and all of our children to be*
> *under the hearing of the Word of God*

Today, a higher percentage of people are literate and have the Bible available in their own native language than ever before in the history of the world. What an enormous encouragement that anyone can place himself, together with the unsaved members of his family, under the hearing of the Bible. In many instances, this can be done by listening to those who faithfully read the Bible and faithfully teach the Bible on radio broadcasts such as those of Family Radio. He can also do this by personally reading the Bible. Indeed, the environment for God to save people is more hopeful than ever before in history. For this reason, we parents want our babies and all of our children to be under the hearing of the Word of God. That is what makes radio an especially valuable and important tool that can be used to make the Gospel available to large multitudes of people.

3. Christ came to save sinners. He did not come to save the self-righteous, those who think of themselves as decent, moral people who trust that their righteous conduct is an inducement for God to look favorably upon them. He came to save sinners! What an encouragement to read about the criminal who was crucified at the same time Jesus was crucified. At first, this criminal showed his utter contempt for Jesus. We read in Matthew 27:41-44:

Likewise also the chief priests mocking him, with the scribes and elders, said, He saved others; himself he cannot save. If he be the King of Israel, let him now come down from the cross, and we will believe him. He trusted in God; let him deliver him now, if he will have him: for he said, I am the Son of God. <u>The thieves also, which were crucified with him, cast the same in his teeth.</u>

Yet marvelously, just a few minutes or hours before this crucified criminal died, he asked Jesus for mercy, and he received the answer that assured him and assures us that, in that most improbable time and location, he had become saved.

We read in Luke 23:39-43:

And one of the malefactors which were hanged railed on him, saying, If thou be Christ, save thyself and us. But the other answering rebuked him, saying, Dost not thou fear God, seeing thou art in the same condemnation? And we indeed justly; for we receive the due reward of our deeds: but this man hath done nothing amiss. And he said unto Jesus, Lord, remember me when thou comest into thy kingdom. And Jesus said unto him, Verily I say unto thee, To day shalt thou be with me in paradise.

This grievous sinner was under the hearing of the Word because he heard Jesus speak to Mary, to the Apostle John, and to God Himself. And right then and there, this despicable sinner was given eternal life. Thus, regardless of how great his sins may be, the unsaved sinner can know that Jesus came for sinners. What a magnificent encouragement!

4. <u>Jesus is not a respecter of persons.</u> That is, no class of people is more likely to become saved than any other. A person may be shunned by society, and regarded as being one of the "untouchables" by his fellow humans, but in the Bible, God gives examples of individuals who became saved who were scorned and despised by the congregation of Jesus' day. We are reminded of this by the salvation of the Samaritan woman (John 4:4-42), the tax collector, Zacchaeus (Luke 19:2-8), the leper (Luke 17:12-19), the criminal who was executed for his crimes (Luke 23:39-43), and the adulterous woman (John 8:1-11). All of these people were looked upon as the scum of society but God saved each one of them. Thus, we see clearly that God is not a respecter of persons. How wonderful this fact should be to any unsaved person.

> *...outside the local congregations, throughout the world God continues to demonstrate His unfathomable mercy.*

5. <u>God is merciful.</u> True, mercy is no longer found in the local congregations where their pastors, elders, deacons, and Bible teachers minister to those poor people. What a terrible truth that is! But outside the local congregations, throughout the world God continues to demonstrate His unfathomable mercy. God is a God of mercy. Remember what we read in Psalm 103:8:

The LORD is merciful and gracious, slow to anger, and plenteous in mercy.

And in Lamentations 3:31-32:

For the Lord will not cast off for ever: but though he cause grief, yet will he have compassion according to the multitude of his mercies.

6. <u>We can personally make known to God our intense desire to become saved.</u> We can beg, beseech, and plead with God for salvation. Praying to God is work that we do, so we know that praying to God will not guarantee or contribute to our salvation. But we can know that as we cry to God, He will know of our desire to become saved. Jesus Himself gives the illustration of the publican who prayed for God's mercy. We read in Luke 18:13-14:

And the publican, standing afar off, would not lift up so much as his eyes unto heaven, but smote upon his breast, saying, God be merciful to me a sinner. I tell you, this man went down to his house justified rather than the other: for every one that exalteth himself shall be abased; and he that humbleth himself shall be exalted.

7. <u>We need never lose the hope for salvation.</u> If God plans to save us, He will do so in His own time. He may save us early in our life, or salvation may come hours before our death. We are never to attempt to dictate to God the time frame of our salvation, if indeed it is God's intention to save us. Remember what we read in Lamentations 3:26:

It is good that a man should both hope and quietly wait for the salvation of the LORD.

And God gives us so much comfort in Psalm 62:5-8:

My soul, wait thou only upon God; for my expectation is from him. He only is my rock and my salvation: he is my defence; I shall not be moved. In God is my salvation and my glory: the rock of my strength, and my refuge, is in God. Trust in him at all times; ye people, pour out your heart before him: God is a refuge for us.

As a person patiently waits upon the Lord, he may be filled with great anxiety. To become saved is a serious and important matter. To remain unsaved is awful.

Wonderfully, God gives us much comfort by the promise of Philippians 4:6:

Be careful [anxious] for nothing; but in every thing by prayer and supplication with thanksgiving let your requests be made known unto God.

Then God gives us the assurance of Philippians 4, verse 7:

And the peace of God, which passeth all understanding, shall keep your hearts and minds through Christ Jesus.

Thus, God is comforting us by encouraging us to rest entirely in Him. He is encouraging us to tell Him all about our anxiety. Marvelously, He is absolutely faithful and trustworthy to do His perfect will. We are to rest in His almighty arms.

In the meanwhile, we can hear God's voice as we continue to carefully and prayerfully read the Bible. And each time anxiety strikes us, again and again, we can come boldly to God's throne of grace to tell God all about it. HOW MERCIFUL GOD IS!

Chronology of the Judges

The Exodus	1447 B.C.
Entrance into Canaan	1407 B.C.
Initial 40 year period in Canaan During this period the conquest of Canaan occurred under Joshua and Othniel delivered Israel	1407-1367 B.C.
Next 80-year period in Canaan During this period Ehud and Shamgar delivered Israel	1367-1287 B.C.
Next 40 year period in Canaan Deborah and Barak were deliverers during this period	1287-1247 B.C.
Gideon judged	1247-1207 B.C.
Abimelech ruled	1207-1204 B.C.
Tola judged	1204-1181 B.C.
Jair judged	1181-1159 B.C.
Jephthah judged	1159-1153 B.C.
Ibzan judged	1153-1146 B.C.
Elon judged	1146-1136 B.C.
Abdon judged	1136-1128 B.C.
Samson judged	1128-1108 B.C.
Eli judged	1108-1068 B.C.
Ark in Philistines' hands	1068-1067 B.C.
Samuel judged	1067-1047 B.C.
Saul reigned as king	1047-1007 B.C.
David reigned	1007-967 B.C.
Solomon reigned	971-931 B.C.
Foundation of temple laid in fourth year of Solomon's reign	967 B.C..

Kings of Judah	Year (B.C.)	Kings of Israel	Year (B.C.)
Rehoboam	931-914	Jeroboam	931-910
Abijam	914-911		
Asa	911-870	Nadab	910-909
		Baasha	909-886
		Elah	886-885
		Zimri	885
		Tibni	885-880
Jehoshaphat	871-846	Omri	885-874
Jehoram (Joram)	854-842	Ahab	874-853
Ahaziah (Jehoahaz)	842-841	Ahaziah	854-853
Athaliah (Azariah)	841-835	Joram (Jehoram)	853-841
Joash (Jehoash)	835-795	Jehu	841-813
Amaziah	796-767	Jehoahaz	813-796
Uzziah (Azariah)	789-737	Jehoash (Joash)	798-782
		Jeroboam	792-751
		Zecariah	751-750
		Shallum	750
		Menahem	750-740
Jotham	738-718	Pekahiah	740-738
Ahaz	730-714	Pekah	738-718
Hezekiah	715-686	Hoshea	718-709
Manasseh	697-642		
Amon	642-640		
Josiah	640-609		
Jehoahaz	609		
Jehoiakim	609-598		
Jehoiachin (Jeconiah, Coniah)	608-597		
Zedekiah	597-587		

Scripture Index
Time Has An End

Who or What is Family Radio?

Family Radio's official name is Family Stations, Inc. It is an altogether unique non-profit corporation begun in 1958 with the express purpose of sending the Christian Gospel into the world. It is a worldwide non-commercial ministry supported entirely by gifts from its listeners. Its president and general manager, Harold Camping is a full time volunteer, receiving no salary or other financial compensation. In reality Family Radio regards the Lord Jesus Christ as its Chief Executive Officer, because it operates altogether under the authority of the Bible. The Board of Directors and all of its employees are regarded as servants who serve Jesus Christ as their King.

We at Family Radio constantly endeavor to send throughout the world all of the teachings of the Bible as extensively and as intensively as possible. Therefore, we broadcast in nineteen of the major languages of the world so that as many people as possible can hear the true Gospel in their own language.

Family Radio also sponsors a correspondence School of the Bible. Anyone may join free of charge to learn Bible Hebrew, Bible Greek, and receive instruction in many books of the Bible.

Family Radio has an intense desire to be altogether faithful to the teachings of the Bible, both in the conduct of its employees and in the Biblical messages it sends into the world. Therefore, the programs sent out by radio broadcasts, the Internet, etc., are constantly reviewed to make certain that the messages being aired are faithful to the Bible.

For most of the years of its existence, Family Radio served as a great help in building up local churches that were reasonably faithful to the Bible. This was so because the Bible indicated that the local congregations were a divine institution made up of those who adhered to the teachings of the Bible. These local churches were divinely mandated to send the Gospel into all of the world.

At Family Radio we emphatically teach that the whole Bible is the Word of God. We believe that, in the original languages in which the Bible was written, every Word was from the mouth of God, and consequently, is never to be altered and must be obeyed. The Bible alone, and in its entirety, is the Word of God. Therefore, we reject the phenomena of tongues, visions, voices, etc., as having any part in the true Gospel since the Scriptures have been completed.

On Family Radio we clearly teach the Biblical truth that all mankind are sinners and, therefore, are subject to God's righteous wrath. We further teach the sad truth that because man by nature is spiritually dead, he will not and cannot come to God on God's terms. However, God in His wonderful love has chosen a people for Himself for whom the Lord Jesus Christ did all the work necessary to save them. In God's own timetable He applies the Word of God to their hearts and saves them. This is the Bible's grand message of salvation that Family Radio wishes to send to every nation of the world.

We also insistently teach the Biblical truth that at the end of the world every human not saved must stand trial at the Judgment Throne of Christ, who is the Judge of all the earth. Those who stand trial will be found guilty of their sins and will be sentenced to eternal damnation.

In its intense study of the Bible ,Family Radio has discovered that a great amount of Biblical evidence points to the all-important fact that the world has come very close to its end. It has also discovered from carefully studying the Bible that, in a sense, this end of the world judgment has already begun, because judgment must begin with the house of God (I Peter 4:17, Hebrews 10:30).

Therefore, now that we have learned from the Bible that God's judgment is upon the house of God, which are the local congregations, we are now compelled to teach the Biblical truth that God has shifted the final task of world evangelism to individual Christians who are outside of a local congregation. In obedience to these Biblical teachings, Family Radio, which is completely outside of any church institution, and which is supported and administered by individual believers, does teach that today, as we are heading for the end of this world's existence, we should not be a part of a local church.

However, we do emphatically teach the Biblical truth that God is still adding to His eternal Church. This eternal Church consists of people all over the world whom God has planned to save as they come under the hearing of the true Gospel.

Therefore, Family Radio continues to send the true Gospel throughout the world-- by shortwave radio, by A.M. and F.M. radio, by the Internet, by satellite broadcasting, by T.V., and by printed materials. Its constant theme is the encouragement of people to carefully read the Bible, praying for obedience to the Word of God.

Listed on this and the following pages are both domestic and international information how you, a loved one or friend may recieve Family Radio.

Family Radio Location and Frequency Guide

Alabama Station
Birmingham	89.5 FM	WBFR

Alabama Translators
Mountain Brook		
	104.1 FM	WBFR
Notasulga/Auburn		
	90.3 FM	KEAR

Arizona Station
Phoenix	88.3 FM	KPHF

Arizona Translators
Phoenix	88.9 FM	KEAR
Prescott	88.1 FM	KEAR

Arkansas Translator
Jonesboro	88.3 FM	KEAR

California Stations
Bakersfield	91.3 FM	KFRB
Chico	89.1 FM	KHAP
El Cajon	910 AM	KECR
Fresno	90.3 FM	KFNO
Le Grand	89.9 FM	KEFR
Long Beach	1280 AM	KFRN
Sacramento	1210 AM	KEBR
	88.1 FM	KEDR
San Francisco	106.9 FM	KEAR
Soledad	89.9 FM	KFRS
Ukiah	89.5 FM	KPRA

California Translators
Banning	91.3 FM	KEAR
Fort Bragg	91.9 FM	KEAR
Garberville	94.9 FM	KPRA
Gonzales	98.7 FM	KEAR
Grover Beach	101.9 FM	KEAR
La Quinta	89.9 FM	KEAR
Laytonville	96.1 FM	KPRA
Palmdale	96.1 FM	KEAR
Palm Springs	101.5 FM	KEAR
Paso Robles	106.9 FM	KEAR
Porterville	91.9 FM	KEAR
Redding	101.5 FM	KHAP
Richvale	90.5 FM	KEAR
Ridgecrest	90.5 FM	KEAR
River Pines	93.3 FM	KEDR
Salida	95.5 FM	KEAR
San Luis Obispo	89.7 FM	KEAR
Smith River	88.7 FM	KEAR
So. Lake Tahoe	92.5 FM	KEAR
Stockton	105.9 FM	KEDR
Tehachapi (Fairmont)		
	91.7 FM	KEAR

Colorado Translators
Grand Junction	90.7 FM	KEAR
Pueblo	88.1 FM	KEAR

Connecticut Stations
Vernon	1170 AM	WCTF

Delaware Translators
Dover	103.3 FM	WFSI

Florida Stations
Florida City	88.5 FM	WMFL

(Continued)

Jacksonville   88.7 FM   WJFR
Okeechobee   91.7 FM   WWFR
Okeechobee
                  Shortwave WYFR
St. Petersburg   91.7 FM   WFTI

Florida Translator
West Palm Beach
                  100.3 FM WWFR

Georgia Station
Columbus   90.5 FM   WFRC

Georgia Translators
Albany   88.5 FM   KEAR
La Grange   91.9 FM   KEAR

Illinois Station
Joliet   91.9 FM   WJCH

Illinois Translator
Rockford   94.5 FM   WJCH

Indiana Translator
La Porte   106.9 FM WJCH

Iowa Stations
Des Moines   91.3 FM   KDFR
Shenandoah   920 AM   KYFR

Iowa Translators
Amana   89.7 FM   KEAR
Ames   89.1 FM   KDFR
Cedar Rapids   95.1 FM   KEAR
Fort Dodge   89.1 FM   KEAR
Ottumwa   88.9 FM   KEAR

Kansas Station
Emporia   90.7 FM   KPOR

Louisiana Translators
Lafayette   89.7 FM   KEAR
Lake Charles   98.3 FM   KTXB

Maryland Station
Annapolis   107.9 FM WFSI

Maryland Translators
Frederick   93.5 FM   WFSI
Hagerstown   93.5 FM   WFSI

Michigan Station
Schoolcraft   89.5 FM   WOFR

Michigan Translator
Wakelee   89.7 FM   KEAR

Minnesota Translator
Duluth   88.5 FM   KEAR

Montana Station
Butte   83.3 FM   KFRD

Montana Translators
Billings   99.7 FM   KEAR
Great Falls   91.3 FM   KEAR
                  102.3 FM KEAR
Shepherd   88.9 FM   KEAR

Nebraska Translators
Grand Island   90.7 FM   KEAR

Nevada Translators
Carson City   89.1 FM   KEAR
Reno   98.7 FM   KEAR

New Jersey Stations
Camden   106.9 FM WKDN
Newark   94.7 FM   WFME

New Jersey Translators
Atlantic City	89.3 FM	WKDN
Cape May	92.3 FM	KEAR

New Mexico Translator
Albuquerque	91.9 FM	KEAR

New York Stations
Buffalo	89.9 FM	WFBF
Kingston	91.7 FM	WFRH
Olivebridge	88.3 FM	*WFSO
Smithtown	88.9 FM	WFRS
Webster	88.1 FM	WFRW

New York Translators
Albany	105.3 FM	WFRH
Catskill/Greenville	90.7 FM	WFRH
East Windham	104.3 FM	WFRH
Hudson/Ravena	104.9 FM	WFRH
Newburgh	90.5 FM	KEAR
Poughkeepsie	90.5 FM	WFME
Rhinebeck	105.7 FM	WFRH

North Dakota Station
Bismarck	91.7 FM	KBRF

Ohio Stations
Cuyahoga Falls	1150 AM	WCUE
Toledo	90.3 FM	WOTL
Youngstown	91.7 FM	WYTN

Oklahoma Translator
Enid	88.3 FM	KEAR

Oregon Station
Springfield	88.9 FM	KQFE

Oregon Translators
Ashland	90.7 FM	KEAR
Black Butte (Sutherlin)	100.1 FM	KEAR
Coos Bay	91.7FM	KEAR
Florence	92.7 FM	KQFE
Newport	89.3 FM	KEAR
Roseburg	88.1 FM	KEAR

Pennsylvania Stations
Erie	88.1 FM	WEFR
Johnstown	88.9 FM	WFRJ

Pennsylvania Translators
Altoona/Bedford	90.7 FM	WFRJ
Bellefonte	88.7 FM	KEAR
Berwick	90.3 FM	KEAR
East Stroudsburg	97.3 FM	WFME
Emmaus/Allentown	88.7 FM	WKDN
Freeland/Hazleton	89.3 FM	KEAR
Harrisburg/Carlisle	101.7 FM	WKDN
Lebanon/Lancaster	97.7 FM	WKDN
Muncy/Williamsport	90.9 FM	KEAR
Pittsburg	97.7 FM	WFRJ
Reading	89.3 FM	WKDN
Scranton	103.9 FM	KEAR
Wilkes-Barre	89.5 FM	KEAR
York	88.7 FM	WKDN

South Carolina Station
Charleston	88.5 FM	WFCH

(Continued)

South Carolina Translator
Myrtle Beach   95.9 FM   WFCH

South Dakota Translator
Rapid City   90.3 FM   KEAR

Texas Station
Beaumont   89.7 FM   KTXB

Texas Translators
El Paso   91.7 FM   KEAR
Galveston   91.1 FM   KEAR

Utah Station
Salt Lake City 91.7 FM   KUFR

Utah Translator
Ogden   91.9 FM   KEAR

Vermont Translator
Burlington   89.3 FM   KEAR

Virginia Translators

Lynchburg   91.7 FM   KEAR
Roanoke   91.9 FM   KEAR
Winchester   91.9 FM   WFSI
Washington Stations
Kirkland   1460 AM   KARR
Longview   89.5 FM   KJVH

Washington Translator
Olympia   90.1 FM   KEAR

Wisconsin Station
Milwaukee   88.1 FM   WMWK

Wisconsin Translator
Eau Claire   89.1 FM   KEAR

Wyoming Translator
Casper   91.7 FM   KEAR
Translator: a means by which
Family Radio's signal is rebroad-
cast from an existing station into a
new area, either directly from the
station or by satellite from KEAR
in Oakland, California.

Satellite to Europe, North Africa & Middle East

Eutelsat Hotbird
3-13 degrees east
· Transponder # 89
· Horizontal LNB polarization
· Satellite frequency: 12.476 GHZ
· Family Radio English:
  channel 951E [SID 10614]
· Family Radio International 1:
  channel 961E [SID 10615]
· Family Radio International 2:
  Channel 966 [SID 10611]

Astra 2B
28.2 degrees east
· Transponder # 36
· Vertical LNB polarization
· Satellite frequency: 12.4024 GHz
· Family Radio Europe : SID 9558

· Family Radio International 1:
  SID 9560
·Family Radio International 2:
  SID 9559

"The Open Forum" A Live Call In Radio Program

The author of this book, Harold Camping, is President and General Manager of Family Radio, and hosts "The Open Forum," a live, call-in program during which he answers questions about salvation and the Bible. **"The Open Forum"** is heard weekdays, Monday through Friday, **8:30-10:00 PM Eastern time, 5:30-7:00 PM Pacific time.** The number is **1-800-322-5385 in the United States.**

On the Internet- *You will find all this and more information regarding Family Radio.*

Visit our web site at *www.familyradio.com*

Family Radio's Bible-based programs are available on the Internet, 24 hours a day, seven days a week. The web site carries a program guide, a shortwave schedule, Bible studies, and audio and text version of the Bible in many languages. Visit Family Radio on the Internet at **www.familyradio.com**. The email address is **familyradio@familyradio.com**.

To receive a free program guide of our Gospel broadcasts, information about our Bible School correspondence courses, free books and materials, write to:

Family Radio
Oakland, CA 94621

or call **1-800-543-1495 in the United States.**

You can also listen to FamilyRadio or download both audio and text Bible study materials from the internet at: www.familyradio.com